Canon Law in Medieval England

Dr. Charles Duggan

Charles Duggan

Canon Law in Medieval England

The Becket Dispute and Decretal Collections

VARIORUM REPRINTS
London 1982

British Library CIP data   Duggan, Charles
                                    Canon law in medieval England. – (Collected
                                    studies series; CS151)
                                    1. Canon law – History   2. England – Church
                                    history
                                    I. Title
                                    262.9'0942   BV760.2

                                    ISBN 0-86078-103-8

Copyright © 1982 by   Variorum Reprints

Published in Great Britain by   Variorum Reprints
                                      20 Pembridge Mews London W11 3EQ

Printed in Great Britain by   Galliard (Printers) Ltd
                                      Great Yarmouth Norfolk

                                      VARIORUM REPRINT CS151

CONTENTS

This volume contains a total of 340 pages

PREFACE

The themes which give coherence to the sixteen chapters and essays reprinted in this volume are those of the reception of canon law in England in the second half of the twelfth century and the role of English ecclesiastics in consolidating the new law. The sub-title, the Becket dispute and decretal collections, suggests two focal points of interest, separate yet inter-related. The Becket dispute was essentially a jurisdictional conflict, in which Becket's position is intelligible only in the context of the post-Gregorian Church, and of its ideological and indeed theological principles, to which the law gave tangible expression. The dispute occurred between the publication of Gratian's *Decretum* at Bologna c. 1140-1, the 'great divide' in the history of medieval canon law, and the initiation of a new era in the history of canonical codification, that is to say the era of the decretal collections. The collections marked a point of departure and fixed the basis of new law primarily in papal letters later in date of issue than Gratian's work. Their earliest traces as separate compilations appear in the years of the Becket dispute and its early aftermath. The importance of the decretal collections in the history of canon law is self-evident, but they are also of crucial importance for more general history. In particular, their relevance to the Becket dispute and the state of the English Church in the decade after his martyrdom has often been undervalued. It is a simple matter of historical fact that a majority of all known collections of the most primitive kind were made in England, based largely on English episcopal archives, in the decade after his death. These English collections provided a formative source for similar collections made on the continent. Moreover, in the skilful process whereby a juristic pattern was imparted to the collections, the English canonists once more played a significant part. The resulting systematic collections were the fountain-head from which the later famous decretal collections flowed. In this way, the judicial records of English bishops and judges delegate left a lasting imprint on the general law of the Western Church. The explanation and context of this remarkable English achievement, and its possible links with the Becket controversy which preceded it, are matters for scholarly debate.

The studies reprinted here are arranged in the following way: a short essay on the significance of the Becket dispute for the English Church sets a general framework of reference. Two chapters, excerpted from a book on the English primitive collections, assess the interest of the decretal investigation for English historians, and suggest a relationship between the work of the English collectors and the Becket dispute. The next six studies deal with individual collections or groups of collections; their primary focus of interest is canonical, but a wider ecclesiastical context is indicated, wherever appropriate. The most familiar single aspect of the Becket dispute, the question of clerical privilege, is treated in studies X and XI, part 2. The eleventh study ranges through various aspects of the reception of canon law in England in the period, and is followed by three articles on the careers of notable personalities from the period of the controversy. Study XV is a broad survey of relations between the English Church and the papacy, from the Conquest to the death of John, and shows in parts how the history of canon law is tightly interwoven in the general history of the twelfth-century Church. Finally there is an address, privately printed, 'in commemoration of St Thomas of Canterbury', delivered in the chapel of the Mercers' Hall in Cheapside, on the site of St Thomas's birthplace. The material is of historical interest, but in view of its more solemn context and phrasing it is placed here as an appendix. Wherever possible errors, typographical or factual, have been corrected in the texts themselves; some more extensive corrections and additional information are to be found in the Addenda at the end of the volume.

It is a pleasant duty to express my thanks to the publishers who have generously given permission for these studies to be reprinted, to the Reverend Editor of the Ampleforth Journal; to the Athlone Press; to the officials of the Manuscript Room in the British Library; to Thomas Nelson and Sons Ltd; to the Fordham University Press; to the Reverend Prefect of the Vatican Library;

to the Director of the Institute of Historical Research; to the Director of the Institute of Medieval Canon Law; to the Royal Historical Society; to Beauchesne Editeur; to the Cambridge University Press; to Burns and Oates Ltd; and to the Mercers' Company. My debts to individual scholars are too numerous to list here, but the following at least must be mentioned: to Walter Ullmann, my supervisor of research at Trinity College Cambridge; to Stephan Kuttner, for exceptional generosity through many years of study at the Institute of Medieval Canon Law, at Yale and Berkeley, and for making available the invaluable Holtzmann papers; to Christopher and Mary Cheney, for scholarly guidance and encouragement in the pursuit of these studies; and to my wife, Dr Anne Duggan, for selfless help at all times, but especially in preparing this volume, which includes one essay published by us jointly.

CHARLES DUGGAN

King's College,
University of London
October, 1981

I

THE SIGNIFICANCE OF THE BECKET DISPUTE IN THE HISTORY OF THE ENGLISH CHURCH

AN EIGHTH CENTENARY COMMEMORATION—1170-1970

The fourth day after Christmas this year will mark an octocentenary of the murder of an Archbishop of Canterbury in his own cathedral, victim of a contemptible quarrel (as some judge) or of reasons of state (as others judge). In life Becket had appeared, as his biographer Herbert of Bosham tells us, above all magnificent, "great of heart, great of physique, great of personal presence"; and in death he appeared no less great as an immediately acclaimed martyr, whose shortfall in sanctity over his lifetime had been abundantly redressed in his last hour. The focus is so often upon this man, commanding of attention as he always is, that we tend to overlook the wider issue, the institutional struggle which was not merely the backcloth but the very marrow of the Becket Dispute. The struggle was itself a piece in the larger process of the emergence of a papally centred Church from national involvements to international predominance. And this process, undergone during the years from 1050 to 1300, was possibly the most crucial in the development of the life of the Church of Rome. Without Becket, it would not have been quite as it is.

Dr Duggan here presents the wider issues with unusual clarity, showing how far England was for a while the principal arena of this important development in the Church's life. He is probably better qualified to do this than any other historian today, as his footnotes indicate. His main work has been concentrated on this period and his special contribution comes from his examination of twelfth century decretal collections. He is a Reader in History, University of London King's College, and Warden of King's College Hall. This paper was read as "The Christmas Lecture" to the Canterbury Archaeological Society on 10th January.

THE Becket Dispute conjures up many diverse images in the minds of those who use or hear that phrase, and most of these images have their validity, but all are not of equal significance in the history of the English Church. The violent death of the archbishop in his own cathedral shocked the astonished senses of Christian Europe, in an age not unacquainted with acts of violence. If the miracles which multiplied around the martyr's tomb and relics are the subject of understandable scepticism in modern times, the cult of the martyr is an historical phenomenon of major importance. Within three years of his death the archbishop's name was inscribed in the catalogue of saints, his canonization having been formally announced in Alexander III's letter *Redolet Anglia*.[1] The mosaic at Monreale in Sicily,

---

[1] Copies of this letter were issued by Alexander III at Segni on 12th and 13th March 1173; cf. *Materials for the History of Archbishop Thomas Becket*, edd., J. C. Robertson and J. B. Sheppard, 7 vols, Rolls Series 67, London (1875-85) : VII, pp. 547-48.

the wall paintings at Tarrasa in the Spanish peninsula, the stained-glass window at Chartres, the counter-seals of Archbishops Hubert Walter and Stephen Langton in England, the proliferation of hagiographical literature, the dedication of numerous chapels to St Thomas of Canterbury—all these and many other indications marked merely the beginnings of a remarkable devotion which continued without abatement to the end of the middle ages, while the shrine of St Thomas at Canterbury rivalled even Rome and Santiago de Compostela as a point of recourse for pilgrims.[2] It was perhaps inevitable that the dramatic aspects of the famous quarrel between Henry II and Becket—their early friendship and its dissolution, Thomas's exile and tragic murder, and Henry's resulting humiliation—should capture the imagination both of their contemporaries and of later ages.[3] Even today this interest remains vital, though necessarily to some extent diminished.

No historian dare neglect the impact of human tragedy and drama in shaping the historical framework in which they are themselves enacted, or in moulding significantly the thoughts and actions of men in later times. It requires no rejection of a moderate historicist view of the forward move-ment of human affairs to recognize at the same time the decisive influences brought to bear on this movement by individuals. The foundation of papal power in the Western Church was not due to Gregory I at the close of the sixth century, nor was the fundamental shift in the balance of Church-State relations in the so-called Gregorian Reform in the eleventh century due simply to the efforts of Gregory VII, but each of these popes by his transcendent spirit and dynamic personality ensured that the pattern of evolution was different from what it would have been without him. And it is in this sense that the problem of their characters and personalities is of central importance in the contest between Henry II and Becket. But the very natural concern with these spectacular considerations attracts dis-proportionately the attention of many modern observers, so that deep currents of conflict between secular and ecclesiastical ideologies and jurisdictions, between contending interests both within the Church itself and in society as a whole, and in the intellectual developments of the period are imperfectly distinguished.[4] Historians, novelists, dramatists,

---

[2] Many examples are discussed and finely illustrated in T. Borenius, *St Thomas Becket in Art*, London (1932). Among more recent studies, cf. R. Brentano, *Two Churches: England and Italy in the Thirteenth Century*, Princeton (1968), p. 58, for evidence of the early Becket cult in Italy; in a commemorative address delivered in Andernach in June 1970, Dom Maurus Münch spoke of "over 150 places of devotion to our saint" in Germany, Austria, Alsace-Lorraine, Denmark, Sweden and Norway; and similar evidence survives for every part of Western Christendom. Cf. also D. J. Hall, *English Mediaeval Pilgrimage*, London (1965), pp. 130-65.

[3] A new biography is now available in R. Winston, *Thomas Becket*, London (1967), reviewed in the Summer 1968 JOURNAL p. 257f; and a biography by Dom David Knowles will be published shortly in the Leaders of Religion series. The *Canterbury Cathedral Chronicle*, No. 65, published in July 1970 (The Friends of Canterbury Cathedral, 8 The Precincts, Canterbury, 6/-), contains a series of commemorative essays to mark the eighth centenary of Becket's death : the first, by Dom David Knowles, is entitled "Archbishop Thomas Becket—the Saint".

[4] Cf. C. Duggan, "From the Conquest to the Death of John", in *The English Church and the Papacy in the Middle Ages*, ed., C. H. Lawrence, London (1965), pp. 63-115, esp. pp. 87-93.

poets and the like have focused attention legitimately but too exclusively on the two human personalities. According to a given writer's standpoint or sympathies, the obstinacy or character failings of Henry II or Becket, or of both, explain the tragedy. The theory that Becket was merely a character actor, playing a part or rather a series of parts, exploiting to the full the role in which he found himself at the several stages of his career, has been advanced among eminent historians by H. W. C. Davis, Zachary Brooke and many others, and among the dramatists by T. S. Eliot.[5] But this is a wholly inadequate explanation, and could not possibly account for the symbolic greatness almost universally attributed to Becket soon after his death, as well as in later centuries, throughout the Western Church. This is not the place to consider those outlandish theories gaining recent literary currency, falsely imputing to Becket weaknesses in personal morality or attaching to his stand against the king a regional or national partisan flavour. Historical truth is certainly not discovered through such inventions.[6]

The Becket Dispute was not merely in its essential aspect a clash of personalities, but a particular quarrel symptomatic of deep-seated conflicts over the nature of authority and its practical applications in Christian society. It echoes and prefigures numerous similar crises in the history of the Christian Church. It has its immediate and contextual interest, but it serves also as a temporary expression of a tension of universal and lasting significance. No approach to the Becket controversy will be satisfactory which does not penetrate the surface crust of local and simply individual interests or arguments. It must be remembered that the English Church was an integral part of the wider Western Church at that time, its evolution and thought processes intermingled with those of Latin Christendom more creatively and more intimately perhaps than at any other phase of its history. Mgr Jedin has aptly observed that the turning point in European history marked by the Gregorian and canonical reforms of the late-eleventh century is in reality more significant from the Church's viewpoint than the more familiar and conventional classifications of periods of European history.[7] Indeed, from that time a dynamic and even aggressive policy was pursued by the Church under papal guidance throughout the length and breadth of Western Christendom, resulting in a

---

5 H. W. C. Davis, *England under the Normans and Angevins*, London (1945 edn), pp. 210-11; Z. N. Brooke, *The English Church and the Papacy from the Conquest to the Reign of John*, Cambridge (1931), pp. 192-96; T. S. Eliot, *Murder in the Cathedral*. Numerous other instances could be cited. Cf. the perceptive essay by Knowles, "Archbishop Thomas Becket. A Character Study", *Proceedings of the British Academy*, XXXV (1949), pp. 177-205, and the immensely scholarly study by R. Foreville, *L'Eglise et la Royauté en Angleterre sous Henri II Plantagenet, 1154-89*, Paris (1943).

6 The imputation of unchastity to Becket in his early career is entirely without substance, and must be judged untrue. The suggestion that Becket was of Saxon lineage has often been discussed but is nowhere seriously considered by scholars today; cf. L. B. Radford, *Thomas of London before his Consecration*, Cambridge (1894), pp. 4-12.

7 K. Baus, *From the Apostolic Community to Constantine*, in *Handbook of Church History*, edd., H. Jedin and J. Dolan, Freiburg/London, I (1965), pp. 6-7.

series of politico-ecclesiastical crises in the relations of the Church with secular rulers. In practical terms the papacy strove for the liberty of the Church and its jurisdictional autonomy, while in the realm of ideas it asserted with increasing confidence its superiority over lay power. The long-waged contest between the popes and emperors, stretching from the deposition of Henry IV in the late-eleventh century to that of Frederick II in the mid-thirteenth century, was the principal front in a wide-ranging general battle. It is sufficient to refer briefly to the Investiture Contest of the late-eleventh and early-twelfth centuries, formally concluded between pope and emperor by the Concordat of Worms in 1122, noting its introduction into England in the reign of Henry I, while Anselm was Archbishop of Canterbury.[8] In a similar way, the Becket Dispute records a high point of crisis within a particular kingdom: it was joined in 1163-64, and concluded in stages in the years 1172-76, within the limits of a critical phase in papal-imperial relations, since the schism inaugurated by Frederick I in 1159 was not settled until the agreement between Frederick and Alexander III at Venice in 1177.[9] Meanwhile, difficult problems arose simultaneously, or nearly simultaneously, in many other parts of the Western Church—in Hungary, for example, and in Scandinavia. It is not without significance that Alexander III linked Becket with Archbishop Lucas of Gran, in naming them the twin buttresses of the Church's liberties.

It was inevitable and understandable that secular rulers would resent these revolutionary changes in the actuality of power in Christian society. They were already accustomed through centuries of usage to a position of dominance in their realms, even in matters of an ecclesiastical nature—in ecclesiastical appointments, in the disposition of Church property and in numerous other ways. The concepts of the *Landeskirchen* and the *Eigenkirchen,* that is to say of regional and proprietary churches, are of central importance here, with the consequent interlocking of secular and ecclesiastical offices, resources and interests, often with manifestly mutual advantages. This delicate balance and the familiar prerogatives were now clearly endangered by the emergent hierocratic principles in the Church, powerfully supported by the new canon law, the most effective weapon in the papal armoury. But, in addition to this, the twelfth century was a vitally important period of development in the conscious realization and practical application of royal power and of secular law. Over the whole front the period was one of evolution and maturity in government and administration, both in practical details and in the conscious ideologies on which they were based. To put the matter more precisely, the reign of Henry II occupies a formative and distinguished place in the history of English law independently of the problems of jurisdictional disharmony

---

[8] For diverse approaches to this problem, cf. N. F. Cantor, *Church, Kingship and Lay Investiture in England, 1089-1135,* Princeton (1958) and R. W. Southern, *Saint Anselm and his Biographer,* Cambridge (1963).

[9] For an account of the papal-imperial struggle, cf. P. Munz, *Frederick Barbarossa: a Study in Medieval Politics,* London (1969) and M. Pacaut, *Frederick Barbarossa,* trans. A. J. Pomerans, London (1970).

between the secular and ecclesiastical courts and legal systems—it was not only with the bishops that Henry II joined issue over his jurisdictional rights. But at that very moment the canon law, the common law of the Western Church, was being consolidated and given a coherent, scientific and juristically mature expression. No one would question the sincerity of Henry II's expressed concern with order and law in his kingdom, still less the extent of his achievements in that field. Equally, one must recognize the interior logic and conviction of the papal ecclesiastics and canon lawyers, based on what they conceived to be transcendent principles which should govern a truly Christian society.

Henry II asserted that the schedule of regulations, the so-called Constitutions drawn up at Clarendon in 1164, represented the customs which had governed relations between the secular and ecclesiastical jurisdictions in England in the days of his grandfather, Henry I. These were the *avitae consuetudines,* which broadly reflected the "barrier" policy successfully devised by William the Conqueror to control the two-way traffic between England and the Roman curia, and which also regulated in the royal interest various matters where the jurisdictions of Church and monarchy might overlap—a policy which had substantially broken down during the troubled reign of Stephen. Among other problems, the Constitutions dealt with the vexed question of appeals to the papal curia, episcopal elections, the excommunication of tenants in chief, the punishment of criminous clerks, disputes over advowsons or presentations to ecclesiastical benefices, the movement of clerks out of the kingdom, tenures in free alms, the profits of vacant bishoprics, and so forth.[10] On most points of actual detail there is general agreement that Henry II's claims were accurate, and in this sense the significance of the dispute from the royal viewpoint can be seen as an attempt to put back the clock, to recover the accustomed rights which had slipped away during a period of weakened secular rule. There was therefore a valid appeal to custom in these claims. It can also be argued to the persuasion of many that most of Henry's statements reflected problems of natural concern to a ruler anxious to establish the integrity of his judicial authority and with it the good order of his realm, and that certainly they deal with matters which an ambitious and self-reliant monarch would hope to manage, or at least substantially control. The judicial aspect of the dispute is clearly disclosed in the words of the Constitutions of 1164. If one were to accept the view, not infrequently propounded, that the strictly legal arguments in the controversy are simply of academic interest, or that they are somewhat empty formulations to give deceptive expression to personal or material ambitions, then it would be necessary to disregard this careful and detailed policy statement by Henry II, and to ignore the king's proposals at their face value. The fact is that they represent a most important and coherent delineation of Henry's conception of his judicial rights *vis-à-vis* the ascendent canon law. Had they been implemented, Henry's regulations would certainly have brought the English Church within his jurisdictional

---

10 The disputed points are fully analysed in Foreville, *op. cit.,* pp. 122-61.

tutelage—a most relevant reflection when assessing the extent of compromise in the aftermath of Becket's death.

But the Church of the mid-twelfth century was no longer the unfreed Church of the previous century, and the appeal to custom or to royal or regional interests could not be effective in resolving a clash of principles, though that is not to say that such an appeal would necessarily be disregarded. Nor should it be forgotten that prudent clerks might acquiesce in much of what they disapproved, provided that they were not required formally to compromise their consciences. Observers were not lacking at the time, nor are they among historians today, who saw the fatal weakness in Henry's calculations in that he forced to a public and most solemn debate issues which for the most part he might have been able to control through diplomatic and tactful compromise.[11] But on the basic principles, for Becket, custom could not contradict justice, and this was the essence of his hostility to the royal policies. The failure of Becket's colleagues to support him *in extremis* should not obscure the fact that, within the framework of the Church's doctrines, Becket's objectives were canonically well supported. Indeed, there is ample evidence that on canonical grounds alone their views were identical with his.[12] It is well known that Alexander III, at a moment of anxious crisis in his relations with Frederick I, condemned nevertheless all the English king's proposals, though he was willing to tolerate a few. Of course, not all of the Constitutions were of equal importance, and almost certainly the most crucial issue was Henry's attempt to subject to his *fiat* the transmission of appeals to the Roman curia. That he did not in practice effectively prohibit appeals in the course of the controversy—except perhaps by the very harsh measures of 1169— does not diminish the significance of his proposal. The question of criminous clerks is among the most familiar individual problems—not only was it the particular question around which the dispute was most bitterly waged, but it provides in miniature an insight into the overall problem. Most historians agree that it was perfectly proper, whatever the legal precedents, that Henry should seek to bring under constraint outrageous clerks, and the majority (though not all) consider that Henry on this point of English practice had a fair case in appealing to custom. But, contrary to the traditional interpretation by historians in modern times, Becket was emphatically supported by canon law in his opposition to the king's suggested procedure, and his opposition was not an exorbitant invention

---

[11] The most striking comment on the unwisdom of Henry's action in committing the Constitutions to writing was by his mother, the Empress Matilda : cf. *Becket Materials,* V, pp. 144-51, a letter of Nicholas of Mont St Jacques to Becket at Christmas 1164.

[12] The views and actions of the English bishops in the course of the controversy are most clearly treated in Knowles, *The Episcopal Colleagues of Archbishop Thomas Becket,* Cambridge (1951). Important studies on individual bishops include A. Morey, *Bartholomew of Exeter,* Cambridge (1937) and *idem* and C. N. L. Brooke, *Gilbert Foliot and his Letters,* Cambridge (1965).

based on his own unreasoning obstinacy.[13] A careful search into the sources of Becket's thought and arguments reveals their faithful reflection of texts devised originally in the ninth-century collection of canon law known as the *Pseudo-Isidore,* or more popularly as the "Forged Decretals", and accepted into the mainstream of canonical collections in the period of Gregorian Reform. To cite just one example, the key texts on which the principle of clerical immunity was debated, though taken in all probability from Gratian's *Decretum* (completed in its vulgate form about the year 1140), were used in the previous century by Gregory VII; some find their ultimate origins in the ninth-century *Pseudo-Isidore,* while the ancestry of others can be retraced into the earliest records of ecclesiastical legislation and of canon law.[14] It can easily be shown that Becket's interpretation of these texts was historically more valid than that of his opponents.

These very specific points of canon law having been argued at Clarendon in early 1164, the political significance of the conflict was made clear at Northampton later in the same year, when Henry mounted a direct and personal attack on Becket on charges and in circumstances involving feudal and financial implications.[15] The course of action chosen by the two protagonists was then, and will remain, a subject of controversial assessment as to their wisdom or lack of statescraft. But it is obvious that an acute crisis of authority had emerged, which could not be explained by the personal failings of the two adversaries—a crisis above all for the leading clergy in a Christian society in which, through a long and gradual process of historical evolution, it was no longer easy to distinguish sharply their duties and their loyalties to their spiritual and their secular superiors. The problem was not confined to England, nor to the period of the Becket controversy. There is no doubt that the nature of the episcopal office was essentially spiritual, but it is a matter of fact that bishops had also become important officials and administrators in the feudal structure of the kingdom. The rival claims of ecclesiastical and secular spheres of interest had their roots far back in Christian history, but this was one moment of high crisis in the long story of that possibly still unresolved dilemma. And it is important therefore to seek an understanding of both sides of the question, as well as of the standpoint of those who preferred to hold aloof as far as they were able from a dangerous commitment.

There is no need here to review in detail the course of the famous quarrel—the archbishop's exile, the many protracted and abortive attempts to secure a solution, the perplexing interplay of numerous incidental conflicts of interest, the final brief reconciliation, and the archbishop's

---

13 The brilliant essay on this subject by F. W. Maitland, in *Roman Canon Law in the Church of England,* London (1898), pp. 132-47, is still an indispensable starting point, but Maitland's conclusions cannot be reconciled with later research; cf. Duggan, "The Becket Dispute and the Criminous Clerks", *Bulletin of the Institute of Historical Research,* XXXV (1962), pp. 1-28; idem, "The Reception of Canon Law in England in the Later Twelfth Century", *Monumenta Iuris Canonici,* Series C: Subsidia I (Vatican City 1965), esp. pp. 359-65 : "The Becket Dispute : William of Canterbury and Clerical Privilege", and pp. 378-82.

14 Duggan, *Criminous Clerks,* pp. 6-18.

15 Cf. Knowles, *Episcopal Colleagues,* pp. 66-90.

return and murder in his cathedral on 29th December 1170. A settlement was hammered out gradually through several years following Becket's death, in which the Compromise of Avranches in 1172 and the negotiations with the papal legate, Pierleoni, in 1175-76 were the most important stages.[16] It is in the aftermath of the dispute that its significance for the English Church can be most clearly estimated, yet it is in this very context that historical judgments are apparently the most divergent. Among earlier historians of distinction, F. W. Maitland and Zachary Brooke argued that the years after 1170 disclose a remarkable posthumous victory for Becket, in which the barriers between the English and the Roman Churches, having been temporarily (as it was thought) re-erected, were entirely demolished, with a resulting and dominating inrush of papal jurisdiction and the consolidation in England of the most advanced theories and practices of the rising canon law.[17] The insights provided by Maitland and Brooke have placed later historians much in their debt, nevertheless some aspects of this theory can no longer be accepted. Among more recent historians of the highest rank, Professor Christopher Cheney has suggested that the Compromise of Avranches settled little in reality, and that the years following Becket's death were a period of effective compromise, with give and take between the rival jurisdictions.[18] Meanwhile, Dom Adrian Morey expressed the conclusion that the quarrel and its settlement ensured that the English Church would not be seriously cut off from continental developments, but would go forward sharing in the advances of the Church as a whole.[19] Dr Henry Mayr-Harting has very recently concluded that the gains were substantially secured by the king, since it is difficult to see (in his evaluation) what Henry II lost in the event, since he was able to secure his objectives by less formal means.[20] The conclusion preferred in this present essay is that a compromise was indeed worked out, but that, for reasons quite different from those advanced by Maitland and Brooke, the Church nevertheless achieved a considerable success, and that therefore in this precise sense it is possible to speak of a defeat for Henry II's policies.

The picture is in fact exceedingly complex, and each of these contrasting or complementary views can be sustained by selected evidence. Historians tend to exaggerate in their controversies the extent of their disagreements, while legitimately underlining the validity of their particular insights into the total problem. The area of agreement is much greater than might appear at first sight. No historian would now seriously challenge the judgment that neither the Church nor the State secured a

---

[16] Duggan, *From the Conquest to the Death of John*, pp. 90-93; *idem*, "Richard of Ilchester : Royal Servant and Bishop", *Transactions of the Royal Historical Society*, 5th Series, XVI (1966), esp. pp. 9-14 : "The Becket Conflict and its Aftermath".

[17] Maitland, *Roman Canon Law*, pp. 122-24; Z. N. Brooke, "The Effect of Becket's Murder on Papal Authority in England", *Cambridge Historical Journal*, II (1928), pp. 213-28; *idem*, *English Church and the Papacy*, pp. 211-14.

[18] The best survey of the decades following Becket's death is C. R. Cheney, *From Becket to Langton*, Manchester (1956); on the Avranches settlement, cf. *ibid.*, p. 108.

[19] Morey, *Bartholomew of Exeter*, pp. 75-78.

[20] H. Mayr-Harting, "Henry II and the Papacy, 1170-1189", *Journal of Ecclesiastical History*, XVI (1965), pp. 39-53.

total victory as a result of the Becket Dispute, or exacted an unconditional surrender. Each side gained some points but lost others. It should be recognized that Henry's concession at Avranches that appeals could go freely to the Roman curia, unless they were detrimental to his own interests, marked a major gain in principle for the Church in a solemn declaration on one of the most crucial points for which Becket had fought. It does not cancel the importance of this concession to say that Henry had not interfered with the process of appeals in the course of the controversy, or that after Avranches he was able to bring pressure to bear effectively in particular cases where his own interests were involved. In contrast, the king was completely successful in gaining his point on other issues, as instanced most obviously by the history of advowsons which were retained within the sphere of secular law;[21] and it is perfectly clear that Henry was able to control the selection of bishops.[22] The question of criminous clerks produced a most interesting compromise in that the king formally conceded the principle of clerical immunity from secular jurisdiction, while the papal legate agreed that clerks would not enjoy this immunity for transgressions of the forest law, a limitation of much material interest to the king.[23]

Nevertheless, through the decades following Becket's death the English Church, and the Roman Church in equal measure, achieved notable advances in influence and in the routine application of its jurisdiction; and this conviction is not weakened by the parallel recognition that Henry II was able to maintain a powerful grip on the Church in England to the end of his reign. If the royal policy adumbrated at Clarendon in 1164 had been literally implemented—that is to say, if Henry II's words are taken at their face value—his constraint of the Church would have been far greater than in fact it grew to be. An analogy in this respect might be seen in the German Church under Frederick I, Henry's contemporary, who was able to sustain a series of anti-popes against the legitimate Alexander. Many royal interests, which Henry's Constitutions sought to protect, he was able in practice to preserve undiminished, notably in the control of episcopal elections and in specific jurisdictional areas involving property rights or with financial implications for the crown. But it is not possible to question that the closing years of the twelfth century reveal the English Church fully participating in the life and organization of the universal Church. Indeed this comment is a considerable understatement. In the vital areas of canon law and papal jurisdiction English bishops and canonists played a part second to none in interest and importance for the Western Church as a whole. The work of English judges delegate—exercising by direct delegation the pope's jurisdictional authority in specific cases—is already very familiar, especially in the careers of distinguished bishops like Bartholomew of Exeter and Roger of Worcester;

[21] Cf. J. W. Gray, "The *ius praesentandi* in England from the Constitutions of Clarendon to Bracton", *English Historical Review*, LXVII (1952), pp. 481-509.

[22] For examples of royal control, cf. Duggan, *Richard of Ilchester*, pp. 13-14.

[23] The agreement is recorded in a letter of Henry II to Alexander III, preserved by Ralph de Diceto, *Opera Historica*, ed., W. Stubbs, 2 vols, Rolls Series, London (1876) : I, p. 410; cf. Duggan, *Criminous Clerks*, p. 22, n. 1.

and increasingly the role of English canonists in codifying decretal law, as expressed in numerous papal letters dealing with general or particular legal problems, and in writing commentaries on the canon law is being disclosed in many manuscripts until recently unexploited.[24] This was the period when English canonists made their most original and distinctive contributions to the history of canon law, their collections and commentaries being of such a nature that they left a permanent imprint on the corpus of law for the whole of the Western Church. It is possible to speculate that these developments would have taken place even without the great legal battle which preceded them, but it is more reasonable to suggest at least a measure of interdependence.

Certainly a quieter period dawned in the history of the rival jurisdictions, in which compromise and harmony contrasted with the former bitter quarrels. Professor Cheney, with particular reference to Archbishop Hubert Walter, has made the interesting suggestion that prelates at the close of the century, by their ability to co-ordinate the interests of both Church and State in their own careers and activities, proved that a compromise was workable, implying that the extreme positions adopted at the earlier time of crisis were unnecessary and there-fore regrettable.[25] This is a most salutary reflection. But it is no less arguable that the balance and moderation which were then achieved would not have been realized in that way if the battle had not been fought, and that the victory would have gone too decisively for the secular power. Moreover, the days of Innocent III, King John and Stephen Langton were also dawning, in which an Archbishop of Canterbury would be selected by the pope against the king's determined opposition, in which the king would be constrained and brought into subjection by ecclesiastical censures, in which the kingdom of England would be submitted to the pope in feudal subjection, and in which among the most decisive personalities during a royal minority in England would be the papal legates. In later days a very different story would be told, but these were not negligible signs of the growth of papal power for the meanwhile.

This brief survey suggests only in broadest outlines the essential nature of the Becket Dispute from the Church's viewpoint. The dispute disclosed in its course many other issues of high political and ecclesiastical importance in addition to those discussed above, and all must be duly assessed in any fully satisfactory account of the controversy. Among these other problems, of outstanding interest is the crisis of authority and primacy within the English Church, symbolized by the re-emergence of conflict between York and Canterbury, and by the preferment of the

---

[24] I have discussed these developments in several publications: *Twelfth-Century Decretal Collections and their Importance in English History*, Athlone Press (1963), esp. pp. 1-12 and 118-51; "Primitive Decretal Collections in the British Museum", *Studies in Church History*, I (1964), pp. 132-44; "English Decretals in Continental Primitive Collections: with Special Reference to the Primitive Collection of Alcobaça", *Studia Gratiana*, XIV (1967): *Collectanea Stephan Kuttner*, IV, pp. 51-72; and other articles mentioned in preceding foot-notes.

[25] Cheney, *From Becket to Langton;* cf. now *idem, Hubert Walter*, London (1967).

metropolitical claims of the see of London by Gilbert Foliot.[26] If all the
relevant problems were to be analysed for their significance in the history
of the English State or monarchy, the emphasis in interpretation would be
necessarily very different from that advanced in this discussion. But that
was not the task envisaged for the present paper. The meaning of the
Becket Dispute for the Church lies in its witness to the strivings of the
Church, in one phase of its evolution, for its freedom from secular
constraint and for its own spiritual integrity, in its forthright assertion of
the hallowed and therefore privileged place of the priestly element in
Christian society and of the primacy of the papacy in the universal Church.
Much of this is obvious enough, yet it tends to be forgotten in more recent
times, when many principles for which Becket fought seem unreasonable,
out of date or unrealistic. But it was still not forgotten in the reign of
Henry VIII, when the issue was rejoined with vastly different consequences, when the shrine of the martyr was desecrated and his hated
name erased from the manuscripts wherever it was encountered, when it
was resolved by the king that "from hense forth the sayde Thomas Becket
shall not be estemed, named, reputed, nor called a sayncte", and when
Archbishop Warham, a successor of Becket in the see of Canterbury,
protested in reply to a charge that he had violated the statute of
Praemunire:[27]

> I intended nothing against the king's highness, but I intend to do
> only that I am bound to do by the laws of God and Holy Church and
> by mine order and by mine oath that I made at the time of my
> profession . . . It were indeed as good to have no spirituality as to have it
> at the prince's pleasure . . . And if in my case, my lords, you think to
> draw your swords and hew me in small pieces . . . I think it more better
> for me to suffer the same than against my conscience to confess this
> article to be *praemunire*, for which St Thomas died.

26 Morey and Brooke, *op. cit.*, pp. 149-62.
27 Citation from F. R. H. Du Boulay, "The Fifteenth Century", *The English Church
and the Papacy in the Middle Ages*, pp. 241-42.

II

Canon Law and the Decretals

THE INTEREST OF THE INVESTIGATION FOR ENGLISH HISTORIANS

THE study of canon law in England has never quite recovered from the attack launched upon it in the sixteenth century, and a burden of suspicion has hindered not only the subject professionally, but even an interpretation of medieval ecclesiastical history in its necessary canonistic setting. The teaching of canon law in the universities was proscribed by Henry VIII's writ of prohibition, and, in addition to this frontal assault, encouragement was given at the same time to an interest in Roman Civil Law through the foundation of Regius Professorships at Oxford and Cambridge.[1] By these means English academic interest ceased in what had been the common law of western Christendom, entailing a sudden catastrophe in the history of the English Courts Christian.[2] For these reasons the story of canon law in the post-Reformation Church of England has no direct connexion with the law of the English Church in the twelfth century. Nor is it intended to attempt here a judgement on the decisions taken in the sixteenth century. But it was undoubtedly a misfortune, historically speaking, that with the eclipse of canon law as a branch of jurisprudence in England, an interest in its history became almost equally suspected. Today it is accepted axiomatically that a knowledge of the development of canon law is central to a true understanding of medieval history. From the eleventh century,

[1] F. W. Maitland, *English Law and the Renaissance* (Rede Lecture, Cambridge, 1901), pp. 8–9; 47, n.14: Injunctions of 1535, *Stat. Acad. Cantab.*, p. 134: 'Quare volumus ut deinceps nulla legatur palam et publice lectio per academiam vestram totam in iure canonico sive pontificio . . .' etc.

[2] Maitland, *Roman Canon Law in the Church of England*, London (1898), pp. 90–3.

at the latest, until the close of the middle ages, ecclesiastical law exerted a profound and far-reaching influence on European thought and civilization, both directly by its control of belief and practice, and indirectly by its provocation of a hostile or critical reaction.[1]

It is no longer possible to estimate the loss of canonical source material through the deliberate destruction of manuscripts, their supersession by more important works, and the lapse of so many centuries.[2] The evidence surviving suggests that such losses have been very great indeed. But the canonistic manuscripts surviving from the twelfth century (and they are still known for the most part in manuscript only) have a richness and variety far exceeding anything thought likely when Maitland restored the study of canon law to a place of central historical interest in England. Now by the exploitation of long neglected manuscripts and the publication of monographs on special aspects of English ecclesiastical history a more balanced interpretation is being gradually achieved. But the detailed research made in recent years (chiefly by continental scholars) on the work of the medieval canonists, strictly in their professional capacity, has not yet been linked satisfactorily with more general interpretations of ecclesiastical history in its social and political aspects. This is particularly true in English history, partly no doubt for the reasons already stated. The work of many scholars provides increasingly an ample basis for the reinvestigation of many familiar problems, and much has been achieved already. Among these scholars, to name only a few, Holtzmann, Kuttner, Ullmann, Le Bras, Plöchl, Stickler, Tierney, Vetulani and many others are both outstanding and characteristic; while, for English history more specifically, Barraclough, Mrs. Cheney, Professor Cheney, Morey, Christo-

---

[1] S. Kuttner, 'Scientific Investigation of Mediaeval Canon Law: the Need and the Opportunity', *Speculum*, xxiv (1949), pp. 493–501: even the critical comments of Roger Bacon, Dante and the satirists reflect 'the actual truth that in the mediaeval world canon law was an all-pervading social and cultural power'. For the development of canon law before Gratian, see P. Fournier and G. Le Bras, *Histoire des collections canoniques en Occident depuis les Fausses Décrétales jusqu'au Décret de Gratien*, 2 Vols., Paris (1931–2); and W. M. Plöchl, *Geschichte des Kirchenrechts*, i, Vienna (1954).

[2] Maitland, *Roman Canon Law*, p. 95: Gentili at Oxford: 'Flammis, flammis libros spurcissimos barbarorum. . . . Flammis omnes, flammis!'

pher Brooke, Kemp, Mlle. Foreville and others like them have already revealed the vital significance of these technical studies in the history of the English Church. But much remains to be done, to be undertaken afresh or brought to completion. There is still some lingering distrust of the subject-matter, and a disinclination to give the preliminary but necessary attention to the minutiae of textual criticism: necessary, not for its intrinsic interest, but so that, when the quarrying has been completed, valid bases may be provided for the broader historical conclusions. At the moment, in so far as these are based on reliable canonical authorities at all, they rest too frequently on a small number of well-known compilations, with little critical understanding of their value as historical, as distinct from legal, source material. Whenever the canon law is consulted to elucidate more general problems, it is misleading to refer simply to one or two of the most famous legal codices however great their professional importance.

It was a failure to realize this danger which misled first Maitland and then Zachary Brooke in their still-basic studies on the twelfth-century church in England, since they relied in their investigations on a small number of canonical codes drawn up somewhat later than the emergence of the problems in which they were interested, and were seemingly insufficiently aware of the nature of the sources on which the codices themselves depended.[1] Both were concerned to trace the course of papal decretal legislation in England, and more particularly the

[1] Maitland, *Roman Canon Law*, pp. 122–31; Z. N. Brooke, 'The Effect of Becket's Murder on Papal Authority in England', *CHJ*, II (1928), pp. 213–29; *idem*, *The English Church and the Papacy*, Cambridge (1931), pp. 211–14. With these the following should be read as a corrective: G. Barraclough, *EHR*, LIII (1938), pp. 492–5 (review of Kuttner, 'Repertorium der Kanonistik, 1140–1234', *Studi e Testi*, LXXI, Vatican City, 1937); Mrs. M. Cheney, 'The Compromise of Avranches of 1172 and the Spread of Canon Law in England', *EHR*, LVI (1941), pp. 177–97; Kuttner and E. Rathbone, 'Anglo-Norman Canonists of the Twelfth Century: An Introductory Study', *Traditio*, VII (1949–51), pp. 279–80. On the other hand, Brooke's arguments are accepted by R. Foreville, *L'Église et la Royauté en Angleterre sous Henri II Plantagenet*, Paris (1943), pp. 389 ff.; and Holtzmann has recently described Brooke's *CHJ* study as 'a short but very weighty paper': W. Holtzmann and E. W. Kemp, 'Papal Decretals relating to the Diocese of Lincoln in the Twelfth Century', *Lincoln Record Society*, XLVII (1954), p. xvi. The whole question is treated on the basis of fresh manuscript evidence in the chapters which follow. For simplicity, the canonists whose work is the basis of this study are described here as 'English', though it is realized that 'Anglo-Norman' is preferred by some historians.

influence of the Becket controversy on the rate of flow of decretals from the Roman Curia to English recipients. To illustrate their methods briefly: Maitland, in discussing the decretal letters which Alexander III sent to English bishops and judges delegate, relied exclusively on the authorized *Decretales*, published by Gregory IX and recommended by him to the canon lawyers at Paris and Bologna on 5 September 1234.[1] Brooke extended the basis of this discussion by examining also the *Quinque Compilationes Antiquae*: the five most important decretal collections made in the preceding half century.[2] Despite the apparent support provided more recently for Brooke's thesis by Holtzmann,[3] it will be shown later how seriously Maitland and Brooke erred in their reliance on these highly specialist productions, which were designed for essentially practical purposes and provide no real guidance in the problems which they were investigating. The fallacy underlying the arguments, which they advanced in consequence, has been noticed briefly by Barraclough and Mary Cheney. It is enough to remark here that the conclusions of general historical importance which were reached by Maitland and Brooke in this context have no necessary connexion with the materials on which they were founded.

Two major adjustments must be made to their method of historical enquiry. Firstly, it must be understood that the *Quinque Compilationes* and the Gregorian *Decretales* are simply the most well-known and highly favoured of a vast family of decretal collections whose genesis can be traced from the eighth decade of the twelfth century. They are the final issues of many generations which succeeded one another in the great schools of canon lawyers, most notably Italian, French and English. Each was not a novel and independent composition based on the papal registers or episcopal records, but rather (at least in most cases) an adaptation or amplification of already existing compilations.[4]

[1] A. van Hove, *Prolegomena ad Codicem Iuris Canonici*, Malines-Rome (1945), p. 358.

[2] *Ibid.*, pp. 355–7.   [3] Holtzmann and Kemp, *op. cit.*, pp. xvi–xvii.

[4] Van Hove, *Prolegomena*, pp. 348–63; but the papal registers left some traces in the decretal collections: cf. Holtzmann, 'Die Register Papst Alexanders III in den Händen der Kanonisten', *Quellen und Forschungen aus italienischen Archiven und Bibliotheken*, xxx (1940), pp. 13–87. See also A. Vetulani, 'L'Origine des collections primitives de décrétales à la fin du XIIe siècle', *Congrès de Droit Canonique Médiéval*, Louvain (1959), pp. 64–72.

From this it follows that the thirteenth-century collections, which provide the customary basis of reference in historical discussions, depend indirectly for their twelfth-century decretals on codices made shortly after the issue of the individual letters, which only very rarely survive in their true originals.[1] The historian's attention must be directed to these early collections rather than to their juridically more important descendants. If we are interested in the decretals which Alexander III issued, the most sensible course is to consult the collections made during his own pontificate. Until quite recently, these have been almost entirely neglected by the general historian.

But even with access secured to these sources more relevant in time to the wider historical problems, a second and equally vital question arises concerning their relevance in species. And it was in this respect above all others that both Maitland and Brooke were mistaken. The decretal collections, as stated already, were professional and specialist compositions. There can be no justification in accepting at its face value the evidence they seem to provide on general historical trends and problems, unless these are corroborated by independent testimony. Before the wider historical significance of a particular decretal collection can be established, many questions must first be settled: questions concerning its provenance and authorship, the motives prompting its composition, and the resources available to the collector. Only with such questions answered is it possible to gauge the value of a collection in reflecting the general policies of the legislator rather than the local or specialist predilections of the compiler.

The problems of interpretation are particularly acute for the

---

[1] For collections already edited or analysed, see E. Friedberg, *Corpus Iuris Canonici*, II, Leipzig (1881); *idem*, *Quinque Compilationes Antiquae necnon Compilatio Lipsiensis*, Leipzig (1882); *idem*, *Die Canonessammlungen zwischen Gratian und Bernhard von Pavia*, Leipzig (1897); the more recent survey by Holtzmann: 'Über eine Ausgabe der päpstlichen Dekretalen des 12. Jahrhunderts', *Nachrichten* (1945), pp. 15–36; *idem*, 'Die Dekretalen Gregors VIII', *Festschrift für Leo Santifaller: Mitteilungen*, LVIII (1950); *idem*, 'Die Dekretalensammlungen des 12. Jahrhunderts: 1. Die Sammlung *Tanner*', *Festschrift zur Feier des 200 jährigen Bestehens der Akademie der Wissenschaften in Göttingen, Phil.-Hist.Kl.* (1951), pp. 83–145; *idem*, 'La collection *Seguntina* et les décrétales de Clément III et de Célestin III', *Revue d'histoire ecclésiastique*, L (1955); *idem* and Kemp, *op. cit.*, pp. ix–xvii; Kuttner, 'Notes on a Projected Corpus of Twelfth-Century Decretal Letters', *Traditio*, VI (1948), pp. 345–51.

twelfth century, when the volume of decretals issuing from the
papal chancery was swelling to previously unheard-of dimen-
sions, but for which the papal registers survive no longer. The
lost registers would doubtless have provided full and incon-
trovertible evidence of trends in papal policies; but their absence
can scarcely justify the uncritical use made of the strictly partial
and selective evidence surviving in the canon lawyers' collections. Both Maitland and Brooke tacitly assumed either that
the Alexandrian letters in the extant decretal collections represent the total significant issue, or at least that they accurately
reflect it in all essentials. Only on the basis of one or other of
these propositions can their conclusions be sustained. In the
event, in can be shown that neither is historically accurate.

Enough has been said, then, to indicate the value of a critical
investigation of the earliest decretal collections available, and
in them an unexpectedly promising field for historical revision
is discovered. More than fifty manuscripts survive from the
twenty years following the death of Becket. Less than half have
been examined so far either for their technical or their political
importance.[1] Many are of the utmost value in English history.
Yet their value is by no means restricted to questions of historical method and enquiry. Setting aside this interest in an
already well-known controversy, the mere numerical recovery
of lost decretals is astonishing. Hundreds of papal letters,
which had passed quite out of knowledge, have been recovered,
though they have yet to be published.

All decretal collections before Peter of Benevento's *Compilatio
Tertia* (1209–10) were private in character, their contents being
subject entirely to the author's caprice and the materials available to him. In the course of a long process of selective development, many letters fell by the wayside, and were never received
into the later, more widely-known, compilations. The Gregorian *Decretales*, itself a selection from the *Quinque Compilationes*
and the most recent papal registers, superseded all earlier collections and drove them out of use and knowledge, though it

---

[1] Holtzmann, *Nachrichten*, pp. 21–4: Holtzmann lists forty collections as pre-
Compilatio Prima, and a further fifteen as pre-*Compilatio Secunda*; and further manuscripts have since been found. Cf. Kuttner, *Projected Corpus*, pp. 345–51. See also the
annual Bulletin of the Institute of Research and Study in Medieval Canon Law,
Traditio, xi–xvii (1955–proceeding).

contained only a fragment of their total contents. Fortunately, many of these rejected or superseded decretals can now be recovered from the twelfth-century collections. Even merely statistically, the gain is striking: Maitland estimated on a basis of the evidence in the *Decretales* that Alexander III had dispatched one hundred and eighty decretal letters to England; and Brooke increased this estimate to two hundred and nineteen by consulting also the *Compilationes Antiquae*. By extracting those decretals discovered afresh in the twelfth-century canonical manuscripts, Holtzmann has shown that no less than three hundred and fifty-nine are now known to have been dispatched to England—and there is no reason to assume that even this provisional estimate is the final figure. In other words, to England alone, during a single pontificate, one hundred and forty forgotten decretals have been made once more available, and many are of considerable historical interest. The quantitative recovery alone, therefore, would justify a detailed analysis of these neglected manuscripts.[1]

But the gain is not quantitative simply. The older collections include fuller and more accurate versions of many decretals already well known. It has often been noticed that many decretal letters, whether in medieval manuscripts or even the best modern editions, are frequently unreliable in historical detail. This defect is due principally to two factors: the one relating to the technical and professional conventions of the canonists themselves; the other resulting from the carelessness or ignorance of medieval copyists. In the first place, a canon lawyer valued a given decretal for its juridical content only;

---

[1] Maitland, *Roman Canon Law*, p. 130; Brooke, *Effect of Becket's Murder*, pp. 219–224; Holtzmann, *Nachrichten*, p. 34; *idem, Dekretalen Gregors VIII*, pp. 113–23; *idem* and Kemp, *op. cit.*, pp. xvi–xvii. The total number of known decretals has to be revised constantly as further letters are discovered in manuscripts previously unnoticed. It must be admitted that Maitland did not claim his figure as an absolute or final total. But his argument does assume the figure to represent the true ratio of letters dispatched to England as compared with other countries. The decretal collections can never provide a complete picture of the total decretal issue, since they are based simply on the selection of letters made by particular canon lawyers. Evidence of numerous decretals never incorporated in professional collections can be discovered in cathedral and monastic cartularies. Moreover, the number of letters rediscovered in the canonical collections is even greater than the statistics given above suggest at first sight: many so-called decretals in the calculations by Maitland and Brooke were merely decretal chapters.

the historical circumstances giving rise to the judicial decision were of little moment to him, and were consequently a fit subject for abbreviation or even total excision. In this way many decretals have been seriously distorted in the process of inclusion in professional collections, the excision being most serious in the hands of the most juristically skilled authors. In diplomatic terms, both protocol and eschatocol were eliminated or drastically curtailed, and even the historical element of the contextus, the *species facti*, was liable to suppression. Further, as the canonist's skill grew, he tended to dissect the longer decretals into their component parts, and these he distributed through the various books and sub-sections into which he divided his collection.[1] In these circumstances, it became increasingly difficult to reconstruct the authentic textual shape of the original entity; and, at the same time, historians from Maitland to Morey have been greatly misled in their statistical calculations.[2] On two counts, therefore, a more accurate version may be discovered if we consult the earlier, more primitive, compositions, designed before the process of excision and dissection had made much headway. So much, then, for the defects due to professional conventions: there remains the problem of scribal inaccuracy.

Maitland noticed long ago how canonistic scribes were prone to distort or misinterpret references to names of persons and places, and his illustrations have been supplemented by later historians. In the many surviving transcripts of a single decretal involving the parishes of Potton' and Sandy, he discovered eighteen variant readings of the former and ten of the latter.[3] And Holtzmann has more recently listed ten variants of Kenilworth, to which one more can be added from a Peterhouse manuscript, where it appears in an unusually accurate version.[4]

[1] Kuttner, *Projected Corpus*, pp. 345–6; Maitland, *Roman Canon Law*, pp. 124–5: showing how Innocent III dealt with a wide variety of topics in a single letter to the bishop of Ely (1204).

[2] Maitland, *Roman Canon Law*, p. 128; A Morey, *Bartholomew of Exeter*, Cambridge (1937), p. 44.

[3] Maitland, *Roman Canon Law*, pp. 122–3: Sandy appears as Sander, Santen, Sandeia, Sandria, Sandinia, Sandeta, Sandaia, Fand and Sandola.

[4] Holtzmann, *Nachrichten*, pp. 25–32: Kenilworth appears as Chinelwi, Chinel Wi, Chimel Wirch, Chimen Wl., Chinel W., Chunbt, Chwith, Exmtwth, Inthwobt and Knieleunede; cf. Peterhouse MS. 193, fol. ii. ra: Kinelworþe. See also W. Ullmann,

The problem hinges chiefly on the use of abbreviated forms of place-names and persons, which were liable to confusion. The slightest acquaintance with the work of decretal scribes will suggest many typical examples: thus London was subject to confusion with Laon, Lyons and Lund, in their Latin versions; York with Evreux; while Exeter was particularly difficult, being confused in specific instances with Lisieux, Brescia, Oxford, Huesca and Osma—and even with Bath, when Bartholomew of Exeter was intended.[1] If such familiar examples as these perplexed the decretal copyists, it is hardly surprising that the Hungarian province of Kolocsa presented even greater difficulties in abbreviated transcription, and was almost invariably re-copied as Cologne;[2] in the same way Dublin was occasionally confused with Durham, Ramsey with Reims, and Salisbury with Salzburg. In many instances the corruption of historical references was so extreme that it is no longer possible to reconstruct them with any conviction. Obviously, the more immediately dependent a transcript was on an original copy or on an archetypal collection, the more accurate was likely to be the abbreviation. The most extravagant misreadings are naturally found (except in a few uncharacteristic instances) in the remoter generations. Here then is another reason for dissatisfaction with the later collections when better texts are available in the ancestral manuscripts.

A precise example affords the most convincing argument. A decretal of Alexander III is included in the Gregorian *Decretales*, in Friedberg's vulgate edition, with the following details:[3]

Idem Herfordensi episcopo et abbati de Forde. Ex literis I. Salabriensis episcopi accepimus, quod defuncta persona ecclesiae de Laton., G.miles qui villam, in qua ecclesia sita est, a monasterio de Vinton. *etc.*

'A Scottish Charter and its Place in Medieval Canon Law', *Juridical Review*, LXI (1949), pp. 225–41; *idem*, 'A Forgotten Dispute at Bridlington Priory in its Canonistic Setting', *Yorkshire Archaeological Journal*, XXXVII (1951), pp. 456–73.

[1] The abbreviations Bathon., Brixen. or Brix., Lexou., Oxon., Oxom., and Oscen. (for Bath, Brescia, Lisieux, Oxford, Osma and Huesca respectively) were frequently confused with Barth. Exon., B.Exon., and Exon. (for Exeter).

[2] The abbreviation for Kolocsa was Coloc., which was very readily confused with Colon., the conventional form for Cologne.

[3] Friedberg, ed., *Corpus Iuris Canonici*, II: *Decretales Gregorii IX*, III. 38. 7.

Experience suggests at once that this letter was sent in reality to the bishop of Hereford and the abbot of Ford, though this could not be taken for granted on the text alone. It is conceivable that a judge delegate at 'Herford' was an intended recipient of this letter, and is referred to wrongly as bishop in the decretal inscription. But a knowledge of scribal failings requires the correction from Herford in Germany to Hereford in England; and this deduction is amply confirmed by the following reference to the abbot of Ford in the diocese of Exeter. With the English provenance of the letter sufficiently established, the reference to 'I. Salabriensis' in the text is soon identified as Jocelin of Salisbury, and the place-name 'Vinton.' is readily recognized as a familiar abbreviation for Winchester. This simple example reveals how the typically distorted details in decretal transcriptions may be corrected by a process of supposition based on probability. But, if the original version is available in an earlier copy, then the deductive process is unnecessary. Deduction is, in any case, a defective instrument in such matters. The decretal discussed above is discovered with fuller and more accurate details in an English decretal collection, the Claudian Collection, made in or shortly after Urban III's pontificate (1185–7).[1] This early manuscript confirms the suggested emendations on all points but one: where Friedberg's version provides the reading 'Vinton.', the primitive collection records 'Wiltona', identifying therefore not Winchester but Wilton. This example merely typifies the numerous corrections which will result from an investigation of the twelfth-century manuscripts, and emphasizes once more the need for further research into the archetypal collections.

One further example illustrates the occasional excitement of an unexpected discovery. In his introduction to Ralph de Diceto's *Ymagines Historiarum*, Stubbs considered at some length the possible etymology of its author's name. The course and con-

---

[1] B.M. Cotton MS. Claudius A. IV, fol. 212rb, n.175. Elementary though such reconstructions seem to be, they depend in many instances on local knowledge: the inscription 'Riwallis et de Beglaus abbatibus et priori de Novoburgo' (*Tanner* VII. 15.15; Holtzmann, *Sammlung Tanner*, p. 143) is easily identified by English historians as addressed to the abbots of Rievaulx and Byland and the prior of Newburgh; but in an otherwise less obvious context the reference 'Beglaus' would clearly present some difficulty.

clusion of his enquiry need not detain us here in detail, but while examining a suggested derivation of the word Diceto from the Norfolk parish of Diss, he cited a lost letter of Alexander III to John of Oxford, bishop of Norwich.[1] The letter could no longer be discovered and was not included among the known collections of Alexander's decretals. Its existence was known only through brief summaries in the *Votaryes* and *Scriptores* of Bale, writing in the sixteenth century. In the decretal, according to Bale, Alexander:

> commaundeth that Wyllyam the new person of Dysse, for clayminge the benefice by inheritaunce, after the decease of his father person Wulkerell which begate him in his presthode, should be dispossessed, no appellacyon admitted.

This letter can now be examined in its authentic form in various decretal manuscripts conventionally associated with Worcester and described in consequence as members of the 'Worcester' family. The letter begins as follows:[2]

> Ad aures nostras sepius pervenisse cognoscas, quod defuncto Wlfkerel sacerdote, qui in ecclesia de Dische multis temporibus personatum habebat, Willelmus filius eius in sacerdotio genitus eiusdem ecclesie administrationem quasi hereditaria successione suscepit, et eam contra fundi dominum violenter detinere contendit. *Etc.*

And in this way accurate details and a little additional illumination are provided for arguments which Stubbs was able to base simply on second-hand and tenuous allusion.

These examples suggest all too briefly how historical enquiry may be furthered in many respects by an exploitation of the neglected manuscripts, both as to general historical problems and details of individual cases. But the manuscripts provide also the materials in which alone can be traced the development of the techniques and traditions in the schools of canon lawyers in the classical period of the emergence of canon law as a true

---

[1] W. Stubbs, ed., *Radulfi de Diceto Decani Lundoniensis Opera Historica*, Rolls Series (1876), I, pp. x–xviii.

[2] Trinity College Cambridge MS. R.14.9, fol. 86r; cf. H. Lohmann, 'Die Collectio Wigorniensis', *ZRG.*, *Kan.Abt.*, XXII (1933), p. 104. The form 'Wlfkerel' is almost certainly corrupt; the variants 'Ulfkutel' and 'Bultekel' are found elsewhere, but the most likely form is 'Wulfketel'.

juristic science. It is for these reasons that the extant manuscripts, and particularly those with English associations, have been chosen as a basis for this present study. Stephen of Tournai, a distinguished canonist and contemporary of Alexander III, referred to the 'inextricabilis silva' of Alexander's decretals. From a canonistic point of view, the chief interest of the twelfth-century collections is their evidence of the way in which the canon lawyers gradually traced a path through this vast forest.

III

THE IMPORTANCE OF THE INVESTIGATION IN ENGLISH HISTORY

The interest of English historians in papal decretal legislation dates from Maitland's famous refutation of Stubbs's thesis that the 'Roman' canon law was not considered binding by the medieval Church in England.[1] We are not concerned here with the central issue of that controversy, and it is enough to note that Maitland's vindication of the contrary opinion has held the field until the present day, and is nowhere seriously called into question. But in the course of his enquiry into the part played by the English Church in the development of ecclesiastical law, he was misled into a position which has vitiated most of the later study of the subject. The nature of his misunderstanding was pointed out briefly in the introductory chapter above, and the broad course of development in decretal legislation and the evolution of the decretal collections have been described in the central chapters, revealing the true pattern of the phenomena which Maitland so grievously misinterpreted. It remains now to draw together these threads and see precisely what modifications must be made to his opinions. Noticing that the Gregorian *Decretales* contained an astonishingly high number of decretals of Alexander III with English inscriptions, more in fact than to any other single part of Europe, Maitland accepted this evidence at its face value, and consulted no earlier sources for confirmation or explanation.[2] It must be admitted that, in the state of historical knowledge of decretal developments then existing, he had no reason to suspect the apparent evidence in a famous official book of law made in Italy with papal authorization. And, therefore, he assumed that Alexander III had in fact sent more decretals to England than to any other part of Christendom:[3]

---

[1] Maitland, *Roman Canon Law, passim.* Maitland's thesis was mainly based on the evidence in the fifteenth-century *Provinciale* of William Lyndwood, Official Principal to Archbishop Chichele, on the decretals, and on the concept of the pope as Universal Ordinary for all Christians. In refuting the arguments advanced by Stubbs, he drew the essential and basic distinction between what the English Church recognized as legally binding and what it was permitted by the secular power to put into practice.

[2] Maitland, *Roman Canon Law*, p. 123.

[3] *Ibid.*, p. 122.

Just at that moment England seems to have demanded, or at any rate to have received a far larger number of papal mandates than would have fallen to her lot, had the supply that was exported from Rome been equally distributed among the importing countries according to their populations.

Armed with this assumption he advanced to the conclusion that more than a third of the permanently important Alexandrian decretals had English cases for their subjects:[1]

> Which is or ought to be one of the most prominent facts in the history of the English Church.

Now, in its strictly literal meaning, this final conclusion was perfectly accurate, but not in the meaning which Maitland intended. The astonishing number of permanently important decretals which were originally received by English bishops was due directly to the formative influence of English canon lawyers in the crucial early phases of decretal codification. There was nothing intrinsically more important or more significant in the decretals received at that time in England than those received elsewhere, and their striking presence in the decretal collections is easily explained in the light of the technical development of the latter. But Maitland's argument was developed still more forcefully by Zachary Brooke who carried the investigation back into the *Quinque Compilationes Antiquae*. It is obvious enough, however, from an understanding of the history of the decretal collections and their technical development that the earlier collections naturally reveal an even higher English content than the Gregorian collection. Brooke raised the proportion of English decretals from one third to one half for Alexander III's pontificate, and to two-thirds for that of his successor Lucius III, with a sharp decline thereafter.[2] Maitland's argument appeared to have been triumphantly vindicated. But let us examine the details of Brooke's analysis more closely: Why, he asked, did the bishops of England more than those of any other country in Europe put so many questions to the pope on points of law at that moment; and why did the

---

[1] *Ibid.*, p. 124.
[2] Brooke, *English Church and the Papacy*, pp. 211–14; *idem, Effect of Becket's Murder*, pp. 216–22.

appeals from England alone require so many legal rulings? The following explanation appeared to him the most convincing: the canon law was fully valid in England only after Henry II's submission at Avranches in 1172, and the English bishops were in need of papal guidance both in matters of law and on points of procedure. Their continental contemporaries, on the other hand, were well abreast of the most recent developments, so that their appeals did not provoke such interesting decisions, and naturally the latter were not incorporated in the decretal collections. But by the end of Lucius III's pontificate this necessary work of instructing the English was completed, and that factor explains the decline in English interest after that date.[1]

At least two major defects in this line of argumentation come instantly to mind: if the continental canonists and ecclesiastical judges were so conversant with the law that they had no need to question the pope in the same way as their English colleagues, why did they also assiduously gather together the resulting papal rescripts, as was certainly their practice even where they had not taken the original initiative in composing the archetypes? And, secondly, if the English ecclesiastics alone in some particular way were in need of such guidance, through lagging behind their continental contemporaries, how is it that later decretals of a similar nature were sent predominantly to European rather than English recipients, once this necessary task of instructing the English had been completed? For this is the conclusion which must be reached if the evidence in the decretal collections is taken consistently at its face value. And, lastly, if the decretals addressed to England were designed simply to bring the regional church into line with the state of law already existing elsewhere in Europe, why did these very letters form so important a part of the great Gregorian collection, a work of universal importance assembled by Raymond of Peñaforte half a century later in Italy?

The answer to these questions has become evident as a knowledge of the history of decretal codification has increased, chiefly through the identification of the sources on which both the most primitive and the later systematic collections ultimately depended. It is clearly misleading to build historical

[1] *Ibid.*, pp. 220–2.

theories on the regional ratios of decretals received into the Gregorian *Decretales*, since this collection depended chiefly on the *Quinque Compilationes Antiquae; Compilatio Prima* in turn was the fruit of the systematic tradition which can be traced still further back through such works as *Lipsiensis* and *Bambergensis* to the *Appendix*; the latter derived its Alexandrian letters from primitive collections such as those examined in the chapters above; the decretals in the primitive collections were drawn more frequently from English sources than from those of any other country, though the influence of the Italian collections was also vital. We have shown above that many of the most primitive of the continental collections were largely indebted to earlier English archetypes for much of their raw material; and that, even where they were not so indebted, they reveal no personal or regional interests in their composition comparable with those so very evident in English collections. Therefore, it is not altogether surprising if more letters of English provenance were ultimately recorded in the most famous decretal collections than those which were sent to any other part of Europe. But this conclusion bears no relationship with the numbers of decretals sent out from the papal chancery. Whenever dependence on a non-English or curial source can be proved in a given collection, the proportion of English decretals contained in it is decidedly different and much less remarkable than that in the decretal collections as a whole. Thus, to revert once again to the register fragment appearing as the 50th Title in the edited version of the *Appendix*: this sequence has only eleven English inscriptions in a total of sixty-seven chapters, which is one sixth of its total contents, compared with one half in *Compilatio Prima* or with nine-tenths in some of the most primitive collections now surviving.[1] The proportion of English decretals increases as the examination is carried back into the primitive period, so that even a non-English work may reveal a third or a half of its total contents with English inscriptions. Thus, the Cambridge Collection in the French family has not less than thirty-seven English items in a total complement of ninety-nine.[2]

---

[1] This has been shown in various collections discussed in Chapter IV, above. Thus, only three decretals with continental inscriptions are found in the first fifty items in *Claud.*: 11, 41 and 50: to Rouen, Reims and Limoges.

[2] Friedberg, *Canonessammlungen*, pp. 5–21.

It is a paradox of the decretal investigation that the further back the examination is retraced in time, and the larger the number of collections analysed, the more convincing does the thesis advanced by Maitland and Brooke appear at first to be: precisely because, in so doing, one approaches more closely that period in which the infusion of English material was at its greatest. The apparent cessation of papal legislative interest in England about the year 1185, if the evidence in the decretal collections were taken at its face value, marks in reality not a change in papal policy but the decisive supremacy which the continental jurists and collectors had by then achieved over the whole range of decretal codification. With this development, the accumulation of rescripts in England, although it continued much as before, ceased to leave any decisive impression on the general corpus of decretals still amassing in the rest of Europe. Therefore, from an examination of the systematic collections composed after that time, it appears as if the stream of papal mandates and commissions flowing into England was suddenly slowed. Whereas in fact the change in decretal provenance reflects merely the closure of a widespread dependence on English archetypes and decretal records, and a more general reliance on decretals addressed to all parts of Europe. In a total of at least one thousand and fifty-five decretals now known from the collections preceding *Compilatio Prima*, seven hundred and thirteen were issued by Alexander III; and of these no less than three hundred and fifty-nine were dispatched to England. Including all Anglo-Norman territories, but excluding Scotland and Ireland, three hundred and ninety-nine of these Alexandrian letters were received in regions subject to English influence. But, in the same general total, one hundred decretals were received in France, eighty-nine in Italy, twenty-one in Spain and Portugal, and only three in Germany. Finally, in a total exceeding four hundred decretals sent by Alexander III to the British Isles and the Angevin empire, none was addressed to Ireland. These proportions merely reflect the relative influence of the canonists in the various countries in providing the raw material for the professional collections. They can have no relationship with the numbers of decretals sent out. To cite one final but most significant example: considering the vital developments in the Irish Church in the period, it would be absurd to suppose that the pitifully small number of Irish decretals preserved in the professional collections reflects in any way the extent of papal legislative interest in the island. Numerous decretals must undoubtedly have been received there, but they have left no traces in the canonical collections.[1]

The raw material suitable for inclusion in the decretal collections existed in fact in most districts if local canonists saw fit to use it, as the systematic Bruges Collection confirms very strikingly. Based largely on the central systematic tradition which included the *Appendix* and the Bamberg Collection, this great compilation was made in France about the same time as *Compilatio Prima* was published in Italy; but it was unknown to the author of that epoch-making Italian collection, and its individual contribution of decretals found no place in the generally accepted corpus of decretals on which the Gregorian *Decretales* ultimately depended. The chief interest of the Bruges Collection in the present context lies in its large number of decretals derived from the regional archives in the province of Reims, relating especially to Reims itself, Amiens, Arras, Châlons, Epernay and other central or northern French districts. Most of these letters were sent out by Alexander III and were found in no other collection so far published, and provide a convincing refutation of the thesis that the large number of decretals to English bishops in most decretal collections suggests that the English were in fact in need of particular instruction. If Brooke's argument were valid as applied by him to the Church in England, then the Bruges Collection provides equally acceptable evidence that the great archbishopric of Reims was similarly out of touch with the latest state of canonical opinion. The theory is of course invalid in either case. At least thirty-five decretals, or parts of decretals, received by French ecclesiastics, or of special interest to them, are found in the Bruges Collection, where they first appeared. So interesting and significant are these examples that it is worth citing a few of their inscriptions in illustration:[2]

[1] Holtzmann, *Nachrichten*, p. 34.
[2] Friedberg, *Canonessammlungen*, pp. 140–70. For other examples, see *Brug.* XXVI, 2; XXVII, 4; XXXI, 2; XXXII, 3; XXXVI, 2 and 6; XXXIX, 2; XL,

Brugensis:

IV, 6.   To the archbishop of Reims.

VIII, 3.   To the bishop of Beauvais and the dean of Reims.

XIII, 5.   To the abbot and chapter of St. Bartholomew's at Noyon.

XIV, 18.   To the provost, dean, chanter and chapter of Reims.

XVII, 7.   To the dean and chanter of Reims.

XIX, 19.   To the bishop of Amiens and the abbot of St. Quentin's at Lille.

XX, 3.   To the archbishop of Reims.

XXIV, 1.   To the archbishop of Reims.

4.   To the bishop of Arras.

5.   To the bishop of Amiens.

XXVI, 1.   To the bishop of Amiens.

And there are many other examples of this kind.

One final consideration now remains. What explanation can be offered for this remarkable English interest in papal decretal legislation, far surpassing in its earliest stages that of all other parts of Western Europe? And, within this wider problem, why was it governed so largely by so few of the English bishops? The classical solution of the first of these problems has been sought in the failure of Henry II's policy to limit the jurisdictional independence of the *ecclesia Anglicana* vis-à-vis the secular government, and in the resulting inrush of decretal letters which signalized the papal victory. The barriers which the Conqueror had raised in his relations with the English Church and the Papacy, to prevent bishops leaving England without his permission and papal legates coming in, had been largely overthrown in the turbulent reign of Stephen; and it was Henry's intention that these should be re-erected as opportunity provided. The early years of Henry's reign witnessed a further advance in the Church's concern for its liberties and jurisdictional freedom, under the guidance of Theobald, and reflected in the increasing reception and study of canon law. But the situation was no longer as favourable to the Church, as it had been during the years of Stephen's weakness; and the parallel growth of secular law and royal administration increasingly now provoked a conflict of ecclesiastical and secular

14 and 15; XLIV, 3; XLV, 8 and 9; XLVI, 6; XLVII, 26; XLIX, 16 and 23; LI, 2 and 5; LIII, 1, 2 and 14; LIV, 3; LVIII, 1 and LIX, 1.

interests.[1] In these circumstances, the right of appeal from the
English ecclesiastical courts to the papal Curia, and the growing practice of referring to the pope on all sorts of questions as
a judge of first instance, in his capacity as Universal Ordinary,
raised the problems of church-state relations in an unusually acute
form. The actual clash between Henry II and Becket arose
over the vexed question of clerical immunity from secular
judgement in criminal cases, ending for Thomas in violent
death in his own cathedral, and for Henry in humiliation and in
the concession at Avranches (1172) of most of what the archbishop had demanded. It is suggested that the 'flood-gates'
were thereby thrown wide open to full-scale papal intervention
after a long period of isolation, in which the English Church
had been cut off from developments taking place elsewhere in
Europe. According to this theory, the English bishops were
through their former isolation in need of special guidance, and
the legally-minded Alexander seized the opportunity to work
out in these ideal circumstances the latest legal theories and
principles, thus explaining his seeming preoccupation with the
English Church. But it is obvious enough from the history of the
decretal collections, as outlined briefly in the preceding chapters,
that such an interpretation is quite misleading in many parti-
culars. It is defective both in respect of fact and in appreciation
of the sources available.[2]

As to the question of fact: the independent records of papal
letters being now made increasingly available from monastic
and cathedral archives provide two major conclusions: the
acceleration of papal legislation through decretal letters, in the
Western Church as a whole, has no necessary connexion with
the peculiar course of developments within the Church in
England. Its origin is independent in motive, and prior in
initiation, to the struggle between Henry II and Becket; and
so to consider the apparent inrush of decretal letters which

[1] A. Saltman, *Theobald, Archbishop of Canterbury*, Athlone Press: University of
London Historical Studies, 2 (1956); Cheney, *From Becket to Langton: English Church
Government, 1170–1213*, Manchester (1956).
[2] This is not to deny the importance of the studies by Maitland and Brooke on
the history of the English Church in the period. Much of their work is valid and of
permanent value. Even within the present context some of their conclusions could
be supported, but not on a basis of the evidence which they cited.

followed the Avranches settlement as a novel departure in papal policy is to misunderstand completely its European context. The new decretal era in papal legislation was an expression of the centralizing tendencies which had increasingly characterized ecclesiastical government from the time of the Hildebrandine Reform in the previous century; and, in its canonistic setting, must be interpreted in the light of the closure of *ius antiquum* and the emergence of a true science of canon law with the publication of Gratian's *Decretum*.

What imparts an aura of peculiar importance to the 1172 settlement for England is its coincidence in time with the floodtide of decretal legislation under Alexander III, coming after a period of confused church-state relations in Europe generally and in England in particular. Still more important is its coincidence in time with the emergence of a novel interest in the professional collecting of papal decretal letters, which is quite a different matter from a change in papal legislative policies. The origin and development of this new canonistic interest have been the main theme of this study, so little further need now be said about it. It was precisely in the period of the Avranches settlement and the years immediately following it that canonists began for the first time to assemble their own collections of contemporary decretal letters. And it seems indisputable from the evidence discussed above that the most striking enthusiasm in the earliest phases of the movement was displayed in England. For these reasons, the large number of decretals then received in England and taken into the professional collections need excite no particular attention in considering the course of central papal policy. Nevertheless, the fact that so many of the earliest collections were devised by English canonists is a matter of the utmost importance for English ecclesiastical historians, illustrating the one phase above all in which English initiative exercised a crucial influence on the development of canon law for the Universal Church.

Herein lies the true importance of the 1172 agreement.[1] If the policy of Henry II had proved successful, the various expressions of papal jurisdictional authority would have been ex-

---

[1] *Ibid.*, p. 108: 'The so-called compromise of Avranches settled nothing; but the next generation was a period of effective adjustment.'

cluded (at least to some extent) from England, and the introduction of decretal letters and commissions to judges delegate
gravely diminished. This could scarcely have influenced the
course of papal legislation in Europe generally, but it would
have effectively prevented that striking contribution which
English bishops and canonists made in the event to the development of the decretal collections. For this reason, it is fitting to
claim for the settlement a place of permanent importance in the
history of the English Church, but even more in the history of
the Church as a whole.

A final word must be said of the personal role of the English
bishops and canonists who had the greatest share in the application of decretal law in England, and the greatest influence
on the development of the English collections. Bartholomew of
Exeter, Roger of Worcester, Baldwin of Ford and Richard of
Canterbury: these are the names which have recurred most
significantly above; these are the men who left their indelible
mark on the English collections. It is scarcely a matter of simple
coincidence that these are also the men who most clearly represent the Becket position or party in the dramatic struggle which
had recently been concluded.[1] Above all other bishops in
England, Bartholomew and Roger are known to have sympathized with the exiled and martyred archbishop: Roger
actually shared his exile (together with John of Salisbury, Herbert of Bosham and others), and finally incurred with Bartholomew the anger of Henry II on this account. Baldwin, too,
maintained close correspondence with the exiled party, and
retired to Ford at the height of the conflict. Richard of Canterbury was not a participant in the conflict, and indeed was sometimes regarded later as too lukewarm in his defence of the rights
for which Thomas had died, yet he may be considered involved
in the Becket position through right of succession in the primatial
see.[2] But, in contrast with this, the famous English bishops
whose share in the systematic extension of papal jurisdiction in
England appears very much slighter than that of these, are

[1] Morey, *op. cit.*, pp. 15–30.
[2] On one occasion Alexander III reproached Richard for endangering the rights
of the Church for which Becket had shed his blood: see the decretal *Qua fronte*,
J-L 14312, 1174–81.

known for the most part as ecclesiastically indifferent or more typically as Becket's opponents: Hugh of Durham, Roger of York, Gilbert of London. It is not unreasonable to suggest a relationship between these phenomena, and to conclude that the pro-Becket bishops played the decisive part after the settlement in clinching the victory through a rapid extension of papal jurisdictional authority. And this is all the more likely since they were naturally more acceptable to Pope Alexander, and were involved personally in what may be called the papalist position in the recent controversy. The prelates of the north and Gilbert Foliot in the south were by no means excluded from the receipt of decretal letters, but it seems that in practice they showed little interest in their professional accumulation. These factors, together with the frequency with which Bartholomew, Roger and Baldwin were commissioned as judges delegate, firmly support our thesis that the chief instruments in the application of decretal legislation in England, as well as in the accumulation of decretal letters in professional collections, were found most conveniently as well as most naturally in the supporters of the late archbishop. By what means precisely the fruits of this English enthusiasm were transmitted into the main streams of contemporary continental developments cannot be established with certainty in the present state of historical knowledge. But we shall end with this speculation: an ideal instrument for their propagation may be seen in the widespread dominions and the numerous diplomatic missions of the Angevin king, exceeding those of any other secular ruler in Western Europe at that time. From Scotland in the north to the Pyrenees in the south, and to the Atlantic coast of Brittany in the west, the Angevin king held direct sway; while, as a result of the political marriages of his daughters, he numbered among his relations King William II of Sicily, King Alphonso of Castile and Duke Henry the Lion of Saxony. The ceaseless and restless diplomatic exchanges and journeyings between England and almost every part of western Europe, conducted for the most part by English clerics, and the councils and arbitrations held under the presidency of the English ruler, afforded an ideal opportunity for the dissemination of material and ideas. The career of John of Salisbury, and his connexions with the schools of

France and with southern Italy and Sicily; the council convened at Westminster in 1177 to arbitrate between the Kings of Navarre and Castile (at which both Bartholomew of Exeter and Roger of Worcester were present, together with Spanish prelates): these are but a few random examples of the numberless points of contact between English bishops and canonists and their continental colleagues.[1] By such means the Angevin Empire played its part in facilitating the spread of English decretal collections throughout the west of Europe. And this is a striking reflection of the failure of Henry II's ecclesiastical policy.

[1] Morey, *op. cit.*, p. 41; Hall, *Roger of Worcester*, p. 47. See also Chapter IV, pp. 116–17, above. The conclusions summarized in this final chapter do not imply that the work of the English collectors ceased after the mid-1180s, but simply that their influence declined in the overall development of decretal codification throughout the Western Church. The Tanner, St Germain and Avranches Collections record later channels of transmission of English or Anglo-Norman influence on collections made elsewhere, and lend further support to the arguments developed above in connexion with the *Appendix*. It is hoped in future studies to trace more closely the interconnexions between the English and continental schools of canonists. See my forthcoming 'Primitive Decretal Collections in the British Museum', *Studies in Ecclesiastical History*, I, Nelson (1963).

IV

Primitive Decretal Collections in the British Museum

ECCLESIASTICAL historians are already aware of the richness of the British Museum in canonical manuscripts of all kinds. The Royal Library alone preserves at least one copy of the greater number of major canonical collections, as well as an imposing range of the works of leading commentators, decretists and decretalists alike, glosses and *summae*, together with the fascinating, if minor, canonistic exercises known as *distinctiones*, *abbreviationes*, *casus*, *quaestiones*, *transformationes* and *notabilia*.[1] A history of the canon law of the medieval Church could in most essentials be written on the basis of these considerable and varied sources. What is perhaps rather less familiar is the particular value of these manuscripts to the historian of the medieval English Church, both in a positive and a negative way: negative in the sense of the ample evidence provided of a rapid and wide-spread reception of ecclesiastical common law in England; and positive in the sense of the record preserved of the initiative and originality revealed by English canonists, and of the contribution which they made in turn to the law of the Universal Church. The copies or abridgements of the ninth-century *Pseudo-Isidore* and Lanfranc's related collection, now in the Museum but belonging originally to English Cathedral chapters in the early-twelfth century, reveal as significantly as any other evidence the dissemination of canon law in the post-Conquest

[1] Cf. G. F. Warner and J. P. Gilson, *Catalogue of Western Manuscripts in the Old Royal and King's Collections*, III (1921): *King's Manuscripts and Indexes*, under 'Canon Law,' 112-4; S. Kuttner, 'Repertorium der Kanonistik, 1140-1234,' *Studi e Testi*, LXXI (1937,) 126, 128, 143, 148, 219, 220, 229, 231, 235, 251, 259, 269-70, 322-44, 477-8, etc. Kuttner lists forty-two volumes in the British Museum each including at least one canonical work from the period 1140-1234.

Primitive Decretal Collections in the British Museum

English Church.[1] The *Quaestiones disputatae*, one of several items in the Royal MS 9 E.VII, record the literary work of English canonists of the later-twelfth century in the circle of John of Tynemouth, Simon of Southwell and others of their school[2]; the copious and systematic lecture notes of Walter Cachepol and an associated group of English decretalists, filling the voluminous Royal MS 9 E.VIII, throw much revealing light on the academic skill of English canon lawyers in the later-fourteenth century[3]; and many other examples of a similar kind could be cited. But second to none of these in interest or importance are the primitive decretal collections of the later-twelfth century, unrivalled numerically in any other single library, English or continental, and preceding in date of composition or technical style the publication of Bernard of Pavia's *Breviarium extravagantium*, or *Compilatio Prima*, completed in or about 1191.[4]

Gratian's *Decretum* had marked a turning point in the history of canonical codification. The literary exposition and interpretation of this quasi-authoritative text began almost immediately after its completion and wide propagation in the mid-twelfth century.[5] Working on this textual basis as an adequate summary of previously defined law, or *ius antiquum*, and influenced also by the rapid development of papal appellate jurisdiction, reflected in the ever-swelling stream of decretals issuing from the papal Curia and the

---

[1] See especially Z. N. Brooke, *The English Church and the Papacy from the Conquest to the Reign of John*, Cambridge 1931, 57-83, 231-45, 247, *et passim*.

[2] Royal MS 9 E.VII, ff. 191-9. Cf. S. Kuttner and E. Rathbone, 'Anglo-Norman Canonists of the Twelfth Century: an Introductory Study,' *Traditio*, VII (1951), 317-21. The volume includes the *Summa* of Johannes Faventinus and a commentary on part of Gratian's *Decretum*; it belonged originally to St Augustine's Canterbury.

[3] Royal MS 9 E.VIII, 198 fols. transcribed on paper. The main element is a set of lectures delivered by Walter Cachepol († 1369) on the Gregorian *Decretales*, the *Liber Sextus* and the *Clementinae*; the notes are preceded on ff. 1-26 by an alphabetical table of topics, and provide a tabulation on f. 172. In addition to Cachepol, the catalogue lists numerous English canonists whose views are referred to in the volume. Cf. A. B. Emden, *Biographical Register of the University of Oxford to A.D. 1500*, Oxford 1957, I, 337.

[4] For *Compilatio Prima*, see E. Friedberg, ed. *Quinque Compilationes Antiquae necnon Compilatio Lipsiensis*, Leipzig 1882; R. Naz, 'Compilationes (Quinque Antiquae)' in *DDC*, 1942, III, 1239-41; etc.

[5] Among many recent studies on Gratian's work, see Kuttner, 'Graziano: L'Uomo e l'Opera,' in J. Forchielli and A. M. Stickler, edd. *Studia Gratiana*, I (1953), 17-29; A. Vetulani, 'Le Décret de Gratien et les premiers décrétistes à la lumière d'une source nouvelle,' *Studia Gratiana*, VII (1959), 273-353.

elaboration of the system of papal judges delegate, the canonists now conceived a new kind of compilation, composed predominantly of the most recent papal rescripts. These works in fact record the gradual accumulation of a corpus of ecclesiastical case law, based on the most up-to-date authoritative judgments, and are known conventionally as *libri extravagantium*, or *libri decretalium*, or more simply as decretal collections. Their formative period extended from the mid-1170s to *c.*1191, culminating at that later date in the publication of Bernard of Pavia's *Compilatio Prima*, mentioned above.[1] With Bernard's work the technical and juristic development of decretal codification reached its full maturity, and the subsequent history of decretal collections is common knowledge. It is for the preceding seminal period that the British Museum collections provide such valuable evidence.

About fifty collections survive in manuscript from this creative phase for the whole of the Western Church, and these are classified in two main styles as primitive or systematic in technical composition. The best of the primitive collections are divided into books, and further sub-divided into titles, on a subject-matter basis; but the systematic collections reveal, in addition to such advantages, a dismemberment and re-classification of the component parts of the longer decretals, which often included many constituent chapters of varied interest in a single letter, a ruthless elimination of passages of non-juridical value, and a thoroughly mature and professional treatment of the whole work. Roughly half the total number of extant collections of all kinds fall within the primitive range; and these in turn can be separated into family or regional groups on a basis of their established provenance or textual inter-connections. More than half of all surviving primitive collections known at present are of English origin, composing three distinct but also inter-related groups, described as the 'English,'

---

[1] Excellent summaries of these developments are provided in W. Holtzmann, 'Über eine Ausgabe der päpstlichen Dekretalen des 12. Jahrhunderts,' *Nachrichten von der Akademie der Wissenschaften in Göttingen, Phil.-Hist. Kl.* 1945, 15-36; idem and E. W. Kemp, *Papal Decretals relating to the Diocese of Lincoln in the Twelfth Century*: Lincoln Record Society, 1954, XLVII, ix-xvii; Kuttner, 'Notes on a Projected Corpus of Twelfth-Century Decretal Letters,' *Traditio*, VI (1948), 345-51; A. van Hove, *Prolegomena ad Codicem Iuris Canonici*, Malines-Rome 1945, 345-57. See also my *Twelfth-Century Decretal Collections and their Importance in English History*, University of London Historical Studies, 1963, XII, for a more detailed examination of many points dealt with very briefly in this essay.

Primitive Decretal Collections in the British Museum

'Bridlington' and 'Worcester' families respectively. And, in a similar way, the continental primitive collections fall into three regional categories, identified by present usage as the Roman or 'Tortosa,' the French and the Italian groups. From an overall total of fifteen extant English primitive collections, no less than eight are now in the British Museum library, including four of seven members in the 'English' family, one of two 'Bridlington' survivors, and three of six collections composing the 'Worcester' group. In addition to these English collections, one member of the Roman or 'Tortosa' family, the Eberbach Collection, is also found in the BritishMuseum now, though it was in all probability a work of continental provenance originally. To sum up this statistical survey: roughly one sixth of all decretal collections surviving from the creative period of their development, or one third of all extant primitive collections from the same period, are now in the British Museum. The palaeographical details of these manuscripts and their bibliographical references are supplied in an appendix below; and their authorship and provenance have been already explored in separate studies.[1] It is enough here to state briefly the salient features of the English primitive collections, and indicate their interest for historians of the English Church.[2]

Four members of the primitive 'English' family reveal with perfect clarity the earliest technical phases in the development of decretal collections in England and the sources on which their authors drew. The Worcester II Collection is among the most basic and original collections now surviving, being perhaps as early as 1175 in date of composition. It is a very short work, comprising no more than ten decretals in all, of certain Worcester provenance and dependent partly on the judicial records of Roger, bishop of Worcester, 1164-79. The Canterbury Collection is in reality three quite separate sections, containing sixty-two, five and twenty-two items respectively, independent alike in composition and transcription, but bound up together with other canonical works in a single volume. Its first group of decretals drew significantly on Canterbury archives; and its third section is supplemented with the canons of

---

[1] Holtzmann, *Nachrichten*, 15-36, especially 21ff.; idem and Kemp, *Lincoln Decretals*, xi-xvi; Kuttner, *Repertorium*, 272ff.; idem, *Projected Corpus*, 345-51; etc.

[2] Duggan, *Decretal Collections*, especially ch. 4: 'The English Decretal Collections,' 66-117.

the Third Lateran Council of 1179. The latest likely date of composition of any of its component parts is 1179-81. The Rochester Collection is a close relation of the Canterbury Collection, but is a more finished or polished work, and transcribed as an entity. Following the canons of the 1179 Lateran Council, roughly the first half of the 'Rochester' decretals are affiliated to the opening sequence in the Canterbury Collection, but these are supplemented with further letters down to 1193, making a total of about one hundred and twenty-five items in addition to the conciliar decrees. It is evident that the Rochester Collection drew on both English and continental sources to expand an English work already existing. The Royal Collection, of uncertain provenance, comprises one hundred and twenty-six decretals or canons in all. Despite its unattractive format and occasional careless details, it is technically more advanced than the other collections in its group, revealing many of the typical features of systematic codification. It has no decretals later than 1181 in date of issue. All four collections are correctly described as primitive: none has achieved a consistent or clearly defined classification of subject-matter, though there is some concentration of decretals of cognate interest in the Canterbury, Rochester and Royal Collections, while the last-named work was assembled with considerable professional skill. The principal interest of these collections lies in their provenance: the Worcester II Collection is clearly of Worcester origin; the Canterbury and Rochester Collections reveal a partial dependence on Canterbury archives, and are completed from the comparable records of Worcester and Exeter more significantly than those of other English sees; the Rochester Collection drew also on non-English sources; the Royal Collection suggests less obviously such immediate regional influences, but it also includes a large proportion of letters received at Canterbury, Worcester and Exeter, with those addressed to Exeter being most significantly grouped in this instance.

The 'Bridlington' family is represented among the Museum manuscripts by the Claudian Collection, which, with the Bridlington Collection in the Bodleian Library, was derived from an English archetype now lost. It is a large and well-integrated work, set out in two hundred and sixteen numerated items, many with several component chapters, and incorporating three groups of conciliar decrees. The collection portrays the typical 'Bridlington' style with

Primitive Decretal Collections in the British Museum

an elaborate system of rubrics for the individual items and some of their constituent parts, a brief gloss commentary and a marginal apparatus of cross-references of a very elementary kind. The first half of the collection was derived from the family archetype, composed about 1181 or shortly after, and dependent on English sources for roughly nine-tenths of its total contents. This 'Bridlington' stock records a Canterbury-Worcester-Exeter predominance of decretals, similar to that noted already in the 'English' works listed above. But the Claudian Collection is completed with further letters down to 1185-7 in date of issue; this supplementary section depended on both English and continental sources, and in one note-worthy sequence of thirty marriage decretals seems clearly derived from a non-English work. Stylistically, the collection advances little beyond the 'English' group already discussed. It has no overall pattern of composition to suit a subject-matter classification, but there is some grouping of letters of related interest, and a measure of technical skill is revealed by occasional decretal dissection and textual abbreviation in the later stages of composition.

The 'Worcester' family is in some respects the most interesting group of English primitive collections. Apart from the very large number of decretals which it preserves, many being re-discovered for the first time in 'Worcester' manuscripts, it also records the evolution of a distinct line of technical development in style and composition. The earliest 'Worcester' phase is exemplified by the Worcester Collection, completed in or shortly after 1181 and devised in seven books on a broad basis of subject-matter classification. The volume incorporating the Worcester Collection includes further letters independent of the main 'Worcester' transmission, continuing the accumulation of material down to 1187 or later. It has clearly some authentic Worcester connections, and almost certainly belonged to a member of the *familia* of Baldwin, successively abbot of Ford in the Exeter diocese, bishop of Worcester and archbishop of Canterbury (†1190).[1] A different line of development from the family archetype is seen in the 'Cheltenham' Collection, in which several separate sources and strata of composition can be distinguished, continuing its elaboration down to 1193 or soon after. The archetypal 'Worcester' matter is set out in this instance

[1] Duggan, 'The Trinity Collection of Decretals and the Early Worcester Family,' *Traditio*, XVII (1961), 506-26.

under many rubricated titles, and supplemented from other sources including a member of the influential Bamberg-Leipzig group of continental systematic collections.[1] In contrast with this, the final phase of the main 'Worcester' tradition is found in the Cottonian Collection, a large work whose several component books disclose a readjustment of the archetypal decretals to secure a more precise arrangement of topics; the books are thus sub-divided into titles and they are also supplemented with further decretals down to 1193 in date of issue. The manuscript is unfortunately damaged by fire and partly illegible, but a large proportion of the lost material can be reconstructed by comparison with a closely related collection in the Peterhouse library in Cambridge. The Cottonian and Peterhouse Collections were completed in that order in or after 1193. The 'Worcester' collections are of more complex ancestry than the 'English' and 'Bridlington' works, and their regional sources are more concealed by the redistribution of letters to suit an analytical concept of subject-matter arrangement; but it is clear that both English and continental collections were intermingled in their composition. The 'Worcester' family in its different phases was linked with important lines of transmission in the systematic tradition—perhaps with the seminal *Appendix Concilii Lateranensis* (*c.*1181-5),[2] and certainly with the Anglo-Norman *Tanner*, *Abrincensis* and *Sangermanensis*, composed about the close of the century,[3] and so left its traces in the principal sources of decretals of the late twelfth century.

One further collection completes the total of nine primitive works preserved in this single library. The Eberbach Collection is a member of the Roman or 'Tortosa' group, and is non-English in authorship and possibly also in transcription. It is certain that the manuscript belonged at an earlier period to the Cistercian abbey of the Blessed Virgin Mary in Eberbach, and was transferred to England in more recent times. The work is set out in twenty-five parts, comprising one hundred and eleven chapters in all, of which

[1] For the Bamberg, Leipzig and other related collections, see Friedberg, *Die Canonessammlungen zwischen Gratian und Bernhard von Pavia*, Leipzig 1897; and, more recently, W. Deeters, *Die Bambergensisgruppe der Dekretalensammlungen des 12. Jahrhunderts*, Doctoral dissertation, Bonn 1956.

[2] Duggan, 'English Canonists and the *Appendix Concilii Lateranensis*; with an analysis of the St John's College, Cambridge, MS 148,' *Traditio*, XVIII (1962), 459-68.

[3] Cf. Holtzmann and Kemp, *Lincoln Decretals*, xii-xv.

Primitive Decretal Collections in the British Museum

the final twenty-seven are canons of the 1179 Lateran Council; its date of completion is c.1179-81. Though by general agreement a work of continental, if debated, origin, the collection can be broken down statistically to provide conclusions of much interest to English historians: at least thirty-two of its first forty-seven decretals were received by English ecclesiastics, and of these no less than twenty were received at Canterbury, while only about one tenth of the decretals in the second half of the work have English inscriptions.[1] This evidence suggests that the Eberbach Collection preserves an expansion of an English archetype in the hands of a continental canonist, a conclusion supported by similar evidence in various other collections in the 'Tortosa' and French groups.[2]

Judged in a context of the total evidence of a similar kind surviving in English and continental libraries, the collections discussed above support conclusions of the highest significance. The origins of primitive decretal collections have been much discussed by continental scholars. Studies by Heckel, Holtzmann, Vetulani and many others have traced the formative influence of the Curia and the papal registers, and evaluated the evidence for the view that there existed a central source of supply from which semi-official archetypes were dispatched widely through the schools.[3] There is no doubt that influences of this kind have left their traces in some collections, and many in fact incorporate express citations from the central registers. But the earliest stages in the emergence of decretal codification can be explained by no single factor simply. The total corpus of decretals surviving from the late-twelfth century records a fusion of many diverse strands of development; and in this fusion the English collections played a distinct and important part. The English collections of the most primitive kind reveal no central or Curial stimulus or source of supply. They disclose on the contrary a creative initiative displayed by English canonists in accumulating

[1] Holtzmann, 'Die Collectio Eberbacensis,' *Zeitschrift der Savigny Stiftung für Rechtsgeschichte, Kanonistiche Abteilung*, XVII (1928), 548-55; idem, *Nachrichten*, 21; Kuttner, *Projected Corpus*, 346; Duggan, *Decretal Collections*, 126-28.

[2] Ibid. 124-35.

[3] Cf. Holtzmann, 'Die Register Papst Alexanders III. in den Händen der Kanonisten,' *Quellen und Forschungen aus italienischen Archiven und Bibliotheken*, XXX (1940), 13-87; Vetulani, 'L'Origine des collections primitives de décrétales à la fin du XIIe siècle,' *Congrès de Droit Canonique Médiéval*, Louvain 1959, 64-72; etc.

the most recent rescripts which they themselves received, and reflect at that stage little assimilation of comparable works produced by other schools, though they were later expanded from non-English sources. They are, without question, the works of English authors, reflecting the activities of English judges delegate and assembled in their primary phases on a basis of English archives. The seminal period in their development was the decade following the death of Becket (1170); and the most striking feature of their growth is a dependence on the judicial records of Exeter, Worcester and Canterbury. The political and juristic implications of this evidence, and its relationship with the course of papal jurisdiction in England after the Avranches settlement in 1172, have been fully discussed in a separate volume.[1] Briefly, it may be suggested that the prelates of these sees were principally, but not exclusively, instrumental in making papal jurisdiction effective in England in that period of settlement; and that the greater juristic concern of the canonists in their circles is reflected in their interest in recording the decretals received by English bishops. The British Museum collections of the English primitive families provide a major part of the evidence by which these conclusions can be sustained; and the Eberbach manuscript preserves a single, though not unique, example of the formative influence of such English works on collections of the same style and period produced in other schools. The creative impulse displayed by English collectors and its resulting impact on significant lines of transmission in continental groups of collections left a lasting mark on the corpus of decretal law surviving from the late-twelfth century. This corpus in turn played its part in shaping the contents of the famous collections of the following century. And in this way the English canonists had made a decisive and permanent contribution to the law of the Universal Church.

[1] Duggan, *Decretal Collections*, 118-51: in the supplement on MSS, appended below, all references to this volume are identified as *Decretal Collections*; in most instances, details are also found *sub nominibus* in Kuttner, *Repertorium*; Holtzmann, *Nachrichten*; idem and Kemp, *Lincoln Decretals*; and *DDC*.

Primitive Decretal Collections in the British Museum

MANUSCRIPTS

1 *The 'English' Family*

(a) The Worcester II Collection: *Wigorniensis Altera :* Royal MS 11 B.II, ff. 97ʳ-102ʳ. Vellum: 10⅛ x 6⅞ ins; double cols. of 34 lines. Initials of inscriptions, decretals and chapters alternately blue and red to f. 98ᵛᵃ; many inscriptions and initials omitted; well-written in several stages in similar hands. Cf. *Decretal Collections*, 46, 69-70, 152-4 and Plate I. MS also includes tracts on legal and theological subjects: *Summa* of Paucapalea; commentary on part of Gratian's *Decretum ;* etc. Belonged to Worcester Cathedral Priory: f. 1, 'Liber monasterii Wygornie.' Cent., xii-early xiii.

(b) The Canterbury Collection: *Cantuariensis :* Royal MS 10 B. IV, ff. 42ᵛᵃ-58ᵛᵇ and 59ᵛᵇ-65ʳᵃ. Vellum: 10⅞ x 7⅞ ins. In four parts: (i) Running on from tract *Quoniam in hac :* Decretals, ff. 42ᵛᵃ-58ᵛᵇ ; double cols. of 33 (aver.) lines; rubricated inscriptions and initials; some inscriptions omitted; marginal rubrics in black in three hands, mostly in flourishing style; (ii) Decretals, ff. 58ʳᵃ⁻ᵛᵇ, independent of previous section; double cols. of 33 and 41 lines; rubricated initials on f. 58ᵛ; transcribed in two or three stages; (iii) Running on from tract *Iudicum est :* Decretals, ff. 59ᵛᵇ-61ᵛᵇ ; double cols. of 41 lines; decretal initials omitted to f. 60ʳᵇ, thereafter rubricated; some inscriptions erased or omitted; (iv) Canons of 1179 Lateran Council, ff. 62ʳᵃ-65ʳᵃ; double cols. of 41 lines; rubricated initials and titles; texts and rubrics suggest transcription in stages. Cf. *Decretal Collections*, 48, 73-6, 162-73 and Plate III. MS includes treatises on civil and canon law: *Ulpianus de edendo ;* tract by Peter of Blois; etc. Belonged perhaps to Christ Church Canterbury. Cent., xii-xiii.

(c) The Rochester Collection: *Roffensis :* Royal MS 10 C.IV, ff. 137ʳᵃ-155ʳᵃ. Vellum: 13¾ x 8½ ins; double cols. of 48 lines. Very fine transcription including: (i) Canons of 1179 Lateran Council, ff. 137ʳᵃ-139ᵛᵇ ; (ii) Decretals, ff. 139ᵛᵇ-154ʳᵇ ; (iii) One appended decretal, f. 155ʳᵃ⁻ʳᵇ. Finely written throughout, with some changes of hand; initials of canons and decretals in red and blue, with flourished initials on ff. 142ʳᵃ, 152ᵛᵃ and 155ᵛᵃ. Cf. *Decretal Collections*, 76-8 and 173-87. MS includes abridgement of Gratian's *Decretum.* Belonged to Rochester Priory: f. 1, 'Decreta abreviata de claustro Roffensi per A. precentorem.' Cent., early xiii.

(d) The Royal Collection: *Regalis :* Royal MS 15 B.IV, ff. 107ᵛᵃ-118ᵛᵇ. Vellum: 8 x 5⅝ ins; double cols. of varying number of lines: 55, 46, 50, 51, 36, etc. Transcribed with much variation of hand and spacing; no rubrication except 'ABCD' on f. 117ʳ; no marginalia, but some titles incorporated in main transcription; extraneous matter on ff. 107ᵛ, 109ʳ and 109ᵛ. Cf. *Decretal Collections*, 81-4 and Plate II. MS includes works on logic and grammar, letters of Peter of Blois, formulary-book for judges delegate, etc. Original provenance uncertain. Cent., xii and xiii.

Other members of the 'English' family are: (i) The Belvoir Collection: *Belverensis:* Oxford Bodleian Library, MS e Mus. 249, ff. 121-35; (ii) The Fountains Collection: *Fontanensis:* Oxford Bodleian Library, MS Laud Misc. 527, ff. 24-45; (iii) The Durham Collection: *Dunelmensis:* Durham Cathedral MS C. III. 1, ff. 5-18. Cf. *Decretal Collections,* 68-84.

2 The 'Bridlington' Family

The Claudian Collection: *Claudiana:* Cotton MS Claudius A.IV, fols. 189ra-216ra. Vellum: 9$\frac{1}{4}$ x 6$\frac{5}{8}$ ins; double cols. of 40 lines. Well-written throughout; items numbered in red in sequence to no. 216; numerous rubricated headings for decretals, canons and some component chapters; marginal rubrics in black and apparatus of cross-references, some details lost through trimming of fols.; initials of inscriptions omitted; Roman caps. I, II and III at bottom verso of three completed quires of eight fols. Cf. *Decretal Collections,* 84-91 and Plate IV. MS now includes: *Tractatus de Calendario,* statutes of Queen's College Oxford, Gratian's *Decretum* and a brief account of holy places in Jerusalem. Provenance uncertain; cf. f. 187^{v}: 'precium istius libri, xii sol.' Cent., decretal collection: end xii.

The other member of the 'Bridlington' Family is the Bridlington Collection: *Bridlingtonensis:* Oxford MS Bodley 357, ff. 80-133; *Decretal Collections,* 84-95.

3 The 'Worcester' Family

(a) The Worcester Collection: *Wigorniensis:* Royal MS 10 A.II, ff. 5^{r}-62va. Vellum: 9 x 5$\frac{3}{4}$ ins; double cols. of 40 lines. List of book headings on f. 4^{v}; written in good small hand throughout; arranged in seven books, each starting on fresh fol. recto with rubricated heading and illuminated initial phrase in first decretal; initial letter of some books omitted by illuminator; book numbers in blue and red at top of each fol.; blank fols. between component books, with one later insertion on f. 21^{v}; items numbered in red through each book; initial letters of items alternately blue and red, with some elaboration; rubricated inscriptions and many rubrics in red; negligible contemporary marginalia, but some references in much later hand, and occasional line-drawings. Supplemented by: (i) Decretals, ff. 1^{r}-3^{r}: double cols. on 1^{r} and 2^{v}-3^{r}, and single on 2^{r}, in typical English hand, differing from main collection; (ii) Decretals, ff. 62^{v} and 63^{v}, double cols., in at least three hands; ending in mid-decretal on f. 63^{v}. Headings 'Decretales epistole' and 'Decretales epistole due' appear on ff. 1^{r} and 4^{v} respectively. For fuller discussions, see H. Lohmann, 'Die Collectio Wigorniensis,' *ZRG., Kan. Abt.,* XXII (1933), 36-187; P. M. Baumgarten, 'Papal Letters relating to England,' *English Historical Review,* IX (1894), 531-41; Duggan, *Trinity Collection,*

Primitive Decretal Collections in the British Museum

506-26; idem, *Decretal Collections*, 49-51, 95-8, 110-5 and Plates V and VI. Provenance: Worcester and (?) Canterbury, belonging perhaps to Archbishop Baldwin († 1190). Cent., late xii.

(b) The 'Cheltenham' Collection: *Cheltenhamensis:* Egerton MS 2819, ff. 18ra-102vb. Vellum: 10 x 7$\frac{1}{8}$ ins; double cols. of 36 lines. Set out under various rubricated groups of titles, from 'De symoniacis *etc*,' f. 17vb, to 'De penitencia,' f. 96ra; beautifully written throughout, in several stages; inscriptions rubricated but some omitted; decretal initials alternately in red and blue; light marginal gloss and rubrics in black in contemporary hands, with cross-references and citations from Gratian; ff. 101^{v}-102^{r} embellished with green, red and gold initials; final decretal a later addition (1193+), f. 102ra-^{vb}. For relevant literature, cf. Kuttner, *Repertorium*, 298; and *Decretal Collections*, 98-103 and Plate VII. MS includes: civil law tracts, collection of legal maxims, canons of 1179 Lateran Council and group of decretals opening with one of Innocent III. Provenance unknown: cf. f. 1^{v}: 'Noverit universitas vestra quod ego Robertus Parvus dedi et concessi Petro Ruffo'; modern owners include William Shaw Mason († 1853) and Sir Thomas Phillipps († 1872). Cent., late xii and early xiii.

(c) The Cottonian Collection: *Cottoniana:* Cotton MS Vitellius E. XIII, ff. 204^{r}-288^{v}. Vellum: 5$\frac{1}{2}$ x 8$\frac{1}{2}$ ins; double cols. of varying number of lines: 47, 48, 49, 51, etc. Well-written throughout, but much damaged by Cotton fire of 1731 and partly illegible; opens with canons of the councils of Tours (1163) and Lateran (1179), followed by decretals arranged in several books; each book begins with elaborate decretal incipit in red and blue, with line ornamentation on lower fol.; material arranged in titles within the books, but headings omitted by rubricator; negligible marginalia; work transcribed perhaps by several hands. MS includes the history by Florence of Worcester. Provenance uncertain. Cent., late xii- early xiii.

Other members of the 'Worcester' family are: (i) The Trinity Collection: *Trinitatis:* Trinity College Cambridge MS R. 14.9, ff. 82-8; (ii) The Klosterneuburg Collection: *Claustroneoburgensis:* Klosterneuburg Stbl. MS XXXII.19, ff. 36-87; (iii) The Peterhouse Collection, *Peterhusensis:* Peterhouse Cambridge MSS 114, 180, 193 and 203, first and final quires. Cf. Duggan, *Trinity Collection*, 506-26; idem, *Decretal Collections*, 95-117.

4 *The Roman or 'Tortosa' Family*

(a) The Eberbach Collection: *Eberbacensis:* Arundel MS 490, ff. 210ra-221rb. Vellum: 11 x 16$\frac{1}{4}$ ins; double cols. of 61 lines. Beautiful later copy; initial letters of inscriptions in red and blue, with some elaboration; rubricated marginal division signs: A I to A XXV; slight marginalia, mostly textual emendations. Analysed by Holtzmann, *Eberbacensis*, 548-

55; cf. Ch. Lefebvre, *DDC*, 1953, v, 134-7; and *Decretal Collections*, 126-8. MS includes Gratian's *Decretum*. Belonged to the Cistercian abbey of the Blessed Virgin Mary in Eberbach. Cent., catalogue suggests xiv.

Other members of the Roman or 'Tortosa' family are: (i) The Tortosa Collection: *Dertusensis;* (ii) The Alcobaça Collection: *Alcobacensis.* For details, see Holtzmann, 'Beiträge zu den Dekretalensammlungen des zwölften Jahrhunderts,' *ZRG., Kan.Abt.*, xvi (1927), 39-77; idem, *Nachrichten*, 21; Kuttner, *Projected Corpus*, 346; and *Decretal Collections*, 126-8.

5 ADDENDUM: *The Frankfurt Collection*

One final twelfth-century collection, a systematic work outside the scope of the present report, completes with *Compilatio Prima* the total number of such works in the British Museum: the Frankfurt Collection: *Francofurtana:* Egerton MS 2901, ff. 1-97. Vellum: $9\frac{1}{2}$ x $6\frac{1}{4}$ ins; one of three related manuscripts, the others being: (i) Frankfurt a.M., Stbl. cod. Barthol. 60, ff. 2-85; (ii) Paris, Bibliothèque Nationale, lat. 3922 A, ff. 173-209. Cf. Kuttner, *Repertorium*, 295-6; Holtzmann and Kemp, *Lincoln Decretals*, xiv; Lefebvre, *DDC*, 1953, v, 878-84; and *Decretal Collections*, Plate VII. Belonged in xvii cent. to the Imperial monastery of St Maximin in Trier; then successively to Frederick North, 5th Earl of Guilford, Thomas Thorpe, Sir Thomas Phillipps and George Dunn. Original provenance: continental with English or Anglo-Norman supplements. Cent., late xii.

V

FACSIMILES OF DECRETAL COLLECTIONS IN THE BRITISH MUSEUM

The following plates will serve to clarify the main phases in the technical development of English primitive decretal collections, and illustrate their wider historical interest. The examples chosen are reproduced from manuscripts now in the British Museum.

PLATE I: The Worcester II Collection

Wigorniensis Altera: B.M. Royal MS. 11 B. II, fol. 101r. Vellum; 10⅛ in. × 6⅞ in. Pp. 46 and 69–70, above.

This folio from the Worcester II Collection records the technical style of the most primitive English collectors, who transcribed their decretals in full, with initial and final protocols, inscriptions and dates. In later collections the longer letters were dissected into their component chapters, and these were redistributed to suit a more convenient method of subject classification. The inscription and initial letter of the decretal *Sicut Romana* have been omitted by the rubricator in the example given here. The Worcester II Collection is a member of the primitive 'English' family, and is one of the earliest decretal collections now extant.

PLATE II: The Royal Collection

Regalis: B.M. Royal MS. 15 B. IV, fol. 107v. Vellum; 8 in. × 5⅝ in. Pp.8 1–4.

The opening folio of the Royal Collection reveals alike the professional advantages and the historical disadvantages of its more advanced technical style. This collection is the most juristically mature member of the 'English' family; and, though correctly described as primitive, it incorporates several notable systematic devices: its longer letters are dismembered in some instances, and their component parts distributed to suit a schematic arrangement of topics; the non-juridical matter is drastically abbreviated or excised in places; decretal inscriptions are entirely omitted from some decretals, but accurately retained in others; conventional abbreviations are freely used to indicate where an excision has been made or to avoid the transcription of repetitive common form. The Royal Collection is much less attractive in format than other decretal manuscripts examined in this study.

PLATE III: The Canterbury Collection

Cantuariensis: B.M. Royal MS. 10 B. IV, fol. 55r. Vellum; 10⅞ in. × 7⅞ in. Pp. 48 and 73–6, above.

The Canterbury Collection is a further member of the primitive 'English' family. The folio selected in this instance reveals the value of such early collections in providing more accurate historical details for decretals already known from other sources in a less reliable form. Thus, the letter addressed in this transcription to Robert Foliot, bishop of Hereford from 1174, was hitherto dated simply by the pontifical years of Alexander III: 1159–81. But now the much narrower limits of Robert's consecration and the death of Alexander, 1174–81, are fixed by this fresh evidence. In many other details also this example typifies the format and style of the earliest collections.

PLATE IV: The Claudian Collection

Claudiana: B.M. Cotton MS. Claudius A. IV, fol. 199v. Vellum; 9¼ in. × 6⅝ in. Pp. 84–91.

The Claudian Collection, a representative member of the primitive 'Bridlington' family, is a careful and finely transcribed collection. Its individual decretals and canons are numbered in a single sequence throughout the work; each item is placed under a rubricated summary of the juridically significant matter contained in it; an apparatus of marginal cross-references correlates passages of cognate interest in different parts of the composition; and points of legal interest are sometimes further discussed in brief marginal gloss commentaries. Although the initial letters have been omitted from decretal inscriptions, the Claudian Collection attains a high standard of accuracy in its personal and place-name references. All these features are illustrated in the single folio selected here.

PLATES V and VI: The Worcester Collection

Wigorniensis: B.M. Royal MS. 10 A. 11, fols. 14r and 63v. Vellum; 9 in. × 5¾ in. Pp. 49–51, 95–8 and 110–15.

Plate V records the typical features of the Worcester Collection, one of the earliest members of the primitive 'Worcester' family. The collection is devised in seven books on a subject-matter basis; the separate decretals are numbered in sequence within these parts; and each book begins on a fresh folio-recto. The professional advantages of this style of composition are clear enough when compared with that of the 'English' and 'Bridlington' families. The example chosen here is the opening folio of Book II. One of the final folios of the volume containing the Worcester Collection is reproduced in Plate VI. The decretals transcribed on this folio were not part of the original scheme of composition, but are later rescripts acquired independently and added to the manuscript already containing the earlier work. They provide significant evidence concerning the provenance both of the Worcester Collection itself and of the completed manuscript volume in which it is the principal part.

sitaſ: indulgeᷤ biennium. niſi forte iudex a quo appellatum fuerit ſcᵭm locorum ⁊ puinciaꝝ diſtanciam. ⁊ qlitatᵉ temporis raſi temp̄ fuerit moderatuſ. infra quod ſi iſ q appellauit cauſam appellationiſ nō fuerit p̄ſecutᵘ tenebit ſentencia. ſi p̄ ſentenciam appellauit. ⁊ a cauſa ſua ceꝛdiſſe iu detur: ⁊ nec ampliᵘ ſuꝑ eodᵉ negocio audietur appellanſ. Si uero abſq̃ oīi grauamine. ⁊ ante litiſ ingreſſū fuerit appellatū huiᵐodi audietur appellanſ. qm ſacri canoneſ paſſim appellare ꝑmittunt. Si uero ān ſentencia appellauit n̄ cogetur illi ſtare iudicio a quo noſcit appellaſſe. Si autē in agꝛo uel aliaſ ān cauſe ingꝛeſſum fuerit appellatū n̄ ſolent dici appellationeſ. ſi ad cauſam uocationeſ. preterea ſi raptoꝛ ſit. uel aliaſ uiolentᵘ detentoꝛ aliene rei ſi q appellat huiuſmodi appellatio facta iniudicio apud eccleſiaſticaſ ꝑſonaſ ſolet audiri niſi forte manifeſtuſ raptoꝛ uel fornicatoꝛ extitit. ſicut ille q abſentem. ⁊ n̄ requiſitū apᶫſ excōmunicauit. Ad b̄ ſi iuna cā alioſq̃ appellauit ⁊ pendente appellatōne aliquod crimen committat uel pꝛi cōmiſiſſe dicat. ut in ⁊ accuſet uel conueniat de alia re de q n̄ fuerit appellatū: nec illa contin gat ad audienciā iudiciſ a q̄ ma iioq̃ negocio appellauit. eum poteſt ſi uo luerit tanq̃ ſuſpectū uitare. Alioqn debebit ſtare iudicio illi a quo appellatū ⁊. maxime ſi iudex ſuuſ ordinariuſ exiſtit. Itᵉ ſi duobz coꝛā ſuo iudice litigan

tibz: alᵗ ad n̄am. alᵗ ad ſui iudiciſ au dienciam ſuꝗ eodem negocio appella tierit. ⁊ ille q ad ſuum iudicᵉ appella uit ad diem appellacioniſ ueniens ad eum ſe appellaſſe ꝓponit eo tacito qd aduerſariuſ eiᵘ ad audienciam Roma m pontificiſ appellaſſet. ſi legitime ci tatuſ neq̃ uenerit. neq̃ aliquᵉ miſe rit reſponſale. Aut ⁊ aliaſ parere con tempſerit. ⁊ in eum excōmunicatōiſ ſñam tulerit. tenebit utiq̃ excōmu nicationiſ ſña ꝓ contumacia quouſq̃ cognouerit iudex eū ad audienciam Romani pontificiſ appellaſſe. Deniq̃ qd in fine qōnū tuaꝝ quiriſ ſi acuiu li iudicᵉ ān iudicium ut ꝓ ad n̄am audienciam fuerit appellatū an hu iuſcemodi appellatio teneat. teneretq̃ dem in hiſ qui n̄re ſunt ſpᵃli iuriſ dictōm ſubiecti. In aliiſ n̄ ⁊ ſi de conſu etudine eccle teneat ſcᵭm iuriſ rigoꝛe n̄re n̄ credim̄. Dat̄. Tuſcuᶫ. xi. k. Apᶫis.

icut Romana

eccla omnium ecclaꝝ diſponente deo mater: ⁊ magiſtra. ita etiam nō q eidem eccle licet imẽi ſu̅e diſpo ſitioniſ ꝓudencia p̄fidem̄ ꝓ ut nobiſ dn̄ſ miniſtrit conſultacionibz reſpon dere cogimur ſinguloꝛ. ⁊ que uiderit dubia apoſtolice circūſpectioniſ pru dencia declarare. Sane queſitū ⁊ a nob ex parte tua utrū ſi aliqn cā infali eſ delegatiſ iudicib; abſq̃ remedio ap pellatioiſ committit. ⁊ altᵃ parſ

V

II. THE ROYAL COLLECTION

B.M. Royal MS. 15 B.iv, fol. 107v.

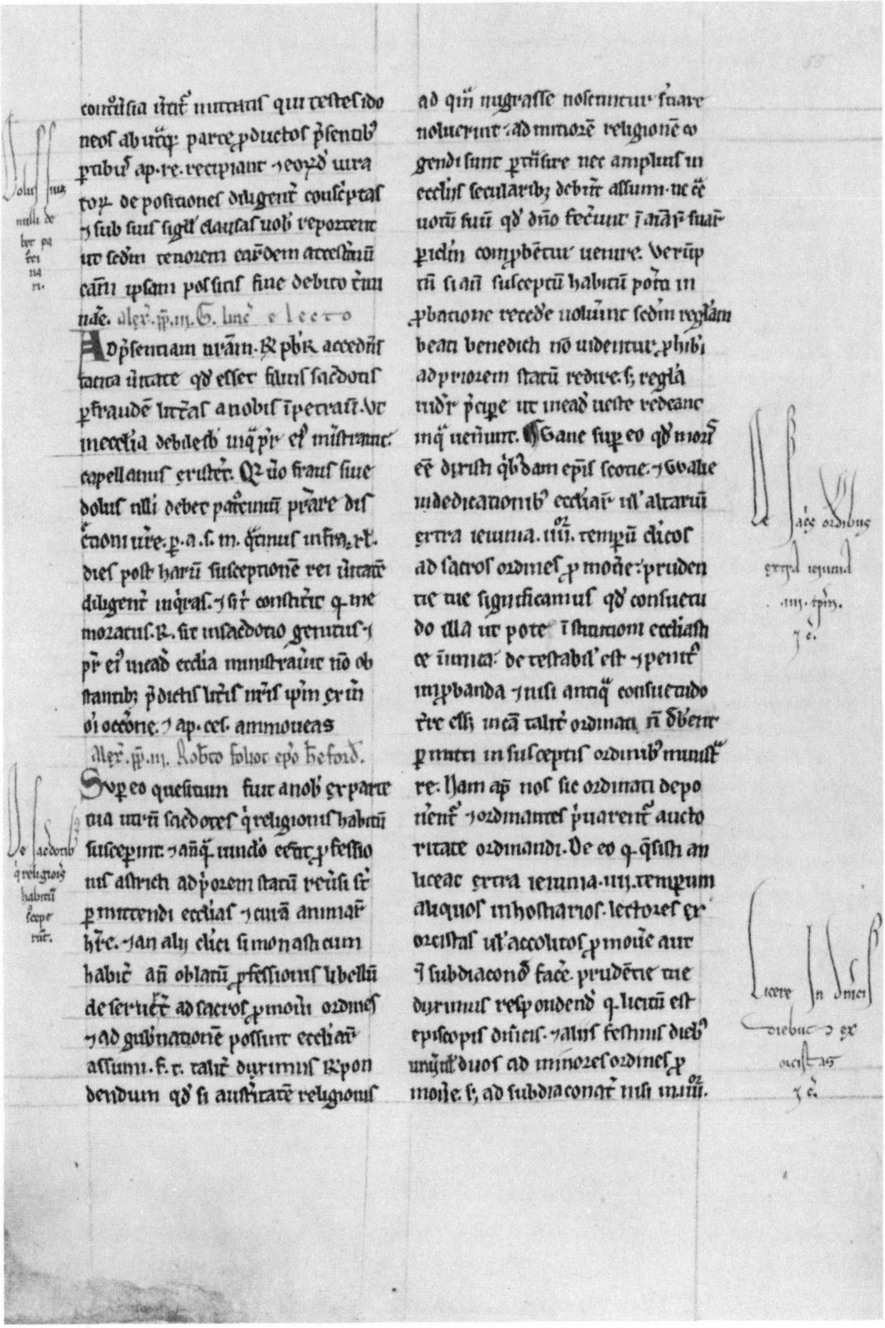

III. THE CANTERBURY COLLECTION

B.M. Royal MS. 10 B.iv, fol. 55r.

IV. THE CLAUDIAN COLLECTION

B.M. Cotton MS. Claudius A.iv, fol. 199v.

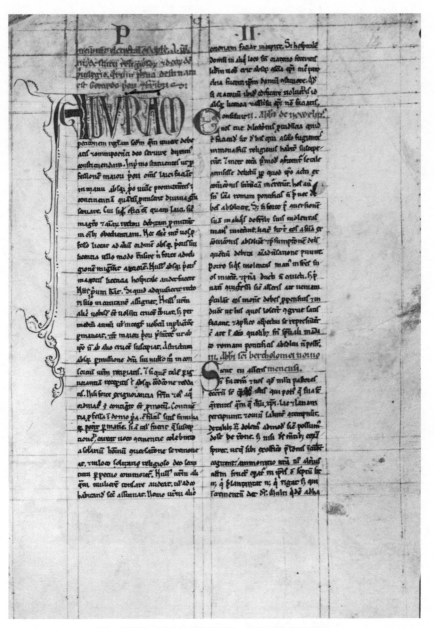

V. THE WORCESTER COLLECTION
B.M. Royal MS. 10 A.II, fol. 14r.

VI. THE WORCESTER COLLECTION
B.M. Royal MS. 10 A.II, fol. 63v.

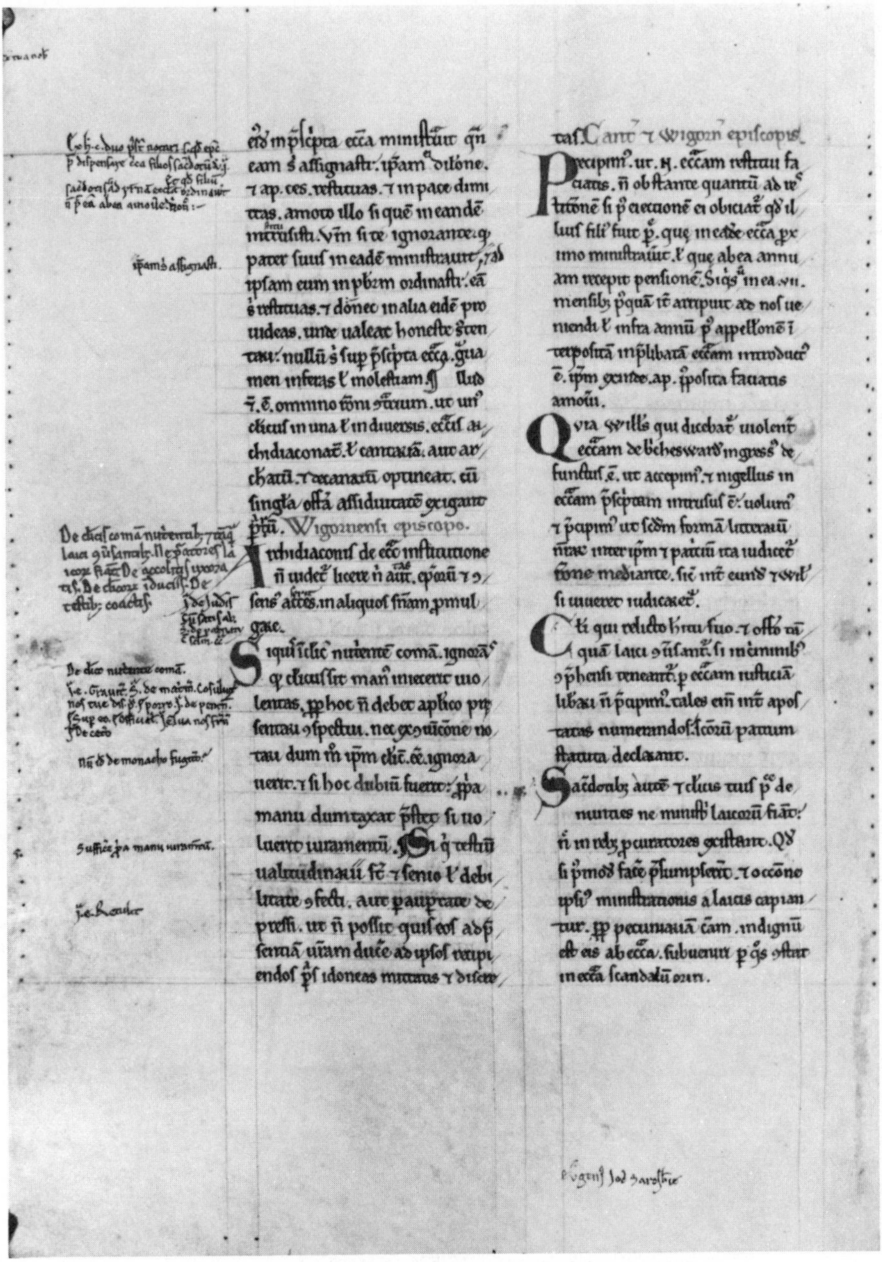

VII. THE 'CHELTENHAM' COLLECTION
B.M. Egerton MS. 2819, fol. 86v.

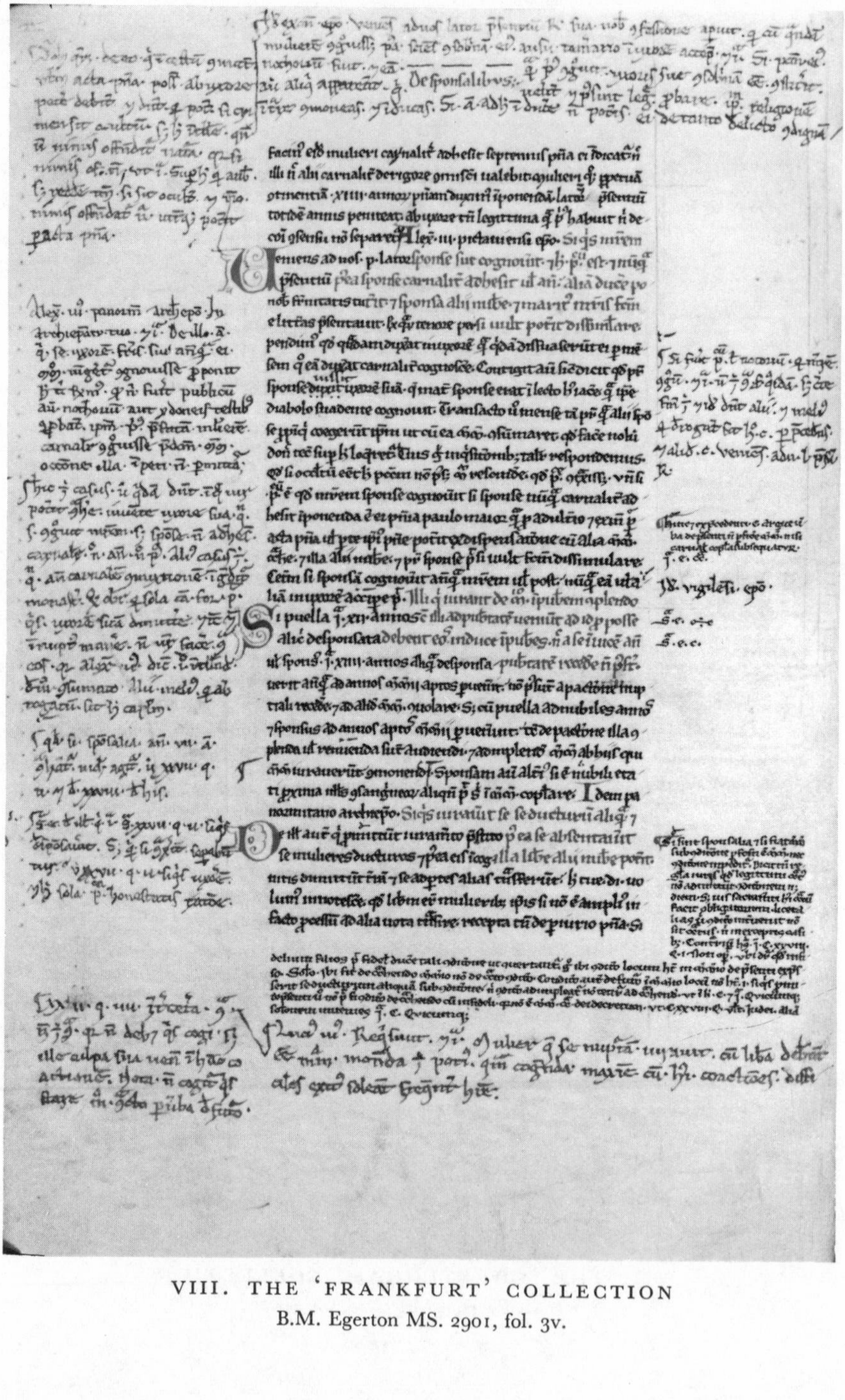

VIII. THE 'FRANKFURT' COLLECTION

B.M. Egerton MS. 2901, fol. 3v.

PLATE VII: The 'Cheltenham' Collection

Cheltenhamensis: B.M. Egerton MS. 2819, fol. 86v. Vellum; 10 in. × 7⅛ in. Pp. 98–103.

The 'Cheltenham' Collection is a large and beautifully transcribed work, recording a distinct line of technical development within the 'Worcester' family. Occasional groups of rubricated titles reveal the extent of juristic skill in the arrangement of its subject-matter. A two-fold dependence on the Bamberg-Leipzig group of continental systematic collections and an early member of the primitive 'Worcester' family is fully discussed in the chapters above. Plate VII provides a typical instance of the grouping of rubricated titles, and also reveals the extent of marginal glossing characteristic of this work.

PLATE VIII: The 'Frankfurt' Collection

Francofurtana: B.M. Egerton MS. 2901, fol. 3v. Vellum; 9½ in. × 6¼ in.

This final example is of outstanding interest in recording the growth and elaboration of a decretal collection in the hands of professional canonists. It is a typical folio from a systematic collection, in which both English and continental sources are intermingled. The layers of composition are patent in the very appearance of the manuscript, and in the different hands of the main transcription and the marginal additions: the latter include both glossatorial commentary and further decretals inserted by a later, characteristically English, hand. The growth of the collectors' professional skill is obvious if this example is compared with the extract from the Worcester II Collection provided in Plate I. The 'Frankfurt' Collection has not yet been fully discussed or analysed; nor is it examined in the present study. It is preserved in three manuscripts, including the Egerton MS. 2901, now in the British Museum but belonging at an earlier date to St Maximin in Trier. For details of the 'Frankfurt' manuscripts, see Holtzmann and Kemp, *op. cit.*, p. xiv.

A Durham Canonical Manuscript of the Late Twelfth Century

THIS paper seeks to present merely a preliminary report on a twelfth-century English canonical manuscript of more than usual interest. The work in question is the Durham Cathedral MS C.III.1, ff. 1^v-18^r, of which a complete analysis with full palaeographical description will be published later, giving clearer definition to the discussions simply outlined here.[1] To deal briefly with the physical appearance of the manuscript first: the folios are 13½ × 9½ in. in size, and the canonical matter is transcribed in double or triple columns with an average of sixty-five lines to the column, carefully written in several different hands of the later twelfth century, with many rubrics and occasional brief marginal references, comments or glosses.[2] It may be said at once that one obvious point of interest in this work is the variety of types of composition, many of them common-place enough individually, gathered together compactly within a few folios of a single volume, revealing the many-sided activities of English canonical collectors at a very creative and formative period in the history of canon law.

The manuscript opens with a canonical compilation of the mid-twelfth century, composed mainly of pre-Gratian material, and

---

[1] For previous references to this MS, see S. Kuttner, 'Repertorium der Kanonistik, 1140-1234,' *Studi e Testi*, LXXI (1937), 280-1; W. Holtzmann, 'Über eine Ausgabe der päpstlichen Dekretalen des 12. Jahrhunderts,' *Nachrichten von der Akademie der Wissenschaften in Göttingen, Phil.-Hist. Kl.*, 1945, 22; idem and E. W. Kemp, *Papal Decretals relating to the Diocese of Lincoln in the Twelfth Century*, Lincoln Record Society, XLVII (1954), xii; C. Duggan, *Twelfth-Century Decretal Collections and their Importance in English History*, University of London Historical Studies, 1963, 78-9.

[2] Triple columns are found on ff. 13^r-14^v; all other folios have double columns, except that f. 11^v is undivided, bearing an *arbor consanguinitatis* and various glosses. Marginalia are found on ff. 5^r, 5^v, 6^r, 7^v, 8^r, 8^v, 9^r, 10^v, 11^r, 11^v, 12^r, 12^v, 15^r, 15^v, 17^r, and 17^v.

comprising varied canonical sources, scriptural and patristic texts, conciliar canons and papal letters. The material is drawn from at least two main sources, of which the first is devised in nineteen short books, the divisions being indicated by marginal numbers;[1] and at least in sections this part discloses a marked penitential character. The second component contains a large proportion of papal decretals, some of them dating from the early and mid-twelfth century.[2] Neither part is dependent on the *Decretum Gratiani*, since they include chapters not incorporated in it, while the second component includes several decretals later in date of issue than the completion of Gratian's work. It is a feature of special interest that certain decretals are found in this second source in significant parallel arrangement with the earliest known appendices in Gratian manuscripts; and, still more strikingly, the grouping of several items here corresponds with their order and sequence in the earliest extant systematic decretal collections: in the Italian *Parisiensis II*, composed perhaps by Bernard of Pavia not later than 1179, and in the seminal *Appendix Concilii Lateranensis*, probably of Anglo-Norman origin and first assembled c.1184-5, from which they passed into the central stream of systematic transmission.[3] On the other hand, these famous systematic collections include many items unknown to the author of the collection in the Durham MS, which is therefore unlikely to be dependent on them in any way. And so it appears that the Durham MS preserves a short canonical collection of the highest interest, later than Gratian's work in completion and linked in origins with the earliest known developments in the codification of twelfth-century papal decretals.

The opening section is followed by a list of popes, under the heading 'Jesus Christus Dei filius sub Augusto Cesare natus est; anno xxxiii sue nativitatis sed xvii imperii Tyberii Cesaris passus est.' The list begins with St Peter, designated in the margin as 'primus

[1] The canonical collection begins on f. 1ᵛ; the first marginal enumeration appears on f. 2ʳ, at the beginning of the second book; the nineteenth book begins on f. 5ᵛᵃ.

[2] Ibid. ff. 6ʳ-7ᵛ; ff. 5-7 are designated *Collectio Dunelmensis* I in Kuttner, op. cit. 280-1, and in Holtzmann and Kemp, op. cit. xii.

[3] For the earliest known appendices to Gratian MSS, see Kuttner, *Repertorium*, 272-6; for analyses of *Parisiensis II* and *Appendix Concilii Lateranensis*, see E. Friedberg, *Die Canonessammlungen zwischen Gratian und Bernhard von Pavia*, Leipzig 1897, 21-45 and 63-84. The Durham MS, f. 6ʳᵇ, includes the group of letters: JL 7401, 9654, and 9506, together with the adjacent marginal comment 'De iuramento calumpnie,' agreeing exactly in sequence and title with *Parisiensis II*, LIII, 2, 3, and 4, and *Appendix*, XXIII, 1, 2, and 3.

A Durham Canonical Manuscript of the Late Twelfth Century

papa,' and continues in order through Linus, Cletus, Clement, Anacletus, and so forth down to Alexander III (1159-81), with whom it breaks off.[1] The first ten popes are numbered individually in sequence; then every tenth pope is numbered down to the ninetieth, until finally the scheme of numeration is abandoned entirely.[2] The length of each pontificate is stated in years, months and days, whenever possible; the reigning emperor is named; the existence of anti-popes is also noted; and marginal references indicate such points of interest as the principal General Councils, inserted by the name of the pope then ruling. Such a work as this is by no means uncommon in the records of the period: a similar, though less informative, list may be seen, for example, in the *opuscula* of Ralph de Diceto, dean of St Paul's at the close of the century;[3] but the present version has a particular dating value for the Durham MS. As noted above, the list ends with Alexander III, who ruled from 1159 until 1181; but the Durham MS in its first completed form recorded only sixteen years for the length of his pontificate, and this was later emended to twenty in a superscript hand: a period, however, which still fell short of the total span of twenty-two years.[4] The evidence thus suggests that the transcription was first made several years before the death of Alexander, then later revised or corrected, but still completed before his death in 1181. But the matter is complicated by the fact that the scribe wrongly dated the beginning of Alexander's pontificate in 1162, instead of 1159: an error which, coupled with the original and emended statements of the length of the pontificate, renders an estimate of the dates of transcription and emendation highly speculative. Nevertheless, the death of the pope was seemingly unknown to the scribe, and there is no reference at this stage to his successor, Lucius III (1181–5), though some of the latter's decretals are found on later folios. And, likewise, the existence of

---

[1] Durham MS, ff. 7va-8rb. The initial letter of the pope's name at the beginning of each entry is missing from the MS; the initials of other names appear in lower case, but are given here in capitals.

[2] There is one further marginal reference: Stephen is numbered 110th pope on f. 8ra.

[3] *Radulfi de Diceto Decani Lundoniensis Opera Historica*, ed. W. Stubbs, RS, 1876, II, 185-91. Diceto provides additional lists of popes with the longest reigns, popes of the same name and a list of schisms: ibid. 192-5.

[4] The full entry for Alexander III is: 'Alexander III genere Thusculano cepit anno
xx
Mclxii. Sedit annis xvi. Imperante Frederico; antipapa Octaviano, postea Guidone,
...
deinde Johanne.' Diceto's list has simply: 'Alexander sedit annis xxii': ed. cit. II, 191.

the anti-pope Innocent III (1179-80) is also unmentioned. From the various possibilities, therefore, the most probable dating limits for the transcription and correction of the Durham list are $c.1178$ to 1179 or shortly after, which tends to be corroborated by the items immediately following in the manuscript volume.

The list of popes is followed by an early decretal collection of English provenance and primitive style. There are in fact three separate collections of this type among the canonical material in the Durham MS; and, for simplicity, it is best to consider these together here, though they are disjoined by other matter in the construction of the manuscript volume.[1] The first collection is composed of thirty-five items; the second begins with the canons of the Council of Tours (1163) and contains forty-five items in all; the third collection follows the second without intermission and now preserves nineteen items, apparently lacking one or more folios, and is supplemented by a short appendix of decretals of Lucius III, transcribed by later hands.[2] Excluding this supplement, the letters are mainly of Alexander III's pontificate, and internal evidence suggests the dating limits of 1179-81 for the completion of the decretal collections,[3] which agrees very well with the date deduced above for the emended reference in the list of popes. The place and significance of these decretal collections, known collectively as the Durham Collection or *Collectio Dunelmensis*, have already been briefly discussed in various publications and will be examined more fully in a later study. Here it will be sufficient to sum up the principal points of interest in general terms. The Durham Collection is a member of the 'English family' of primitive decretal collections: the most rudimentary, and therefore in some ways the most interesting historically, of the decretal families known at present. It is related in part to six other extant manuscripts, of which two are in the Bodleian Library in Oxford and four are in the British Museum, being respectively the Belvoir, Fountains, Worcester II, Canterbury, Rochester and Royal

[1] Durham MS, ff. $8^{va}-10^{vb}$, $14^{rb}-16^{vb}$, and $17^{ra}-18^{ra}$. But see also the Durham Collection, *Collectio Dunelmensis* I-III, in Kuttner, op. cit. 280-1, and in Holtzmann and Kemp, op. cit. xii.

[2] The canons of the Council of Tours are on ff. $14^{rb}-14^{vb}$; the decretals of Lucius III are on f. 18ra. The second and third groups of decretals could perhaps be treated as a single collection, but there is undoubtedly a break in continuity between them. One folio, or more, is missing between ff. 17^v and 18^r, so the original number of items in the third group of decretals was probably much higher than the estimate given here.

[3] Duggan, *Decretal Collections*, 78-9.

A Durham Canonical Manuscript of the Late Twelfth Century

Collections.[1] These works reveal very clearly how the earliest English decretal collections were made, recording the initiative taken by English collectors in the most elementary phase of technical development, showing especially the influence of the bishops of Worcester and Exeter and of Richard of Canterbury, or more probably of the canonists in their circles, in this work of codification.[2] The Durham Collection discloses all these features no less than the other members of its group. But the light that is thrown on the canonists of the Canterbury province is all the more significant considering that the manuscript here discussed is of northern provenance: nineteen of the thirty-five items in the first group of decretals were received at Exeter, Worcester or Canterbury, whereas no more than nine decretals in the total collection were received in the province of York. A further point of interest lies in the appendix of four letters of Lucius III, added by at least two different scribes, and recording how the collectors supplemented their work letter by letter as they came to hand.[3]

Meanwhile, the first component part of the Durham decretal collection is followed by a transcription of the canons of the Third Lateran Council of 1179,[4] beginning in the most customary way with the decree *Licet de vitanda*, laying down the requirement of a two-thirds majority in papal elections. There is little of significance to note here concerning these canons, as they are very well known and found in numerous manuscripts of the period. But within the folios on which the conciliar canons are transcribed is found a diagrammatic *arbor consanguinitatis*, with instructions on its interpretation.[5] The same folio preserves a number of glosses of considerable interest, one in particular listing the powers reserved by the pope to himself. It is worth briefly summarising this analysis, which provides an illuminating insight into a late twelfth century view of papal prerogatives. The gloss begins 'Hec sunt que specialiter reservavit sibi summus pontifex,' and lists the following rights: the summoning of a general council; the confirmation of a new religious order;[6] the

---

[1] The MSS references are respectively: MS Bodley e Museo 249, ff. 121-35; MS Bodley Laud Misc. 527, ff. 24-45; British Museum, Royal MS 11 B.II, ff. 97-102; BM, Royal MS 10 B.IV, ff. 42-58 and 59-65; BM, Royal MS 10 C.IV, ff. 137-55; BM, Royal MS 15 B.IV, ff. 107-18. Cf. Holtzmann and Kemp, op. cit. xii; and Duggan, *Decretal Collections*, 68-84.

[2] Ibid. 68-117 (*passim*), 118-24 and 149-51; see also my 'Decretal Collections in the British Museum,' SCH, 1 (1964), 132-44.   [3] Durham MS, f. 18[ra].

[4] Ibid. ff. 11[ra]-12[vb].   [5] Ibid. f. 11[v].   [6] Ibid. f. 11[v]: 'Confirmatio nove religionis.'

deposition of bishops; the restoration of the deposed; the absolution of those guilty of striking clerks; the settlement of problems of faith; the absolution of excommunicates; the hearing of appeals made to the Roman see; the authoritative interpretation of the Church's laws; the right of the pope to alter his own decisions; the union of different dioceses; the settlement of cases involving the laws of consanguinity; the restoration of the defamed; the ordination of clerks subject to another; the right to choose a successor; the power to lay down decrees; the translation of bishops; the conferring of the pallium; and the power to judge without fear of appeal. The greater number of these claims are supported by references to chapters in Gratian's *Decretum* (though some of the references have been transcribed inaccurately), in which either the papal right is itself directly discussed or the pope is revealed acting in such a way as to give substance to the claim of right. But it must be conceded that in some instances the glossator seems to claim more than what appears in the original text, and indeed more than what the popes of the period would themselves have defined.[2]

Following the canons of the Third Lateran Council is an abbreviation of Gratian's *Decretum*.[2] This is an extremely condensed summary of most of the principal topics treated by Gratian, and is little more than a table of contents, the whole abbreviation spanning merely seven columns with an average of sixty-five lines each. Certain parts of the *Decretum* are omitted entirely, as are Distinctions XV-XXI, while others are summarised in a single brief entry: such as 'A quibus sint eligendi et consecrandi prelati' for Dist. LXII, and 'De lapsis et penitentibus' for Dist. XLVIII.[3] To cite a familiar example, Causa XI, Questio 1, dealing at length with the difficult subject of clerical immunity, is recorded here simply by the one sentence 'Si cause vel contentiones inter clericos fuerint et laicos apud quos conveniri et convenire debeant et aliis capitulis.'[4] Yet, despite such drastic brevity, the Durham abbreviation should not be undervalued, as it provides a useful and speedy reference list for most of the important problems discussed by Gratian.

---

[1] A critical commentary on these claims and on the canons cited by the Durham glossator in support of his definitions will be published later. Similar lists of papal prerogatives in other decretist MSS are now discussed in J. A. Watt, 'The Theory of Papal Monarchy in the Thirteenth Century: the Contribution of the Canonists' *Traditio*, xx (1964), 259-60.   [2] Durham MS, ff. 13ra-14ra.
[3] Ibid. f. 13ra.   [4] Ibid. f. 13va.

A Durham Canonical Manuscript of the Late Twelfth Century

There remains only to note in the folios reviewed in this paper a transcription of the canons of the Council of Tours of 1163, as mentioned above, providing a prooemium to the second English decretal collection, and various other short entries and canonical exercises.[1]

[1] I must thank Mr J. E. Fagg for most courteous advice on various matters of detail in the Durham MS.

THE TRINITY COLLECTION OF DECRETALS AND THE EARLY WORCESTER FAMILY*

All primitive decretal collections composed in England are conventionally classified in three main groups, described as the English, Bridlington, and Worcester Families respectively.[1] These names are admittedly matters merely of convenience, and are open in all cases either to question or qualification.[2] The Worcester Family (the most advanced of English primitive collections in technical construction) is named after the Worcester Collection, on the mistaken assumption that this, authentically Worcester, composition is the oldest surviving member of the group; whereas in fact a hitherto undiscussed manuscript in the library of Trinity College, Cambridge, reveals an earlier derivation from their common origin, and there are good reasons for doubting if the family archetype was dependent in any way on the Worcester school of canon lawyers.[3] Six members of this once-numerous family are known at present

---

* This is the first of several studies on twelfth-century decretal collections; in the next issue of this Bulletin an analysis of the hitherto unknown collection in the St. John's College, Cambridge, MS 148 will be given. Meanwhile, the Athlone Press will shortly publish my study on *Twelfth-Century Decretal Collections and their Importance in English History*, including a review of all English primitive collections known at present, together with brief analyses of the Worcester II, Belvoir, Canterbury, and Rochester collections.

[1] W. Holtzmann, 'Über eine Ausgabe der päpstlichen Dekretalen des 12. Jahrhunderts,' *Nachrichten Akad. Göttingen* (1945) 15-36; idem and E. W. Kemp, *Papal Decretals Relating to the Diocese of Lincoln*, (Lincoln Record Society; 1954) xii-xiii; S. Kuttner, 'Notes on a Projected Corpus of Twelfth Century Decretal Letters,' *Traditio* 6 (1948) 345-51.

[2] The description 'English Family' is particularly liable to confusion, since all three groups could equally aptly be so described. The 'Bridlington Family' is so identified because the earlier of its two surviving members belonged originally to Bridlington Priory, but the family archetype was produced in the province of Canterbury. The suitability of the name 'Worcester Family' is discussed below.

[3] For the Worcester Collection: British Museum Royal MS 10.A II, fols. 5-62; H. Lohmann, 'Die Collectio Wigorniensis,' ZRG Kan. Abt. 22 (1933) 36-187. For the Trinity Collection: Trinity College Cambridge MS R.14.9, fols. 82-87. The Worcester Collection is described as the oldest member of the family in Holtzmann-Kemp, *op. cit.* xii, and C. N. L. Brooke, 'Canons of English Church Councils in the Early Decretal Collections,' *Traditio* 13 (1957) 475. But see also Holtzmann, *Nachrichten* 22; and idem, 'Die Dekretalensammlungen des 12. Jahrhunderts: 1. Die Sammlung Tanner,' *Festschrift zur Feier des 200jährigen Bestehens der Akademie der Wissenschaften in Göttingen*, Phil.-Hist. Kl. (1951) 98-99: in these earlier studies Holtzmann's list of Worcester Family members apparently agrees with the suggestion made here that the Trinity Collection is the earliest extant derivative.

in manuscript, and two of these are also familiar in published analyses.[4] All are technically primitive in composition, being either divided into books or *libri* simply, or in the most mature examples subdivided also into titles or *tituli*, but without the systematic device of dismemberment of the longer decretals. In systematic collections the longer letters, dealing frequently with several different and quite unrelated topics within the limits of a single decretal, are dissected into their component chapters, which are arranged analytically according to subject matter and distributed under various headings. None of the Worcester Family is systematic in this sense, though some record an advanced stage of technical development within the primitive conventions.

The earliest members of the group are three closely interrelated compositions, whose manuscripts are now preserved respectively in the British Museum, at Trinity College, Cambridge, and in the priory of the Augustinian Canons at Klosterneuburg in Austria. The provenance of the first of these can be safely attributed to Worcester, and the manuscript reveals unmistakable evidence of association with Baldwin of Ford, successively bishop of Worcester and archbishop of Canterbury: it is therefore aptly described as the Worcester Collection. But the second and third manuscripts are of uncertain authorship and provenance, and are identified accordingly as the Trinity and Klosterneuburg Collections, after their present locations.[5] All three works were composed in 1181 or shortly after, and provide the earliest surviving evidence of their family origins, recording the first extant phase of technical development within the group, being divided into several books but without further formal subdivision into titles.[6] A fourth member of the family is an Egerton manuscript in the British Museum, again of uncertain provenance and known as the Cheltenham Collection because of its place in the Egerton Library. This is a work of more complex pattern and composite origin, and was certainly much later in completion than the collections mentioned so far, being derived from several mutually independent sources assembled between 1181 and 1193 or shortly after: its origins lie partly within the 'Worcester' tradition, and partly also within the systematic traditions of the great Bamberg-Leipzig group of continental collections.[7] The final stages of technical development within the

---

[4] Holtzmann, *Nachrichten* 22. Only the Worcester and Klosterneuburg Collections have been analyzed. For the latter: Klosterneuburg Stiftsbibl. MS 19, fols. 36-87; F. Schönsteiner, 'Die Collectio Claustroneoburgensis,' *Jahrbuch des Stiftes Klosterneuburg* 2 (1909) 1-154.

[5] The full details of these three works are given in nn. 3 and 4, above. For the connection with Baldwin of Ford, see Lohmann, *art. cit.* 53 n.1; S. Kuttner - E. Rathbone, 'Anglo-Norman Canonists of the Twelfth Century,' *Traditio* 7 (1951) 282-83; and Brooke, *art. cit.* 475.

[6] Lohmann, *art. cit.* 51-53: the family archetype included one decretal issued on Jan. 23, 1181 (*Wig.* 7.59 and *Claustr.* 291), but no decretals later than the death of Alexander III on Aug. 30, 1181, are found in any of these three collections. For the technical structure of the Worcester Collection: Lohmann, *art. cit.* 39-40 and 43-53; see also A. van Hove, *Prolegomena* 350-52.

[7] British Museum Egerton MS 2819, fols. 11-102; Holtzmann, *Nachrichten* 22; Kuttner, *Repertorium der Kanonistik* 346; van Hove, *op. cit.* 353; L. R. Misserey, 'Collection de Cheltenham,' *DDC* 3 (1942) 682-83; E. Rathbone [unpublished London Ph. D. thesis], *Bishops and Cathedral Bodies in England*, 1066-1215 (1935) 509ff. The collection includes

Worcester Family itself are recorded in the Cottonian and Peterhouse Collections, closely interrelated and now located in the Cottonian Manuscripts in the British Museum and in various scattered positions in the library at Peterhouse in Cambridge.[8] These are also named by their modern locations, and are both large collections, set out carefully in books and titles, and completed at the earliest in 1193 and 1194 respectively.[9]

The Klosterneuburg Collection was analysed by Schönsteiner in 1909, and the Worcester Collection by Lohmann in 1933; and it is evident from these published works that both sprang from a common origin (now lost), which was in fact the archetype of the so-called Worcester Family.[10] Their collation

---

one decretal of Clement III: *Chelt.* fol. 101rb, *Referentibus canonicis*, JL 16181 (1187-91); and the final item in the manuscript is a decretal of Celestine III: fol. 102ra, *Bone memorie Alanus*, JL 17055 and 17675 (1193).

[8] For the Cottonian Collection: British Museum Cotton MS. Vitellius E. XIII, fols. 204-88; L. Falletti, 'Collectio Cottoniana,' DDC 4 (1949) 725-26; this MS was severely damaged in the Cotton fire of 1731: many fragments were destroyed or are now illegible, but much can be reconstructed by collation with the Peterhouse MSS. For the Peterhouse Collection: Peterhouse Cambridge MSS 193 (last quire), 114 (first and last quires), 193 (first quire), 203 (last quire) and 180 (first and last quires); M. R. James, *Descriptive Catalogue of the Manuscripts in the Library of Peterhouse, Cambridge* (1899): James was mistaken in describing these fragments as parts of a volume of Cistercian Ordinances; the full collection no longer exists, but the seven fragments listed here have been rediscovered in the endbindings of various Dyngley volumes in the Peterhouse Library. For the Peterhouse Collection, see also Kuttner, *Projecta Corpus* 348; *idem* and Rathbone, *art. cit.* 283 n.14; Holtzmann, *Nachrichten* 22; *idem* and Kemp, *op. cit.* xiii; and Ch. Lefebvre, 'Collection de Peterhouse,' DDC 6 (1957) 1438. A fragment discovered by Kolsrud among the MSS of Oslo University was provisionally classified as a member of the Worcester Family, but this view has been abandoned: Holtzmann-Kemp, *op. cit.* xiii; Holtzmann, 'La collection "Seguntina" et les décrétales de Clément III et de Célestin III,' RHE 50 (1955) 401 n.2; Ch. Lefebvre, 'Fragment d'Oslo,' DDC 6 (1957) 1180.

[9] Holtzmann's classification of these collections as 'Pre-Compilatio Prima' is chronologically misleading, since both works were completed later than Bernard of Pavia's *Compilatio prima*. Falletti, *art. cit.* 725-26, dates the Cottonian Collection by the pontificate of Clement III (1188-91), but at least two decretals in the closing folios were issued by Celestine III in 1193, though their inscriptions are no longer legible in the MS: fol. 287^v, to the prior and chapter of Huntingdon, *Bone memorie Alanus*, JL 17055 and 17675 (1193); fol. 286^v, to John, dean of Rouen, *Prudentiam tuam*, JL 17019 (June 17, 1193). Similarly, Lefebvre, *art. cit.* 1438, dates the Peterhouse Collection at least five years too early in 1188: see Peterhouse MS 193 (first quire), fol. 2vb: 'Celestinus papa J(ohanni) Rothomagensi decano. A nobis fuit *etc.* Dat. Lat. xix. Kl. Decembris, pontificatus nostri anno tertio.' At least one other decretal in this collection was sent by Celestine III to Hubert Walter as archbishop of Canterbury, its earliest possible date being that of Hubert's elevation in 1193: Pet. MS 193 (first quire), fol. 1ra.

[10] Lohmann, *art. cit.* 43-48 and 164-87; and Appendix I, below. Lohmann's analysis is defective at the close of *Wig.* II, *ibid.* p. 100, where he states that the transcription breaks off abruptly through scribal oversight at 'privilegium nostrum,' but the decretal (*Wig.* 2.37) is correctly concluded to 'integre solvunt' on the folio-verso, and is followed by a further decretal transcribed in a different hand, and concerned with the Church in Hungary.

reveals the scope and pattern of the archetype in substantial detail, and proves that the archetype itself as well as its earliest derivatives were each divided into seven books on a subject matter basis, and that each derivative augmented the archetype with additional letters acquired independently. Each derivative can, therefore, be broken down into two or more major component sources: firstly an ancestral basis common to all members of the family, and secondly an appendix or series of appendices peculiar to each descendant. There is conclusive evidence that the archetype was itself expanded from time to time in its place of origin, and that various transcriptions were taken from it at different stages in its own development. It was transcribed in all probability on a series of unbound folios, to which additions were made periodically to provide the material for a more substantial collection to be completed in due course.[11] These are factors of some importance, which seriously complicate the problems of filiation between the surviving descendants.

The collation of *Claustr.* and *Wig.* (the Klosterneuburg and Worcester Collections respectively) reveals this significant difference in the manner of their completion: the supplementary decretals in the former appear as a single appendix transcribed at the end of the work as a whole; whereas they are themselves classified and distributed according to their subject matter in the latter, where they appear as appendices to its several component parts.[12] Moreover, the supplementary sections in the two collections were independent of one another in provenance and acquisition, since the author of each completed work showed no knowledge of the later additions provided by the other.[13] The collation also suggests at first sight (though misleadingly) that the earlier derivative is preserved in *Claustr.*, since it reveals intact the greater part of the archetype as a single and compact entity, whereas *Wig.* does not.[14] But Lohmann has argued conclusively that *Wig.* in fact preserves the earlier derivation, though it was completed independently of the archetype, and in a different place; whereas *Claustr.* was composed where the archetype was itself accessible, but after the *Wig.* transcription had been taken from it.[15] His conclusion is justified by the following consideration: a group of decretals became misplaced from their correct position at some early stage in the assembly of the common stock (due no doubt to that loose folio arrangement described above), and the resulting error in the sequence of material is reflected in both derivative collections in significantly contrasting ways: whereas the entire misplaced group is found intact though out of true order within the archetypal stratum in *Wig.*, it is found only partly so in *Claustr.*, where the remaining items are found within the supplementary appendix. This factor, combined with the clear evidence that the author of *Wig.* had no knowledge of the supplementary decretals in *Claustr.*, makes it quite certain that the version recorded by *Claustr.*

---

[11] Lohmann, *art. cit.* 45-48.

[12] Cf. Schönsteiner, *art. cit.*, Appendix, and Lohmann, *art. cit.* 44-48 and 164-87. See also Appendix I (b) and (c), below: thus, in Book III the family archetype is represented by *Wig.* 3.1-25 and *Claustr.* 114-41; but *Claustr.* 142 = *Wig.* 4.1, and *Wig.* 3.26-40 are interpolated at this point.

[13] Thus, *Wig.* 2.27-37 and 3.26-40 were, with only four exceptions, all omitted from *Claustr.*

[14] Lohmann, *art. cit.* 48.

[15] *Ibid.* 45-48.

was transcribed from their common source after the *Wig.* version had been taken from it. And this argument is the basis of the true conclusion that *Wig.* is earlier in derivation than *Claustr.*, and also of the resulting supposition that *Wig.* is therefore the oldest surviving member of their family as a whole.

The Trinity Collection was unknown when Schönsteiner and Lohmann published their analyses of *Claustr.* and *Wig.* respectively, and disproves the common assumption resulting from their work. It is unfortunately now merely a fragment of the original collection, but sufficient in substance to justify certain concrete conclusions [16] It is closely related to *Wig.* and *Claustr.* in contents and arrangement, and was almost certainly composed in the same period as they were.[17] It records the same technical phase of Worcester Family development, and was derived from their common stock, which it augmented in the same way as *Wig.* by adding decretals to its several component books. Its relationship with *Wig.* is indeed very striking: the supplementary decretals in both collections have common features both in contents and arrangement which are absent from *Claustr.*, so that the connections between *Trin.* and *Wig.* are closer than those between either of them and *Claustr.*; and this is also true of their textual details, though there is no immediate textual interdependence between any two of the three works.[18] But although every addition to the archetypal source in *Trin.* is found also in a corresponding position in *Wig.*, the converse is not true, and their collation proves that *Wig.* cannot be earlier in derivation than *Trin.*, though both are members of a single strand of development which did not include *Claustr.*[19]

A complete analysis of the Trinity Collection is set out for the first time below, and provides the full evidence on which these conclusions are based. The most reasonable assumption, combining this fresh evidence with Lohmann's arguments, is that the Trinity Collection is earlier in derivation than either

---

[16] A complete analysis is given in Appendix I, below. The whole of Book I is lost, and the remaining fragment begins abruptly towards the end of Book II, breaking off equally abruptly early in Book IV; the whole of Books V, VI and VII are missing.

[17] On internal evidence alone, the dating limits for the Trinity fragment are 1178 and 1181; the earlier limit is fixed by the presence of the decretal *Cum essemus Venecie* (*Trin.* 3.5), JL 14334 (1178); and the later by the absence of any material dated after the death of Alexander III. But since the archetype included one decretal of Jan. 23, 1181, this date must also be accepted for *Trin.*

[18] The textual relationship between the extant MSS is extremely complex. Despite the greater correspondence between *Wig.* and *Trin.*, a closer agreement exists in some details between *Trin.* and *Claustr.* For examples and further comparative details, see Appendix I (a) below. The Klosterneuburg MS is seriously defective in certain respects: decretal inscriptions are omitted, and details of names and places are often inaccurate: see Schönsteiner, *art. cit.* nn. 66, 104, 110, 135, 145, 197, 224 and 290.

[19] Thus, *Trin.* 2.26-29 agree exactly with *Wig.* 2.27-30, but only the second of these items is found also in *Claustr.*; and even that is not in the corresponding position: *Claustr.* 344. Again, none of the decretals *Wig.* 2.31-37 and 3.26-40 are found in *Trin.*; and only two are found in *Claustr.*, and these are not in the corresponding positions: *Wig.* 3.28 and 36 = *Claustr.* 343 and 300.II; *Wig.* 3.39 repeats 3.24 = *Trin.* 3.25 and *Claustr.* 140. It must be assumed that the decretals now discovered in *Wig.* alone were not included in the family archetype.

Wig. or *Claustr.* and may therefore be fittingly described as the oldest extant member of their family, since these three works together record the first known phase of technical development within the group.[20] It follows that the suitability of the family name is called into question on two considerations. Lohmann had already argued that the Worcester Collection was completed where the family archetype was not accessible, and now it is further suggested that the Trinity Collection is closer to their common origin. But, since *Wig.* was almost certainly of Worcester provenance at some stage in its history, whereas there is no evidence that either *Trin.* or *Claustr.* was dependent on Worcester at any phase in its development (though *Claustr.* was composed where the archetype was itself available), then, equally there is no persuasive evidence that the family archetype sprang in reality from Worcester origins. The provenance of the archetype must, therefore, remain a matter of some speculation, and in its earliest known form had already combined both English and continental sources.[21]

All three remaining members of the family (*Chelt. Cott.* and *Pet.*) were completed in their extant form in the period 1193-94 or shortly after. For this reason, and also because all three are technically more advanced than *Trin. Wig.* and *Claustr.*, it seems unlikely at first sight that they could throw further light on the earliest phases of development within the group. But there is ample evidence within them to prove the contrary, and that in *Chelt.* is particularly significant. The Cheltenham Collection was first described by Hampe over sixty years ago, later cursorily analysed by Seckel, and more recently referred to by Kuttner and Holtzmann.[22] On the basis of Seckel's incomplete analysis, it has been described as a member of the Bamberg-Leipzig filiation of continental systematic collections, though Hampe noticed some affinity between it and the Worcester and Cottonian Collections, and most recently Holtzmann has listed it as a member of the primitive Worcester Family.[23] Both descriptions are in part correct: a descendant of the 'Worcester' archetype is combined in *Chelt.* with various independent sources including an element from the Bamberg-Leipzig systematic tradition. The opening decretals follow the arrangement of the Leipzig Collection itself very closely, and together with sundry later acquisitions tend to obscure the formative 'Worcester' influence pervading the greater part of the work as a whole.[24]

---

[20] As argued below, the Cheltenham Collection also preserves a very early derivation from the original source, but the Trinity Collection was certainly completed earlier. Even the Cottonian and Peterhouse Collections were not textually dependent on *Trin. Wig.* or *Claustr.*; and all members play their part in helping to reconstruct the authentic details of the family archetype.

[21] This is clear in the decretal inscriptions in the Trinity Collection: see Appendix I, below.

[22] K. Hampe, 'Reise nach England,' *Neues Archiv der Gesellschaft für ältere deutsche Geschichtskunde* 22 (1897) 388-415; E. Seckel, 'Ueber drei Canonessammlungen des ausgehenden 12. Jahrhunderts,' *Neues Archiv* 25 (1900) 523-25 and 529-31; Kuttner, *Repertorium* 346; Holtzmann, *Nachrichten* 22.

[23] Misserey, *art. cit.* 682-83: 'une collection systématique, satellite du groupe de la collection de Bamberg.' Cf. Holtzmann, *loc. cit.* and *Die Sammlung Tanner*, 92-94; *idem* and Kemp, *op. cit.* xii.

[24] The opening folios are clearly dependent on the Bamberg-Leipzig tradition: cf. *Chelt.*

As far as this 'Worcester' material is concerned, its arrangement in *Chelt.* differs significantly from that of the corresponding parts in *Trin. Wig.* and *Claustr.*; and many smaller groups of letters are found widely scattered in this collection, in contrast with the simple seven-fold book formation revealed in *Wig.*[25] By collating the common elements in *Trin. Wig. Claustr.* and *Chelt.*, it is seen that all agree in many details of arrangement and text, but that some features are common to all except *Claustr.*; and so there is a closer kinship between *Trin. Wig.* and *Chelt.* than that between any one of them and *Claustr.*, though the exact nature of their interrelationship is complex and cannot be explained in the absence of so many intermediate collections which have not survived.[26] Thus, *Wig.* and *Chelt.* have decretals in common where *Trin.* has not;[27] while *Trin.* and *Wig.* have decretals in common which are absent from *Chelt.*;[28] and *Wig.* has still further decretals which are present in neither *Trin.* nor *Chelt.*[29] Though not fully conclusive on all points, the evidence suggests that *Trin. Wig.* and *Chelt.* were all members of a single tradition of family development, in which neither *Trin.* nor *Chelt.* was later in derivation than *Wig.*

Moreover, it has already been explained above that certain decretals were misplaced from their intended sequence at an early stage in the assembly of the common stock; that these letters were transcribed out of true order in *Wig.* but preserved intact within the ancestral stratum; and that they are found also out of true order in *Claustr.* but split into two sections, of which one was in-

---

fols. 17vb-21, and the first items in the Leipzig Collection: Friedberg, *Canonessammlungen* 119-20; and in the Bamberg Collection, *ibid.* 93-94.

[26] The Cheltenham Collection is set out under various rubricated headings typified by the following: fol. 17^v: 'De simoniacis et indebitis exactionibus tam in ecclesiasticis quam castris et scolis regendis. De transactionibus et patronatu in quibus quandoque notatur simonia'; fol. 22^v: 'De transactionibus et iure patronatus'; fol. 29^v: 'De iuramento calumpnie, et ut clerici non iurent'; etc. Other similar examples are found on fols. 31^r, 36^r, 40^r, 58^v, 63^r, 66^r, 67^v, 73^r, 75^v, 81^v, 86^v, 91^r, 96^r. A further sub-heading 'De capellanis castrorum' appears on fol. 21^v; and a list of titles is found on fol. 1^v. A few examples will show the correspondence between the Worcester and Cheltenham Collections: *Chelt.* fols. 25^v-27^v = *Wig.* 7.73 and 76-79; fols. 63^r-64^v = *Wig.* 4. 1, 2, 8, 9, 10, 11, 30, 13, 23; fols. 84^r-86^v = *Wig.* 3.1-3, 5-8, 19, 21-23, 26, 29, 32, 35, 36; etc.

[26] There is a close agreement in many decretal inscriptions between *Wig.* and *Chelt.*: cf. *Wig.* 1.33-44 and *Chelt.* fols. 48rb-51rb; but there is no consistent textual correspondence between them, or between either of them and *Trin.* Thus, *Wig.* 2.22 has the inscription 'Remevensi archiepiscopo,' where *Trin.* 2.22 has no inscription, and *Chelt.* fol. 62vb has 'Eliensi episcopo'; many other similar variants could be cited. At the same time, a close agreement is frequently discovered between *Wig.* and *Trin.*, as the analysis of the Trinity Collection in Appendix I, below, reveals. In contrast, the decretal inscriptions are entirely omitted from *Claustr.* See also Appendix I (c), below: *Trin.* 2.25-27 = *Wig.* 2.26-28, and these three decretals are found also in *Chelt.* fols. 62ra, 60rb and 60va; in addition, *Wig.* 2.25 is found on fol. 63ra.

[27] App. I: *Wig.* 3.26, 29, 32, 35, 36 are found in *Chelt.* fols. 86ra, 86rb, 86va, 86va, 86va respectively. None of these decretals occurs in a corresponding position in *Trin.*

[28] App. I: *Trin.* 2.28-29 = *Wig.* 2.29-30; but neither item exists in a corresponding position in *Chelt.*

[29] App. I: *Wig.* 2.31; 3.27-28, 33-34 and 37-38.

serted within the appendix of later acquisitions. The relevant sequence does not appear in the surviving fragment of *Trin.*; but a third arrangement is found in *Chelt.*, in which the decretals occur in a sequence identical with that in *Claustr.* but preserved intact in a single unbroken sequence as in *Wig.*[30] Finally, as far as textual comparisons are concerned, the closest agreement exists between *Wig.* and *Chelt.*; and it is clear that the 'Worcester' material in *Chelt.* is earlier in derivation than that in *Claustr.* and independent of that in *Wig.*[31] For all these reasons, it is also evident that the Cheltenham Collection is of the utmost value in helping to reconstruct the authentic details of the common source, and it is possible that the Cheltenham manuscript preserves the most accurate version of the family archetype now surviving.[32]

But in displacing the Worcester Collection from its allegedly formative role in the development of the Worcester Family as a whole, the collection loses little of its historical interest or value in the process. It is a work of outstanding and unique significance, revealing to quite an unusual degree substantial evidence of authorship and provenance. The decretal collection is the principal item in a manuscript volume which also includes further papal letters transcribed on the opening and closing folios.[33] In both the decretal collection itself and in the additional letters, transcribed independently, a connexion with the career of Baldwin of Ford (archdeacon of Exeter and abbot of Ford, bishop of Worcester and archbishop of Canterbury successively) is quite distinctly reflected.

It is well known that distinguished schools of canon lawyers flourished at Exeter and Worcester in the later twelfth century;[34] and it is only to be expected that the canonists of those dioceses were closely interested in the judicial work of their own respective bishops. Bartholomew of Exeter and Roger of Worcester were among the most famous ecclesiastical judges and papal judges delegate in England at that time, and their work has left an unsurpassed impression on the material contents of the primitive English decretal collections. Two associations of Exeter and Worcester help to explain the use and inter-

---

[30] *Chelt.* fols. 48rb-51rb. If these items are numbered i-xv, for convenient reference to their order of transcription in *Chelt.*, the corresponding arrangements in *Wig.* and *Claustr.* are as follows: *Wig.* 1.33, 34bc, 35, 36, 41, 38, 37, 39, 40, 42-45, 34a, or *Claustr.* 70-75 and 309-15. *Chelt.* vi is not found at this point in either *Wig.* or *Claustr.* though it does occur as *Wig.* 7.55; and *Chelt.* xiv-xv are not included in *Claustr.* It is obvious from the MSS that the scribes were aware that a misplacement of decretals had occurred, since both *Wig.* and *Chelt.* include cross-references where the readjustments are necessary: see Lohmann, *art. cit.* 86, at *Wig.* 1.37; and *Chelt.* fols. 48rb, 49vb and 51rb.

[31] Cf. *Wig.* 2.37 (Lohmann, *art. cit.* 86) and *Chelt.* fol. 49vb; etc. See also n.26, above.

[32] This conclusion has been suggested also by W. Ullmann, 'A Forgotten Dispute at Bridlington Priory in its Canonistic Setting,' *Yorkshire Archaeological Journal* 148 (1951) 460: 'one may even suggest that the decretal in *Coll. Cheltenhamensis* presents to us the nearest approximation to the original'; and Rathbone, *op. cit.* (n.7) 509ff.

[33] The Worcester Collection is Royal MS 10.A II, fols. 5r-62v. Further letters are transcribed independently on fols. 1r-3r and 62v-63v, the latter group breaking off abruptly owing to the loss of one or more folios. For details of these letters, see P. M. Baumgarten, 'Papal Letters relating to England,' EHR 9 (1894) 531-41.

[34] Kuttner-Rathbone, *art. cit.* 282-83 and nn.10-11; A. Morey, *Bartholomew of Exeter* (Cambridge 1937), 100ff; M. Cheney, 'The Compromise of Avranches of 1172 and the Spread of Canon Law in England,' EHR 56 (1941) 177-97.

mingling of their decretal records in canonical collections. Firstly, there was the well-known collaboration of the two bishops in legal cases: they were not only the most frequently appointed judges delegate in England during Alexander III's pontificate, but they were sometimes jointly commissioned by the pope to deal with particular problems.[35] And, secondly, there was the no less significant link between the sees provided by Baldwin, a friend of both bishops and a member of Bartholomew's *familia*.

Baldwin first emerges clearly in English history as archdeacon of Totnes (*c.* 1161-70), master of the cathedral school of Exeter, and a friend and confidant of Bartholomew and John of Salisbury. There is little doubt that his sympathies were with the archbishop, Thomas Becket, in the great politico-ecclesiastical struggle of the period; and at the height of the bitter controversy he retired (*c.* 1169) to the Cistercian abbey at Ford, where he was abbot by 1173 at the latest.[36] As abbot of Ford he was commissioned as papal judge delegate by Alexander III on several occasions.[37] Already well-acquainted with both Bartholomew and Roger in the political and judicial affairs of the English Church, he was promoted to the bishopric of Worcester in 1180, following Roger's death in 1179. Four years later, on the death of Archbishop Richard, Becket's successor, he was elected to the archbishopric of Canterbury, and died on Crusade at Acre in 1190. These principal phases in Baldwin's career provide a remarkable commentary on the provenance of the manuscript volume, which (as already described) includes the decretal collection as its principal component.[38]

It was explained above that the Worcester Collection can be broken down analytically into two main sources: the 'Worcester' archetype, and a series of appendices to its several component books. Now, in each of these principal elements more decretals are found addressed to the bishops of Exeter and Worcester than to any other persons: some of these letters were sent to Exeter or Worcester individually, and others were sent jointly to both.[39] This striking

---

[35] In *Wig.* alone the following decretals were received jointly by Worcester and Exeter: 1.31 (JL 14167); 4.4 (JL 13928); 4.44; 4.47 (JL 13923); 4.50; 7.22; and 7.70. *Wig.* 3.22 (JL 14224) is addressed to Exeter and Winchester in this collection, but sometimes to Exeter and Worcester elsewhere.

[36] For Baldwin while at Exeter and Ford, see Morey, *op. cit.* 23-29 and 105-9; on the alignment of English bishops during the Becket controversy, see D. Knowles, *The Episcopal Colleagues of Archbishop Thomas Becket* (Cambridge 1951) 1-52.

[37] F. W. Maitland, *Roman Canon Law in the Church of England* (London 1898) 128: Maitland noticed the large number of decretals sent by Alexander III to the abbot of Ford, but was unaware of their significance in the provenance of the decretal collections. Cf. Kuttner-Rathbone, *art. cit.* 282-83. But it cannot be assumed that all decretals addressed to Ford and included in the collections were received by Baldwin: cf. Ullmann, *art. cit.* 465.

[38] Lohmann, *art. cit.* 53 n.1. For details of Baldwin's career, see R. Foreville, *L'Eglise et la Royauté en Angleterre sous Henri II Plantagenet,* 1154-89 (Paris 1943), 384-87 and 533-54: Roger died on Aug. 9, 1179; Baldwin succeeded him on Aug. 10, 1180; Baldwin was promoted to Canterbury on Dec. 16, 1184, and died at Acre on Nov. 19, 1190. See also n.33, above.

[39] A list of *Wig.* decretals with Exeter and/or Worcester inscriptions is given in Appendix II, below. It is well known that decretal inscriptions are not always reliable in any given MS; but the margin of possible errors of this kind in *Wig.* could not invalidate the general conclusions suggested here.

feature is not in fact unusual in English primitive collections in general. But, whereas the decretals to Exeter and Worcester provide only a minority, however significant, of the total number of letters in the family archetype, they form a remarkably large proportion of the additions in the supplementary appendices.[40] Moreover, whereas the decretals to Exeter outnumber those to Worcester in the archetype, the reverse is true in the later additions.[41] Both Exeter and Worcester decretals are significantly present in each of the major sources of the completed work, and the abbot of Ford is named no less than eight times in decretal inscriptions: five times in the archetype and three times in the supplements.[42] There can be little doubt that Baldwin was the abbot who received the decretals addressed to Ford, but that Roger was the bishop who received those addressed to Worcester.[43] Roger died in August 1179, and Baldwin succeeded him in August 1180. The archetype was assembled in its earliest known form some time later than January 1181. The Worcester Collection itself, though necessarily completed later than its source, contains no decretals later than 1181 in date of issue. It must be assumed, therefore, that the Worcester Collection was completed at Worcester after Baldwin's arrival there, and that in its composition the 'Worcester' archetype (or rather a derivative from the archetype) was supplemented with further decretals drawn from the episcopal records of Baldwin's predecessor, and to some lesser extent from the similar records of the diocese of Exeter from which he had been recently promoted.[44] Exactly how these resources were brought together can no longer be determined with any certainty, though Baldwin's own career suggests the most obvious explanation. On internal evidence alone it could not be assumed that the family archetype was made at Worcester, though there is every reason to believe in the Worcester provenance of the extant collection. And this conclusion agrees entirely with Lohmann's theory that the Worcester Collection was completed where the family archetype was not accessible. The known details of Baldwin's career, and the contrasting emphasis in the provenance of the two main sources of the completed Worcester Collection, thus jointly support the conclusion that his influence can be traced in either part.

---

[40] Appendix II, below: notice especially the concluding items in Books III, IV and VII.

[41] *Ibid.* 1.2-47 and 4.35-50. Many of the supplementary decretals received at Worcester were previously unknown when Lohmann analysed *Wig.* in 1933: *Wig.* 1.48; 2.34; 3.38 and 40; 4.39, 44, 45, 48, 49, 50; 7.70, 72, 73, 79, 80. It is significant that none of these items was included in the family archetype.

[42] *Ibid.*, 1.43; 7.2, 14, 15, 26, 65, 77, 78. It is possible that 7.11 was also received by Baldwin, being addressed to the archdeacon of Exeter.

[43] But cf. n.37, above: Ullmann, *art. cit.* 465.

[44] Since Baldwin became bishop of Worcester in August 1180, and the latest positive date in both the archetype and *Wig.* is Jan. 23, 1181, it is most unlikely that any decretals of Worcester provenance included in *Wig.* were received by Baldwin as bishop. Since Roger died in August 1179, and the earliest possible date of composition of *Wig.* must be later than Jan. 23, 1181, the absence of so many of Roger's decretals from the archetype, and their very substantial supplementation of the archetype in *Wig.* strongly support the conclusion that the archetype was not itself of Worcester provenance.

But if this supposition, based entirely on evidence within the decretal collection, falls short of full conviction, there can be no reasonable doubt about
Baldwin's connection with the completion of the manuscript volume as a whole.
Letters of later popes, received in England between 1181 and 1187, are transcribed on the folios at either end of the volume, bound up with the Worcester
Collection, but independent of it in composition and transcription. Five letters
of Lucius III (1181-85) are entered on the closing folios: three to Baldwin as
bishop of Worcester, one to Rapolla and one further fragment of English provenance but without inscription.[45] Five letters of Urban III (1185-87) are
transcribed on the opening folios: three to Baldwin as archbishop of Canterbury,
one to the Canterbury clergy to advise them of Baldwin's legatine status, and
one letter to Henry II on the same subject.[46] And, finally, one letter of Clement
III, issued in 1187 on the subject of his own election, is found on the closing
folios, addressed in this transcription to the English bishops generally.[47] These
varied letters were written by different hands and at different times. At least
six, and almost certainly seven, were received by Baldwin personally as bishop
of Worcester or archbishop of Canterbury between 1181 and 1187; and two
further letters are concerned with his legatine status.

The personal factors here are obvious: the parallel stages in his own career
and the gradual completion of the manuscript volume are too close for mere
coincidence. If not his personal possession, this manuscript now in the British
Museum must surely have belonged to a member of Baldwin's circle. No other
member of the Worcester Family reveals such clear evidence of provenance
and authorship as this. Where the other collections augment the common
stock with later letters independently acquired, they show no comparable
emphasis, personal or regional, in the selection of decretals so appended. Among
the members of the Worcester Family in particular, and among English primitive decretal collections in general, the Worcester Collection retains its place
of unusual importance. But for reasons sufficiently explained above it can no
longer be described as the oldest member of its family group.

APPENDIX I: THE COLLECTIO TRINITATIS

The *Collectio Trinitatis* is the fifth item in the Trinity College MS R.14.9,
fols. 82r-87v.[48] Now merely a fragment of the original, the collection is transcribed
in a characteristic English pointed hand of the later twelfth century, set out
in a single column with an average of forty lines on each folio side. In addition
to many rubricated comments, the decretal inscriptions and the initial letters

---

[45] The letters of Lucius III to Baldwin are: Royal MS 10 A.II, fol. 63va, *Ex conquestione*,
JL 15205 (Dec. 13, 1181); fol. 62va, *Fraternitati tue*, JL 15204 (1181-83); fol. 63vb, *Significavit
nobis*, JL 14964 (June 5, 1182-83).

[46] The letters of Urban III to Baldwin are: *ibid.* fol. 1r, *Celestis altitudo*, JL 15518 (Jan. 12,
1186); fol. 2va-b, *Sinceritas devotionis* (Dec. 13, 1185); fol. 3rb, *Sicut tue littere* (June 23,
1186-87). To the Canterbury clergy: fols. 2vb-3ra, *Divine sapientie* (Dec. 18, 1185); and
to Henry II: fol. 2r, *Ab oculis Romane* (Dec. 17, 1185).

[47] *Ibid.* fol. 62v, *Illud operata* (Dec. 1187).

[48] The older folio numbers, recently changed to 83-88, have been retained here.

of decretals and their component chapters are transcribed in red. The folios have been trimmed at the edges in process of binding, with the result that parts of the marginal rubrics are now lost; in these circumstances, the following analysis includes a suggested reconstruction of the missing words and letters, placed in parentheses. Similarly, wherever the MS omits the decretal inscriptions, these also are inserted within parentheses, if they are known from other sources. The whole of the first book is lost, and the extant fragment begins in mid-decretal at 'indulgentiam sedis' towards the end of Book II, ending abruptly at 'iamdicte' soon after the beginning of Book IV. For reasons explained above, it must be assumed that the original collection included seven books, and that the whole of Books V, VI and VII have not survived. The individual decretals are not numbered in this MS according to their order within each book, but a plan of numeration is adopted in the analysis for convenience in collation with *Wig.* and *Claustr.*, and for reference purposes, accepting as far as possible the system of numeration existing in *Wig.* (Royal MS 10 A.II). According to this arrangement, therefore, the extant fragment of *Trin.* extends from Book 2.21 to Book 4.7. There are no decretals in this surviving fragment of *Trin.* which are not already known in *Wig.*; but there are textual variants in their decretal inscriptions, and, wherever these are significant, they are noted in the following analysis.

(a) *Analysis*

TRIN. II

(21) (Eboracensi archiepiscopo et Lincolnensi et Cestrensi episcopis.
Audivimus et audientes ...)
indulgentiam sedis ... representent. [fol. 82^r]

    (a) indulgentiam sedis ... observari.
    (b) *Rubric*: Infra septa monasterii nullus violentiam inferat. Quod si fecerit, excommunicetur.
    Ad hec presentium auctoritate ... representent.

Not in JL. — 1166-79. — Lohmann p. 96; Holtzmann, *Papsturkunden in England* I (1930) n. 160. Rubric for *Trin.* (a) no longer legible: 'Monachi albi [...] habent decimationum.'

(22) (G. Ravennati archiepiscopo.)
Rubric: Si electio in episcopum colla(ta) valet.
Causa que vertitur inter moniales ... existat.

JL 14070. — 1159-77. — Addressed to Guido (1158-69) or Gerard (1170-90), archbishops of Ravenna. Cf. *Wig.*: 'Remevensi archiepiscopo. Causam ... existit.'

(23) Cant(uariensi) archiepiscopo.
Rubric: Sicut de pascuis ita ad (fertilitatem) redactis.
Commisse nobis a Deo ... persolvi.

JL 11660. — 1162-70.

(24) Londoniensi episcopo.
Rubric: Monachi inquieti corr(ipiantur).
Delatum est auribus nostris ... convertantur.

JL 13997. — 1159-81. — Cf. *Wig.*: 'Relatum est.'

(25) Abbati et fratribus de monasterio Loregio. [82ᵛ
Suggestum est ex parte vestra ... proponunt.
JL 14004. — 1159-81. — Cf. *Wig.*: 'Abbati et fratribus monasterii de Loregio.'

(26) (Abbati et fratribus Ramecensibus.)
Licet de benignitate ... compellat.
JL 14068. — 1159-81. — Lohmann p. 97; the decretal is addressed to Rameiges in the province of Sens.

(27) Tracensi archiepiscopo.
Ex parte tue fraternitatis ... vendicare.
JL 14117. — 1159-81. — Cf. *Wig.*: 'Trecensi episcopo.'

(28) Dulinensi archiepiscopo.
Contingit interdum quod ... optinere.
  (a) Contingit interdum ... revocare.
  (b) *Rubric*: Nil iuris habere in ecclesia ex carta laicorum. [83ʳ
      Super eo vero quod ... optinere.
JL 13868. — 1159-81. — Cf. *Wig.*: 'Dunolmensi episcopo.'

(29) (Abbati sancte Genovephe.)
Ex tuarum litterarum tenore ... expiare.
JL 13940. — 1159-81. — Lohmann p. 98.

TRIN. III

Rubric: Tertia partitio de personis ecclesiarum et earum institutione et earum ornatu.

1. Cant(uariensi) archiepiscopo.
   Cum in Cantuariensi provincia ... percellas.
   (a) *Rubric*: Clerici fornicarii ab ecclesiis removeantur.
       Cum in Cantuariensi ... spoliare.
   (b) *Rubric*: Christiani non famulentur Judeis.
       Ad hec cum cautum sit ... percellas.
   JL 13810 and 13976. — 1174-81.

2. Turonensi archiepiscopo.
   Rubric: Nec servi nec spurii ordinentur.
   Consuluit nos tua fraternitas ... presumas.
   JL 14121. — 1159-81.

3. Universis suffraganeis Cant(uariensis) ecclesie.
   Rubric: Archiepiscopus iure legationis omnes causas subditorum audire potest.
   Cum non ignoretis ... transferre.
   JL 11665. — 1166-70.

4. Universis suffraganeis Cant(uariensis) ecclesie. [83ᵛ
   Rubric: (S)i appellatio in aliquo articulo interpo(n)iatur ab episcopo, licet tota diocesis (s)ub protectione pape constituatur, tamen ex(c)essus nihilominus corripiantur.
   Significavit nobis venerabilis ... revocare.
   JL 12378. — May 14, 1174.

5. Nobilissimo duci Venecie.
   Rubric: (Priv)ilegium personale ut clerici secundum (cons)uetudinem loci in causa pecuniaria iu(di)centur.
   Cum essemus Venecie ... durare.
   JL 14334. — 1178.

6. Romorensi episcopo.
   Rubric: (Si) excommunicati divina celebra(ver)int, poterunt de iure deponi.
   Consuluit nos fraternitas ... promulgare.
   Not in JL. — 1159-81. — Cf. *Wig.*: 'Remorensi episcopo.'

7. Lucensi episcopo et eius capitulo.
   Rubric: (Pe)na presbiteri qui in conflictu lapi(des) misit, licet non percusserit.
   Presentium lator J. ... admittatis.
   JL 14006. — 1159-81.

8. Fuscentino archiepiscopo.   [84^r
   Rubric: Laicus dum insileret diacono, letale vulnus accepit, ideoque non prom(o)veatur sine licentia pape, nec ministret.
   Continebatur in litteris ... patiaris.
   JL 13856. — 1159-81. — Cf. *Wig.*: 'Cusantino archiepiscopo.'

9. Exoniensi episcopo.
   Rubric: Causa criminis in personis presentibus non solet ab apostolico alii committi.
   Suggestum est auribus nostris ... ammovere.
   JL 13913. — 1162-81.

10. Cant(uariensi archiepiscopo) et suffraganeis episcopis.
    Rubrics: Officiales episcoporum ius inst(i)tuendi habere.
    Invasores ecclesiarum quater in anno excommunicandi.
    Ex frequentibus querelis ... presumatis.
    JL 13817. — 1159-81.

11. Cant(uariensi) archiepiscopo.
    Rubric: Filii clericorum nulla persona media, paternam non retineant ecclesiam, et si plures habuerint una sola contenti sint.   [84^v
    Ad exstirpandas successiones ... noscatur.
    JL 13802. — 1159-81.

12. London(iensi) episcopo.
    Ad aures nostras noveris ... servarent.
    (a) *Rubric*: (In)stituti ab archidiacono post prohi(biti)onem episcopi removeantur.
        Ad aures nostras ... interdicere.
    (b) *Rubric*: Canonici in servitio episcopi manentes de omnibus preterquam de victualibus communiter accipiant.
        De cetero quia dignum ... servarent.
    See *Trin.* 3.13, below.

13. Salubiriensi episcopo.
    Si vero aliquando ordinatio ... terminari.
    (a) *Rubric*: (Si contro)versia fuerit de iure advo(cati)onis episcopus

instituat, et postea victor presentet.
Si vero aliquando ... evicerat.

(b) *Rubric*: Causam delegatam delegare posse.
Porro si pro debilitate ... terminari.

Trin. 3.12 and 13 = *Wig.* 3.12.
JL 13990, 13992, 13996, and 14181. — 1159-81. Cf. *Wig.*: 'Lundonensi episcopo.'

14. Panibergensi electo.
Rubric: Non consecratum uti mitra et pontificalibus.
Non sine gravibus sumptibus ... facultatem.
Not in JL. — 1159-81. — Lohmann p. 102; the decretal is addressed to Bamberg, and is hitherto known only in *Wig.* and *Claustr.* Cf. *Wig.*: 'Pambergensi episcopo.'

15. Winton(iensi) episcopo.   [85ʳ
Suggestum est nobis quod quidam ... puniatur.
(a) *Rubric*: In maioribus ordinibus constituti si mulieres non abiecerint ab officio removeantur.
Suggestum est nobis ... apparere.
(b) *Rubric*: Post appellationem enormiter delinquentes et scandalum facientes, appellatione non defendantur.
Preterea de clericis ... puniatur.
JL 14152. — July 21, 1177. — *Wig.* has an additional chapter: Porro de his ... parere. Cf. note at *Trin.* 3.16, below.

16. Exon(iensi) episcopo.
Rubric: Si ex separatione suspicari p(otest) deterius contingere, subdiaconi (cum) uxoribus manere poterint dis(si)mulari. Quod si ecclesias habent eas dimittant.
Significatum est nobis ... cogendi.
JL 13904. — 1162-81. — The MS has the single word 'Porro' above the opening word 'Significatum'; cf. note at *Trin.* 3.15, above.

17. Will(el)mo Norwigensi episcopo.
Ex tenore tuarum litterarum ... suscipias.
(a) *Rubrics*: Persone ecclesiarum autenticis scriptis episcopi et domini fundi muniantur, ne illis descendentibus alii preripiant facultatem institutionis.   [85ᵛ
Appellationi terminus constituatur infra quem si non prosequatur iudicio stare compellantur.
Ex tenore tuarum ... constringas.
(b) *Rubric*: Complices in testimonio non producantur.
Verum si coram ... recipiantur.
(c) *Rubric*: Falsatores litterarum apostolici a beneficio et officio deponantur, et monasteriis tradantur.
Ad hec de sacerdote ... suscipias.
JL 12253 and 14146. — 1160-74.

18. Lincoliensi archidiacono.
Rubric: (Si) aliquis tacito quod sit filius sacerdo(tis) et super ecclesia in qua pater mi(ni)stravit litteras recuperavit, (eam) amittat.
Ad presentiam nostram accedens R... amoveas.

JL 13982. — *c*. 1170-73. — The decretal is addressed to Geoffrey Plantagenet, archdeacon of Lincoln. Cf. *Wig*.: 'Lincolnensi archidiacono Galf'do.'

19. Cant(uariensi) archiepiscopo.
   Rubric: (Offi)cialis si non ex deliberatione sed (ex cas)u clericum leserit, similiter ali(quis si) cum sibi coniuncta consanguinita(te a)dulterantem clericum leserit, (non in)cidit in datam sententiam.
   Officialis pro iniectione ... immunis.
   JL 12180. — Jan. 31, 1171-2. — The inscription here is inaccurate, the decretal being sent to the bishop of Exeter.

20. Norwicensi pontifici. [86.
   Rubric: Filii sacerdotum in sacerdotio geniti ab ecclesiis removeantur^r
   Ad aures nostras sepius pervenisse ... incumbere.
   Not in JL. — 1159-81. — The decretal is hitherto known only in *Wig*. and *Claustr*

21. Exon(iensi episcopo).
   Rubric: Pignora restituantur si ex fructibus consecuti sunt sortem.
   Cum non solum viris ... districtione.
   JL 13819. — 1162-81.

22. Decano et capitulo Salubriensi.
   Rubric: Filius curam animarum non potest su(s)cipere quam pater prius habuit, ma(xime) si in minori etate fueri(t) collata (*MS*: collate).
   Cum Hugo Huvet ... ducere.
   JL 14098. — 1159-81. — Cf. *Wig*.: 'Cum Hugo Buvet'; *Claustr*.: 'Cum Hugo Hinnet.'

23. Exon(iensi) et Wint(oniensi) episcopis.
   Rubrics: Decretum apostolici contra filios sacerdotum tam promulgatum.
   Constitutiones futuris dant formam negotiis.
   Ante Concilium Turonense.
   Significavit nobis O. presbiter ... impetratis.
   JL 14224. — 1164-81.

24. Salubriensi et Exon(iensi) episcopis. [86^v
   Rubrics: In sacerdotio geniti nisi in claustris probabiliter vixerint non sunt promovendi.
   Testes super manifestis non producantur.
   Suggestum est nobis quod J. ... sit.
   JL 14097. — 1159-81. — Cf. *Wig*.: 'Salesburiensi et Wigorniensi episcopis.'

25. Exon(iensi) episcopo.
   Rubrics: (Fi)lius sacerdotis in subdiaconatu promotus, (bene)ficium ecclesiasticum habere potest.
   (So)lus sacerdos non potest divina celebrare.
   Proposuit nobis R. ... celebrare.
   JL 14217. — 1162-81.

26. Eborac(ensi) archiepiscopo.
   Fraternitati tue duximus ... recipere.
      (a) *Rubric*: (Cleri)ci causa studiorum vel alia iusta causa (ab)sentes beneficiis non spolientur, (lic)et vocati ab episcopo non venerint.
      Fraternitati tue ... debeant.

(b) *Rubric*: Clericos alterius episcopi sine commendaticiis non retinendos.
Preterea clericos alterius ... recipere.
JL 13879. — 1159-81.

TRIN. IV.

Rubric: Incipiunt decretales epistole Alexandri pape tertii de statu et iure ecclesiarum. Quarum prima destinata est Eborac(ensi) archiepiscopo.

1. *Rubric*: (Con)cessiones ecclesiarum viventibus (per)sonis irritas esse.
Ea que honestatis ... decernas.
JL 15171. — 1159-81.

2. Abbatibus et prioribus et aliis viris ecclesiasticis (per Eboracensem archiepiscopatum constitutis).   [86ᵛ
Rubric: Donatione ecclesiarum a laicis facta prescriptionem valere vel episcopi consensum.   [87ʳ
Cum pastorali sollicitudine ... sanctimus.
JL 13893. — 1159-81. — Cf. *Wig.*: 'Cura pastorali.'

3. Cant(uariensi) archiepiscopo et suffraganeis eius.
Ad aures nostras noveritis ... spolietis.
   (a) *Rubric*: Puniantur archidiaconi qui in ecclesias vacantes se intrudunt; et eis remotis, personis congruis ordinentur.
   Ad aures nostras ... punire.
   (b) *Rubric*: Ius advocationis vendi non potest; unde si venditum fuerit ab episcopo auferetur.
   Ceterum quia clerici ... spolietis.
JL 13909 and 13954. — 1159-81.

4. Exon(iensi) et Wigorn(iensi) episcopis.
Rubric: Decimas sine diminutione a la(i)cis solvendas; quod si non fecerint, anatheme percellantur.
Cum homines de Hortuna ... exhibeant.
JL 13928. — 1162-81.

5. Eboracensi archiepiscopo.
Ex parte abbatis et canonicorum ... evitari.
Not in JL. — 1159-81. The decretal is hitherto known only in *Wig.* and *Claustr*.

6. Exon(iensi) episcopo.   [87ᵛ
Rubric: Heres sacerdotis cogatur luere de rebus ecclesie quam sacerdos pignoravit.
Presentium latoris insinuatione ... cohercere.
JL 13911. — 1162-81.

7. Wigorn(iensi) episcopo.
Rubrics: Ubi aliquis et voluntaria et necessaria sacramenta percipit, ibi decimas persolvat.
Transactio nisi fuerit ab apostolico confirmata videtur inter personas et non ecclesias facta.
De omnibus proventibus decimas (i)ntegre esse solvendas.
Veniens ad apostolice sedis clementiam ... iamdicte (... decernas.)
JL 14137. — 1159-81. — The MS ends abruptly at 'iamdicte.'

(b) *Comparative Table of Claustroneoburgensis,*
Trinitatis, and Wigorniensis

Since the Trinity MS is now merely a fragment, beginning in Book II and ending in Book IV, comparison between the three collections is necessarily limited to that extent, although both *Claustr.* and *Wig.* have survived intact. In external appearance, *Claustr.* is not set out in book-form, as *Trin.* and *Wig.* are, but this difference between them is merely superficial, and its underlying pattern of composition is the same as that in the other two collections. For collating purposes, therefore, it is most convenient to treat *Claustr.* as if it were set out in clear divisions, though these have no formal existence in the MS.

Claustr.	*Trin.*	*Wig.*	*Claustr.*	*Trin.*	*Wig.*
Book II					
110	21a	21a	—	28b	29b
111	b	b	—	29	30
112	22	22	—	—	31a
113	23	23	—	—	b
114.I	24	24	—	—	32
—	—	25.I	—	—	33
—	—	II	—	—	34
107	25	26	—	—	35
—	26	27	—	—	36
344	27	28	—	—	37
—	28a	29a			
Book III					
114.II	1a	1a	131	16	15
III	b	b	132.I	17a.I	16a.I
115	2	2	II		II
116	3	3		II	b
117	4	4	III	b	c
118	5	5	IV	c	d
119	6	6	133	18	17
120	7	7	134	19	18
121	8	8	135	20	19
122	9	9	136	21	20
123	10	10	137	22	21
124	11	11	138	23	22
125.I	12a	12a.I	139	24	23
II		II	140	25	24
III	b	b	141	26a	25a
126	13a	c		b	b
127	b	d	—	—	26
128	14	13	—	—	27
129	15a	14a	343	—	28
130	b	b	—	—	29
—	—	c	—	—	30

Clausrt.	Trin.	Wig.	Claustr.	Trin.	Wig.
—	—	31a	—	—	34
—	—	b.1	—	—	35
—	—	11	300.11	—	36
—	—	c	—	—	37
—	—	32a	—	—	38
—	—	b	140	25	39
—	—	c	—	—	40
—	—	33			

Book IV

142	1	1	145	4	4
143	2	2	146	5	5
144.1	3.1	3.1	147	6	6
11	11	11	148	7	7

The Comparative Table provides the following conclusions:

(a) Book II. The three collections correspond in this book as far as *Wig.* 2.24, at which point *Claustr.* passes to Book III, but *Trin.* and *Wig.* continue their parallel arrangement down to *Wig.* 2.30. At that stage, *Trin.* also passes to Book III, and *Wig.* continues alone to 2.37. (*Wig.* 2.26 = *Trin.* 2.25 = *Claustr.* 107.)

(b) Book III. Full correspondence between all three collections is resumed in this book, and is maintained down to *Wig.* 3.25b, at which point both *Claustr.* and *Trin.* pass to Book IV, but *Wig.* again continues alone to 3.40.

(c) Book IV. Once more the full correspondence is resumed between all three collections, but collation in this book is possible only down to *Wig.* 4.7, at which point the *Trin.* MS is abruptly concluded.

(c) *Comparative Table of Claustroneoburgensis, Trinitatis, Wigorniensis, and Cheltenhamensis.*

	Claustr.	Trin.	Wig.	Cheli.
Book II				
	113	23	23	fol. 61vb
	114.1	24	24	61vb
	—	—	25.1	63ra
	—	—	11	
	107	25	26	62ra
	—	26	27	60rb
	344	27	28	60va
	—	28	29	—
	—	29	30	—
	—	—	31	—
Book III				
	140	25	24	fol. 67rb
	141	26	25	67va

Claustr.	Trin.	Wig.	Chelt.
—	—	26	86ra
—	—	27	—
343	—	28	—
—	—	29	86rb
—	—	30	64vb
—	—	31	74vb
—	—	32	67va + 86va
—	—	33	—
—	—	34	—
—	—	35	86va
300.ii	—	36	86va
—	—	37	—
—	—	38	—
140	25	39	67rb

APPENDIX II: DECRETALS WITH EXETER AND WORCESTER INSCRIPTIONS
IN THE COLLECTIO WIGORNIENSIS

The following list provides statistical details of decretals received by the bishops of Exeter and Worcester and by the abbot of Ford, as recorded in *Wigorniensis*. It is well known that the details of proper names are frequently unreliable in the inscriptions preserved in any given manuscript. Therefore, in the list below, the inscriptions recorded in *Wig.* are noted first, but, if variant readings have been found in other manuscripts, these are also listed in parentheses. Unless otherwise stated, the references in this list apply to the bishops of the sees mentioned, and all other relevant details are found in Lohmann's analysis already published. To distinguish clearly the two principal source strata in *Wig.*, all items which were not included in the 'Worcester' common stock are listed in italics.

BOOK I

2. Norwich (Exeter).
4. No inscription (Exeter).
8. Exeter (Lisieux).
9. Winchester (Worcester).
11. Exeter.
13. Hereford (Worcester).
14. Worcester.
16. Exeter.
17. Exeter.
29. Exeter.
30. Exeter.
31. Exeter and Worcester.
43. Exeter, Winchester, and the abbot of Ford.
47. Exeter (repetition of 8).
48. *Worcester.*
49. Winchester (repetition of 9).

BOOK II

8. Worcester.
11. Worcester and the abbot of Evesham.
34. *London and Worcester.*
37. *Worcester and Hereford.*

BOOK III

9. Exeter.
14. Winchester (Worcester).
15. Exeter.
18. Canterbury (correctly: Exeter).
20. Exeter.
22. Exeter and Winchester (Exeter and Worcester).
23. Salisbury and Worcester (Salisbury and Exeter; or Canterbury).
24. Exeter.

35. *Worcester.*
36. *Bath* (Bath and Exeter; or Exeter).
38. *Worcester.*
39. Exeter (repetition of 24).
40. *Canterbury and Worcester.*

BOOK IV

3. Canterbury and suffragans (Exeter; or Hereford and abbot of Ford; or Worcester).
4. Exeter and Worcester.
6. Exeter.
7. Worcester.
8. Canterbury and Exeter
17. Exeter.
25. Worcester (Exeter and Worcester).
35. No inscription (*Worcester*).
36. *Canterbury and Worcester.*
39. *Worcester.*
40. *Worcester and the prior of Pentney.*
41. *Worcester.*
42. *Exeter.*
43. *Worcester and Norwich*
44. *Exeter and Worcester.*
45. *Worcester.*
46. *Exeter.*
47. *Exeter and Worcester.*
48. *Worcester and Hereford.*
49. *Worcester and the abbot of Eynsham.*
50. *Exeter and Worcester.*

BOOK VII

2. The abbots of Ford and Evesham.
7. London and Worcester (London and Norwich; or Toledo).
9. London and Winchester (London and Worcester; or Worcester).
11. The abbot of Ramsey and the archdeacon of Exeter.
12. Exeter and the dean of Chichester (Exeter and the elect of Chichester).
14. York, Exeter, and the abbot of Ford.
15. The abbots of Ford, Evesham, and St Albans (Chichester and the abbot of Ford).
19. Worcester
22. Exeter and Worcester.
25. Winchester and Exeter (Bath and Exeter).
26. Exeter and the abbot of Ford.
28. Exeter.
29. Lisieux (Exeter).
32. Worcester.
37. No inscription (Exeter and the dean of Lincoln).
39. Worcester and the abbot... (MS incomplete; elsewhere: Worcester and the archdeacon of Ely).
43. Worcester and the abbot of Evesham.
51. Canterbury (Exeter).
52. Norwich (Exeter).
56. Exeter and the abbot of St Albans.
65. *Hereford and the abbot of Ford.*
66. *Worcester and the prior of Kenilworth.*
70. *Worcester and Exeter.*
72. *Worcester.*
73. *Worcester.*
77. *Exeter and the abbot of Ford.*
78. *Exeter and the abbot of Ford.*
79. *Worcester and the abbot of Kenilworth*
80. *Worcester and the prior of Kenilworth.*

No decretals to Exeter or Worcester are found in Books V and VI, which comprise thirteen and four decretals respectively. Six inscriptions in Book VII refer to Kenilworth: two in the common stock (7.20 and 21), and four in the later additions to it (7.66, 67, 79 and 80). In addition to the decretals with Worcester inscriptions, others refer to Worcester within the texts: e.g. 7.64, 75 and 81.

King's College,
University of London.

VIII

ENGLISH CANONISTS AND
THE 'APPENDIX CONCILII LATERANENSIS'

With an Analysis of St. John's College, Cambridge, MS 148

The formative role of the *Appendix Concilii Lateranensis* in the development of twelfth-century decretal collections is already familiar to historians of canon law.[1] This important collection begins in its vulgate edition with the canons of the Lateran Council of 1179, followed by forty-nine titles, which, with the exception of the final two, are systematic in technical style. The collection as preserved in the *editio princeps*, based by B. Laurens on a manuscript now lost, was built up in a series of successive stages, the basic work being completed within the limits *c.* 1181-5, and the final form including material as late as 1188-90. But the concluding title in this *editio princeps*, or vulgate edition, is not discovered in any of the surviving *Appendix* manuscripts, and has been shown by Holtzmann to depend on an excerpt from the lost register of Alexander III.[2] It must be assumed, therefore, that this title had no place in the original collection, but was a special supplement to the manuscript on which Laurens based his edition, being discovered elsewhere only in the material at the end of *Orielensis I*, a related work.[3] Since the collection in its earliest version (*c.* 1181-5) was the fountainhead of the main tradition of decretal transmission, its provenance and authorship are clearly of historical interest.[4]

---

[1] The text is in P. Crabbe, *Concilia omnia tam generalia quam particularia* II (2nd ed. Cologne 1551) 836-944; J.-D. Mansi, *Sacrorum conciliorum nova et amplissima collectio* 22.248-454; etc. See also Friedberg, *Canonessamlungen* 63-84; A. Amanieu, 'Appendix Concilii Lateranensis,' DDC 1 (1935) 833-41; S. Kuttner, *Repertorium der Kanonistik* 290-1, including a critical bibliographical report on relevant work by E. Seckel, F. Heyer, J. Juncker, and others; W. Holtzmann, 'Die Register Papst Alexanders III. in den Händen der Kanonisten,' *Quellen und Forschungen aus italienischen Archiven und Bibliotheken* 30 (1940) 13-87; *idem*, 'Über eine Ausgabe der päpstlichen Dekretalen des 12. Jahrhunderts,' *Nachrichten Akad. Göttingen* (1945) 23; *idem* and E. W. Kemp, *Papal Decretals Relating to the Diocese of Lincoln* (Lincoln Record Society; 1954) xiii; etc. For generous advice in preparing this paper, I am much indebted to Professor Stephan Kuttner, and for information kindly given at an earlier stage my thanks are due to Dr. Eleanor Rathbone.

[2] Holtzmann, *Quellen und Forschungen* 18ff.; *idem* and Kemp, *op. cit.* xiii-xiv.

[3] *Ibid.* xiv.

[4] Cf. S. Kuttner and E. Rathbone, 'Anglo-Norman Canonists of the Twelfth Century,' *Traditio* 7 (1951) 283-4.

The origin of the *Appendix* has been the subject of divergent theories, but the evidence for its English provenance seems most convincing at present. An Italian origin was thought most likely by Van Hove;[5] a continental, rather than English, origin has been preferred by Holtzmann, who correctly established the curial source of the final title of the vulgate edition;[6] but Kuttner and Rathbone have argued persuasively the alternative theory of its English authorship.[7] The justification for this theory lies in the use made of the *Appendix* by English or Anglo-Norman canonists in their commentaries, and its seemingly total neglect for this purpose by the canonists in other schools. But support for their thesis is not confined to this discovery alone. It is clear that the *Appendix* in its earliest deducible version was already a work of complex ancestry, drawing on both English and continental sources for its raw materials. Thus, the continental systematic *Parisiensis II*[8] and the English collections of the primitive 'Worcester' family alike throw light on the varied earlier strands which were drawn together in this work. But the evidence in the 'Worcester' group is the more significant in the present context.[9]

The 'Worcester' family is the most technically advanced group of English primitive collections, and is so called on the doubtful assumption that the Worcester Collection, a work of well-authenticated Worcester connections, completed in or shortly after 1181, is its earliest surviving member.[10] While the Worcester Collection reveals no immediate or direct filiation with the *Appendix*, a collation of the two works suggests their partial dependence on a common source of supply. The Worcester Collection can be broken down analytically into two main sources: the family archetype, divided into seven books on a subject-matter basis; and a series of additions made to these component parts.[11] A comparison of the two collections shows that the great majority of all decretals in the 'Worcester' archetype are included in the *Appendix*;[12] that further decretals supplementary to the archetype in the Worcester Collection are also found in the *Appendix*;[13] and, most significant of all, that both collections have

---

[5] A. Van Hove, *Prolegomena* 352.

[6] Holtzmann, *Quellen und Forschungen* 16 n. 1 and 18ff.; *idem*, 'Die Benutzung Gratians in der päpstlichen Kanzlei im 12. Jahrhundert,' *Studia Gratiana* 1 (1953) 332; *idem* and Kemp, *op. cit.* xiii.

[7] Kuttner and Rathbone, *art. cit.* 283-4.

[8] Cf. Friedberg, *Canonessammlungen* 21-6 and 71-84.

[9] The English primitive collections are discussed in my *Twelfth-Century Decretal Collections and their Importance in English History* (University of London, Athlone Press, 1962); for the 'Worcester' family, see *ibid.* 95-110.

[10] Duggan, 'The Trinity Collection of Decretals and the Early Worcester Family,' *Traditio* 17 (1961) 506-13.

[11] H. Lohmann, 'Die Collectio Wigorniensis,' ZRG, *Kan. Abt.* 22 (1933) 36-187, esp. 45-8.

[12] Decretals or chapters in the 'Worcester' archetype but not in *Appendix*: Wig. 1.3a.II, 12, 40, 41b, 42 and 43; 2.1.II, 3, 6, 13d-f, 19 and 21; 3.6, 12b, 13, 14a, 16a.I and 19; 4.5, 8, 12, 13, 16a, 17, 20a and 24; 5.2; 6.1a; 7.1-8, 11b, 14, 15, 18, 20-3, 25, 26, 27d-f and 1, 44a, 59 and 61. All other items are found in both collections.

[13] Decretals or chapters supplementary to the archetype in *Wig.* but not in *Appendix*: Wig. 1.45 and 48; 2.25.I, 31b, 32, 33, 34 and 36; 3.34, 38 and 40; 4.34, 39, 41-6 and 48-50; 7.55, 64, 66, 67 and 70-80.

many decretals in common which were unknown to the authors of all other primitive collections examined by Lohmann in his meticulous analysis of the Worcester Collection, except for some decretals which were also known to the author of the Klosterneuburg Collection, its close relation.[14]

A further point of circumstantial evidence is supplied by the *Appendix* in its 44th Title. This group of letters is placed under the heading 'De preeminentia Lundoniensis et Eboracensis,' an interest deriving from the well-known letter of Gregory I to St. Augustine in 601, advising him on the future provincial structure of the English Church.[15] The revival of controversy over the primacy in the English Church in the course of the twelfth century creates an assumption in favor of an English background in the original selection of this heading, especially since an adjacent and additional heading 'De discordia Turonensis ecclesiae cum Dolensi' was introduced into the derivative French *Bambergensis*, referring with similar regional emphasis to the quarrel between Tours and Dol.[16] It might seem at first sight that this English emphasis in the 44th Title is counterbalanced by the curial origin of the 50th Title. But, as mentioned above, the final title in the vulgate edition was not included in the original work, is not found in the extant manuscripts, and therefore provides no evidence on the provenance of the archetypal *Appendix*. The point is exemplified by the Lincoln Cathedral MS 121, one of the three main surviving *Appendix* texts.[17] The Lincoln manuscript includes in place of the 50th Title further decretals closely corresponding with the later additions to the Cottonian and Peterhouse Collections, in the 'Worcester' family, completed in or after 1193-4,[18] and with similar additions in the English systematic *Tanner*, composed towards the close of the century.[19] The Lincoln manuscript preserves a textually interesting

---

[14] Items listed by Lohmann in *Wig.* and *Appendix* only: *Wig.* 1.34a; 2.25.II, 30 and 37; 3.26, 27, 30, 31b-c, 32, 33 and 35; 4.25b, 28, 29, 31, 32, 36-8, 40 and 47; 7.65. In addition, the following items are listed in *Wig. Claustr.* and *Appendix* only: *Wig.* 1.2, 4, 7, 11, 30, 35, 41a and 44; 2.9, 10a, 11, 12, 15, 17, 20 and 24; 3.9, 22, 24, 25, 28, 36 and 39; 4.2, 4, 6, 7, 9-11, 15, 19, 25a and 35; 5.10 and 13; 6.3 and 4; 7.9, 11a, 12, 13, 17, 24, 32, 34-9, 42, 43, 45, 46, 53, 58, 62 and 63. But no direct interconnection existed between the Worcester Collection in its completed form and the *Appendix*: the items listed in nn. 12 and 13, above, reveal a significant element in the Worcester Collection unknown to the author of the *Appendix*.

[15] Friedberg, *Canonessammlungen* 65 and 110 n. 1. For the English background, see R. Foreville, *L'Eglise et la Royauté en Angleterre sous Henri II Plantagenet* (Paris 1943) 48-60, 64-76 and 276-326.

[16] Friedberg, *Canonessammlungen* 110, *Bamb.* 48.

[17] Lincoln Cathedral MS 121, fols. 1-61; Holtzmann and Kemp, *op. cit.* xiii.

[18] Lincoln MS 121, fols. 58v-61. The Cottonian Collection is B. M. Cotton MS Vit. E. XIII, fols. 204-88; the Peterhouse Collection is distributed in binding folios in Peterhouse, Cambridge, MSS 114, 180, 193 and 203; cf. Holtzmann and Kemp, *op. cit.* xii-xiii; see also n. 19, below.

[19] *Tanner* is Oxford Bodl. MS Tanner 8; Holtzmann, 'Die Dekretalensammlungen des 12. Jahrhunderts: 1. Die Sammlung Tanner,' *Festschrift zur Feier des 200jährigen Bestehens der Akademie der Wissenschaften in Göttingen*, Phil.-Hist. Kl. (1951) 83-145. Typical of late additions common to all four collections mentioned here is the decretal *Prudentiam*

transcription of the *Appendix*, and certainly records a continuation in the hands of English canonists.[20]

It is evident that each of these arguments, considered in isolation, would not place the English authorship of the *Appendix* beyond a reasonable doubt; but, considered together, they afford persuasive evidence. A related collection, hitherto undiscussed and now merely a fragment, is found in the library of St. John's College, Cambridge, in MS 148 (F. 11), fols. 61ᵛ-84. The St. John's Collection does not allow the investigation of the authorship of the *Appendix* to be pressed much further, but it does throw some light on the collection at an early stage in its formation. It is conceivably linked with the earliest recension of the *Appendix* deducible from present evidence. The manuscript volume is briefly described in the library catalogue by M. R. James as follows: 'Sermones, etc. Vellum, $6\,^1/_8 \times 4\,^1/_2$, ff. 84+2, 20 lines to a page. Cent. xii-xiii, well written in several different hands. Vellum wrapper. Donor, T.C.S.'[21] The medieval ownership of the volume has not been established, nor is it listed in the standard reference books of medieval libraries. But the final flyleaf has the medieval inscriptions 'De Straford' and 'Stredford,' suggesting perhaps that the volume belonged originally to the Savigniac-Cistercian abbey of the Blessed Virgin Mary at Stratford-Langthorne in Essex.[22] The post-medieval binding bears the arms of St. John's College and the inscription 'E libris Gulielmi Crashaw,' identifying the volume as a gift by Thomas Wriothesley, Earl of Southampton, to St. John's College, following his purchase of the library of William Crashaw, a fellow of St. John's College from 1593.[23]

The canonical matter of interest in this report, analyzed in full below, is transcribed in a single column on folios 61ᵛ-84ᵛ, varying between 20 and 25 lines to the folio-side. The canons of the Lateran Council of 1179 appear first, with brief headings and occasional marginal comments written in black, while the heading and initial letter of the seventh canon are in red. The first three canons occur in the same position and order as in the vulgate *Appendix*,[23a] but there is less significant correspondence between their arrangements thereafter. The conciliar canons are followed by three separate groups of decretals, or canons

---

tuam, JL 17019, Jun. 17, 1193: Lincoln, MS 121, fol. 58ᵛ; Cott. Vit. E. XIII, fol. 286ᵛ; Pet. MS 203, final quire, fol. 2ʳᵇ; Tanner, App. 1: Holtzmann, *Sammlung Tanner* 143.

[20] The Lincoln MS is sometimes unusually full and accurate in its decretal inscriptions, including such clear forms as *Giseburne, Bridlingtun, Rameseia, Lichesfeld, Frethesvide, Oseneia* and so forth; but in many instances Laurens' edition is better or more complete. A report on the Lincoln MS will be published later.

[21] M. R. James, *Descriptive Catalogue of the Manuscripts in the Library of St John's College Cambridge* (Cambridge 1913) 182-3.

[22] D. Knowles and R. N. Hadcock, *Medieval Religious Houses: England and Wales* (London 1953) 116. The place-name Stratford is found so frequently that this attribution is speculative; cf. E. Ekwall, *Oxford Dictionary of English Place-names* (Oxford, 1947 ed.) 428.

[23] James, *op. cit.* 182-3; M. Cowie, *Descriptive Catalogue of the Manuscripts and Scarce Books in the Library of St John's College Cambridge* (Cambridge Antiquarian Society 6; 1842) vi.

[23a] On the sequence of canons of the Third Lateran Council, see Kuttner, *Traditio* 13 (1957) 505-6, notes from an unpublished dissertation by W. Herold (Bonn 1950).

and decretals, which may for convenient reference be called Parts I, II and III. Part I follows the Lateran canons immediately, in mid-folio, and comprises three well-known letters of Alexander III, which are not in the *Appendix*, being respectively *Redolet Anglia*, announcing the canonization of Becket in 1173; a letter to Prester John in 1177; and *Ex antiqua*, in which Alexander explained the symbolism of the Golden Rose to Louis VII in 1163. Among primitive collections, none of these letters are found in the earliest members of the various English families, though two at least occur in later members of the 'Worcester' group;[24] nor are they found in the Italian *Berolinensis*;[25] but all three occur in the French *Parisiensis I* and *Aureaevallensis*;[26] and all are found in the Spanish *Dertusensis*, at Tortosa, a member of the Roman-Spanish group.[27] The fullest correspondence exists between the St. John's Collection and *Dertusensis*, in which latter the three letters are found in close proximity, within a single sequence of seven chapters, in a part of the collection dependent in all probability on an Italian or curial source.[28] Among systematic collections, the letters were not received into collections in the Italian tradition; but one or more is found in each of the Anglo-Norman collections *Tanner*, *Sangermanensis* and *Abrincensis*; and all three occur in a single manuscript of the French *Brugensis*.[29] Part I of the St. John's Collection may, therefore, suggest a link between primitive collections of the French and Roman-Spanish families and later primitive and systematic collections of the French and Anglo-Norman schools. But it does not stand directly between any of their surviving members, and it is unconnected with the *Appendix* and its most direct descendants.[30] The letters in question are not otherwise unknown in English non-canonical sources, all three being discovered in the *Ymagines historiarum* of Ralph de Diceto, dean of St. Paul's from 1180 until the early years of the thirteenth century.[31]

---

[24] *Redolet Anglia* and *Ex antiqua* are in the Cottonian Collection: B. M. Cott. MS Vit. E. XIII, fols. 246ʳ and 283ʳ; *Redolet Anglia* is also in the 'Cheltenham' Collection: B. M. Egerton MS 2819, fol. 93ᵛᵃ. This letter is in fact included in one member of the 'English' family: *Belverensis*, Oxford Bodl. MS e Mus. 249, fol. 131ᵛ, but addressed to the prelates, clergy, and people of England, and in a sequence of decretals peculiar to that work.

[25] J. Juncker, 'Die Collectio Berolinensis: Ein Beitrag zur Geschichte des kanonischen Rechts in ausgehenden zwölften Jahrhundert,' ZRG *Kan. Abt.* 13 (1924) 284-426.

[26] *Parisiensis I*: Friedberg, *Canonessammlungen* 45-63; *Aureaevallensis*: Holtzmann, 'Beiträge zu den Dekretalen-Sammlungen des 12. Jahrhunderts,' ZRG *Kan. Abt.* 16 (1927) 77-115. See Comparative Table (b), below.

[27] *Dertusensis*: Holtzmann, *Beiträge* 39-77. See Comparative Table (b), below.

[28] *Dertus.* 58, 54 and 52; cf. Holtzmann, *Beiträge* 39-54 and Analysis 42-61. See also Comparative Table (b), below.

[29] Comparative Table (c), below. For *Tanner*, see Holtzmann, *Sammlung Tanner*; for *Sangermanensis* and *Abrincensis*, H. Singer, 'Neue Beiträge über die Dekretalensammlungen vor und nach Bernhard von Pavia,' *Sb. Akad. Wien* 171. 1 (1913) 68-400; for *Brugensis*, Friedberg, *Canonessammlungen* 136-170; cf. Holtzmann and Kemp, *op. cit.* xiv-xv. Information on the Vatican MS of the *Brugensis* was kindly supplied by Professor Kuttner. The decretals *Redolet Anglia* and *Ex antiqua* are also found in the systematic *Francofortana*, B. M. Egerton MS 2901, fols. 93ᵛ-94ʳ.

[30] For *Bambergensis*, see Friedberg, *Canonessammlungen* 84-115; and W. Deeters, *Die Bambergensisgruppe der Dekretalensammlungen des 12. Jahrhunderts* (Bonn 1956).

Part II comprises two further decretals, of Eugenius III and Honorius II respectively, under the rubricated heading 'De iuramento calumpnie a clericis secundum canones non prestando'; and the initial letter of the first decretal and the inscription of the second are also in red. These letters are frequently found in other canonical sources, in some of the oldest appendices of Gratian manuscripts,[32] and in both primitive and systematic decretal collections. They appear together, and unaccompanied, in at least one of the early Gratian manuscripts;[33] and they appear together, but with further letters, in the 53rd Title of *Parisiensis II* and the 23rd Title of the *Appendix*, under the similar though shorter heading 'De iuramento calumpnie.'[34] But their order in the St. John's Collection is the reverse of that in these other canonical sources. Part II of the St. John's Collection is, therefore, also linked with well-known lines of decretal transmission, but is not itself a part of their main tradition.

The third and final part, comprising seven decretals and conciliar canons, completes the collection in its extant fragmentary state. These chapters appear under a long heading 'De simonia et ne merces pro ecclesie consecratione recipiatur ...' etc., agreeing exactly, except for minor textual variants, with that of the second Title in the vulgate *Appendix*, which follows immediately the Lateran canons in that version. The seven chapters likewise agree with the first nine in the *Appendix* second Title, except for a single extra item in the latter.[35] In heading and chapters alike, the correlation between this part of the St. John's Collection and the corresponding *Appendix* title is so exact that there can be little doubt of their kinship. But there is no direct interrelationship between the St. John's Collection as a whole and the vulgate *Appendix*, since each includes material unknown to the other or incorporated in a significantly different way. The St. John's Collection does not, therefore, stand in the central line of decretal transmission, but it is in part connected with the *Appendix* tradition at an early and formative stage in the evolution of the latter.

APPENDIX: THE ST. JOHN'S COLLECTION
St. John's College, Cambridge, MS 148 (F. 11), fols. 61ᵛ-84ᵛ.

(a) *Analysis*

CONCILIAR CANONS, fols. 61ᵛ-77ᵛ.

1. Non nisi a duabus partibus electus Romanus pontifex habeatur.
   Licet de vitanda ... recursus haberi.

---

[31] W. Stubbs, ed. *Radulfi de Diceto Opera omnia: Ymagines historiarum* 1 (Rolls Series, 1876) 369, 440 and 310.

[32] Kuttner, *Repertorium* 273-6.

[33] *Ibid.* 274-5: Montecassino MS 64, 333.

[34] Cf. Friedberg, *Canonessammlungen* 41 and 64. See Comparative Table (d) Part II, below.

[35] Comparative Table (d) Part III, below. The correspondence of *App.* 2.7, 9 and *Bamb.* 4.2, 3 does not appear from Friedberg's analysis, where by contamination of two chapters 4.2. is omitted; cf. E. Seckel, rev. of Friedberg, *Canonessammlungen*, in *Deutsche Literaturzeitung* (1897) 664; Deeters, *op. cit.* 58.

2. Ordinationes hereticorum irritas esse.
   Quod a predecessore ... manere suspensos.

3. Quid circa promovendos attendi debeat.
   Cum in cunctis sacris ... ordinetur.

4. De publicanis et defensoribus et receptoribus eorum.
   Sicut ait beatus ... sepulturas.

5. De Breibenconibus et his qui eos adduxerint et tenuerint vel foverint.
   De Breibenconibus ... optineant.

6. Onera ecclesiis a laicis non imponi.
   Non minus pro ... competentem.

7. *Rubricated*: De his qui Sarracenis et piratis necessaria sumministrant.
   Rubricated initial: Ita quorundam ... subiacere.

8. Clericos, religiosos, commeantes, agricolas cum animalibus suis continua securitate letari.
   Innovamus autem ... Christiana.

9. De Treugis.
   Treugas a quarta ... incurrat.

10. De torneamentis.
    Felicis memorie ... sepultura.

11. De ponendis in sede vel introducendis in ecclesia vel de sacramentis ecclesie nichil requiri.
    Margin: Nota. Novos census non imponendos ecclesiis, nec veteres augendos.
    Cum in ecclesie ... habeatur.

12. Monachos sine precio recipi, sine peculio vivere, singulos per villas vel ecclesias non constitui.
    Margin: Priores sine causa non mutandos.
    Monachi sine precio ... transferendi.

13. Magistris necessaria sumministrari et pro licencia docendi nichil exigi.
    Quoniam ecclesia ... impedire.

14. Clericos procurationibus vel exactionibus non gravari.
    Cum apostolus ... indultam.

15. Subditos nulla ammonitione promissa suspendi non debere, nec ante cause ingressum provocare.
    Reprehensibilis valde ... iniunctum.

16. Nulli ecclesiastica beneficia promitti antequam vacent; nec vacantia ultra vi menses in suspenso manere; nec aliquem in diaconum vel presbiterum sine certo titulo promoveri.
    Nulla ecclesiastica ... habere.

17. Quod pluribus et sanioribus visum fuerit, ab omnibus observari; nisi rationabile aliquid fuerit obiectum.
    Cum in cunctis ... existat.

18. Mulierculas a clericis in sacris ordinibus constitutis in domibus suis non teneri.
Clerici in sacris ... immunis.

19. In sacris ordinibus constitutos vel stipendiis ecclesiasticis sustentatos coram seculari iudice advocatos non fieri, vel procuratores villarum aut iusticiarios, nec iurisdictiones seculares exercere.
Clerici in subdiaconatu ... attemptare.

20. Per ecclesiam adquisita in alios non transferri; nec pro pecunia episcopalem iurisdictionem exerceri.
Cum in officiis ... amittat.

21. De excessibus Templariorum et Hospitalariorum et aliorum religiosorum.
Margin: Ecclesias (*MS* Ecclesia) vel decimas de manu laicorum non recipi et sic recepta (*MS* recipta) dimitti.
Presbiteros in ecclesiis episcopis inconsultis non institui; et institutos amoveri.
Cum et plantare ... habeatur.

22. Leprosos propriis ecclesiis, cimiteriis, presbiteris, sine veterum ecclesiarum iniuria iuvari.
Cum dicat apostolus ... cogantur.

23. Usurarios ad communionem altaris non admitti, repulture non tradi, illorum oblationem non recipi.
Quoniam in omnibus ... suspensus.

24. A Iudeis sive Saracenis Christiana mancipia non haberi; Christianorum testimonium contra illos recipi; conversos possessionibus suis non privari.
Iudei sive Saraceni ... exhiberi.

25. Diversas dignitates vel plures ecclesias parochiales ab uno non possideri.
Quia nonnulli ... sullevari.

26. Illum (*MS illegible* ...) ecclesie prefici, qui maioribus iuvatur meiitis aut illum (*MS* illā) ab episcopo si id sine scandalo fieri nequiverit, vel si dissidentibus patronis post tres menses vacaverit, ordinari.
Quoniam in quibusdam ... privetur.

The above canons in the St John's MS, 1-26, are found in the vulgate *Appendix* in the following sequence: 1, 2, 3, 27. ɪ, 27. ɪɪ, 19, 24, 22, 21, 20, 7, 10, 18, 4, 6, 8+5, 16 11, 12, 15, 9, 23, 25, 26, 13+14, ɪ, 17+14. ɪɪ.

DECRETALS

PART I, fols. 77ᵛ-81.ʀ

1. De canonizatione beati Thome martiris Cant(uariensis) archiepiscopi.
Alexander papa tercius Universis in Christo credentibus, salutem et apostolicam benedictionem.
Redolet Anglia ... intercedat.

JL 12203, 12204 and 12218. — Mar. 12 - Ap. 2, 1173. — Cf. title in *Tann.* 6.9 and *Abr.* 7.15: 'Quod necessaria sit auctoritas Romani pontificis ad hoc ut aliquis pro sancto habeatur.'

2. Epistola Alexandri pape III missa Johanni Presbitero Indorum regi.
Alexander papa III karissimo in Christo filio Johanni illustri et magnifico.
Apostolica sedes ... lucrifacere.
JL 12942. — 1178.

3. Quid significet rosa aurea quam gestat dominus papa singulis annis in dominica qua cantatur Letare Jerusalem.
Alexander papa III illustri Francorum regi Lod(ovico), salutem et apostolicam benedictionem.
Ex antiqua ... largiatur.

JL 10826. — Mar. 3, 1163. — Cf. title in *Tann.* 6.10 and *Abr.* 7.16: 'De mistica significatione rose auree quam summus pontifex gestare consuevit.'

PART II, fols. 81ʳ-82ᵛ.

Rubricated: De iuramento calumpnie a clericis secundum canones non prestando.

1. *No inscription*.
Rubricated initial: Dilectionis tue ... procedat.
JL 9654. — 1145-53. — Cf. JL: 'Eugenius III Arditioni Romane ecclesie subdiacono et magistro Omnibono.'

2. *Rubricated*: Honorius urbis Rome episcopus.
Inherentes maiorum ... annuimus.

JL 7401. — 1125-30. — Cf. JL: 'Honorius II omnibus episcopis.'

PART III, fols. 82ᵛ-84ᵛ.

De simonia, et ne merces pro ecclesie consecratione recipiatur, vel exigatur, vel pro monachatione, vel pro sacramentis ecclesie, vel pro licencia docendi, et ne prelati ecclesie vices suas ad causas terminandas, vel ad regimen ecclesiarum sub annuo precio aliis committant, nec subditos suos taliis vexent vel pena pecuniaria multare presumant.

1. Alexander in Turon(ensi) concilio.
Quoniam in quibusdam ... percellatur.
Tours c. 17. — 1163.

2. Idem in Turon(ensi) concilio.
Quoniam enormis ... habetur.
Tours c. 5. — 1163.

3. Idem Ric(ardo) Cantuariensi archiepiscopo.
Licet iuxta ... observari.
JL 14315. — 1174-81.

4. Idem Vigiliensi episcopo.
Cum sit Romana ... exigere potes.
JL 14126. — 1159-81.

5. Idem in capitulo quod incipit Ea que de av(aritia).
Cum autem collectas ... visitare.

JL 14172 = 12578a. — 1160 or 1173-6. — Lohmann pp. 68 and 111: 'Archidiaconis in quorum archidiaconatibus ecclesiae monasterii Ramesiensis consistunt.'

6. Idem.
Pervenit ad audientiam ... abstinebunt.
JL 14192. — 1159-81. — Cf. JL: 'quibusdam.'

7. Idem archidiaconis et decanis.
Ad nostram noveritis ... in eorundem (.. pervenerit.)
JL 13956. — 1159-81. — The MS ends abruptly at 'eorundem.'

(b) *Comparative Table of Part I of the St. John's Collection,
Parisiensis I, Dertusensis, Aureaevallensis, and Diceto's Ymagines Historiarum*

St. John's MS	Pa. I	Dertus.	Aureae.	Diceto.
1	39	58	14	1.369
2	40	54	30	1.440
3	178	52	44	1.310

(c) *Comparative Table of Part I of the St. John's Collection,
Sangermanensis, Abrincensis, Tanner, and Brugensis*

St. John's MS	Sang.	Abr.	Tann.	Brug.
1	7.146	7.15.1	6.9.1	App. 3*
2	—	—	—	1.1
3	—	7.16.1	6.10.1	8.6

* Only in the *Brug.* MS Vatican Ottobon. lat. 3027.

(d) *Comparative Table of Parts II and III of the St. John's Collection,
Parisiensis I, Parisiensis II, the Appendix, and Bambergensis*

St. John's MS	Pa. I	Pa. II	Appendix	Bamb.
PART II				
1	106	53.3	23.2	35.2
2	—	53.2	23.1	35.1
PART III				
1	139	26.6	2.1	2.1
2	85	—	2.2	2.2
3	—	—	2.3	4.1
4	41	—	2.4	1.1
5	95	—	2.5-6	1.7(8)
6	—	—	2.7	4.2
—	—	—	2.8	—
7	—	—	2.9	4.3

*King's College,
University of London.*

IX

ENGLISH DECRETALS IN CONTINENTAL PRIMITIVE COLLECTIONS WITH SPECIAL REFERENCE TO THE PRIMITIVE COLLECTION OF ALCOBAÇA

SUMMARIUM: Non paucae collectiones decretalium, quae inter annos 1170-1200 compilatae sunt, adhuc prostant et iuxta earum modum exarationis forma primitiva vel systematica describuntur. Quarum auctores et ortus obscuri sunt. Palam admittitur quasdam syllogas priores " appendices " fuisse, quarum primae confectae sunt, ut *Decretum Gratiani* complerent, quaedam vero ex posterioribus, ut *Breviarium extravagantium* Bernardi Papiensis perficerent. Quandoque dictum est collectiones priores ex regestis litterarum SS. Pontificum, quae nunc deperditae sunt, ortum habuisse; sed has non solos collectorum fontes fuisse certum est. Multae adhuc hodie prostant syllogae originis anglicae quibus demonstratur auctores frequenter usos esse tabulariis regionalibus Angliae itemque patet quosdam compilatores terrae continentis suos textus desumpsisse ex istis exemplaribus anglicis. Collectio primaria Alcobacensis, quae iacet in cod. ms. Alcob. 144 (314), fol. 1v-39v Bibliothecae Nationalis Ulixiponensis, nova argumenta affert dicentibus litteras decretales anglicas in Europa continenti diffusas esse. Haec collectio originis Lusitanae ad familiam Romanam seu " Dertusam " collectionum pertinet et nexum habet cum collectionibus Dertusensi et Eberbacensi; analysi tamen critica decretalium, quae inibi continentur, eam fontibus anglicis derivare ostenditur allatis decretalibus eminentibus quae Cantuariam et Exonium missae fuerant.

---

* My thanks are due to Professor Kuttner and the Institute of Medieval Canon Law at Yale University. Since beginning the present and other related studies, I have been able through Professor Kuttner's generosity to consult the Holtzmann papers and research materials now deposited at the Institute. As a result of this opportunity it has been possible to refine many details which would otherwise have been incomplete. Throughout this essay,

54

Perhaps no branch of canonistic studies has made more significant advances in recent years than the investigation of twelfth-century decretal collections. But this progress has been made possible only by the fruitful labours of many earlier scholars, dating in their inception from the later nineteenth century. Outstanding in this context was the work of Emil Friedberg, and later that of Hampe, Seckel, Singer and others of like quality (1). It is increasingly clear that many of the most important conclusions at present being reached in this field of interest were in fact already implicit in their seminal studies. In more recent times the decisive contributions have been made by Walther Holtzmann, most eminent of decretal scholars, and Stephan Kuttner, in honour of whose unique position in the international community of canonical historians the present volume is presented (2). Studies of central importance have been published also by Lohmann, Fransen, Vetulani, Mme Rambaud-Buhot and many others (3).

in foot-notes and in the appendix, I have adopted Holtzmann's numeration of decretals in the various manuscripts cited, even where the numbers diverge substantially from those in my own previously published analyses. I must thank also the Trustees of the Twenty-seven Foundation for a generous grant to help with the purchase of photostatic copies of decretal manuscripts.

(1) E. FRIEDBERG, *Die Canonessammlungen zwischen Gratian und Bernhard von Pavia*, Leipzig (1897); K. HAMPE, *Reise nach England* in: *Neues Archiv*, xxii (1897), 225-86 and 337-415; E. SECKEL, *Ueber drei Canonessammlungen des ausgehenden 12. Jahrhunderts* in: *Neues Archiv*, xxv (1900), 523-25 and 529-31; H. SINGER, *Neue Beiträge über die Dekretalensammlungen vor und nach Bernhard von Pavia* in: *Sitzungsberichte der kaiserlichen Akademie der Wissenschaften in Wien, Phil.-Hist. Kl.*, clxxi (1913).

(2) For HOLTZMANN, see especially *Über eine Ausgabe der päpstlichen Dekretalen des 12. Jahrhunderts* in: *Nachrichten von der Akademie der Wissenschaften in Göttingen, Phil.-Hist. Kl.* (1945), 15-36; and *Kanonistische Ergänzungen zur Italia Pontificia* in: *Quellen und Forschungen aus italienischen Archiven und Bibliotheken*, xxxvii (1957), 55-102, and xxxviii (1958), 67-175: published also in a separate volume (Halle 1958). For KUTTNER cf. *Repertorium der Kanonistik, 1140-1234 (Studi e Testi* lxxi, 1937); and *Notes on a Projected Corpus of Twelfth-Century Decretal Letters* in: *Traditio*, vi (1948), 345-51.

(3) H. LOHMANN, *Die Collectio Wigorniensis* in: *Zeitschrift der Savigny Stiftung für Rechtsgeschichte, Kanonistische Abteilung (ZRG, Kan. Abt.)*, xxii (1933), 36-187; A. VETULANI, *L'Origine des collections primitives de décrétales à la fin du XIIe siècle* in: *Congrès de Droit Canonique Médiéval*, Louvain (1959), 64-72; J. RAMBAUD-BUHOT, *Les paleae dans le Décret de Gratien* in: S. KUTTNER and J. J. RYAN, *Proceedings of the Second International Congress of Medieval Canon Law: Monumenta Iuris Canonici, Series C, Subsidia*, i (1965), 23-44. These studies are cited as having special reference to the present essay. For an important new survey, cf. G. LE BRAS, CH. LEFEBVRE and J. RAMBAUD, *Histoire du Droit et des Institutions de l'Eglise en Occident, Tome VII: L'Age Classique, 1140-1378: Sources et Théorie du Droit*, Paris (1965).

Yet, despite the richness of the source materials and the illuminating insights provided by so many experts, many of the basic problems remain unresolved and the subjects of continuing controversial interest. One such problem is that of the origins and authorship of the decretal collections, and the extent of their derivation, directly or otherwise, from the papal registers or alternatively from regional or private archives.

Twelfth-century decretal collections are classified conventionally as primitive or systematic according to their juristic skill in composition (4). The systematic collections are divided into numerous sections or titles on a subject-matter basis, and also disclose such professionally accomplished techniques as the dismemberment of the longer decretals dealing with several different topics and the distribution of the resulting component parts through the various titles. It has long been clear that this classification is open to criticism, but the now traditional distinction is retained in the present discussion because it is familiar to most scholars concerned with the subject (5). The primitive collections are the most rudimentary in technical style, but they are not necessarily the earliest in date of composition. Some primitive collections were devised as supplements to Bernard of Pavia's *Breviarium extravagantium*, or *Compilatio prima*, completed not earlier than 1192, whereas the earliest primitive collections were designed as appendices to Gratian's *Decretum*, and date from c. 1170 or slightly later (6). The "appendix" character of primitive collections has been most revealingly discussed by Holtzmann, Vetulani and Mme Rambaud-Buhot. In the course of her work on the *paleae* in Gratian manuscripts, Mme Rambaud-Buhot has instanced numerous short sequences of decretals inserted as supplements

---

(4) Holtzmann, *Kanonistische Ergänzungen* (*QF*, 1957), 58-65; idem and E. W. Kemp, *Papal Decretals relating to the Diocese of Lincoln in the Twelfth Century*, Lincoln Record Society, xlvii (1954), ix-xvii; C. Duggan, *Twelfth-Century Decretal Collections and their Importance in English History*, University of London Historical Studies, xii (1963).

(5) Cf. J. J. H. M. Hanenburg, *Decretals and Decretal Collections in the Second Half of the Twelfth Century* in: *Tijdschrift voor Rechtsgeschiedenis*, xxxiv (1966), 585-99. In my brief survey published in 1963 (cf. n. 4, above) I accepted the conventional distinction, while noting its weaknesses. It then appeared likely that Holtzmann's projected studies would be completed with the same conventions, and therefore it would have been merely confusing to introduce variant categories.

(6) Rambaud-Buhot, *art. cit.*, 30-31.

to the main *Decretum* text, interpolated sometimes in the body of the collection, or transcribed quite literally as appendices to the completed work (7). The purpose of such insertions was to incorporate significant texts which Gratian had omitted or to bring the work up to date with citations from more recent papal rulings. It was from such simple beginnings as these that the tradition of decretal codification developed. Both Holtzmann and Vetulani agreed that this " appendix " practice marked a decisive turning point in the history of canonical collections: " le point de départ de toute la tradition des collections de décrétales " (8). By the mid-1170s decretal collections were appearing as a *genre* in their own right, often independently of Gratian manuscripts, and thereafter they swiftly became the dominant form of canonical compilation.

To identify the sources from which the decretal collectors derived their letters is a task of more than merely technical interest. More than fifty decretal manuscripts have been classified by Holtzmann as pre-*Compilatio prima*, but none can be attributed with any certainty to a known author; in many instances even their general provenance is uncertain and its evidence complex (9). Nineteen further manuscripts are listed by Holtzmann as pre-*Compilatio secunda*, some of these dating from the early thirteenth century. Both these groups are sub-divided into primitive and systematic categories (10). The primitive collections are the most interesting from a provenance viewpoint, since they preserve more direct evidence of their authors' sources, recording a stage of compilation before the process of analysis, classification, dissection and distribution under titles had made much progress. The judgment has been widely held that the ancestry of the decretal collections, especially of the primitive collections, should be attributed to the papal registers, which no longer survive. According to this theory, there existed a curial source of supply from which register transcripts were disseminated to collectors to enable them to supplement their records with selections from the most recent

---

(7) *Ibid.*, 23-44.

(8) Vetulani, *art. cit.*, 66-67; cf. Holtzmann, *La collection ' Seguntina ' et les décrétales de Clément III et de Célestine III* in: *Revue d'histoire ecclésiastique*, l (1955), 400-53, esp. 401-02.

(9) Holtzmann, *Kanonistische Ergänzungen* (*QF*, 1957), 58-63.

(10) *Ibid.*, 58-65.

papal decisions. And there is no doubt that some collections, both primitive and systematic, contain clear evidence of register derivations of this kind. The most convincing proof of this practice has been found in the primitive decretal collections from the closing years of the twelfth century, but the evidence is by no means confined to these works. Again, both Holtzmann and Vetulani have made significant contributions to the elucidation of this problem. In two important articles, published respectively in 1940 and 1955, Holtzmann examined the evidence of register derivations in specific collections: the former article included an analysis of the letters in the concluding title of the *editio princeps* of the *Appendix Concilii Lateranensis* and in the *Collectio Orielensis II*, while the later study was based on the highly interesting *Collectio Seguntina*, a primitive collection then recently discovered in Sigüenza by Fr. Gérard Fransen and composed of decretals derived from the registers of Clement III and Celestine III (11). And in 1958 Vetulani adduced still further proof of register derivations in primitive collections, while diverging from Holtzmann's views on certain points of detail. For this purpose Vetulani used as his principal basis of reference the primitive *Collectio Cracoviensis*, presenting a fascinating insight into the process of formation of a decretal collection in the hands of a group of Bolognese masters with access to the curial records (12). Like the *Seguntina*, this collection also contains many letters from the registers of Clement III and Celestine III. Within their terms of reference these most scholarly studies establish beyond dispute that certain collections were based on register extracts, but their conclusions cannot be generally applied to all collections, even of the primitive style. With the progress of his researches, Holtzmann himself withdrew from any universal or comprehensive theory that the origins of all decretal collections could be ascribed to the papal registers. He stated so explicitly, and it is also implicit in his treatment of the numerous individual collections which he classified in regional or family groups. The total problem of the origins of the decretal collections, as well as that of their gradual development, is too complex to permit any single or simple gen-

---

(11) HOLTZMANN, *Die Register Papst Alexanders III. in den Händen der Kanonisten* in: *Quellen und Forschungen*, xxx (1940), 13-87; and cf. n. 8, above.

(12) VETULANI, *art. cit.*, 64-72.

58

eralization. And it is in this context that the English primitive collections, and the continental collections partly dependent on them, are of such unique importance.

Twenty-seven primitive collections are included in Holtzmann's pre-*Compilatio prima* category, though a small number of these are later than Bernard's collection in date of completion (13). Fifteen of these collections are of English authorship, being grouped respectively into the English, Bridlington and Worcester families, while the remaining twelve collections are of continental provenance, and are identified by Holtzmann as the Tortosa, French and Italian groups (14). The composition and contents of the English collections are now rather familiar, and it will be sufficient here to summarize their salient characteristics from the authorship and provenance viewpoints (15). Certainly it is not possible to explain the origins of the English primitive collections by the supposition of their derivation from the papal registers, since they are English in every sense of that description. They are not merely English transcripts, largely derived from continental archetypes: they are English in composition, authorship and transcription, incorporating large numbers of decretals addressed to English bishops or English judges delegate. It is true that all but the most rudimentary reveal an assimilation of continental material, but there is little doubt that the English collectors drew most heavily on records available in their own country (16). It is not surprising therefore that a very large proportion of decretals in the English collections can be assigned to identifiable English recipients. And it is a striking matter of fact that a high percentage of these letters were received by four well-known English ecclesiastics: namely, Richard of Canterbury, Roger of Worcester, Bartholomew of Exeter and Baldwin, successively archdeacon of Totnes, abbot of Ford, bishop of Worcester and archbishop of Canterbury. The possible political and jurisdictional implica-

---

(13) HOLTZMANN, *Kanonistische Ergänzungen* (*QF*, 1957), 58-60; DUGGAN, *Twelfth-Century Decretal Collections*, 60, n. 2; and 107, nn. 3 and 4.

(14) HOLTZMANN, *Kanonistische Ergänzungen* (*QF*, 1957), 58-60.

(15) DUGGAN, *Twelfth - Century Decretal Collections*, 1-12, 66-125 and 140-51; IDEM, *Primitive Decretal Collections in the British Museum* in: C. W. DUGMORE and C. DUGGAN, *Studies in Church History*, i (1964), 132-44; IDEM, *The Reception of Canon Law in England in the Later-Twelfth Century* in: KUTTNER and RYAN, *ed. cit.*, 365-71 and 382-88.

(16) For continental material in English primitive collections, cf. *ibid.*, 365-71.

tions of this evidence have been already discussed elsewhere, and
will doubtless remain a subject for further reflection and controversial interest; but it seems safe at least to assume either that
the judicial activities of these four prelates provided an unusual
stimulation to the English collectors, or that for one reason or
another their decretal archives were more readily accessible to
them (17). It must be emphasized that these conclusions are not
suggested on any crude or uncritical statistical basis; their justification lies rather in the collectors' manner of incorporating the
individual items. Various earlier theories erected on the basis
of a statistical analysis of the decretals in the *Quinque Compilationes Antiquæ* or in the Gregorian *Decretales* can be proven unconvincing, because the merely mathematical data were not in-
formed by a knowledge of the ancestry of the collections being
examined, or by a true consideration of the relative disposition
of the decretals they contained (18). The evidence in the English
primitive collections is of a far different and more compelling
kind. Thus, when a decretal manuscript of definite Canterbury
provenance includes nine letters received at Canterbury in its
opening thirteen decretals, or when a collection of certain Worcester associations supplements the several component sections
of its archetypal source with further letters of which a high proportion were received at Worcester, or when a collection contains
an unbroken run of eight or nine decretals addressed to the bishop
of Exeter, then it seems most reasonable to conclude that excerpts
from the records of Canterbury, Worcester and Exeter provide
the most acceptable explanation of such insertions (19). And this
brings us finally to a consideration of the reception of English
decretals into primitive collections of continental provenance.

It is regrettably true that the continental primitive collections
of the pre-*Compilatio prima* period are still very imperfectly

(17) DUGGAN, *Twelfth-Century Decretal Collections*, 118-24 and 140-51.

(18) *Ibid.*, 1-12 and 140-51.

(19) These examples are cited respectively from the following MSS: British Museum
Royal MS 10 B.IV, fols. 42v-45r: the Canterbury Collection; British Museum Royal MS 10
A.II: the Worcester Collection; British Museum Royal MS 15 B.IV, fols. 115v-116r: the Royal
Collection (*Regalis*). Cf. DUGGAN, *Twelfth - Century Decretal Collections*, 110-117: *Baldwin of
Ford and the Worcester Collection*; and IDEM, *The Trinity Collection of Decretals and the Early
Worcester Family* in: *Traditio*, xvii (1961), 506-26.

known, except in their manuscripts, and this is particularly true of the important Italian collections. Of the three families of continental collections, two of the three " Tortosa " members have been analysed, three of the four French collections, but only two of the five Italian (20). A brief consideration of these printed analyses, published as a pilot survey in 1963, suggested nevertheless certain provisional conclusions with some basis of justification (21). Thus, the continental primitive collections examined at that time revealed only to a very insignificant degree such regional and personal influences on composition as those disclosed by their English counterparts, except where they incorporated English material. There is in them no continental feature comparable with the Canterbury-Exeter-Worcester element in the English works. They seem much less likely therefore to have drawn very significantly on the regional records of the countries of their origin. Some collections reveal minor, though highly interesting, exceptions to this generalization, but broadly speaking the distinction is valid (22). Moreover, at least where the " Tortosa " collections are in question, the incorporation of English decretals into the continental collections could be rationally explained only on the assumption that their authors were acquainted with English sources; and this is true also of the French collections, but much less so of the Italian collections on the slender evidence until now available (23). Once more, this conclusion was not based on faulty principles of merely numerical analysis, but on an examination of the character of the English material in the continental collections, and on the order and disposition of the individual decretals. The evidence of unbroken sequences of Canterbury decretals in the " Tortosa " collections and the extraordinary dominance of English decretals in the greater part of *Parisiensis I*, in the French

---

(20) For full details of MSS and printed analyses, see HOLTZMANN, *Kanonistische Ergänzungen* (*QF*, 1957), 58-59.

(21) DUGGAN, *Twelfth-Century Decretal Collections*, 124-35; IDEM, *Reception of Canon Law*, 365-71.

(22) The Tortosa Collection is an interesting exception: cf. HOLTZMANN, *Beiträge zu den Dekretalensammlungen des zwölften Jahrhunderts* in: *ZRG. Kan. Abt.*, xvi (1927), 39-77; see especially items 65-69. Cf. also DUGGAN, *Twelfth-Century Decretal Collections*, 124-35.

(23) Cf. J. JUNCKER, *Die Collectio Berolinensis* in: *ZRG. Kan. Abt.*, xiii (1924), 284-426; KUTTNER, *Repertorium* 279-80; DUGGAN, *Twelfth-Century Decretal Collections*, 124-135, esp. 130-35; IDEM, *Reception of Canon Law*, 368-70.

group, give particular justification to this view (24). At the same time, most primitive collections, whether English or continental and except only the most simple works, suggest some indebtedness to Italian and possibly curial sources. Nevertheless, the transmission of decretals from English sources into the continental collections is clearly a matter of outstanding historical importance, leading to the conclusion that the organization of their local material by English collectors was familiar to canonists widely placed in the Western Church, and in consequence helped to shape the *corpus* of decretals which provided the common stock from which later canonists composed their more mature collections. As further research now goes forward on these problems the important and independent tradition of the Italian collectors becomes ever more clear, as might be expected, though even within this family there are occasional remarkable instances of English derivations, as exemplified by the St. Florian Collection which contains one sequence of decretals, otherwise unknown, concerning a dispute over the church of Bungay in Suffolk (25). Only one member in each of the French and " Tortosa " families now remains unexamined, being respectively the collection of St. Victor in Paris and that of Alcobaça in Portugal; and it is with a preliminary report on this latter collection that the present essay is concluded (26).

The primitive decretal collection of Alcobaça, the *Collectio Alcobacensis I*, is now found in the National Library at Lisbon in MS Alcob. 144 (314), fols. 1v-39v. A complete analysis with palaeographical description will be published in a later study, and in the present context the following brief details will suffice. The Portuguese provenance of the codex is not in doubt: it belong-

---

(24) For the ' Tortosa' collections, see HOLTZMANN, *Beiträge zu den Dekretalensammlungen* in: *ZRG. Kan. Abt.*, xvi (1927), 39-77; IDEM, *Die Collectio Eberbacensis* in: *ZRG. Kan. Abt.*, xvii (1928), 548-55; DUGGAN, *Twelfth-Century Decretal Collections*, 126-28. For *Parisiensis I*, see FRIEDBERG, *Die Canonessammlungen*, 45-63, esp. 52-59; JUNCKER, *Die Collectio Berolinensis* in: *ZRG. Kan. Abt.*, xiii (1924), 297-301; DUGGAN, *Twelfth-Century Decretal Collections*, 128-30.

(25) St. Florian, Stiftsbibliothek MS III 5, fols. 173-83, items 168-72. I am preparing an edition of this interesting group of letters.

(26) The Alcobaça Collection is discussed below; the St. Victor Collection, *Collectio Victorina I*, is Bibliothèque Nationale (Paris) MS lat. 14938 (St. Victor), fols. 226-66; it will be shown later that this MS also contains evidence of the reception of decretals from English sources.

ed originally to the Cistercian abbey at Alcobaça; it contains
Portuguese subject-matter independently of the canonical collection;
and there is one letter of singular Portuguese interest incorporated
in the decretal collection itself. The canonical material opens
with the canons of the Third Lateran Council of 1179 under the
heading: *Incipiunt decreta et consultationes Alexandri pape tercii*.
The Lateran canons are transcribed right through the first quire
of eight folios, but break off abruptly at that point, where some
folios are now missing, and the transcription resumes on the present fol. 9r, in the middle of the decretal *Meminimus*, to the bishop
of Worcester (27), after which the decretals continue without
interruption until the work is completed on fol. 39v. The collection is transcribed in double columns throughout, except that
the final *folio verso* is written in a single column stopping short
of the bottom of the folio, and so confirming that the collection
was completed. The conciliar canons can be numbered 1-26,
and the decretals 27-125 (28). Of particular interest is item 45,
which is the letter *Cum in quibusdam* sent by Alexander III to
the king of Portugal, in the period 1179-81, dealing with questions
of tithe payment and exemption affecting the Order of Calatrava
and the Knights of St. James (29). This is an important detail
helping to establish the Portuguese provenance of the collection
in its completed form. The date of final composition cannot be
earlier than 1179, but the collection contains no letters or canons
later than the death of Alexander III in 1181.

Holtzmann has associated this collection principally with the
Tortosa and Eberbach collections, grouping them under the family
name Roman (Tortosa), or simply Tortosa, family (30). Collat-

---

(27) JL 13162.

(28) This is the numeration adopted by HOLTZMANN in his unpublished papers.

(29) MS Alcob. 144 (314), fol. 14v; cf. C. ERDMANN, *Papsturkunden in Portugal* in:
Abhandlungen der Gesellschaft der Wissenschaften in Göttingen, N.F. 20, 1, Berlin (1927), 254,
n. 81.

(30) Cf. n. 24 above; see also HOLTZMANN, *Kanonistische Ergänzungen* (*QF*, 1957), 58:
Die Dertusensisgruppe. But in IDEM and KEMP, ed. *cit.*, xi, HOLTZMANN describes the Alcobaça Collection as a member of " the earliest, probably Roman, group of primitive collections
previous to the *Compilatio I* "; this description seems appropriate to one archetypal source
of the ' Tortosa ' group, but not to the completed collections. In HOLTZMANN, *Nachrichten*,
21, the collections are called "Die römische (Dertusensis) Gruppe". For a valuable comment,
see KUTTNER, *Projected Corpus of Twelfth-Century Decretal Letters* in: *Traditio*, vi (1948), 346.

ion of their contents certainly establishes a kinship between these three works, though each has also features which distinguish it from the other two. Particularly significant in considering the provenance of the Tortosa Collection itself are the three decretals to Hungary and the five to recipients in the Spanish peninsula with which the collection ends (31). The presence of the Hungarian decretals is a factor suggesting a possible derivation from the papal registers, while further decretals within the " Tortosa " common stock point possibly in the same direction; and the Spanish decretals appended to the whole reflect the place of its final composition. The Spanish provenance of the Tortosa Collection is clear enough, as is the Portuguese authorship of the completed Alcobaça Collection, but that of the Eberbach Collection is less certain. The latter collection belonged to the Cistercian abbey of Eberbach in the middle ages, but is now in the British Museum; nevertheless, its relationship with the " Tortosa " collections is undoubted. The now fragmentary Alcobaça Collection reveals its kinship with the other " Tortosa " collections by its corresponding arrangement of decretals. Thus, its first twenty-three letters, with very few exceptions, correspond very closely in sequence with their arrangement in the Tortosa and Eberbach Collections; and the pattern of this evidence suggests that the decretals now lost from the Alcobaça manuscript were at least in part derived from the " Tortosa " common stock. So much is made clear in a table of comparison in the appendix below (32). But, for present purposes, attention is directed simply to those letters which in fact survive, and which are in a truly remarkable proportion of English provenance; and in this respect also the Alcobaça Collection reveals a feature in common with the other members of its family group.

The presence of significant numbers of English decretals in the Tortosa and Eberbach Collections has already been noticed in earlier publications, in which the probability that such letters

---

There is no intention in the present essay to deny that the ' Tortosa ' collections were partly derived from an Italian source, possibly from the papal registers; this essay is concerned with the significance of the English decretals in these collections.

(31) HOLTZMANN, *Beiträge zu den Dekretalensammlungen*, ZRG. Kan. Abt., xvi (1927), 65-68; the Hungarian decretals are items 62-64, and the Spanish decretals items 65-69.

(32) Appendix: Comparative Table I; the correspondence between the collections is not confined to this sequence.

were derived from English sources has been suggested (33). The Alcobaça Collection has not so far been discussed in any comparable detail, but some limited evidence that a similar English element might be found in it has been provided in studies by Dom Adrian Morey and Canon E. W. Kemp. In an important study on Bartholomew of Exeter, Morey printed two decretals of Alexander III to Bartholomew, which had been discovered in the Alcobaça manuscript but were otherwise unknown; and Kemp drew significantly on the texts of five English decretals in the same manuscript for his edition of decretal letters concerning Lincoln in the twelfth century. Both these scholars worked in collaboration with Holtzmann in providing these valuable texts (34). But this tenuous evidence of English decretals in the Alcobaça collection can now be greatly expanded. The collection now contains a total of 99 items, in addition to the conciliar canons. Disregarding a very small number of letters with general inscriptions, not less than 82 of these items, including duplications, are of English provenance: at least 30 (possibly 33) were received at Canterbury, 15 at Exeter, and 17 at Worcester, though in some instances a single letter was addressed to more than one recipient (35). Such details by no means exhaust the English interest of this Portuguese manuscript, but the Canterbury-Exeter-Worcester emphasis is once more very striking. Recalling the sound analytical principles mentioned above, it must be noticed that the order and disposition of the letters are much more significant than their mere numbers. Thus, the Canterbury decretals in the Alcobaça Collection appear as follows: *Alcob.* 31, 34-37, 39-42, 51, 52, 57, (64), (68), 70, 78, 95-105, 107, 111, 112, 116, 120 and 122-24; the Exeter decretals appear as *Alcob.* 56, 66, 73-83, 85 and 89; and the Worcester decretals as *Alcob.* 27, 52-56, 60, 61, 63, 65, 66, 71, 85, 92, 94, 117 and 118. The unbroken sequences of Canterbury and Exeter decretals are especially significant. A heavy

---

(33) DUGGAN, *Twelfth-Century Decretal Collections*, 126-28.

(34) A. MOREY, *Bartholomew of Exeter: Bishop and Canonist*, Cambridge (1937), 130-35, letters 4, 8 and 9 (cf. *Alcob.* 66, 77 and 76): the texts of MOREY's *epp.* 8 and 9 were found only in the Alcobaça Collection. HOLTZMANN and KEMP, *ed. cit.*, 2-3, 6-9, 18-19, 28-29 and 40-41: *epp.* 1, 4, 7, 12 and 16, corresponding with *Alcob.* 125, 90, 92, 63 and 91.

(35) In other words, the total number of letters in the collection which are addressed to Canterbury, Exeter or Worcester is less than the sum of the numbers cited here.

concentration of Canterbury decretals has been noted in English primitive collections already discussed elsewhere, especially in the Canterbury Collection itself, and in the Bridlington and Claudian Collections whose archetype was almost certainly assembled in the Canterbury province (36). It has been noted also in the " Tortosa " collections closely related to the manuscript under review. It is all the more significant therefore that a comparison of the Alcobaça Collection and the English primitive collections leaves little room to doubt their inter-relationship. For example, twelve of the Canterbury decretals (two of them in fact appearing twice) in the Alcobaça Collection are found in the first book of the Canterbury Collection as follows: *Cant.* I, 33, 9, 4, 35, 39, 33, 34, 11, 10, 9, 12, 7, 13 and 1. With the same two duplications, twenty-one are found in the Bridlington Collection as *Brid.* 70, 36, 68, 82, 137, 76, 46, 109, 83, (15), 65, 70, 74, 75, 36-38, 60, 77, 73, 78, 178 and 128; and eighteen in the Claudian Collection as *Claud.* 51, 44, 49, 65, 57, 97, 66, (15), 51, 55, 56, 48, 44-47, 58, 54, 59 and 119. The correspondence between the collections is even more striking than these figures suggest, if selected brief sequences are consulted in the appendix tables below. But the tables also reveal some correspondence between all families of primitive collections, whether English or continental, for some of these Canterbury decretals. The parallel grouping of letters is particularly interesting in the St. Victor Collection of the French group (37). And therefore it might be argued that a final judgment should be deferred on the direction of their lines of transmission. It is against this consideration that the evidence of the Exeter decretals in the Alcobaça collection is of such exceptional importance.

Twelve decretals to Bartholomew of Exeter appear in a single sequence of thirteen items as *Alcob.* 73-83 and 85. This group of letters is found in its entirety in no other decretal collection; two of the letters are quite unknown except in this manuscript; some of the individual letters are found in English primitive col-

---

(36) Duggan, *Twelfth-Century Decretal Collections*, 66-117, esp. 73-79 and 84-95.

(37) Appendix: Comparative Tables 2 and 3; among many interesting parallel arrangements, notice especially the correspondences at *Alcob.* 39-42 and 95-105. For the St. Victor Collection, cf. Comparative Table 3.

lections, sometimes with interesting parallel arrangements; but no other continental primitive collection of the pre-*Compilatio prima* period contains more than two of these twelve decretals, and the majority of the continental primitive collections, including the Tortosa and Eberbach Collections, contain none of the twelve (38). Here then is a uniquely convincing instance of an English regional source disclosed in a collection of continental authorship, a further strong support for the theory that English decretals were disseminated from insular records and used by continental collectors. It could not be rationally supposed that such a grouping of Exeter decretals was derived from the papal registers or any curial source of supply; its unique and personal flavour suggests a very individual and particular transmission from English sources. How, and in what circumstances, the transmission was accomplished remains at present a matter of speculation. On the other hand, eight of these twelve decretals were received into the *Appendix Concilii Lateranensis*, a systematic collection of fundamental importance in the central tradition of decretal codification which culminated in Bernard of Pavia's *Compilatio prima*, although the majority were unknown to the authors of all surviving continental primitive collections of the period, except that of Alcobaça (39). It could scarcely be argued that the Alcobaça Collection was directly a source of the great *Appendix Concilii Lateranensis*, but it is very probable that both were indebted in some way to English sources for their decretals. Such considerations raise once more that fascinating but still unresolved problem of the authorship of the *Appendix Concilii Lateranensis*, and suggest one more clue to its possible English origins (40). This difficult and complex, but critically important, question must remain open for further investigation. But, mean-

---

(38) Appendix: Comparative Table 4.

(39) *Alcob.* 73 and 76-78 are not in the *Appendix Concilii Lateranensis;* but *Alcob.* 74, 75, 79-83 and 85 appear respectively as: *ACL,* 45.2; 29.1; 19.6; 16.10; 18.13; 12.7, 35.3, 6.33 and 50.43; 8.23; and 47.9

(40) Cf. HOLTZMANN, *Register Papst Alexanders III.* in: *Quellen und Forschungen,* xxx (1940), 16; KUTTNER, *Projected Corpus* in: *Traditio,* vi (1948), 349; IDEM and E. RATHBONE, *Anglo-Norman Canonists of the Twelfth Century: an Introductory Study* in: *Traditio,* vii (1951), 283-84; DUGGAN, *English Canonists and the " Appendix Concilii Lateranensis ''; with an Analysis of the St. John's College, Cambridge, MS 148* in: *Traditio,* xviii (1962), 459-68.

English Decretals in continental primitive collections 67

while, the decretal collection of Alcobaça exemplifies in a most remarkable way the reception of English decretals into the continental collections, at least in their early primitive phase.

The following abbreviations have been used to identify decretal collections in the appendix: *Alcob.* = *Alcobacensis I* (Alcobaça); *Dert.* = *Dertusensis I* (Tortosa); *Eber.* = *Eberbacensis* (Eberbach); *Belv.* = *Belverensis* (Belvoir); *Cant.* = *Cantuariensis* (Canterbury); *Roff.* = *Roffensis* (Rochester); *Roy.* = Royal or *Regalis* (Royal MS); *Dunl.* = *Dunelmensis* (Durham); *Font.* = *Fontanensis* (Fountains); *Brid.* = *Bridlingtonensis* (Bridlington); *Claud.* = *Claudiana* (Cotton Claudius MS); *Claust.* = *Claustroneoburgensis* (Klosterneuburg); *Wig.* = *Wigorniensis* (Worcester); *Chelt.* = *Cheltenhamensis* (Cheltenham MS); *Cott.* = *Cottoniana* (Cotton Vitellius MS); *Berol.* = *Berolinensis* (Berlin); *Cus.* = *Cusana* (Cues); *Duac.* = *Duacensis* (Douai); *Flor.* = *Florianensis* (St. Florian); *Par. I* = *Parisiensis I* (Paris B.N. MS); *Cantab.* = *Cantabrigiensis* (Cambridge); *Vict.* = *Victorina I* (St. Victor); *Aur.* = *Aureaevallensis* (Orval). For details of MSS and analyses, see W. HOLTZMANN, *Kanonistische Ergänzungen zur Italia Pontificia* in: *Quellen und Forschungen aus italienischen Archiven und Bibliotheken*, xxxvii (1957) 58-60.

APPENDIX: COMPARATIVE TABLES

The following tables of comparison are merely extracts from the complete tables which will be published later. They are selected to illustrate the various points discussed in the essay above. In all cases the numeration of items given here follows that adopted by Holtzmann.

1. This table collates the opening items of the Alcobaça Collection with the corresponding items in the Tortosa and Eberbach Collections.

Alcob.	Dert.	Eber.
27	17	12.1
—	18	12.2
28	19	1.2 = 7.3–4
29) 30)	20	13.1–5
31	21	7.5
32	22	13.6
—	23	8.1
33	24	8.2
34 = 101	25	8.3
(103)	26	8.4
(102)	27	8.5
(100)	28	9.1
35	29	9.2
36	30	9.3
37	31	10.1
(98)	32	10.2
—	33	1.7
38	34	2.1
39	35	2.2
40	36	3.3 = 10.3
41	37	3.4 = 10.4
42	38	10.5
—	39	5.2 = 10.6
43	40a	3.2 = 11.1
	b	1.6 = 11.2
—	41	14.1
—	42	14.2
44	43	14.3
45	—	—
46	44	15.1
47	45	15.2
48a	46	15.3
b	47	15.4
—	48	15.5
49	49	15.6

2. This table collates the Canterbury decretals in the Alcobaça Collection with the corresponding items in English primitive collections of the English, Bridlington and Worcester families.

Alcob.	English						Bridlington			Worcester		
	Belv.	Cant.	Roff.	Roy.	Dunl.	Font.	Brid.	Claud.	Claust.	Wig.	Chelt.	Cott.
96 = 31	—	1.33	65	—	—	—	70	51	253	7.30	17.11	3.37
101 = 34	—	1.9	77	—	—	—	36	44	—	4.34	2.19	5.58
35	—	1.4	34	—	—	—	68	49	123	3.10	11.13	3.17
36	—	—	—	—	—	—	82	65	—	3.34	—	—
37	—	1.35	68	38	3.49	—	137	—	168	4.21	—	4.89
39	—	—	—	37	—	—	76	57	26	1.1	—	2.78
40	—	1.39	—	41	2.31	—	46	—	278	7.51	6.15	3.34
41	—	—	—	—	—	—	109	97	177	5.4	15.4	3.9
42	—	—	—	—	—	—	83	66	124	3.11	11.14	6.26
51	—	—	—	—	(3.56)	(1.33)	(15)	(15)	(173)	(4.26)	(4.10)	(6.38)
52	—	—	—	—	—	—	—	—	—	—	—	6.29
57	—	—	—	117	—	2.52	—	—	290	7.58	6.19	7.19
70	—	—	—	—	—	—	—	—	—	7.81	—	—
78	—	—	—	—	—	—	—	—	149	4.8	11.3	7.100
95	—	1.33	65	(127)	(3.50)	(1.32)	65	—	116	3.3	16.16	6.86
31 = 96	—	—	—	—	—	—	70	51	253	7.30	17.11	3.37
97	—	—	—	—	—	—	74	55	—	—	17.28	3.14
98	—	1.34 (1.64)	74	—	—	—	75	56	—	—	(9.48)	(3.15)
34 = 99	49	1.11	33	—	3.43	1.15	—	48	176	5.3	15.3	3.16
100	—	1.10	29	8	3.29	—	36	44	170	4.23	11.9	6.30
101	56	1.9	77	—	—	—	37	45	169	4.34	2.19	5.58
102	51	1.12	27	—	—	—	38	46	102	4.22	13.18	6.62
103	—	1.7	28	—	2.17	—	60	47	166	2.14	10.16	6.61
104	—	1.13	56	87	—	—	77	58	—	4.19	13.16	4.1
105	53	—	—	122	—	—	—	—	113	—	—	—
107	50	1.1	76	—	—	—	73	54	97)	2.23	10.12	4.21
111	—	—	—	131	—	2.38	78	59	98)	2.10	10.2	4.48
112	—	—	—	—	—	—	—	—	195	—	—	—
116	—	—	—	—	—	—	178	—	—	7.4	15.26	3.33
120	—	—	—	—	—	—	—	—	—	—	7.14	6.56
122	—	—	—	—	—	—	128	119	328	2.36	—	—
123	—	—	—	—	—	—	—	—	—	—	(11.10) (19.18)	(6.32)
124	—	—	83	—	—	—	—	—	—	3.27	2.15	5.17

3. This table collates the Canterbury decretals in the Alcobaça Collection with the corresponding items in continental primitive collections of the 'Tortosa', Italian and French families.

Alcob.	'Tortosa'		Italian					French		
	Eber.	Devt.	Berol.	Cus.	Duac.	Flor.	Par. I	Cantab.	Vict.	Aur.
96 = 31	7.5	21	67	191	—	157	5	—	118	18
101 = 34	8.3	25	—	—	—	—	1	—	120	—
35	9.2	29	—	—	—	—	4	—	117	—
36	9.3	30	68	—	—	—	—	—	—	—
37	10.1	31	—	51	—	152	3	82	38	34 = 125
39	2.2	35	42	14	54	155	—	20A	40	—
40	10.3	36	—	15	55	119	—	20B	41	52 = 43c
41	10.4	37	—	—	—	120	44	—	—	—
=	3.4	—	—	—	—	—	—	—	—	—
42	10.5	38	—	—	—	—	—	27	49	(107)
51	—	—	—	—	—	—	—	—	—	—
52	—	—	—	—	—	—	—	—	—	—
57	—	—	—	—	—	—	—	—	—	—
70	—	—	—	—	—	—	—	—	—	—
78	—	—	—	—	—	—	—	—	—	—
31 = 95	5.3	72	43	16	56	121	5	21	42	18
96	7.5	21	67	191	—	157	—	23	118	56
97	—	—	—	17	57	122	—	83	44	—
98	10.2	32	59	50	19	153	—	25	46	—
99	3.5	—	81	87	30	66	20	24	47	—
100	9.1	28	—	166	—	77	1	—	45	29.I = 81
34 = 101	8.3	25	—	167	31	—	6	26	120	19
102	8.5	27	—	—	—	78	—	—	48	—
103	8.4	26	—	1	32	—	19	—	119	—
104	—	—	—	—	—	79	—	—	114	—
105	—	—	52	26	—	—	—	—	—	—
107	—	—	—	171	—	—	—	—	—	—
111	—	—	—	—	—	—	—	—	—	—
112	—	—	—	—	—	—	—	—	—	—
116	—	—	—	61	—	—	—	—	—	—
120	—	—	—	—	—	—	—	—	—	—
122	—	—	—	52	—	—	—	—	—	99
123	—	—	—	60	—	—	—	—	—	—
124	—	—	—	—	—	—	—	—	—	—

4. This table collates twelve Exeter decretals in the Alcobaça Collection with the corresponding items in English primitive collections of the English, Bridlington and Worcester families.

Alcob.	English					Bridlington			Worcester		
	Cant.	Roff.	Roy.	Dunl.	Font.	Brid.	Claud.	Claust.	Wig.	Chelt.	Cott.
73	—	—	115	—	1.41	—	—	—	4.46	4.6	—
74	1.31	97	—	—	1.39	—	—	67	1.30	9.27	2.64
75	1.16	36	116	—	1.40	—	—	147	4.6	8.9	4.75
76											
77			117					149	4.8	11.3	6.100
78			112					140	3.24	12.6	6.27
79						53			= 3.39		
80	—		75		1.42	20	20			12.2	
81	1.27	89			= 3.17	4	4	131	3.15	= 9.71	5.47
82	1.28	95	76) 40)	2.29	1.43	54) 5)	138) 5) 146)	44) 45)	1.17	9.18	2.45
83	1.29	96	77		1.44	6	6	66	1.29	9.26	2.24
85	—	—	—			3	3		4.47		6.47

Only three of these decretals are found in continental primitive collections. The maximum possible collation is as follows:

Alcob.	Cus.	Par. I	Vict.	Aur.
81	—	81	127	—
82	169.11	82) 83)	128	—
83	173	—	—	121

X

The Becket Dispute and the Criminous Clerks

INTRODUCTION: THE JURISDICTIONAL CONFLICT

No FICTION DIES so hard in English history as the well-known theory that, in their famous quarrel over the privilege of clergy, Henry II could argue a better case in canon law than Becket. The spectacular course of the conflict and the dramatic interest of the principal contestants tend to obscure its underlying causes, but nothing could be less related to reality than the common assumption that the controversy was merely a personal issue between king and archbishop, or that Becket alone was responsible for the formulation of those doctrines in canon law which he defended so vigorously, and for which he finally paid with his life. The personal factors were undoubtedly important, and controlled the pattern of the dispute as it developed in England, but it is not easy to see how the conflict could have been averted entirely as the rival spheres of ecclesiastical and secular jurisdiction clashed at their many points of contact or interlocking interests.

It was the object of Henry II's policies to erect a ring-fence round his kingdom, and to restore the traditional Norman barrier against the encroachment of papal influence in England, to strengthen his jurisdictional authority, and so to give tangible expression to his natural ambitions as a strong-minded secular ruler. But the reformed papacy, with its Gregorian traditions of ecclesiastical superiority and independence, the aftermath of the Investiture Controversy, the far-reaching doctrinal, intellectual, legal and administrative movements in the Church, all combined to produce a remarkable advance of centralized government, with repercussions throughout Christian society, under the guidance of the pope, and made effective by canon law. Each of these parallel streams reflected something of the creative ferment which distinguished the European intellect at that time, but their twin growth made inevitable a conflict of claims and interests between them, a conflict heightened in England by insular and personal associations. The circumstances of Stephen's reign had been peculiarly favourable to the advance of the Church's interests in a period of weakened secular government, and it was Henry II's desire to restore as far as possible the conditions which prevailed in the reign of Henry I, his grandfather, to reinstitute the 'avitae consuetudines', and so to re-establish the barrier breached in the reign of his predecessor. But the status and claims of the Church were irretrievably altered, in many respects quite independently of Stephen's weakness, so that it was not merely a defect of Becket's character, or of Henry's, which produced the dramatic crisis forever associated with them.[1]

The dispute over clerical immunity was not the crucial issue between the two contestants, but it was the single aspect around which the quarrel was waged most bitterly. The ever-widening jurisdiction of papal judges delegate, freedom of appeal from the English ecclesiastical courts to the papal Curia, the passage of bishops and papal legates between the island and the continent: these were far greater obstacles to the realisation of Henry's policies, and were naturally viewed with much disquiet by him; and, in comparison with these, the question whether criminous clerks should be subjected to secular jurisdiction and punishment, or not, was of minor importance intrinsically. But symptomatically its importance can scarcely be exaggerated, for it provided a *point d'appui* for the controversialists in a wider and more fundamental quarrel.[2]

Yet even historians most sympathetic to Becket on all other conceivable issues believe that in this single respect he passed beyond the accepted canonical doctrines of his time; and their reasons are not hard to find. The policies which Henry wished to make effective commend themselves as both reasonable and realistic; the royal appeal to custom is defensible on the extant historical evidence; the ultimate triumph of the secularist

[1]On the ideological conflict in England, see D. Knowles, *The Episcopal Colleagues of Archbishop Thomas Becket* (Cambridge, 1951), pp. 140–56. For the European context, see M. Pacaut, *Alexandre III* (Paris, 1956), pp. 153–71; and W. Ullmann, 'The medieval interpretation of Frederick I's Authentic *Habita*', in *Studi in memoria di Paolo Koschaker* (Milan, 1953), pp. 102–10 (*L'Europa e il Diritto Romano*, vol. i.) See also Z. N. Brooke, *The English Church and the Papacy* (Cambridge, 1931); R. Foreville, *L'Église et la Royauté en Angleterre sous Henri II Plantagenet, 1154–89* (Paris, 1943), pp. 77–161. On the development of canon law in England, see S. Kuttner and E. Rathbone, 'Anglo-Norman canonists of the twelfth century', *Traditio*, vii (1951), 279–358. For varying estimates of Becket's character and its influence on the controversy, see Knowles, *Archbishop Thomas Becket: a Character Study* (Raleigh Lecture, 1949); Foreville, pp. 107–15; H. W. C. Davis, *England under the Normans and Angevins* (12th edn., 1945), pp. 210–15; A. L. Poole, *From Domesday Book to Magna Carta* (2nd edn., Oxford, 1955), pp. 196–209; I. P. Shaw, 'The ecclesiastical policy of Henry II on the continent', *Church Quart. Rev.* (1951), 137–8.

[2]Knowles, *Episcopal Colleagues*, pp. 55 and 60–66; Foreville, pp. 125–31 and 137–51; F. W. Maitland, *Roman Canon Law in the Church of England* (1898), pp. 132–47; R. Génestal, *Le Privilegium Fori en France* (2 vols., Paris, 1921–4), ii. 95–114; C. R. Cheney, 'The punishment of felonous clerks', *Eng. Hist. Rev.*, li (1936), 215–36; L. C. Gabel, *Benefit of Clergy in England in the Later Middle Ages* (Smith College Studies, Northampton, Mass., 1929); A. L. Poole, 'Outlawry as a Punishment of Criminous Clerks', in *Historical Essays in honour of James Tait*, ed. J. G. Edwards *et al.* (Manchester, 1933), pp. 239–46; H. W. R. Lillie, 'St Thomas of Canterbury's opposition to Henry II', *Clergy Rev.*, viii (1934), 261–83.

viewpoint obscures in some instances a retrospective vision.[1] Most precisely, the domination of Maitland's brilliant but misconceived thesis has hindered a more just evaluation: Maitland himself, Génestal, Lillie, Poole, Cheney, Knowles, even the sympathetic Foreville, all these merely typify the many distinguished scholars who argue that in one respect or other Becket's case was weaker in canon law than the king's, or at least advanced beyond the canonical positions already defined.[2] It is with some natural diffidence that the considered judgment of so many scholars is called into question here, but the argument proposed in the following pages is this: that Henry II had little justification (if any) in canon law, that Becket's case was canonically better grounded than has been conceded in the past, and that Becket was certainly not the inventor of the canonical doctrines so frequently attributed to him.

CRIMINOUS CLERKS: HENRY II'S PLAN AND BECKET'S RESPONSE

The king's proposals for dealing with suspected felonous clerks are recorded briefly in the third clause of the Constitutions of Clarendon (1164) as follows:

Clerici rettati et accusati de quacunque re, summoniti a iusticia regis venient in curiam ipsius, responsuri ibidem de hoc unde videbitur curiae regis quod ibidem sit respondendum; et in curia ecclesiastica unde videbitur quod ibidem sit respondendum; et ita quod iusticia regis mittet in curiam sanctae ecclesiae ad videndum qua ratione res ibi tractabitur. Et si clericus convictus fuerit, non debet de cetero eum ecclesia tueri.

The phrasing of the clause is unfortunately ambiguous, but historians are in full agreement on the following interpretation: all clerks accused of serious crimes, not specifically ecclesiastical, but crimes like robbery and murder which are breaches of the king's peace as well as God's law, should first be summoned before a royal justice to answer the charge; sent from there without trial to the court of the Church, where they should be tried, deposed in the presence of the royal officer after condemnation; and finally sent back to the royal court to be punished as laymen would be. Expressed in technical terms, this conventional interpretation

---

[1] G. M. Trevelyan, *History of England* (1943 imp.), p. 156: 'Supported by the high papal claims from overseas, the Church courts now threatened to invade many provinces not their own.'

[2] Maitland, p. 145; Génestal, ii. 102–4; Lillie, *ubi supra*, pp. 268–71 and 276; Poole, *From Domesday Book to Magna Carta*, p. 206; Cheney, *ubi supra*, p. 216; Knowles, *Episcopal Colleagues*, pp. 144–5; Foreville, pp. 146 and 149; J. J. Dwyer, *St. Thomas of Canterbury* (Catholic Truth Soc., 1948 imp.), p. 17. Nevertheless, Mlle Foreville's view is that Becket's case was canonically better than the king's, and the present article agrees with her conclusions (p. 151) on most aspects of the controversy; this view is also briefly supported in Davis, p. 213. For a recent brief analysis of the dispute, see G. Greenaway, *The Life and Death of Thomas Becket* (Folio Society, 1961), pp. 9–22.

4   THE BECKET DISPUTE AND

can be stated succinctly as follows: accusation and plea in the secular
court; trial, conviction and deposition in the ecclesiastical court; and
sentence to a layman's punishment in the secular court.[1]

Confronted with this plan, Becket resisted the king on a broader front
than is sometimes recognized, and his answer can be broken down into
three component parts.[2] He objected, firstly, to the summoning of clerks
before a secular justice in the initial stage of the king's procedure, and
there is little doubt that canonical opinion was firmly on his side in this.[3]
He argued, secondly, that no secular punishment should follow the
deposition of a guilty clerk, since secular judges had no jurisdiction over
clerks; but if a guilty clerk committed a further felony in his degraded
state, the secular judge could both try and punish him in that condition:
'Curiae enim traditus est regiae et seculari jurisdictioni suppositus, curiae
perpetuo serviturus'.[4] And he maintained, thirdly, that deposition was
itself the penalty for the crime in question, to which no secular punishment could be legitimately added, for this would involve a double punishment, and 'God does not judge twice in the same matter'.[5]

But the validity of his argument was contradicted by his opponents,
and has been denied by most recent historians. It is objected, firstly, that
the 'traditio curiae' implied at the time of the dispute the delivery of a
degraded clerk to secular punishment; that, whatever the phrase had
meant in earlier ages, the common opinion of contemporary canonists
was against him in this; and that, on this point at least, his interpretation
was exceptional.[6] It is maintained, secondly, that his theory of the double

---

[1] Maitland, pp. 132–7; Génestal, ii. 99–100; Foreville, pp. 136–7; Lillie, *ubi
supra*, pp. 261–7. See also *Radulfi de Diceto Opera Historica*, ed. W. Stubbs
(2 vols., Rolls Ser., 1876), i. 313 (hereafter referred to as Diceto).

[2] Lillie, *ubi supra*, pp. 271–9.

[3] Foreville, pp. 148–9. Note FitzStephen's comment on Henry II's plan: 'Ut
clericus accusatus de furto, vel rapina, vel huiusmodi, primo veniat in curiam
regis . . . Et alia in hunc modum, quae palam cum sacris canonum constitutionibus
dissonantiam resonabant': *Materials for the History of Thomas Becket*, ed. J. C.
Robertson and J. B. Sheppard (7 vols., Rolls Ser., 1875–85), iii. 47 (hereafter
referred to as *Materials*).

[4] Becket's full argument on this point is recorded by Herbert of Bosham:
Materials, iii. 270: 'Curiae enim traditus est regiae et saeculari jurisdictioni
suppositus, curiae perpetuo serviturus. Hoc est enim quod canon dicit "Traden-
dum curiae", quod ex historiis unde verbum hoc sumitur manifestum; unde
postquam sic traditus, nobis et illi, iam curiae servo, nihil. Et ideo si qua deinceps
poena infligitur, iam non erit poena nostri, tanquam alicuius de clero, sed erit
poena vestri, tanquam unius de populo.'

[5] Many variant accounts of Becket's argument on this point are recorded:
Herbert of Bosham, *Materials*, iii. 281: 'Et quod adhuc poenalis servitutis accedit
cumulo, contra Domini in propheta mandatum clerici bis iudicabuntur in idipsum,
et duplex eorum consurget tribulatio.' Cf. William of Canterbury, *Materials*,
i. 28; Edward Grim, *ibid.*, ii. 386–8; Auctor Anonymus II, *ibid.*, iv. 96; *Summa
Causae inter Regem et Thomam*, *ibid.*, p. 202.

[6] The canonical support for the king's policy is also recorded by Herbert of
Bosham: *Materials*, iii. 266: 'Hoc ergo rex, quorumdam fretus consilio utriusque

punishment had not previously been applied to this particular problem; that the principle admittedly existed elsewhere in canon law, but that Becket's use of it in this context was new and bold.[1] Moreover, Maitland argued that Henry's plan was not in conflict with canon law in reality, since he had no wish to draw clerks as such to secular judgments. According to this theory, the opening stage of the king's procedure, when a clerk was presented to the royal justice to make his plea, involved no trial; and the final stage, when the guilty one was punished after deposition, involved no clerk.[2] But, if the issue could truly be resolved in such a simple fashion, the conflict resulting would certainly be inexplicable.

Two aspects of Henry's plan were clearly obnoxious to the Church: the summoning of clerks before a secular magistrate was contrary to canon law, whether a trial or judgment was involved at that procedural stage or not, quite independently of the prospect of a secular punishment later; and the presence of a royal official during sentence and deposition in the ecclesiastical court was an affront to the jurisdictional immunity of the Church.[3] For Becket at least, the trial and punishment of a criminous clerk were an entity, in which the ecclesiastical judgment was itself the penalty. Within the single case he recognized no distinction between the status of the accused before and after deposition; within the single case a clerk was protected by his privileged status from all secular physical punishments, so that he could suffer neither mutilation nor a capital sentence, 'lest in man the image of God should be deformed'.[4] If he were not so protected in practice, then what else was this, Becket demanded, but to draw clerks to secular judgments?[5] Two questions, therefore,

iuris se habere peritiam ostentantium, instantissime postulat ut tales mox summoti a clero curiae tradantur . . . Et hoc esse tradi curiae, judici videlicet saeculari relinqui ab eo puniendos; unde et bene in canone sequitur, "Et recipiat quod inique gessit."' Cf. Maitland, p. 145; Génestal, ii, pp. xxxiv–xxxix and 98–100; Poole, *From Domesday Book to Magna Carta*, p. 206.

[1] Génestal, ii. 102–4; Knowles, *Episcopal Colleagues*, p. 145; Brooke, p. 205; Foreville, p. 149.

[2] Maitland, pp. 134–40.

[3] Lillie, *ubi supra*, pp. 271–2.

[4] Herbert of Bosham, *Materials*, iii. 269: 'ita et in peculiari Dei portione et spirituali coertio spiritualis seorsum per se et a saeculari coertione separata. Et inde est quod absque membrorum mutilatione et sine omni deformatione corporis est, spiritualis est enim. Adeo etiam quod ordinis privilegium excludat cauterium; quam tamen poenam communiter inter homines etiam ius forense damnat, ne videlicet in homine Dei imago deformetur.'

[5] *Ibid.*, p. 281: 'iuxta funestum canonem hunc clerici tam in criminali quam in civili causa ad saeculare iudicium pertrahuntur. Et de novo iudicatur Christus ante Pilatum praesidem.' Cf. William of Canterbury, *ibid.*, i. 25; Grim, *ibid.*, ii. 386. Herbert of Bosham also records the king's argument: *ibid.*, iii. 266: 'ad nocendum promptiores fore adiiciens nisi post poenam spiritualem corporali poenae subdantur, et parum curare de ordinis amissione, qui contemplatione ordinis a tam enormibus manus continere non verentur.' Maitland certainly oversimplified this issue; cf. Foreville, pp. 138–9.

remain to be answered in assessing the legality of Becket's case: what was the true canonical significance of the 'traditio curiae'; and what was the historical justification of his objection to a double punishment?

THE DOCTRINE OF CLERICAL IMMUNITY IN
GRATIAN'S *DECRETUM*

How far Gratian's *Decretum* was accepted as the standard work of reference by Becket or by Henry's supporters can no longer be decided with certainty, though it is indisputable that earlier canonical collections were still used by individual ecclesiastics in England at that time.[1] Despite the primacy of authority which the *Decretum* swiftly secured, many other famous collections were still frequently studied and cited; and it cannot be assumed that any single text in Gratian, still less any *dictum Gratiani*, provides a definitive canonical ruling on a given problem.[2] But Gratian was certainly familiar to the writers who recorded the controversy, and has been accepted as a basis of discussion by modern historians. Two canons especially touch on the issues of the English dispute concerning clerical privilege, and purport to be decretal letters of Popes Pius and Fabian respectively:

Rubric: Clericus suo inobediens episcopo depositus curiae tradatur.
Canon: Si quis sacerdotum vel reliquorum clericorum suo episcopo inobediens fuerit, aut ei insidias paraverit, aut contumeliam, aut calumpniam, vel convicia intulerit, et convinci potuerit, mox depositus curiae tradatur, et recipiat quod inique gessit.

Rubric: Qui episcopo insidiatur semotus a clero curiae tradatur.
Canon: Statuimus, ut, si quis clericorum suis episcopis infestus aut insidiator fuerit, eosque criminari voluerit, aut conspirator fuerit, mox ante examinatum iudicium submotus a clero curiae tradatur, cui diebus vitae suae deserviat, et infamis absque ulla restitutionis spe permaneat.

The relevance of these passages to the Becket dispute is clear enough: both canons deal with clerks deposed for certain offences, and both refer to the much-debated 'traditio curiae'.[3] But it could hardly be overlooked

---

[1] Brooke, p. 112; Diceto, ii. 32–3, 298, 305 and 413.

[2] *The Summa Parisiensis on the Decretum Gratiani*, ed. T. P. McLaughlin (Toronto, 1952), pp. xvi-xvii. Numerous examples could be cited of 12th-century canonists refuting Gratian's arguments: Huguccio, Cambridge, Pembroke Coll. MS. 72, fo. 128vb: 'et ideo non approbo quod hic dicit magister nisi de talibus intelligat'; Anglo-Norman canonists, Cambridge, Caius Coll. MS. 676, fo. 142rb: 'Gratianus hic sompniasse videtur'; etc.

[3] The following editions of Gratian have been consulted: *Corpus Iuris Canonici*, ed. E. Friedberg (2 vols., Leipzig, 1879–81), i; *Decretum Gratiani*, ed. J. H. Boehmer, in *Patrologia cursus completus, series Latina*, ed. J. P. Migne, CLXXXVII (Paris, 1891), hereafter cited as *Pat. Lat.*; *Corpus Iuris Canonici emendatum et notis illustratum, Gregorii XIII Pontificis Maximi iussu editum*, ed. J. P. Lancelotti (Paris, 1618). The canons quoted above are *Decretum*, C. XI, Qu. 1, cc. 18 and 31. The conventional dates for the publication of Gratian's *Decretum* and the earliest

that the offences specified involve disobedience or resistance to ecclesiastical authority, and that the second canon speaks of the degraded clerk being delivered to the 'curia' to serve there all the days of his life, remaining defamed without hope of restitution. Two further canons broaden the terms of reference by defining that no one may accuse a bishop or clerk before a secular magistrate, and that no judge may distrain or condemn priests or clerks except with their bishops' consent. The first of these canons is attributed to Pope Caius; the second is a *Palea*, and therefore not included in Gratian's first draft, but it is in fact a canon of the 615 Council of Paris[1]:

Rubric: Apud saecularem iudicem nullus clericus conveniatur.

Canon: Nemo unquam episcopum apud iudicem saecularem aut alios clericos accusare praesumat.

Palea: Nullus iudicum neque presbiterum, neque diaconum, aut clericum ullum, aut iuniores ecclesiae sine licentia pontificis per se distringat aut condemnare praesumat.

Finally, two more canons, attributed respectively to Pope Boniface and a Roman synod convened by Pope Sylvester, deal with both civil and criminal cases involving bishops, and prohibit all public examination of clerks except in the Church[2]:

Rubric: Neque pro civili, neque pro criminali causa episcopus apud civilem iudicem producatur.

Canon: Nullus episcopus neque pro civili, neque pro criminali causa apud quemvis iudicem, sive civilem, sive militarem producatur vel exhibeatur.

Rubric: Quilibet clericus non est in publico examinandus.

Canon: Testimonium clerici adversus laicum nemo recipiat, nemo enim clericum quemlibet in publico examinare praesumat nisi in ecclesia.

These six canons are merely a selection from the numerous authorities assembled by Gratian on the subject of clerical immunity, but they provide an insight into the essential doctrines; and his own conclusions and commentary are summarized in a series of explanatory *dicta*:[3]

Quum ergo his omnibus auctoritatibus clerici ante civilem iudicem denegentur

commentaries on it are accepted in this study, but it should be noticed that these have been recently challenged by A. Vetulani, who argues that the earliest recension of the *Decretum* must be dated much earlier than has hitherto been supposed. Nevertheless, the vulgate version of the *Decretum* cannot be earlier than 1139, as it incorporates material from the Second Lateran Council of that year: see A. Vetulani, 'Le Décret de Gratien et les premiers Décrétistes', in *Studia Gratiana post octava Decreti saecularia*, ed. J. Forchielli and A. M. Stickler (Bologna: Institutum Gratianum, 1959), vii. An excellent summary of the history of the 'traditio curiae' is found in R. Laprat, 'Livraison au bras séculier', in *Dictionnaire de droit canonique*, ed. R. Naz (Paris, 1937), ii.

[1] *Decretum*, C. XI, Qu. I, cc. 1 and 2.
[2] *Ibid.*, cc. 8 and 9.
[3] *Ibid.*, *dicta Gratiani* post cc. 26, 30 and 47.

producendi, quum (nisi prius depositi, vel nudati fuerint) curiae non sint repraesentandi, patet, quod ad saecularia iudicia clerici non sunt pertrahendi.

In criminali vero causa non nisi ante episcopum est clericus examinandus. Et hoc est illud, quod legibus et canonibus supra definitum est, ut in criminali videlicet causa ante civilem iudicem nullus clericus producatur, nisi forte cum consensu episcopi; veluti quando incorrigibiles inveniuntur, tunc detracto eis officio curiae tradendi sunt.

Ex his omnibus datur intelligi, quod clericus ad publica iudicia nec in civili, nec in criminali causa est producendus, nisi forte civilem causam episcopus decidere noluerit, vel in criminali sui honoris cingulo eum nudaverit.

Thus the canons clearly define the basic principle that clerks may not be accused, examined, constrained or condemned by secular judges without the consent of their bishops; and the canons concerned with the 'traditio curiae' deal specifically with offences committed by clerks against their bishops. The meaning of the 'curia' is not easily discovered in the texts alone, which refer to different concepts in different contexts: the 'traditio curiae' involves a punishment following deposition in one instance, and a servile status resulting from deposition in another; and a further canon (not cited above) speaks of the 'curia' in its most usual meaning as a place or court of law.[1] In Gratian's commentary the 'traditio curiae' includes the notion of deposition and delivery to secular punishment, but Gratian does not explicitly equate these concepts, and it cannot be assumed that he believed this to be the necessary or invariable meaning of the canons. The delivery of clerks to secular justice is conceded by him in certain conditions, after deposition and subject to episcopal consent; and the example selected to illustrate the procedure is the delivery of an incorrigible clerk. On the evidence of the *Decretum* alone, it seems that neither Henry II nor Becket was entirely justified by the canons or by Gratian's *dicta*: Becket's basic principle is firmly stated, but with some qualification and with no mention of the objection to a double punishment; and Henry's procedure is in part permitted, but subject to a different control and in restricted circumstances. On balance, the evidence is more favourable to Becket than to Henry, but a final verdict requires a fuller understanding of the historical background of the canons themselves.

PSEUDO-ISIDORE AND THE 'TRADITIO CURIAE'

It is a remarkable fact that all but one of the six canons discussed above were either forgeries or recorded in Gratian with false inscriptions: the canon of the 615 Council of Paris is a genuine conciliar canon; the so-called letter of Pope Boniface is a text from Roman law with a false inscription; the synodal decree of Pope Sylvester is apocryphal; the

---

[1] *Decretum*, C. XI, Qu. 1, c. 33: 'Nullus clericus, vel diaconus, vel presbiter propter quamlibet causam intret in curiam, nec ante iudicem civilem causam dicere praesumat.'

decretals of Popes Caius, Pius and Fabian are pseudo-Isidorian fabrica-
tions.[1] This revelation does not invalidate their force as legal texts in the
twelfth century, but it does throw light on their original meanings and on
the intentions of their authors. The forged letters of Pius and Fabian
are best suited to a more detailed examination, since these two texts
refer to the 'traditio curiae'.

The pseudo-Pius is first found in the ninth-century Frankish *Pseudo-
Isidore*; it is an undoubted forgery, and it would in any case be absurd
to suppose that Pius I could have legislated in such a sense in the conditions of the second century. But the Frankish forger drew skilfully on
both Roman and canonical models in concocting his spurious text. On
the issue of clerks in opposition to their bishop, the substance of the
canon can be retraced to a decision of the Council of Chalcedon of 451;
and in the matter of procedure, the delivery of clerks to the 'curia', the
canon can be retraced to an epitome of the Breviary of Alaric, and ultimately to a constitution of Arcadius and Honorius in the Theodosian
Code. The result of this conflation of canonical and Civilian authorities
can be seen in the texts of the forged letters of Pius and Fabian (the
prototypes of the texts in Gratian) and a further letter attributed by
Pseudo-Isidore to Pope Stephen[2]:

Pseudo-Pius: Et si quis sacerdotum vel reliquorum clericorum suo episcopo
inobediens fuerit aut ei insidias paraverit aut contumeliam aut calumniam, et
convinci poterit, mox curiae tradatur.

Pseudo-Fabian: Ut si aliquis clericorum suis episcopis infestus aut insidiator
fuerit eosque temptaverit aut conspirator fuerit, ut mox ante examinatum
iudicium submotus a clero curiae tradatur, cui diebus vitae suae deserviat.

Pseudo-Stephen: Clericus ergo qui episcopum suum accusaverit aut ei
insidiator extiterit, non est recipiendus, quia infamis effectus est et a gradu
debet recedere aut curiae tradi serviendus.

All three canons deal with clerks in opposition to their bishops; two
canons make no mention at all of deposition, but all three refer to the
delivery of a guilty clerk to the 'curia'; in two canons the 'traditio curiae'
is so expressed that the guilty clerk will 'serve' in his resulting condition.
This notion of the 'traditio curiae' springs directly from the Roman law
procedure described in the Theodosian constitution already mentioned[3]:

Quemcumque clericum indignum officio suo episcopus iudicaverit et ab
ecclesiae ministerio segregaverit . . . continuo eum curia sibi vindicet.

---

[1]*Pat. Lat.*, CLXXXVII, cols. 821–2, *Notationes Correctorum* C. VIII (h) and
n. 23, C. IX (i) and n. 27; *ibid.*, cols. 819–20, n. 1, cols. 823–5, n. 64 and cols.
829–30, n. 118.

[2]*Decretales Pseudo-Isidorianae et Capitula Angilramni*, ed. P. Hinschius (Leipzig,
1863), pp. 120, 165 and 186; cf. *Decretum*, C. XI, Qu. 1, cc. 18 and 31. See
Génestal, ii, pp. xiii–xvii; Maitland, pp. 140–3; Foreville, pp. 149–50.

[3]Génestal, ii, pp. xiv–xvii; Maitland, pp. 142–3; *Codex Theodosianus*, ed.
P. Krüger (Berlin, 1923–6), XVI, ii. 39.

It is quite obvious, therefore, that the 'traditio curiae' bore no implication whatever of delivery to secular judgment, either in its Roman law context or in its pseudo-Isidorian derivative. In its Roman law origin it meant that a condemned clerk, being deprived of office, should as a 'curialis' be liable to civil burdens for the future, and should be subject in that condition to secular justice.[1]

But it is more than likely that the Frankish forger wished to limit even this degree of secular meaning, when adapting the Roman text to his purpose. The motives underlying his work are well known: the advance of papal authority throughout the Church, the rights of bishops against their metropolitans and over their own subject clerks, the privileges of clerks in Christian society. It is inconceivable that such an author devised a text to subject clerks in any way to secular judgments; and it is improbable that he would have troubled to forge a canon merely to restate the Roman concept of translation to a curial status.[2] Génestal believed that the 'traditio curiae' implied in *Pseudo-Isidore* that a degraded clerk should be transferred to a condition of slavery or public servitude; and Gregory VII certainly used the phrase with this intention.[3] But it is equally likely that the pseudo-Pius was designed as an expression of episcopal authority and ecclesiastical superiority, a theory fully supported by the full text of the decretal, from which the familiar canon is merely a brief extract[4]:

Audet aliquis vestrum, habens negotium adversus alterum, iudicari apud iniquos et non apud sanctos? An nescitis quoniam sancti Dei de mundo iudicabunt? Et si in vobis iudicabitur mundus, indigni estis quidem ut de minimis iudicetis, nescitis quoniam angelos iudicabimus? Quanto magis saecularia! Saecularia igitur iudicia si habueritis contemptibiles sunt in Ecclesia illos ad iudicandum ... De cetero salva in omnibus apostolica auctoritate quaecumque sunt ad religionis pertinentia, locis suis et a suae dioeceseos sinodis audiantur. Et si quis sacerdotum vel reliquorum clericorum suo episcopo inobediens fuerit, aut insidias ei paraverit, aut contumeliam, aut calumniam, et convinci potuerit, mox curiae tradatur. Qui autem facit iniuriam, recipiat hoc quod inique gessit. 'Corrumpunt enim mores bonos colloquia mala. Evigilate iusti et nolite peccare.'

Centuries later an Anglo-Norman canonist defined the 'curia' in this context as an ecclesiastical prison.[5] One conclusion is certain: the 'traditio curiae' in *Pseudo-Isidore* was related in no way to the notion of the delivery of degraded clerks to secular judgment.

---

[1] Maitland, p. 143.

[2] Cf. W. Ullmann, *The Growth of Papal Government in the Middle Ages* (1955), p. 181.

[3] Génestal, ii, pp. xvii and xxxiv–xxxv; *Das Register Gregors VII*, ed. E. Caspar, in *Mon. Germ. Hist.*, *Epistolae* (Berlin, 1920–3), ii. 461; *Pat. Lat.*, CXLVIII, cols. 546–7: Reg. VII, ep. 2.

[4] *Pat. Lat.*, CXXX, col. 114.

[5] Cambridge, Caius Coll. MS. 676, fo. 109rb: 'nomine curie hic ergastulum ecclesie designatur'.

CLERICAL IMMUNITY: FROM *PSEUDO-ISIDORE* TO GRATIAN

The many collections published between *Pseudo-Isidore* and Gratian reveal no consistent tradition either in their selection of canons or in textual detail within them.[1] It would be rash to build too much on the evidence of any single source, but a selection of characteristic canons from some of the most well-known collections will serve to illustrate their general treatment of the subject of clerical privilege. Of the three relevant forgeries discussed above, *Anselmo Dedicata* (882–96) received the pseudo-Pius, with its concluding phrase 'curiae tradatur', but omitted the other two. Since the pseudo-Pius is the one text which does not include the words 'serviendus' or 'deserviat' in association with the 'traditio', this selection led Génestal to the supposition that a delivery to secular judgment, rather than a translation to curial or servile status, was already implied by this canon in the ninth century.[2] But there is no firm evidence to support this theory, though *Anselmo Dedicata* also received a Roman law decision that a secular magistrate could judge a clerk, provided that he was first degraded.[3]

The *De Ecclesiasticis Disciplinis* (*c.* 906) of Regino of Prum and the *Decretum* (*c.* 1012) of Burchard omit all three of the forged decretals, but include other canons revealing the doctrine of clerical immunity as then received. Their inclusion of a canon of the Twelfth Council of Toledo is especially relevant[4]:

Si quis presbiter ab episcopo suo fuerit degradatus, aut ab officio suo pro certis criminibus suspensus, et ipse per contemptum et superbiam aliquid de ministerio sibi interdicto agere praesumpserit, et postea ab episcopo suo correptus in coepta praesumptione perduraverit, hic omnimodis excommunicetur et ab Ecclesia expellatur. Et quicunque cum eo communicaverit scienter, similiter

[1] Excellent surveys of the many collections assembled in this period are found in P. Fournier and G. Le Bras, *Histoire des Collections Canoniques en Occident depuis les Fausses Décrétales jusqu'au Décret de Gratien* (2 vols., Paris, 1931–2); and A. van Hove, *Prolegomena ad Codicem Iuris Canonici* (2nd edn., Malines/Rome, 1945), pp. 305–48. To illustrate the textual variants in the transmission of the pseudo-Pius: *Anselmo Dedicata*, the *Decretum* of Ivo of Chartres, and the *Collectio Trium Partium* all agree with the original version in *Pseudo-Isidore* in omitting the word 'depositus'; but Anselm of Lucca's *Collectio Canonum*, Cardinal Gregory's *Polycarpus*, and Gratian's *Decretum* all include this significant term. But in other respects, both Ivo and Gratian agree exactly in textual details where both diverge from *Pseudo-Isidore* and Anselm. On textual problems in Gratian, see S. Kuttner, 'De Gratiani opere noviter edendo', *Apollinaris*, xxi (Vatican City, 1948), 118–28; Kuttner, 'The scientific investigation of medieval canon law: the need and the opportunity', *Speculum*, xxiv (1949), 495; and Pius XII's address to the Gratian Congress at Bologna in 1952: *Acta Apostolicae Sedis*, xliv (1952), 368–9.

[2] Fournier and Le Bras, i. 234–43; Génestal, ii, pp. xvii–xviii. The canon is *Anselmo Dedicata*, IV. 49.

[3] Génestal, ii, p. xviii.

[4] *Pat. Lat.*, CXXXII, col. 364: *Reginonis Prumiensis Abbatis de Ecclesiasticis Disciplinis et Religione Christiana*, II, 420; *Pat. Lat.*, CXL, cols. 654–5: *Burchardi Wormaciensis episcopi Decretorum libri XX*, II, 179.

se sciat excommunicatum. Similiter de clericis, laicis, vel feminis excommunicatis observandum est. Quod si aliquis ista omnia contempserit, et episcopus emendare minime potuerit, regis iudicio exsilio damnetur.

The interest of this canon is that the royal judge is permitted to constrain a degraded clerk, if the latter has shown himself incorrigible and beyond the control of the Church. The nature of the crimes in question is not made clear, but the initiative is held securely by the bishop, who is supported by the royal authority when his own decisions would otherwise be frustrated. Further canons included by Burchard bring the issue still more directly into the arena of rival jurisdictions, variously ruling that all clerks are exempt from the imputation of crimes by laymen; that priests and deacons should be deposed if guilty of murder, whatever the provocation; and that no secular judge may presume to distrain any ecclesiastical person.[1] The selection of texts by Burchard is all the more significant in view of his well-known desire to promote as far as possible the rights and jurisdictional independence of the Church. In the same way, it must be taken for granted that Gregory VII had no wish to subject clerks in any way to secular justice, unless the interests of the Church were involved or at its own discretion, and his conception of the 'traditio curiae' is made clear in a letter to the bishop and people of Lucca in 1079, and in the legal process which resulted from it. In this letter the false decretals provide a basis of canonical authority, and the penalty imposed was public slavery[2]:

Iudicio totius sanctae sinodi curiae traduntur. Tunc fidelis et prudens marchionissa Mathilda servos illos appellans, in servitutem curiae vocavit eos.

In contrast with this, the letters of Ivo of Chartres reveal a different and novel interpretation. The 'traditio curiae' certainly implied for him in some instances the delivery of clerks to secular punishment. A letter of Ivo to the bishop of Orleans in 1096 rebuked the bishop for the confinement of a clerk in a secular prison, uncondemned and undegraded, where he remained 'curiae traditum'; the bishop should either release the clerk himself or take measures to secure his liberation[3]:

Per manus servorum trahi fecistis ad carcerem, et curiae traditum nulla consolatione refovistis, neque de eius liberatione curare voluistis . . . quam clericus vester non iudicatus, non damnatus a vobis curiae traderetur ubi more furis,

---

[1] *Pat. Lat.*, CXL, col. 593: *Burchard*, I, 151; *ibid.*, col. 777: *Burchard*, VI, 47; *ibid.*, col. 912: *Burchard*, XVI, 22. Cf. *Decretum Gratiani*, C. XI, Qu. 1, c.2.

[2] Génestal, ii, pp. xvii and xxxiv–xxxv; *Das Register Gregors VII*, ii. 461; *Pat. Lat.*, CXLVIII, cols. 546–7. For Anselm of Lucca, see Génestal, ii, pp. xxi–xxii; *Anselmi episcopi Lucensis Collectio Canonum*, ed. F. Thaner (Innsbruck, 1906), or *Pat. Lat.*, CXLIX; for relevant canons in Anselm's collection, see *Anselmi Collectio Canonum*, ed. Thaner, col. 444: VIII, 16; *ibid.*, col. 128: III, 23.

[3] Génestal, ii, pp. xxxvi–xxxix; *Pat. Lat.*, CLXII, col. 64: *Ivonis Carnotensis episcopi Epistolae*, ep. LIII; see also *ibid.*, col. 85: ep. LXVI, and col. 146: ep. CXXXVII.

contumeliis et iniuriis quotidianis cruciaretur. Non est officium pastoris, sed mercenarii . . . Unde si vultis amplius nos amicos habere et adiutores, aut diaconum curiae traditum liberate, aut pro eius liberatione, quod exigit cura pastoralis sine dilatione perficite.

It is evident that the clerk had been cast into prison; but it is equally evident that Ivo did not approve of this action. Nor can it be assumed that he understood the 'traditio curiae' to have this meaning in every context; still less that he believed that degraded clerks should be delivered to secular punishment after deposition. The canonical texts which he incorporated in his *Decretum* differ in no discernible respect from those in earlier collections: one canon declared that recalcitrant clerks might be punished 'per potestates exteras' when no other remedy remained to the Church; and his authorities were brought up to date with a recent ruling by Pope Urban II that no secular lord could exercise power over clerks, who were subject to their bishops only.[1]

Finally, the evidence in Alger of Liége's *Liber de Misericordia et Iustitia* (*c.* 1106) has been curiously neglected. Alger died a single decade before Gratian's work was published, and it is well-established that Gratian made direct use of Alger's canons and comments in composing his own *Decretum*.[2] Alger included one rubric dealing with the 'traditio curiae', and this is found at the head of the pseudo-Fabian text derived from *Pseudo-Isidore*; but the pseudo-Fabian, which was also received by Gratian, is scarcely susceptible of the new meaning of the 'traditio curiae' discovered in Ivo's letter discussed above. It is inconceivable that the notion of a secular judgment and punishment was in Alger's mind when he transcribed his text and rubric[3]:

Rubric: Quod proditores et laceratores episcopum infames fieri, deponi et curiae tradatur.

Pseudo-Fabian: . . . submotus a clero curiae tradatur, cui in diebus vitae suae deserviat, et infamis absque ulla restitutionis spe permaneat.

Thus, from *Pseudo-Isidore* to Gratian, the canons define the doctrine of clerical immunity in confident terms, but they do not altogether exclude the operation of secular jurisdiction. The punishment of degraded clerks

---

[1] Génestal assumed that Ivo's meaning would be consistent (ii, p. xxxvii and n. 4, citing *Decretum Ivonis*, V, 243). But see also *Pat. Lat.*, CLXI, col. 496: *Decretum*, VI, 238 and *ibid.*, cols. 532–3: *Decretum*, VI, 408: 'Ut nullus saecularis super clericos habeat potestatem. Urbanus II Radulpho comiti: Nosse te volumus quia nulli saeculari domino potestatem in clericos habere licet; sed omnes clerici episcopo soli esse debent subiecti. Quicunque vero aliter praesumpserit, canonicae procul dubio sententiae subiacebit.'

[2] *Pat. Lat.*, CLXXX: *Algeri Scholastici Leodiensis Liber de Misericordia et Iustitia*; van Hove, 'Quae Gratianus contulerit methodo scientiae canonicae', *Apollinaris*, xxi (Vatican City, 1948), 14–17 and 22; van Hove, *Prolegomena*, pp. 334–5; Le Bras, 'Alger de Liége et Gratien', *Revue des sciences philosophiques et théologiques*, xx (1931), 5–26.

[3] *Pat. Lat.*, CLXXX, col. 922: *Alger*, II, 45.

by secular officers is permitted by some canons, though in restricted circumstances and with definite limitations: an incorrigible clerk has proved recalcitrant and beyond the control of the Church, and so the secular arm will make effective the judgment of the Church; alternatively, the secular action is legitimate with the consent of the bishop. The circumstances which give rise to these definitions are mostly where the interests of the Church are involved, or its authority resisted. The matter can be fairly expressed in this way: the secular judgment or punishment of degraded clerks is permitted by the canons, subject to the interests or consent of the Church; and the principle of immunity is not undermined by these exceptions. But the history of the 'traditio curiae' presents a more complicated problem. Many canonists included in their collections one or more of the relevant forged decretals, but seldom with sufficient evidence to reveal its meaning as they understood it. At least four variant meanings have been discussed above in connexion respectively with the original Roman law procedure in the Theodosian constitution, the intention of *Pseudo-Isidore* in composing the spurious decretal, the concept of public servitude as received by Gregory VII and the notion of delivery to secular punishment as implied in some passages in the letters of Ivo of Chartres.

Gratian received the canons susceptible of so many diverse interpretations, and the memory of these conflicting opinions helps to explain both the lack of precision in the *Decretum* itself, and the controversy which broke out on this issue in England. Herbert of Bosham records that Henry II's supporters boasted of their skill in either law; and, though it is clear that Herbert utterly scorned their pretensions, his faithful account reveals both sides citing the same canonical texts with widely divergent constructions placed on their common phrases. Henry's supporters argued that the canons required a secular penalty for a degraded clerk, who should be left by the Church to be punished by secular authority.[1] But Becket maintained against them that no such punishment was intended by the canons, that the 'traditio curiae' implied a translation to curial status, in which a degraded clerk would be subject to secular justice for the future, and would remain in that condition for ever.[2] It is obvious that Becket's interpretation was historically more accurate, agreeing with the Theodosian constitution in its procedure and definition, and with the spirit of *Pseudo-Isidore* in its purpose. But Henry's supporters

---

[1] *Materials*, iii. 268; Poole, *From Domesday Book to Magna Carta*, p. 206; Génestal, ii. 98, n. 2; Maitland, p. 145. Poole and Génestal assert simply that Henry was relying on the advice of men learned in both Civil and canon law, basing this belief on Herbert of Bosham's account of the controversy; but Herbert in fact related that Henry's advisers boasted of their skill in either law, whereas in his opinion they were 'scienter indocti'. Maitland clearly understood these implications when he spoke of the 'sneers of Master Herbert of Bosham.'

[2] *Materials*, iii. 270; a detailed canonical justification of Becket's stand is found in William of Canterbury, *ibid.*, i. 25–9.

received the historically more recent interpretation, a more novel concept winning wider recognition at that time.

THE THEORY OF THE DOUBLE PUNISHMENT

It remains next to consider how far Becket was canonically justified in opposing the delivery of degraded clerks to secular judgment because this involved a double punishment, and 'God does not judge twice in the same matter'. It is quite true that no text in Gratian or in any earlier canonical collection used this specific text and argument when discussing the principle of clerical privilege; and for this reason Becket's use of the maxim in this context has been described as extravagant and revolutionary. But the subjection of clerks to secular justice, without the consent of the Church, was forbidden by numerous other texts and arguments, as abundantly illustrated already above; and the *Presbiter* canon, received by Gratian, is much more relevant to Becket's case than has been generally realized in the past[1]:

Rubric: In crimine captus presbiter vel diaconus deponatur, non tamen communione privetur.

Canon: Presbiter aut diaconus, qui in fornicatione, aut periurio, aut furto, aut homicidio captus est, deponatur, non tamen communione privetur: dicit enim Scriptura: Non vindicabit Dominus bis in id ipsum.

As long ago as the sixteenth century the *Correctores Romani* noticed that this text had been altered since its first appearance as the twenty-fifth canon of the *Canones Apostolorum*, remarking that murder had not been mentioned in the original version, but had been interpolated by the Council of Tribur (895) on the understanding that what applied to lesser crimes should apply *a fortiori* to murder. The *Correctores* assumed that Gratian and other collectors inserted the word 'homicidio' in their versions for this reason.[2] The textual history of this canon from its origin to its reception by Gratian is self-evident from the following select examples[3]:

[1] Génestal, ii. 104; Brooke, p. 205; Knowles, *Episcopal Colleagues*, p. 145; Foreville, pp. 146 and 149: all these historians argue that Becket passed beyond the established canonical theories in applying the principle of the double punishment to criminous clerks, or even that he was the inventor of the doctrine in this context. On the use of the maxim in other connexions, see Génestal, ii. 104, n. 3; the best existing discussion of this subject is by Lillie, *ubi supra*, pp. 276–80. The *Presbiter* canon in Gratian is: *Decretum*, D. LXXXI, c. 12; see also *ibid.*, D. III, *dicta* post cc. 39 and 42.

[2] *Corpus Iuris Canonici*, ed. Lancelotti: *Correctores Romani*, D. LXXXI, c. 12, comment at *aut homicidio*.

[3] *Didascalia et Constitutiones Apostolorum*, ed. F. X. Funk (Paderborn, 1905), i. 570–1: *Constitutiones Apostolorum*, VIII, 47, 25; *Pat. Lat.*, LXVII, col. 144: *Dionysii Exigui Codex Canonum Ecclesiasticorum: Regulae Ecclesiasticae Sanctorum Apostolorum*, XXV; *Sacrorum Conciliorum Nova et Amplissima Collectio*, ed. J. D. Mansi, xviii (1767), col. 138: *Concilium Triburiense*, c. 11; *Pat. Lat.*, CXXXII, col. 209: *Regino*, I, 86. See also *Pat. Lat.*, CXL, cols. 657 and 926–7: *Burchard*,

Canones Apostolorum: Episcopus aut presbiter aut diaconus, qui in fornicatione aut periurio aut furto captus est, deponatur, nec vero segregetur; dicit enim scriptura: Non vindicabis bis in idipsum; similiter et reliqui clerici.

Dionysius Exiguus: Episcopus, aut presbiter, aut diaconus, qui in fornicatione, aut periurio, aut furto captus est, deponatur: non tamen communione privetur. Dicit enim Scriptura: Non vindicabit Dominus bis in idipsum.

Council of Tribur: Si quis clericus, quamvis nimium coactus, homicidium fecerit, sive sit presbiter, sive diaconus, deponatur. Legimus in canonibus apostolorum, quod episcopus, presbiter, et diaconus, qui in fornicatione, aut periurio, aut furto captus est, deponatur: quanto magis is, qui hoc immane scelus fecerit, ab ordine cessare debebit. Qui enim Christum sequi desiderat, debet sicut ille ambulavit, et ipse ambulare.

Regino of Prum: Presbiter aut diaconus qui in fornicatione aut periurio aut furto aut homicidio captus est, deponatur, non tamen communione privetur. Dicit enim Scriptura: Non iudicat Dominus bis.

It is interesting to notice that the *Presbiter* canon was not included in *Pseudo-Isidore*, and that Regino's version conflated the Dionysian text and the declaration of Tribur. There was no further significant modification after that time, and the new form of words was accepted with no substantial change by Burchard, Anselm of Lucca, Ivo, Cardinal Gregory and many other canonists down to Gratian.

Now, it is perfectly obvious that this canon could not literally justify Becket in his use of the maxim 'Non iudicat Deus bis in idipsum' in objecting to the secular punishment of degraded clerks. Both in its original intention and in its later variants the *Presbiter* canon was concerned with the punishment of clerks within the Church, and no question of secular jurisdiction was involved. It was even conceded in Becket's day that the canon no longer accurately described the policy which the Church itself consistently pursued.[1] Nevertheless, the freedom of clerks from secular jurisdiction, except with the Church's consent, was firmly established quite independently of this authority; and it is scarcely surprising if the familiar maxim was now adapted to an unfamiliar context when the essential principle of clerical immunity was itself subjected to a new attack. The argument has been well expressed by Lillie in this way: a canon in Gratian, *Quaesitum est ab aliquibus*, declared that communion should not be refused to a criminal awaiting execution, for God does not judge twice in a single matter; and the *Presbiter* canon had stated centuries earlier that a guilty clerk should not be excommunicated after degradation, since there should not be a second penalty for the same offence. If, therefore, a felonous layman should be spared a double punishment, one secular and one ecclesiastical, for a single crime, then *a fortiori* a clerk

II, 189 and XVII, 39; *Pat. Lat.*, CXLIX, col. 526: *Anselm*, II, 29; *Pat. Lat.*, CLXI, cols. 495–6: *Ivo*, VI, 234. For Anselm, Gregory and Gratian, see *Pat. Lat.*, CLXXXVII, cols. 389–90.

[1] E.g. *Summa Parisiensis*, ed. McLaughlin, p. 65: D. LXXXI, c. 12: 'his capitulis canonum Apostolorum, datis in primitiva ecclesia, derogetur per subsequentia.'

should enjoy a comparable immunity. Moreover, since the *Presbiter* canon forbade a double ecclesiastical punishment of a degraded clerk, then the latter, once punished by the Church, should not be punished again by the inferior jurisdiction of the state.[1] Somewhat surprisingly, Lillie overlooked the fact that the *Presbiter* canon was also included in the *Decretum*, and his argument would have been all the more convincing had he realized this.[2] Briefly, the matters involved in the case were these: a clerk has been found guilty by the Church of serious crime, perhaps of robbery or murder, and has been deposed by the Church as a penalty for his misdeeds; but the Church will impose no further punishment, since God does not judge twice in a single case. The crimes are those of chief concern to secular judges also; and the scriptural maxim is recalled to prohibit the double penalty. Of course, the canon was not designed to ward off secular intervention, but other canons asserted repeatedly that clerks were not liable to secular jurisdiction, except where the interests of the Church were involved, or with its consent.

Moreover, it is already well-known that Stephen of Tournai discussed the theory of the double punishment, as one of several divergent arguments then current, when composing his *Summa* on Gratian at some uncertain date, roughly contemporaneously with the dispute in England; and it has been assumed too readily in the past that Stephen's commentary followed rather than preceded Becket's adoption of the theory.[3] The *Summa Parisiensis* (c. 1160), though conceding that the *Presbiter* canon had been superseded by later legislation, discussed the delivery of degraded clerks to secular punishment in the same context.[4] Most striking testimony of all, the *Policraticus* of John of Salisbury, composed and presented to Becket in 1159, when the latter was still the royal chancellor and not yet even in priestly orders, embodied a clear-cut statement of that very principle whose invention is so commonly attributed to Becket himself[5]:

Nam privati legibus publicis, quae constringunt omnium vitas, facile cohercentur; in sacerdotem tamen, etsi tirannum induat, propter reverentiam sacramenti

---

[1] Lillie, *ubi supra*, pp. 277–80; *Decretum*, C. XIII, Qu. ii, c. 30; *ibid.*, C. XXIII, Qu. v, c. 6. See also *ibid.*, D. LXXXI, c. 12 and D. III, *dicta* post cc. 39 and 42.

[2] Lillie, *ubi supra*, pp. 278–80. Although Lillie refers to both the Apostolic Canon 25 and Gratian's D. LXXXI, c. 12, his discussion suggests no awareness of the fact that the latter is merely a derivative version of the former.

[3] E.g. Génestal, ii. 104.

[4] *Summa Parisiensis*, ed. McLaughlin, pp. 65–6.

[5] *Joannis Saresberiensis Episcopi Carnotensis Policratici sive de Nugis Curialium et Vestigiis Philosophorum Libri VIII*, ed. C. C. I. Webb (Oxford, 1909), ii. 788. In a general way, the letters of Becket, John of Poitiers and John of Salisbury reveal their identity of basic view in the jurisdictional conflict; FitzStephen alleges that the king secured the exile of John of Salisbury and the transference of John of Poitiers to his continental bishopric, so to deprive Becket of their advice and help: *Materials*, iii. 46. See also the cross-bearer's lament in a moment of crisis at Clarendon: 'Where shall now be found a place of abiding for innocence or resistance, or who may conquer in the fight, since the captain is felled?': E. Magnússon, *Thómas Saga Erkibyskups* (Rolls Ser., 1875–83), i. 171.

gladium materialem exercere non licet, nisi forte, cum exauctoratus fuerit, in Ecclesiam Dei cruentam manum extendat; eo quidem perpetuo optinente ut ob eandem causam non consurgat in eum duplex tribulatio.

The canonical sources of John's phrases are not difficult to find, and it is clear that the long established use of the scriptural maxim and the problem of criminous clerks have been drawn together in his hands.[1] Here was one obvious source of Becket's later thought, and the judgment must be finally abandoned that the argument was personal to him. Nevertheless, the principle for which he fought received the highest confirmation after his death, in the decretal *Licet praeter* (*c.* 1178), which Alexander III sent to the archbishop of Salerno, including the ruling that a degraded clerk should not be delivered to secular punishment: 'nec debet eum duplici contritione conterere.'[2] Although Alexander did not directly cite the familiar maxim in support of this definition, his vicar, Walter of Albano, had done so some time previously in a letter to Gilbert Foliot and the chapter of Rochford: a certain sub-deacon had committed a murder, and came forward for absolution; Walter released him from excommunication and imposed a detailed course of penance; the crime would normally have merited removal from his sub-diaconal status, but, because 'God does not judge twice in the same matter', the pope had dispensed with this ruling, and allowed him to return to his benefice; and he should suffer no further vexation.[3]

CRIMINOUS CLERKS IN DECRETIST COMMENTARIES

The earliest surviving decretist commentaries are those of Paucapalea (*c.* 1140–8) and the canonist Rolandus (*c.* 1148), whose discussion of the subject of criminous clerks is very slight in substance, but for that reason all the more significant in the emphasis selected[4]:

[1] *Decretum, dictum* post *De Poenit.*, D. III, c. 42: 'Non iudicabit Deus bis in idipsum, de his tantum intelligi oportet, quos praesentia supplicia in melius commutant, super quos non consurget duplex tribulatio.'

[2] *Corpus Iuris Canonici*, ed. Friedberg, ii: *Decretales Gregorii IX*, II, 1, 4; for the date of *Licet praeter*, see Génestal, ii. 20–26.

[3] Oxford, Bodl. MS. e Mus. 249, fo. 129r: 'Et quia non iudicat Deus bis in idipsum, licet idem Petrus pro petrato crimine non in subdiaconatu sed in acolitatu deinceps Deo et ecclesie servire valeat, tamen ex dispensatione et benignitate sacrosancte Romane sedis concessit ei dominus noster ecclesiasticum beneficium integrum retinere.' The letter is undated but found in the decretal collection *Belverensis*, completed not much later than 1175. It is an interesting fact that the *Glossa Ordinaria* of Bartholomew of Brescia cited the *Licet praeter* decision of Alexander III when glossing the *Presbiter* canon in Gratian's *Decretum*: Cambridge, Univ. Library MS. Dd. VII. 20, fo. 89va, and Cambridge, Caius Coll. MS. 6, fo. 58vb: *Decretum*, D. LXXXI, *Presbiter*: *Scriptura, Extra, De Iudicibus. Ac si clerici.*

[4] *Die Summa des Paucapalea über das Decretum Gratiani*, ed. J. F. von Schulte (Giessen, 1890), p. 78; *Die Summa Magistri Rolandi nachmals Alexander III*, ed. F. Thaner (Innsbruck, 1874), p. 25; van Hove, *Prolegomena*, pp. 433–4.

Paucapalea: In criminali causa ante civilem iudicem nullus clericus est producendus, nisi forte cum consensu episcopi sui, veluti quando incorrigibilis invenitur; tunc detracto ei officio, auctoritate Fabiani papae curiae tradendus est.

Rolandus: In criminali causa ad saecularem iudicem nullus omnino clericus est trahendus, nisi a proprio episcopo ante proprio fuerit nudatus honore.

It seems fair to conclude that both wished to stress the dependence of secular action on a preceding ecclesiastical decision, and that a secular judgment was subject, and not merely subsequent, to the Church's consent. But the work of an unknown author, completed at some uncertain date in or after 1154, included the very different opinion that, if a clerk is accused of a criminal offence, he should be summoned before his bishop, who ought to degrade him after conviction, and so deliver him to secular justice[1]:

Auctor Incertus: Quando impetit eum super civili criminali, debet eum producere coram episcopo, qui debet eum, si constiterit eum admisisse, exauctorare, et sic iudicis cognitioni tradere.

This is a commentary very favourable to Henry II's procedure, leaving little to ecclesiastical discretion when secular crimes have been committed; but the provenance and date of composition of the work are so uncertain, and its doctrine so untypical, that its significance as canonical evidence must be assessed with caution.

It is otherwise with the *Summa* of Rufinus (*c.* 1157–9), a work of outstanding interest and influence, which is conventionally assumed to favour Henry's policy rather than Becket's. Rufinus conceded that a Roman law *Authentic* declared that a layman could summon a suspected criminous clerk before a secular tribunal, provided the judge did not punish him before degradation by his bishop. But, he continued, the canons deal more mercifully with clerks than this, so that even in a criminal case a clerk must not be drawn to secular judgment without his bishop's consent[2]:

Canones tamen in hac causa clericis clementius provident, ut scilicet etiam in ista causa criminali non possint trahi ad forense iudicium . . . nisi cum permissione proprii episcopi. Sed quid si episcopus permiserit, clericus tamen trahi noluerit? Et putem clericum in hac parte non esse cogendum. Episcopi autem et sacerdotes nulla ratione pro aliqua causa apud iudicem saecularem possunt accusari, quia de eis iudicare non possunt. Quid igitur faciendum erit? Conveniatur clericus vel episcopus ante iudicem ecclesiasticum, et postquam ibi fuerit de crimine forensi legitima probatione convictus, et si adeo horrendum crimen fuerit, spoliabitur propriae dignitatis officio et dimittetur post haec, a saeculari iudice secundum leges publicas puniendus.

---

[1] *Die Summa Magistri Rolandi*, p. 293: *Incerti auctoris quaestiones*; Génestal, ii. 16; van Hove, *Prolegomena*, p. 441, n. 3. Van Hove, following Schulte, suggests Bologna as the place of composition of this work, within the dating limits 1154–79.

[2] *Die Summa Decretorum des Magister Rufinus*, ed. H. Singer (Paderborn, 1902), p. 307; van Hove, *Prolegomena*, pp. 428 and 434.

And so it appears that the teaching of Rufinus has been only partly understood. The immunity of clerks in criminal cases is stated by him emphatically, and an initiative or compulsive action by the secular ruler is
excluded. On the other hand, a guilty clerk should be deposed in certain
serious cases, and so delivered to secular punishment by the decision of the
Church. The procedure so described has admittedly much in common
with Henry II's intentions, but with this crucial difference that for
Rufinus the initiative remains with the Church.[1]

The commentary by Stephen of Tournai was very similar to that of
Rufinus on all essential details, noting the Roman law *Authentic* and its
curtailment by canon law in favour of clerks. But Stephen developed his
discussion with striking relevance to the dispute in England by listing
the various views then current on the theory of the double punishment:[2]

In criminali forensi secundum Authenticum ante iudicem civilem debet reus
clericus conveniri et pronuntiare potest civilis iudex, sed punire non potest,
nisi prius condemnatum clericum episcopus ordine et gradu spoliaverit. Canones
non permittunt id, cum in omni crimine prius sit ante iudicem ecclesiasticum
conveniendus et condemnatus ab eo curiae tradendus sit, i.e., reliquendus, ut
curia puniat eum secundum quod leges praecipiunt. Sed quaero: utrum
degradatus a iudice ecclesiastico iterum sit accusandus pro eodem crimine ante
civilem? Quidam dicunt nec accusandum, nec ab eo puniendum, ne saepius
de eodem quaeratur, quod lex prohibet. Alii dicunt, non esse opus, ut accusetur
ante civilem iudicem, sed ex quo condemnatus et degradatus ab ecclesiastico,
statim sine ulla cognitione potest puniri a civili. Sed melius dicitur non puniendus nisi iterum inscribatur et a civili iudice legitime cognoscatur et sic secundum
leges damnatio vel absolutio sequatur.

It is clear from this that Stephen was not in favour of a secular punishment
of a degraded clerk within a single process, although in reaching this
conclusion he made explicit reference to the contrasting arguments of
Becket and his opponents on this vexatious problem. His commentary
is an admirably succinct summary of the issues involved in the dispute,
and a proof of the uncertainty of canon lawyers at that time. But there
was no such ambiguity in the *Summa Parisiensis* (*c.* 1160), which argued
that a clerk should not be brought before a secular judge unless first
deposed by his bishop; and that, if he were deposed and delivered as a
result to the 'curia', it was not for execution, but so that he should be
defamed and subject to its authority.[3] And John of Faenza (*post* 1171)

---

[1] Génestal, ii. 16–17; Poole, *From Domesday Book to Magna Carta*, p. 206;
Lillie, *ubi supra*, p. 274. The discussions by Poole and Lillie are misleading:
Lillie certainly oversimplifies the matter in describing Rufinus as 'a writer who
says in so many words that a clerk is to be degraded and then handed over for
punishment'; he also wrongly dates the *Summa Rufini* 1160–70.

[2] *Die Summa des Stephanus Tornacensis über das Decretum Gratiani*, ed. J. F.
von Schulte (Giessen, 1891), pp. 211–2; van Hove, *Prolegomena*, p. 343; Génestal,
ii. 17–18; Lillie, *ubi supra*, p. 275.

[3] *Summa Parisiensis*, ed. McLaughlin, p. 147: 'Pro criminali ergo, nisi prius
deponatur ab episcopo, coram iudice saeculari non stabit'; *ibid.*, p. 148, gloss at

later declared that a degraded clerk should never be delivered or abandoned to a secular punishment unless his obstinacy is such that he cannot be corrected by the Church[1]:

Nec unquam curiae tradendus est vel reliquendus est ut puniatur, nisi in eo casu dumtaxat cum tanta est eius pertinacia ut per ecclesiae corrigi non valeat disciplinam.

This was a confident doctrine entirely unfavourable to Henry II's intentions, and one whose formulation was wrongly dated by Génestal as late as Huguccio's *Summa* (*c.* 1188–90) in origin.[2]

The decretists who published their commentaries after Becket's death cannot fairly be cited to illustrate the state of canonical opinion during the controversy, but their major arguments have a retrospective value. Simon of Bisignano (1177–9) observed that earlier canonists had written many useful things on the subject of clerical immunity, but somewhat confusedly and obscurely; and since the 'moderni' delight in brevity he would try to abbreviate the earlier prolixity.[3] Simon was at pains to emphasise that clerks were in practice judged in secular courts in some instances, as in feudal matters, but that this was by custom only and was not true law. Laws which had been devised for the benefit of clerks should not be twisted to their disadvantage: the general rule was that clerks could be summoned before ecclesiastical judges only, and only contumacious clerks should be delivered to secular constraint.[4] Huguccio's

---

curiae: 'non ut interficiatur sed infamis sit curiae exsecutori, ut habebimus.' The sources and date of composition of the *Summa Parisiensis* are not positively established: McLaughlin suggests that the works of Ivo, Peter Lombard, Paucapalea and Rolandus were known to the author, but that there is no evidence that Rufinus was used, and no proof that Stephen of Tournai's commentary was known to him. McLaughlin concludes (pp. xx–xxxii) that *c.* 1160 is the most probable date of composition.

[1] Brit. Mus., MS. Royal 9 E. VII, fo. 85rb; van Hove, *Prolegomena*, pp. 434–5. See also the Anglo-Norman gloss on Gratian in Cambridge, Sidney Sussex Coll. MS. 101, fo. 103va; this gloss reveals marginal and interlineal comments in several different hands: at *curie tradatur* one glossator wrote: 'Id est seculari iudici relinquitur, ab eo puniendus'; to which another added: 'Ita dico si omnino incorrigibilis existat'; the gloss is at least in part post-Rufinus.

[2] Génestal, ii. 28.

[3] Van Hove, *Prolegomena*, p. 435; Brit. Mus., Additional MS. 24659, and MS. Roy. 10 A. III.

[4] Brit. Mus., Add. MS. 24659, fo. 19va–vb: 'Laicus similiter si voluerit clericum convenire, conveniet eum coram ecclesia secundum regulam que dicit actor forum rei sequetur, nisi ratione alicuius cause forum istorum clericorum mutetur, ut in feudo quod iure consuetudinario regitur, non iure scripto. Unde quicumque convenitur de feudo, coram domino feudi conveniendus videtur. Sic enim hodie principum consuetudo se habet . . . Cum enim propter favorem clericorum statutum sit ne inviti ad iudicium trahantur, non debet in eorum dampnum retorqueri, quod propter eorum utilitatem est introductum; . . . id est auctoritatem et licentiam ut possent de iure punire clericos contumaces, et hic est unus casus in quo clericus potest a iudice seculari puniri . . . Hoc capitulum ad hoc inducitur quod clericus potest a seculari puniri, cum per ecclesiasticam disciplinam teneri

treatise was still more explicit, and the exceptions which some writers had allowed to the general principle of clerical immunity were refuted by him. In civil matters a clerk could be brought to secular judgment, if both clerk and bishop agreed; but never in criminal matters except as a final resort. Whatever the law might say on this point was untrue except for incorrigible clerks. Clerks taken in public and outrageous crimes were deposed in practice, and the secular magistrate was allowed, or even ordered, to judge and punish them by secular laws; but this was by custom and as a deterrent to others, rather than true law. For Huguccio, the 'traditio curiae' implied that a degraded clerk should be taken by the secular judge and punished if he had sinned, or subjected to public servitude if he had not.[1] In interesting comparison, an Anglo-Norman gloss

ad correptionem non potest.' See also Sicard of Cremona, Brit. Mus., Add. MS. 18376, fo. 37rb–va: 'Queritur utrum clericus ante civilem iudicem sit producendus. Videtur quod non, quia nec in causa criminali nec in civili. . . . Proponat itaque accusationem suam sive clericum sive laicum accusare voluerit ante iudicem ecclesiasticum. Quod si eam iudex recipere noluerit, adeat principem, non ut postulet cognitionem publicorum iudiciorum, sed ut impetret iudicium episcopale, et mandet alicui episcopo iudicare de causa secundum canones . . . Attendum quod si clericus invitus trahitur ad non suum iudicem, et contra eum sententia fertur, nullas vires habebit. Si sponte inerit fueritque causa criminalis deponetur, quamvis innocens a seculari iudice iudicetur.' Sicard's *Summa* (1179–81) is wrongly dated 1150 by Lillie, *ubi supra*, p. 275, n. 72.

[1] Vatican Libr., MS. Arch. S. Petro, C. 114, fos. 184vb–186rb: 'quidam excipiunt causam de feudo de quo sive clericus sive laicus conveniat clericum vel laicum, ut dicunt debet eum convenire coram domino feudi, sed non est verum . . . quia et quod observetur in laicos de iure eorum consuetudinario tamen clericus ratione feudi nunquam mutabit forum suum. . . . Interveniente ergo consensu episcopi et clerici potest clericus produci ad civilem iudicem, et hoc dumtaxat in causa civili, nam in criminali, quamvis episcopus consentiat et clericus velit, non debet produci ad secularem iudicem. . . . In nullo ergo casu clericum invitum potest secularis iudex iudicare nisi sit incorrigibilis . . . Sed quicquid lex dicat vel innuat, non credo esse verum nisi essent incorrigibiles . . . Ideo magister subicit illum casum in his tribus capitulis, scilicet cum omnino incorrigibiles et per ecclesiam corrigi non possunt, tunc de licentia ecclesie iudex secularis potest eum capere et coercere. . . . Ergo tunc demum clericus tradendus est si per ecclesiam corrigi non potest, de consuetudine tamen est ut clericus deprehensus in publico et enormi (*MS.*: enormissione) crimine deponatur et statim permittatur vel etiam iubeatur iudici seculari ut eum iudicet et puniat secundum leges humanas; sed hoc potius sit de consuetudine ut ceteri terreantur quam de mero iure canonico; et nota quod clericus depositus ita traditur (*MS.*: dicitur) curie quandoque ut ibi serviat quandoque ut ibi puniatur . . . idem debere suppleri per gladium materialem quod non potest fieri per spiritualem.' In an English context, it is interesting to note that the papal legate Pierleoni reached a compromise agreement with Henry II in 1175/6 on the subject of clerical immunity: Henry agreed to recognize the general principle, and the legate consented to exclude feudal matters and forest offences: Diceto, i. 410; the angry outburst of the author of the *Gesta Regis Henrici II* is worth recording: 'Ecce membrum Sathanae! ecce ipsius Sathanae conductus satelles! qui tam subito factus de pastore raptor, videns lupum venientem fugit et dimisit oves sibi a summo pontifice commissas, pro quarum tutamine missus erat a Romana sede in Angliam' (*Gesta Regis Henrici II*, ed. W. Stubbs (Rolls Ser., 1867), i. 105).

at the close of the century defined the 'curia' in one gloss-layer as an ecclesiastical prison; and limited the 'traditio' to incorrigible clerks in another. According to the same source, a secular judge did not infringe the canon *Si quis suadente* when laying violent hands on a clerk in the circumstances described, since he did so with the consent of the Church.[1]

Starting from a period of meagre comment, even of doubt and uncertainty in some cases, the decretists had gradually worked out a satisfactory and comprehensive theory of clerical privilege, limited only by the discretion of the Church. The strict letter of the law could be neglected in certain circumstances, if the interests of the Church itself were implicated, or when the guilty clerk had shown himself beyond control. In other instances, a departure from true law was conceded in recognition of local custom or exceptional conditions, the basic principle remaining unaffected by such concessions. No single interpretation of the 'traditio curiae' is common to all decretist commentaries, and no less than four variant meanings have been noted in the brief review above. At the same time, the decretists attached no great importance to the theory of the double punishment; and their teachings show that secular intervention was considered reconcilable with a most extreme concept of clerical immunity, provided only that the Church consented, and was not itself constrained in this.

DECRETAL LEGISLATION ON CLERICAL PRIVILEGE

It is hardly necessary for the present study to trace the course of papal legislation dealing with the punishment of criminous clerks in the period following Becket's death. But two decretals have been the subject of much historical comment in connexion with the Becket controversy, and therefore must be briefly mentioned here. It is commonly stated that the first official pronouncement, condemning the secular punishment of degraded felonous clerks because this involved a double penalty, was made in Alexander III's decretal *Licet praeter* (c. 1178) to the archbishop of Salerno. It would be more accurate to describe this as the first extant entry of such a definition in familiar canonical collections, for it cannot be assumed that the doctrine appeared for the first time as an authoritative ruling in that letter. But *Licet praeter* remains important legislatively, since it was the text commonly accepted by canon lawyers for inclusion in their decretal collections; and so it ultimately passed into the Gregorian Decretals of 1234, and became definitive law in this form[2]:

---

[1] Cambridge, Caius Coll. MS. 676, fos. 108va–109vb; fo. 109rb: 'nomine curie hic ergastulum ecclesie designatur; vel hic de incorrigibilibus'; *ibid.*: 'Si ergo iudex secularis comprehendat clericum depositum incorrigibilem, non incidit in canonem illum, Si quis suadente, quia hoc non est violentas manus in eum mittere, si auctoritate ecclesie dico id faciat.'

[2] *Decretales Gregorii IX*, II, 1, 4; Génestal; ii. 20–26. Alexander's ruling is commonly described as the decretal *At si clerici*, but this description is not strictly accurate: *At si clerici* is one of many chapters in the decretal *Licet praeter*; see

Si vero coram episcopo de criminibus de iure confessi sunt, seu legitima probatione convicti, dummodo sint talia crimina, propter quae suspendi debeant vel
deponi, non immerito suspendendi sunt a suis ordinibus, vel ab altaris ministerio
perpetuo removendi . . . sed non debet quemlibet depositum pro suis excessibus,
quum suo sit functus officio, nec duplici debeat ipsum contritione conterere,
iudici tradere saeculari.

The decretal *Novimus expedire*, issued by Innocent III in 1209, has
excited still further comment. In this letter Innocent noted that his
predecessors had spoken diversely on the subject of the 'traditio curiae',
and so to avoid ambiguity he laid down an official definition: the act of
degradation should take place in the presence of the secular officer, who
should be bidden to receive the degraded clerk into his jurisdiction. But
the Church should intervene effectively to ensure that no risk of capital
punishment was involved[1]:

Degradatus, tanquam exutus privilegio clericali saeculari foro per consequentiam
applicetur, quum ab ecclesiastico foro fuerit proiectus; eius est degradatio
celebranda saeculari potestate presente, ac pronunciandum est eidem, quum
fuerit celebrata, ut in suum forum recipiat degradatum, et sic intelligitur tradi
curiae saeculari; pro quo tamen debet ecclesia efficaciter intercedere, ut citra
mortis periculum circa eum sententia moderetur.

This passage has been widely interpreted as an *ex post facto* justification
of Henry II's case against Becket, and as a reversal of the principle defined
by Alexander III in *Licet praeter*; more precisely, it was this letter which
induced Maitland to conceive his imaginative picture of Henry claiming
in anticipation that he could not hope to be a better canonist than Pope
Innocent would be.[2] It must be admitted that Innocent's procedure
closely resembled that desired by Henry II, and the 'traditio' is
certainly defined by him as a delivery to secular jurisdiction; he not only
accepted the presence of a secular officer at the act of degradation, but
laid this down as the correct procedure. With these points conceded, it is
equally evident that there were crucial distinctions between the papal
definition and the English king's intentions: the papal procedure was
dependent on ecclesiastical authority, the offences in question were harmful to the Church's interests, the punishment inflicted should be limited
by ecclesiastical intervention, and the rules which the pope himself
defined were dispensed with by him in this very decretal.[3] It was Henry's
intention that the Clarendon procedure would be made effective by secular
action in both the opening and the closing stages, that the offences dealt

---

Regesta Pontificum Romanorum, ed. P. Jaffé (2nd edn., Leipzig, 1885-8), ii, no.
14091. For other relevant papal rulings, see *Decretales*, II, 1, 8 and 9; and V,
20, 3 and 7.

[1] *Decretales*, V, 40, 27.

[2] Poole, *From Domesday Book to Magna Carta*, p. 206 n. 7; Maitland, pp. 144-5.

[3] *Decretales*, V, 40, 27: the guilty clerk had forged a papal letter, but was not
in fact delivered to secular judgment. Moreover, Innocent's phrase was explicitly 'et sic intelligitur tradi curiae *saeculari*.'

with would be those of chief concern to secular judges, that degradation and delivery should be the automatic and invariable sentence, and that the secular authorities should not be limited by the Church in imposing a penalty. With so many essential differences, it could scarcely be argued persuasively that Henry was as good a canonist as Pope Innocent, since they were speaking of different problems. With a curious lack of perception Maitland failed to realize that, if Innocent's procedure appeared an exception to the essential principle for which Becket fought, it was an exception which the Church had consistently recognized. Nor could it be justly argued that Innocent cancelled or contradicted the decision expressed by Alexander III in *Licet praeter*, since both these rulings were incorporated by Raymond of Peñaforte in the Gregorian Decretals of 1234; and in this way both were accepted as authoritative in canon law.[1]

THE INFLUENCE OF ROMAN LAW ON HENRY II'S PROCEDURE

In a general way the influence of Roman law is clear enough in both the secular and ecclesiastical systems of law in the twelfth century, when the revival of Civilian studies coincided with the scientific development of canon law. The conflict of secular and ecclesiastical authorities in the various European countries, as well as throughout western Christendom generally, can be argued in certain aspects on a basis of the disharmonies existing between these two distinct but related jurisprudential traditions. And within the wider framework the problem of criminous clerks reveals the conflict in miniature. Génestal has traced the impact of Roman and Frankish constitutions on the legal traditions permitting secular action in dealing with felonous clerks in specified conditions.[2] It is well-known that secular constitutions and capitularies dealing with this subject were frequently received by canon lawyers, and incorporated in their collections. In this way, secular doctrines touching on the punishment of criminous clerks were accepted into the traditional *corpus* of ecclesiastical law, complicating the problem from the canonists' viewpoint, and producing a dichotomy in post pseudo-Isidorian collections on the twin subjects of clerical immunity from secular jurisdiction and clerical superiority in Christian society. But it could hardly be claimed that the presence of such secular constitutions in the many unofficial canonical collections gave them authoritative sanction from the Church's point of view.

The relevance of these reflections to the quarrel between Henry II and Becket is greater than may appear at first sight. In the first place, the very notion of the 'traditio curiae' sprang from procedures worked out originally in Roman law; and the canonists at the time of the Becket dispute were well aware of the influence of Civilian concepts in the controversy: both Rufinus and Stephen of Tournai rejected specifically

[1] *Decretales*, II, 1, 4, and V, 40, 27.
[2] Génestal, ii, pp. iii–xx.

the doctrine of the Roman *Authentic* permitting the summons of a sus-pected clerk before a secular magistrate in the first instance: a direct witness of the fact that its authority was appealed to at that time. In the same way, Herbert of Bosham recorded how Henry II's supporters boasted of their skill in either law; and the importance of this comment has been recognized often enough in its canonical setting, but overlooked perhaps as far as its Civilian implications are concerned.

Two Roman texts are of outstanding interest in this connexion: the eighty-third and the one hundred and twenty-third *Novellae* in the *Corpus Iuris Civilis*. The first of these texts is also the eighty-fourth *Authentic* so much discussed by twelfth-century canonists, and defines that, if a bishop is unable to decide a case involving a clerk, the suit should go forward to the secular judges to be decided freely by them, the privileges of clerks being nevertheless protected; but, if the matter is a criminal one, the secular judges should fix a term within which the issue must be decided; and, if the judges determine that the defendant clerk is guilty in such a case, he should be deprived of his office by the bishop, and made subject in this way to the power of the laws. The second *Novella* is even more instructive: if a clerk is accused before his bishop and convicted of crime, he should be deprived of rank or honour by the bishop, and the secular judge may take him, examine him in due legal process, and impose a sentence. But, if the clerk is examined in due form first before the secular magistrate and the accusation proved, the magistrate should set the record before the local bishop. The bishop should then, if he agrees with the justice of the record set before him, deprive the clerk of rank or honour; and the secular judge may then take the clerk and impose a sentence. If, however, the bishop considers the record presented to him an unjust one, he may defer a decision, and with the secular magistrate submit the matter to the emperor's ruling[1]:

Novella LXXXIII: Si tamen de criminibus conveniantur, si quidem civilibus, hic quidam competentes iudices, in provinciis autem harum praesides sint iudices, non transcendente lite mensium duorum spatium ex quo litis contestatio fit, quatenus brevis imponatur causae terminus. Illud palam est, si reum esse putaverit eum qui convenitur provinciae praeses et poena iudicaverit dignum, prius hunc spoliari a Deo amabili episcopo sacerdotali diginitate, et ita sub legum fieri manu.

Novella CXXIII: Si vero crimen fuerit quod adversus quamlibet memo-ratarum reverentissimarum personarum inferatur, si quidem apud episcopum aliquis accusatur et ipse veritatem invenire potuerit, ab honore aut gradu hunc secundum ecclesiasticas regulas eiciat, et tunc competens iudex hunc comprehen-dat et secundum leges litem examinans finem imponat. Si vero prius civilem

---

[1]*Corpus Iuris Civilis: Novellae*, ed. R. Schoell (Berlin, 1895), pp. 409–11: Nov. LXXXIII (Auth. LXXXIV); *ibid.*, pp. 609–11: Nov. CXXIII, c. 21; *The Liber Pauperum of Vacarius*, ed. F. de Zulueta (Selden Soc., 1927), p. 9: Lib. I, Tit. 3, c. 32; E. Caillemer, *Le Droit Civil dans les Provinces Anglo-Normandes au XIIe Siècle* (Paris, 1883), pp. 12–14; Foreville, p. 145. Cf. *Decretum*, C. XI, Qu. 1, c. 18.

iudicem adeat accusator et crimen per legitimam examinationem potuerit approbari, tunc episcopo locorum gesta monumentorum palam faciat, et si ex eis cognoscatur proposita crimina commisisse eum, tunc ipse episcopus hunc secundum regulas ab honore seu gradu quem habet separet, iudex autem ultionem ei inferat legibus congruentem.

It can hardly be doubted that the Roman *Novellae* afforded a far better legal precedent for Henry II's procedure than did the canonical texts in Gratian. The principle of clerical immunity was recognized both in the Roman edicts and in Henry's constitution; and it was conceded in each case that deposition was a necessary preliminary to secular penalties. At the same time, the initiative and final control were retained by the secular authorities; and there was no intention that the procedure described related merely to offences against ecclesiastical authority, or that the secular penalty was imposed as a last resort.

GENERAL CONCLUSIONS

Had Henry II simply claimed that degraded clerks could be delivered to secular judgment in certain cases, his claim would not have conflicted with established canonical theories; and it is obvious that a resemblance existed between his proposals and the treatment of degraded clerks described by Gratian. Moreover, in the short-term background of his quarrel with Becket, support for the legality of the king's intentions is found in the writings of individual commentators, though these are a minority and their works of doubtful provenance. But, if it was Henry's intention that clerks should be dealt with invariably in this fashion, when secular interests were involved, subject to the control of his own officials, and with penalties determined by secular judges (and it is surely indisputable that these were in fact his intentions), then his plan was undoubtedly in conflict with the meaning and spirit of the canons; and, if his procedure was in reality based on the famous texts in canon law most commonly cited in its support, then it was no less certainly a misinterpretation of them.[1]

---

[1] The conclusion suggested here is that Becket's interpretation was canonically the correct one, but it is quite evident that canon lawyers were themselves in disagreement at that time: some held that Becket was an innovator; others that Alexander III did reverse the doctrine found in Gratian. Cf. Cambridge, Caius Coll. MS. 676, fo. 76va: 'Iudex secularis non habet fidem ecclesiastico, ergo nec ecclesiasticus debet habere seculari; sed idem cancellavit beatus Thomas sanguine suo'; an anonymous primitive gloss in the Durham Cathedral MS. C. III. 1, fo. 8vb, inserted 'contra' by the decretal *Licet praeter* (*Ac si clerici* clause), together with a cross-reference to the pseudo-Pius in Gratian. Many other examples of the same kind could be cited. But there is no doubt that the views of some individual canonists were inaccurate: cf. Cambridge, Sidney Sussex Coll. MS. 101, fo. 232va: 'Clericus apud civilem iudicem convictus ab episcopo suo degradandus est, ut sic puniatur a civili iudice, nisi ecclesiasticum sit crimen, ut C. XI, Qu. 1, Si quis'.

But Becket's arguments were, in contrast, a faithful index of the true purpose of the canons and of the broad stream of canonical tradition concerning them, even if his expression was somewhat rigorous and extreme in the emotional circumstances of the bitter dispute in which he was involved. His view of the 'traditio curiae' was historically sounder than the king's, though divergent interpretations and gradual shifts of meaning had produced some confusion on this subject even with canon lawyers, so that it could be truthfully argued that the state of law was itself uncertain at that time. Moreover, his objection to the double punishment involved in the king's procedure was better grounded than has been conceded in the past; and it is perfectly clear that he was not himself the inventor of this doctrine, though there is little doubt that his support won wider recognition for it. Had Becket argued that the Church could in no conceivable circumstances deliver a degraded clerk to secular justice, it would be impossible to reconcile his opinion with familiar canonical tradition either before or after his own involvement in the controversy (though even this hypothesis could not justify in canon law the procedure which Henry II desired); but there is no convincing evidence that so extreme a theory was accepted by him. He did not argue that the rights and privileges of clerks could not be varied at the Church's volition, or if its interests were at stake, for the canons clearly permitted such a procedure, and his own description of the 'traditio curiae' no less envisaged its possible application. He was not concerned in the heat of the controversy with the Church's discretionary use of its own immunities, but with the assertion of the essential basis of those immunities in face of a secularist conception and limitation of them.[1] There is no doubt that Henry's intentions can be supported by excellent and realistic considerations, but these are not easily found in the teachings or traditions of canon lawyers. As far as canonical considerations are concerned, reversing Maitland's judgment, the better opinion was not that of King Henry but that of Becket.

---

[1] Knowles, *Episcopal Colleagues*, p. 66; Irene Ott, 'Der Regalienbegriff im 12 Jahrhundert', *Zeitschrift der Savigny Stiftung für Rechtsgeschichte*, Kan. Abt., lxvi (1948), 234–304; A. Nissl, *Der Gerichsstand des Clerus in Frankischen Reich* (Innsbruck, 1886), pp. 45–6: in Nissl's judgment the struggle between church and state for the power to punish clerks was not a struggle of the state against an already-existing clerical privilege, but one in defence of its old rights fallen partly into abeyance. An argument based on custom had little weight with Becket: 'Invenitur enim Christus aliquando dixisse "Ego sum veritas". Sed numquam dixit "Ego sum consuetudo"'; cf. Génestal, ii. 101, n. 2. In this he was merely repeating the words of Gregory VII in the previous century: see G. Tellenbach, *Church, State and Christian Society*, trans. R. F. Bennett (Oxford, 1948), p. 164, n. 2.

XI

THE RECEPTION OF CANON LAW IN ENGLAND
IN THE LATER-TWELFTH CENTURY

For the purpose of this paper, the title 'The Reception of Canon Law in England in the Later-Twelfth Century' is interpreted in the following sense: the introduction of books of canons and canonical commentaries from the continent into England, together with the composition of canonical works by English canonists and the inter-relations between the canonists of English and continental schools. Three topics have been chosen to illustrate the principal themes of this study: firstly, the evidence of canonical sources in one of the most familiar records of the Becket dispute; secondly, the inter-relationship of English and continental decretal collections, with special reference to the influence of continental collections in England, to complement the converse emphasis in recent publications; and, thirdly, the work of English decretists in the closing decade of the century, as seen in the glosses on Gratian's *Decretum* in the Caius College, Cambridge, MS 676.

I. The Becket Dispute: William of Canterbury and Clerical Privilege

Any interpretation of the conflict between Henry II and Becket, favorable to the archbishop in its canonical setting, is sure of an unwelcome reception by many historians. So deeply-rooted is this continuing antipathy to Becket's stand, that it is useful to say something briefly on its complex nature. At the highest level of consideration, Becket's arguments are seen as too extreme, inconsiderate of other legitimate interests, somewhat unrealistic in the circumstances of the time, passing beyond the limits of what the Church had itself laid down in theory, certainly beyond the limits which had previously been accepted in practice. So many historians of integrity and learning have accepted one or other of these arguments that their conclusions demand respect and stimulate a re-appraisal of every aspect of the question. But, at a lower level, the canonical arguments are ruled out of court at the outset, and mentioned with condescension as matters of 'merely academic interest.' Such an attitude reduces to nonsense the conflict in its original setting, prejudges the issues in favor of the ultimately triumphant secular viewpoint, and cancels totally the ideological justification of one of the two conflicting systems. Bereft of its canonical basis, Becket's stand is devoid of meaning. It is not necessary, however, for historians to decide objectively on the respective merits of the claims of archbishop and king; it would in any event be impossible to adjudicate in any absolute sense between the two contestants, for each can be justified from his appropriate viewpoint. It is important rather to understand the thought processes, as well as the material interests, which governed and moulded the divergent theories. And for this reason an examination of the conflict retains its significance.

The canonical basis of Becket's defense of clerical immunity has recently been rediscussed, leading to the following principal conclusions: that Henry II had little justification (if any) in canon law for his proposals for dealing with criminous clerks; that Becket's response to the King was better grounded in canon law than has sometimes been conceded in the past; and that Becket was certainly not the inventor of canonical arguments so frequently attributed to him.[1] If further support for these conclusions is still required, a few selected examples may serve in illustration: a letter of Archbishop Theobald to Pope Adrian IV in 1156 records one instance of conflicting claims of jurisdiction over archdeacon Osbert of York, retracing the origins of this case into Stephen's reign;[2] a letter of John of Poitiers to Becket in 1163 reveals the introduction of the wider jurisdictional issues into Henry II's continental lands with the arrival of royal mandates 'of unheard-of harshness,' independently of any personal quarrel between the king and Becket in England.[3] On the theory of the double judgment, or double punishment, to which Becket objected, a single *dictum* in Gratian's *Decretum* (*c.* 1140/1), following many earlier sources, links the two phrases 'non iudicabit Deus bis in idipsum' and 'super quos non consurget duplex tribulatio', though not with reference to the problem of conflicting jurisdictional claims;[4] but John of Salisbury applied the latter almost verbatim to the problem of felonious clerks in his *Policraticus*, dedicated to the Chancellor Becket in 1159;[5] and Herbert of Bosham again linked both phrases in the context of the Becket dispute in

---

[1] C. Duggan, 'The Becket Dispute and the Criminous Clerks,' BIHR 35 (1962) 1-28.

[2] W. J. Millor and H. E. Butler, edd., revised by C. N. L. Brooke, *The Letters of John of Salisbury* I (Nelson's Medieval Texts; 1955) 26-7; see also *ibid.* xxxvi, 42, 43, 92, 97, 98, 138, 139 and 261.

[3] J. C. Robertson and J. B. Sheppard, edd., *Materials for the History of Thomas Becket*, (Rolls Series, 7 vols.) V (1881) 37-41.

[4] *Decretum Gratiani: de poen.* D. 3 d.p. c.42: 'Non iudicabit Deus bis in idipsum, de his tantum intelligi oportet, quos praesentia supplicia in melius commutant, super quos non consurget duplex tribulatio.' The two phrases are often in fact discovered together in earlier works, but not in connexion with the criminous clerks dispute.

[5] C. C. I. Webb, ed., *Joannis Saresberiensis Episcopi Carnotensis Policratici sive de nugis curialium* II (Oxford 1909) 788: ' . . . . eo quidem perpetuo optinente ut ob eandem causam non consurgat in eum duplex tribulatio.'

his retrospective narrative.[6] The wisdom or validity of the 'double judgment' theory is not under consideration here, but simply its origin and development independently of Becket's initiative. Again, the *Summa* of Rufinus, completed at Bologna *c.* 1157-9, is sometimes cited to prove that Henry II's proposals for dealing with criminous clerks were supported by the leading contemporary canonists, but Génestal argued long ago, surely correctly, that in Rufinus' judgment the secular action was subject to the Church's consent.[7] As far as Rufinus is concerned, the most striking point of interest in an English context has so far been overlooked: this conflict of claims of jurisdiction over felonious clerks was a problem already vexing the foremost Italian canonists by 1159 at the latest, and the variant interpretations in their canonical, civilian and feudal frameworks were already set side by side in their decretist commentaries.[8] Becket was not an original thinker: his greatness from the Church's viewpoint lay in his strength of character and singleness of purpose, not in any original or inventive cast of mind. The doctrines which he advanced, and for which he died, were formulated and familiarized before his own involvement in the controversy. In a more restricted and insular setting, Becket evoked an echo of Gregory VII's life and doctrines.[9] The principles for which he stood had already long been called into question.

The most frustrating hindrance to a final evaluation of Becket's support for the principle of clerical immunity is the absence of an official record, complete in terms and strictly contemporary in composition. The proposals of Henry II for dealing with criminous clerks are preserved in the third clause of the chirograph of the Constitutions of Clarendon of 1164, expressed in terms of well-known ambiguity.[10] But Becket's arguments, in contrast, though found in numerous versions, remain in derivation only, second-hand at best, with the inevitable risk of *ex post facto* reconstructions. Yet among these records the *Vita et Passio S. Thome* of William of Canterbury remains of outstanding and unique importance: this is the work among the many familiar Becket sources which preserves the most professional canonical argument, complete with texts and expounded in technical phraseology.[11] The date and provenance of William's work has been much discussed. The established

---

[6] *Becket Materials* III (1877) 281: 'Et quod adhuc poenalis servitutis accedit cumulo, contra Domini in propheta mandatum clerici bis iudicabuntur in idipsum, et duplex eorum consurget tribulatio.'

[7] Rufinus, ed. Singer 306-12, esp. 307; R. Génestal, *Le Privilegium fori en France* II (Paris 1924) 16-17.

[8] Duggan, *Becket Dispute* 19-20.

[9] For a striking instance of this, cf. *ibid.* 28 n.1.

[10] A full discussion of the Constitutions is given by Herbert of Bosham: *Becket Materials* III 279-84 and 288.   [11] *Ibid.* I (1875) 25-9.

details of his career make it most unlikely that he was a first-hand witness of the events of 1164; but he was certainly a monk of Christ Church on Becket's return from exile, undoubtedly in Becket's circle or company in the period immediately before the murder, and therefore familiar with the archbishop's mind at the time of the final crisis.[12] A single manuscript preserves the complete *Vita et passio*, transcribed much later than the original composition; the manuscript itself belonged in the later-fourteenth century to William of Wykeham, from whom it passed into the possession of Winchester College, its present owners.[13] The relationship of William's work with the other surviving accounts of Becket's life and death has been subjected to meticulous scrutiny by many scholars: Robertson, Magnússon, Morris, Dom A. L'Huillier, Halphen, Walberg and Foreville, to mention the more familiar.[14] And the result of their studies at present suggests that the *Vita et passio* occupies an important place as one of the earliest and independent *Lives* of Becket, that it stood to one side of the principal manuscript transmissions of Becket sources, and was composed in all probability within the limits 1172-4, within a very few years of the archbishop's death.[15] But the strictly canonical matter in William's work has not been examined in comparable detail.

---

[12] For William of Canterbury, see *ibid.* I xxvi-xxx; E. Magnússon, *Thomas Saga Erkibyskups* (Rolls Series, 2 vols) II (1883) lxxxv-lxxxvii; D. Knowles, *The Episcopal Colleagues of Archbishop Thomas Becket* (Cambridge 1951) 70 n.

[13] Winchester College MS 4: 422 pp., 12 × 8 1/4″, double cols.; gatherings mostly of 8 fols., numbered in sequence at bottom of final fol. verso, with catchwords; neat hands, with many corrections of text and rubrics, some of the rubric corrections in black; very slight marginalia but frequent marginal 'nota' at significant passages; many decorated initial letters, with varying degrees of elaboration: large initial letters at the beginning of each major section, and an illuminated representation of Becket on p. 2ᵇ; probably thirteenth-century hand; the volume was rebound in 1951. I am indebted to Mr. J. M. G. Blakiston, Librarian of Winchester College, for his great kindness in making possible my use of this MS. A related MS, from Clairvaux, is now found at Montpellier, but reliable information on this is not yet available: Montpellier École de Médecine MS 2.

[14] J. C. Robertson, *Becket Materials* I (1875): *Vita et Passio S. Thomae, auctore Willelmo monacho Cantuariensi*, xxx; Magnússon, *Thomas Saga* II (1883) lxxxv-lxxxvii; John Morris, *The Life and Death of Saint Thomas Becket, Archbishop of Canterbury* (2nd ed. London 1885) xviii-xix; Dom A. L'Huillier, *Saint Thomas de Cantorbéry* (2 vols. Paris 1891) I 418-20; M. L. Halphen, 'Les biographes de Thomas Becket,' *Revue historique* 52 (1909) 35-45; E. Walberg, *La tradition hagiographique de Saint Thomas Becket avant la fin du XIIᵉ siècle* (Paris 1929) 122-4; R. Foreville, *L'Église et la Royauté en Angleterre sous Henri II Plantagenet* (Paris 1943) xxv-xxxii. My thanks are due to Miss Anne Heslin for advice on the narrative sources of Becket's life; Miss Heslin is preparing a study on the MS transmission of the Becket correspondence.

[15] Cf. n. 14, above: for the date of composition, Robertson suggested 1174 or later; Magnússon, 1174-6; Halphen, after 1172; and Walberg, 1172-4. On quite independent evidence, the present study tends to confirm the earlier dates: cf. n. 21, below.

William's account of the discussion between Henry II and Becket on the subject of clerical immunity begins with a brief statement of the king's alleged proposals that clerks guilty of specified crimes should be drawn to secular judgment so that, after confession or conviction, they should be deprived of office and delivered to the secular court.[16] Against this, the archbishop, after considering the appropriate competence of secular and ecclesiastical judges, argued that the secular power had no jurisdiction over ecclesiastical criminal matters. His thesis is then supported by a long series of canonical texts dealing with various aspects of the question and problems arising from it; the canons themselves are linked together by a parallel series of brief comments: identifications, definitions or elaborations; and the record is completed with a re-statement of the archbishop's objections to the king's proposals, including his familiar attack on the double penalty which the proposals entailed. The account is presented as Becket's argument in the debate at Clarendon in 1164. But, setting aside the introductory and concluding phrases, the record thus briefly described falls neatly into two main elements: the canonical texts and the linking or connecting phrases. There can be no doubt that the texts themselves were acquired from a canonical codex, and little doubt that this was Gratian's *Decretum*: with a single exception all are readily found in the *Decretum*, and almost exclusively in the first *questio* of *Causa* 11, where Gratian dealt with these problems most directly; the extant manuscript actually opens the discussion with a canonical rubric.[17] On the other hand, not all the canons are found in Ivo's collections, the only alternative feasible source for the period; and therefore the use of Gratian's work as the source book can be confidently accepted. It has long been known that Gratian's *Decretum* was used in England from the late 1150's and provided the textual basis for some at least of the arguments recorded in the Becket dispute.[18] On this point, therefore, William's account does not increase existing knowledge, though it exemplifies the development with unusual precision. The linking phrases are far more significant.

The connecting or linking phrases are in many instances verbatim transcripts from Rufinus' *Summa*: the definition of 'crimen forense' and the dictum that the canons deal more mercifully with clerks than does the secular law on such a matter; the pre-requisite of episcopal permission if a clerk is

---

[16] Winchester MS 4, p. 20ª; *ed. cit.* 25. The full text is printed in Appendix A, below.

[17] Winchester MS 4, p. 20ª: 'Quod clericus non est trahendus ad seculare iudicium'; Robertson omitted to mention that this sentence is rubricated in the MS.

[18] John of Salisbury's knowledge of the *Decretum* is discussed by Z. N. Brooke, *The English Church and the Papacy* (Cambridge 1931) 110-12; and by C. N. L. Brooke, in *Letters of John of Salisbury* I xx, 99, 157, 231 *et passim*. See also A. Saltman, *Theobald Archbishop of Canterbury* (University of London Historical Studies 2; 1956) 125 and 176.

to be subjected to a secular penalty; the proviso that a clerk may not be subjected unwillingly to secular judgment, even with episcopal consent; the ruling that a secular judgment against an unwilling clerk is devoid of force: such points compose the greater substance of the phrases connecting the canonical texts in a continuous exposition. Their textual similarity, amounting in some passages to identity, with the corresponding sections in Rufinus' *Summa* is so close that their dependence on the latter may be accepted as proven, and is demonstrated at length in an appendix to this essay.[19] It is obvious from this evidence that William's version of Becket's argument is a conflation of the relevant canons in Gratian's *Decretum* and Rufinus' commentary on them. If it were certain that William's account preserves a faithful transcription of the thesis advanced by Becket in 1164, as he asserted, it would be a most striking witness of the use in England of the most advanced canonical works of that time. But William was not present at Clarendon when the issue was argued, and his exactly documented version is preserved in no other surviving manuscript; and therefore its authenticity is called, at least to some extent, into question. On the other hand, it is well known that Becket continued his canonical studies with zeal while in exile at Pontigny, and it is established that several canonists, including Italians, were found in his *familia*.[20] If not earlier, the work of Rufinus was doubtless familiar to him during that period; and, if not his original argument, William's version may well preserve its final elaboration. But so exact is the correspondence between this record in the *Vita et passio* and the relevant passages of both Gratian and Rufinus that it was almost certainly composed with the canonical manuscripts open before its author. Who the original author may have been

---

[19] Appendix A, below: William's version follows the text of Rufinus very closely, with minor modifications to suit his narrative; thus, where Rufinus has 'Denique notandum est quod cum clericus apud non suum iudicem convenitur, 'etc., William has 'Denique perpendit archiepiscopus quod cum clericus apud non suum iudicem convenitur, 'etc. In this context, Génestal cited Rufinus and William of Canterbury on adjacent pages, but failed to notice their interrelation: *op. cit.* II 102-3. At the same time it should be noted that William's text omits those passages in Rufinus which permit the *traditio curiae* in certain circumstances, possibly because these might appear to weaken the archbishop's case; cf. Duggan, *Becket Dispute* 19-20. Rufinus clearly experienced some difficulty in dealing with the relevant canons in Gratian; notice the most interesting comment: 'si adeo horrendum crimen fuerit, spoliabitur proprie dignitatis officio et dimittetur post hec, a seculari iudice secundum leges publicas puniendus. Quod videtur quodammodo conici ex sensu illius capituli *Statuimus* et item ex illo capitulo *Si quis sacerdotum*' (ed. Singer 309); cf. C. 11 q. 1 cc. 31 and 18.

[20] These matters are already discussed in many works; see, for example, Knowles, *Episcopal Colleagues* 148, referring to Becket's canonical studies under Lombard of Piacenza at Pontigny. Knowles suggests that it was there that Becket probably acquired his familiarity with Gratian.

remains at present a matter of mere conjecture: at the earliest extreme, it is conceivable that William's version preserves in fact the argument advanced at Clarendon by Becket; at the latest extreme, it is possible that William invented the argument for the first time in his record; it is no less feasible that he derived his material from an intermediary source devised between these limits.[21] It is possible therefore that Becket never advanced the defense of clerical privilege in the precise form which William of Canterbury attributed to him. But the importance of the record for the history of canon law in England is only very slightly reduced as a consequence. For it seems established beyond dispute that Becket's case was argued by one of his acquaintance on a basis of the most influential canonical commentary of the time, and completed at the latest within a very few years of the archbishop's martyrdom.

II. ENGLISH AND CONTINENTAL DECRETAL COLLECTIONS

No instrument was more effective in bringing the latest rules of canon law into the provinces of the Western Church in the later-twelfth century, or in bearing witness to the general recognition of papal jurisdictional authority, than the papal letter. An ever-swelling stream of confirmations and rulings of all kinds flowed out from the Curia to almost every part of the Church at that time: privileges, mandates, judicial commissions and decretal letters. The many thousands of items listed in the *Regesta pontificum Romanorum*, supplemented by the more recent volumes of the Göttingen *Papsturkunden* and the hundreds of decretal letters rediscovered in long-neglected decretal collections, provide ample confirmation for this truth.[22] The English Church, no less than any other, shared in this development, but it was in the receipt and codification of papal decretals that English canonists made their most original contribution.

The broad outlines of the emergence of the decretal collections to an important place in canonical history are sufficiently known and need no lengthy re-description. Starting from the most rudimentary beginnings in the

---

[21] Cf. n. 15, above. The canonical matter is unlikely to have been interpolated in William's *Vita* much later than these suggested limits: the decretist commentaries coming rapidly to hand from the early 1170's would have provided a forger with far more decisive arguments to support his case: notice especially Johannes Faventinus (*post* 1171), Simon of Bisignano (1177-9) and so forth: see Duggan, *Becket Dispute* 20-3.

[22] P. Jaffé, ed., *Regesta Pontificum Romanorum*, 2 vols. (2nd ed. 1885 and 1888); W. Holtzmann, *Papsturkunden in England* (3 vols. Abh. Gesellsch. [Akad.] Göttingen, N. F. 25, Dritte F. 14-15, 33; 1930, 1935 and 1953), and similar vols. for other parts of the Western Church, by P. Kehr, etc; W. Holtzmann, 'Über eine Ausgabe der päpstlichen Dekretalen des 12. Jahrhunderts,' *Nachr. Akad. Göttingen* (1945) 15-36.

mid-1170's, the decretal collectors by degrees worked out a satisfactory method of codifying the latest canonical doctrines and judicial rulings, defined for the most part in contemporary or recent papal letters: a technical process completed with the publication of Bernard of Pavia's *Breviarium extravagantium*, or *Compilatio prima, c.* 1190/1.[23] Exactly how this juristically acceptable pattern was achieved can be traced in the many unofficial decretal collections made in the intervening period: more than fifty are known at present, recording almost every stage of technical growth, and these are classified in two main groups as 'primitive' or 'systematic' according to their level of juristic competence, the latter incorporating the device of individual decretal dissection as well as the division of the whole work into books or titles.[24]

The twelfth-century decretal collections, both primitive and systematic, are of exceptional interest for the historians of the English Church. Not only do they reveal the very large number of permanently important decretals received by English ecclesiastics, but they establish beyond dispute the formative role which English canonists played in decretal codification at its most creative period.[25] It may now be taken as proven that no mere freak of chance entails that a clear majority of all surviving primitive collections are of English provenance; and it is no less well established that English collections left their mark on many collections of continental authorship.[26] The fact of this English initiative has been explored in recent studies, from which it is clear that the canonists in the circles of several distinguished English prelates, supporters for the most part of Becket in the jurisdictional conflict, played an original role in recording for professional use the decretal letters which they themselves received.[27] It seems certain that their frequent commissions as papal judges delegate stimulated an interest in this work, in a striking illustration of the effective application of canon law in England in the decade following Becket's death. Their earliest collections are English in every sense of the description: the decretals themselves were almost exclusively received in England; their codification and transcription were the work of English collectors and of English *scriptoria*; it is only in the secondary stages of compilation that the influence of comparable works by continental canonists is detected.[28] But, in contrast with this, the primitive collections of the French

---

[23] Holtzmann and E. W. Kemp, *Papal Decretals relating to the Diocese of Lincoln in the Twelfth Century* (Lincoln Record Society 47; 1954) ix-xvii; *Compilatio prima* ed. Friedberg, *Quinque Compilationes* 1-65; individual collections are discussed *sub nominibus* in Kuttner, *Repertorium*; the subject is now rediscussed in my *Twelfth-Century Decretal Collections and their Importance in English History* (University of London Historical Studies 12; 1963).

[24] Duggan, *Decretal Collections* 45-65.

[25] *Ibid.* 118-24 *et passim.*   [26] *Ibid.* 124-35.

[27] *Ibid.* 118-24 and 149-51.   [28] *Ibid.* 66-117, esp. 76-8, 92-5, 110-17, etc.

and Roman/Spanish families reflect only slightly a similar local initiative, revealing very markedly in many instances their direct assimilation of decretals from the English works.[29]

This highly significant English contribution to canonical history can be traced from the mid-1170's in such simple short works as the Worcester II and Belvoir Collections, and continued with increasing technical skill to the end of the century, recording in the process many stages of growth in the so-called 'English', 'Bridlington' and 'Worcester' families; and culminating in the systematic compilations of the Anglo-Norman school: Tanner and the St. Germain and Avranches Collections.[30] The interlocking of English and continental sources is apparent at an early stage of development, revealing a mutual interchange of material by c. 1179 at the latest.[31] If it is accepted that the *Appendix Concilii Lateranensis* (c. 1181-5), a fountain-head in the main systematic transmission, is also in fact of English authorship, both the exchange of material between the schools and the formative role of the English canonists are further supported in a most interesting way.[32]

Now, it was stated above that the earliest English collections show little trace of continental influence: in the so-called 'English' family, the Worcester II Collection (*post* 1175) contains no more than ten decretals, of which all but one are of English provenance;[33] the Belvoir Collection (about the same date of composition) includes three small blocks of decretals, making a total of twenty-seven items in all, in which only a single item bears a continental inscription, and that is Norman;[34] the primary component of the Canterbury Collection (1179-81) is made up of sixty-two chapters, of which no more than seven were received by continental prelates;[35] the collections of the 'Bridlington' family depend on an archetype (c. 1181), now lost, of whose opening fifty items no more than three were of non-English origin.[36] A similar pattern can be discovered in almost all the earliest English collections in their first

---

[29] *Ibid.* 124-35.

[30] For the English primitive families, see *ibid.* 66-117; for the systematic Anglo-Norman collections, see Holtzmann and Kemp, *op. cit.* xiv-xv. See also H. Singer, *Neue Beiträge über die Dekretalensammlungen vor und nach Bernhard von Pavia* (Sb. Akad. Vienna 171.1; 1913): pp. 68-354 for the St. Germain Collection, and 355-400 for the Avranches Collection; and Holtzmann, 'Die Dekretalensammlungen des 12. Jahrhunderts: 1. Die Sammlung Tanner,' *Festschrift zur Feier des 200jährigen Bestehens der Akad. Göttingen* (1951) 83-145.

[31] Duggan, *Decretal Collections* 134-5.

[32] *Idem*, 'English Canonists and the *Appendix Concilii Lateranensis*; with an Analysis of the St. John's College, Cambridge, MS 148,' *Traditio* 18 (1962) 459-68; *idem, Decretal Collections* 135-9.

[33] *Decretal Collections* 46 and 69-70; analysis: 152-4.

[34] *Ibid.* 46-7 and 69-73; analysis: 155-62.

[35] *Ibid.* 73-6; analysis: 162-73.   [36] *Ibid.* 84-95, esp. 91-4.

recensions. But in their secondary phases the insular matter is expanded with letters from abroad: the Rochester Collection (1179-81 to 1193) is dependent on one source in common with the Canterbury Collection, but its concluding forty-eight items, appended to the 'Canterbury' stock, include no less than twenty-three received by continental ecclesiastics;[37] the 'Bridlington' archetype (c. 1181) records only ten non-English inscriptions in its opening ninety-four chapters, in contrast with eight in the concluding thirteen;[38] the Claudian Collection (1185-7) expanded the 'Bridlington' archetype from several different sources, including a book of marriage decretals, of whose thirty items at least twenty-three were of continental origin.[39] The Worcester Collection (c. 1181), in the 'Worcester' family, is of special significance: in its extant form it is so clearly of English provenance that its connections with Baldwin (successively archdeacon of Exeter, abbot of Ford, bishop of Worcester and archbishop of Canterbury) have been conclusively established;[40] but lying behind the collection is the 'Worcester' archetype (c. 1181) in which the intermingling of English and continental sources is clearly revealed in Lohmann's analysis: in Book I, containing marriage decretals, an unbroken sequence of eleven decretals with continental inscriptions is discovered.[41] Once more the pattern is clear enough: the English collections, though dependent at first on insular records, quickly afforced the native resources with further matter from the continental families. The influence of the continental collections on the early English works was not as great as the reverse movement at that stage, but it is clear and significant. It remains to examine in greater detail the relevant sequences of continental decretals in the English collections to identify, where possible, the collections on which the English canonists drew. For this purpose, comparison is possible with the printed analyses of the Cambridge, Paris I and Orval Collections of the French school, with the Tortosa and Eberbach Collections of the Roman/Spanish School, and with the Berlin Collection of the Italian school.[42] Unfortunately, the Italian col-

---

[37] *Ibid.* 76-8; analysis: 173-87.   [38] *Ibid.* 92.

[39] *Ibid.* 89-91 and 93-4.

[40] Duggan, 'The Trinity Collection of Decretals and the Early Worcester Family,' *Traditio* 17 (1961) 506-26; *idem, Decretal Collections* 110-17: 'Baldwin of Ford and the Worcester Collection'; Kuttner and E. Rathbone, 'Anglo-Norman Canonists of the Twelfth Century,' *Traditio* 7 (1949-51) 282-3; the analysis of the Worcester Collection is by H. Lohmann, 'Die Collectio Wigorniensis,' ZRG Kan. Abt. 22 (1933) 36-187; the MS is British Museum MS Royal 10 A. II, fols. 5-62.

[41] Cf. Lohmann, *Wig.* 1.18-28.

[42] For details of continental primitive collections, see Holtzmann, *Nachrichten* 21-2; *idem* and Kemp, *op. cit.* xi-xii; Duggan, *Decretal Collections* 124-35. For analyses of individual collections, see Friedberg, *Die Canonessammlungen*: Cambridge Collection, 5-21, and Paris I Collection, 45-63; Holtzmann, 'Beiträge zu den Dekretalensammlungen des zwölften

lections *Duacensis, Cusana, Floriana* and *Ambrosiana* are not yet available in completed analyses, but significant collation with them is possible on a basis of Holtzmann's supplements (*Kanonistische Ergänzungen*) to the *Italia pontificia*.[43]

The opening book of the Worcester Collection, comprising fifty-six items in all, contains twenty-two letters with continental inscriptions, of which thirteen are found, in whole or in part, in the Paris I Collection in this order: 180-1, 145ab, 107, 137, 79a-c=85A, 77=88, 96, 138, 133, 157ab, 97, 21-9 and 168;[44] over the more restricted area of ten of these items included in Holtzmann's *Kanonistische Ergänzungen*, all but one of the decretals in the Worcester Collection are found in the Italian *Cusana* as follows: 180, 18, 159, 204, 122, 203, 165, 133 and 63;[45] and, of these, eight are also found in the Cambridge Collection in this sequence: 89, 78, 93BC=81, 87, 46, 91, 94=48, and 75.[46] In the Rochester Collection, the final forty-seven items include fourteen continental decretals listed in *Kanonistische Ergänzungen*; and, of these, no less than ten are found also in *Cusana* in the order: 180, 203, 160, 161, 20=16, 159, 180, 164, 206 and 204. The relationship between the continental derivative in the Rochester Collection and *Cusana* is therefore very striking;[47] but there is also a lesser degree of correspondence between the Rochester Collection and the French family, most notably in the Cambridge Collection in the following items: 91, 47, 3b, 81=93BC, 89, 87 and 75.[48] It is perhaps most probable that the English and French collections alike were dependent here on Italian sources. Again, the continental block of marriage decretals in the Claudian Collection has only five of its opening eighteen letters

---

Jahrhunderts', ZRG Kan. Abt. 16 (1927): Tortosa Collection, 39-77, and Orval Collection, 77-115; *idem*, 'Die Collectio Eberbacensis,' *ibid.* 17 (1928), 548-55; J. Juncker, 'Die Collectio Berolinensis,' *ibid.* 13 (1924), 284-426. The most recent discussion of the Italian Family is by Holtzmann, 'Zu den Dekretalen bei Simon von Bisignano,' *Traditio* 18 (1962) 450-59.

[43] Holtzmann, 'Kanonistische Ergänzungen zur Italia Pontificia,' *Quellen und Forschungen* 37 (1957) 55-102 and 38 (1958) 67-175; publ. also separately as book (Halle 1958). Subsequent references to *Kanonistische Ergänzungen* in the present essay are to items, according to their consecutive numeration in these two articles and the book.

[44] For Worcester Collection, see Lohmann, *Wig.* 1.3, 10, 12, 15, 18-28, 32, 36, 38-42 and 45; for Paris I, see Friedberg, *Canonessammlungen, sub numeris.*

[45] The *Cusana* references correspond with *Kanonistische Ergänzungen* 191, 186, 105, 218, 21, 35, 176, 132 and 133; and with *Wig.* 1.3, 18, 22, 23, 24, 25, 28, 38 and 40.

[46] Cf. *Wig.* 1.3, 18, 22, 23, 24, 25, 28 and 36.

[47] For Rochester Collection, see Duggan, *Decretal Collections* 76-8 and 173-87; the *Cusana* references correspond with Rochester items 107, 109, 115, 116, 124, 127, 137, 139, 147 and 148; and with *Kanonistische Ergänzungen* 191c, 35, 29, 28, 57, 105, 191a, 150, 217bc and 218.

[48] Cf. Rochester Collection, 109, 116, 126, 137, 138 and 149; and *Kanon. Ergänz.* 35, 28, 195b, 105, 191a, 150 and 167.

in common with the *Kanonistische Ergänzungen*; so little collation with the Italian collections is possible at present in this instance; but three of the five letters appear significantly in *Cusana* as items 203, 204 and 133;[49] on the other hand, seven of the Claudian letters are found in Paris I as items 145ab, 107, 168, 157, 82 and 156;[50] and five appear in the Cambridge Collection as 91, 87, 75, 77=78, and 156.[51] Much detailed collation and further analysis remain to be done, but this preliminary survey justifies the following conclusions: both the Italian and the French collections were used by English collectors in the primitive phases; this use is established in English collections by *c.* 1179-81 at the latest; the Italian *Cusana* (or a close relation) appears more than any other extant collection to have been accessible to English collectors; but there are interconnections between all the schools, both English and continental, and the continental parents of the primitive French collections also played their part in shaping the English works.

In proportion as the most primitive phases of decretal codification were left behind, the use of local records and the interrelations between regional schools became obscured. The imposition of a pattern of composition based on a juristic analysis of the contents of the collections broke up the blocks of letters drawn from local archives. But the continuance of exchange between the English and continental schools is clear enough. The principal systematic collections left their traces on collections assembled in England to the end of the century: occasionally an early copy of a systematic collection survives from the twelfth century in an English manuscript. And, conversely, the English and Anglo-Norman collections, primitive and systematic, continued to play their part in amassing a corpus of decretal law disseminated through the schools of the Western Church. By way of illustration of these claims: the Cottonian and Peterhouse Collections (*post* 1193) of the 'Worcester' family reveal the most advanced English collections of the primitive type influenced by important strands of transmission in the systematic tradition;[52] the Anglo-Norman systematic collections Tanner and the St. Germain and Avranches Collections record still more strikingly the intermingling of English and continental material towards the close of the century;[53] a copy of the Frankfurt Collection in the British Museum clearly discloses a systematic col-

---

[49] The Claudian Collection is British Museum MS Cotton Claudius A. IV, fols. 189-216; the individual items are numbered in the MS; *Claud.* 124, 125, 126, 130 and 132 = *Kanon. Ergänz.* 35, 218, 40, 167 and 132; *Claud.* 124, 125 and 132 = *Cusana* 203, 204 and 133. Cf. Duggan, *Decretal Collections*, 84-95

[50] The Paris I items correspond with *Claud.* 123, 128, 130, 131 and 137, 138 and 156.

[51] Cf. *Claud.*, 124, 125, 130, 135 and 139.

[52] Duggan, *Decretal Collections* 95 and 103-110; cf. Comparative Table, *ibid.* 189-91.

[53] Cf. n. 30, above; Holtzmann and Kemp, *op. cit.* xiv-xv.

lection of probable continental origin expanded from an English source;[54] if the authorship of the seminal *Appendix Concilii Lateranensis* is still in doubt, yet there is no doubt about the English provenance of the Lincoln version of it with its appended letters of indubitable Anglo-Norman provenance.[55] But the most striking instance of all is perhaps the 'Cheltenham' Collection in the primitive 'Worcester' family: this 'Cheltenham' Collection is dependent for a major part of its contents on an early derivative of the 'Worcester' family archetype (*c.* 1181), but it is expanded from various sources down to 1193; its opening sixteen items were taken from a systematic collection in the Bamberg-Leipzig tradition, following very closely the arrangement of the Leipzig Collection itself.[56] The use by English canonists, in the closing decade of the century, of collections in their insular traditions together with a very mature collection of the continental systematic transmission could hardly be more clearly demonstrated than by this example. With the turn of the century a new phase opened in the history of the English collectors; their interest in this work continued as before, but now their most significant contribution was made in a different setting; the famous collections of Gilbert and Alan, and the still more influential *Compilatio secunda* of John the Welshman, were made in Italy and less dependently on the traditions of the regional schools.[57] The most striking English contribution to decretal codification was therefore integrated directly within the central tradition from that time.

III. The Glossators of the Caius College, Cambridge, MS 676

There is no need to traverse again the ground so ably covered by Professor Kuttner and Dr. Rathbone in disclosing the extent and variety of Anglo-Norman canonical interests in the late-twelfth century.[58] Their study marks a turning point for English historians of canon law, and a stimulation to many scholars to press further many of the lines of enquiry on which they briefly touched: the literary as well as the already familiar practical interests of

---

[54] *Ibid.* xiv; Duggan, *Decretal Collections* 195 and plate VIII; cf. British Museum MS Egerton 2901.

[55] Lincoln Cathedral MS 121; cf. Duggan, *English Canonists* 461-2.

[56] *Idem, Decretal Collections* 95 and 98-103; these claims are fully supported in Appendix B, below: Analyses and Comparative Tables.

[57] But see Kuttner and Rathbone, *Anglo-Norman Canonists* 339, for the suggestion that Alanus relied on the tradition of collections in the St. Germain group. For Gilbert and Alanus, see R. von Heckel, 'Die Dekretalensammlungen des Gilbertus und Alanus,' ZRG Kan. Abt. 29 (1940); for John the Welshman, see Friedberg, *Quinque Compilationes*, 66-104; cf. Holtzmann and Kemp, *op. cit.* xv-xvi.

[58] Kuttner and Rathbone, *Anglo-Norman Canonists* 279-358

English canonists; their connections with the Rhineland schools as well as the French and Italian; the careers of significant individuals like Gerard Pucelle and Master Honorius; the work of the English canonists in the circle of John of Tynemouth; these and many similar topics provide a more certain foundation for historians to build on in the future. For the present report, the so-called Oxford School of canonists in the circle of John of Tynemouth and its connections with the Caius College, Cambridge, MS 676 afford the basis for a more substantial evaluation.

The Caius MS is a twelfth-century transcription of Gratian's *Decretum* with numerous marginal glosses inserted in several independent stages down to the close of the century. A number of separate layers of gloss comment are readily identified in these additions, both physically from the obvious differences of hands in their writing, and substantially from the differing and sometimes contradictory interpretations which they contain. In some instances at least four distinct hands can be identified in a single margin and two separate hands are seen at times within a single paragraph;[59] and, in addition to these twelfth-century insertions, many folios bear a further gloss stratum of a later period. Moreover, in addition to the various gloss layers palpably revealed in the physical appearance of the manuscript, the work of several canonists is often integrated within one paragraph transcribed by a single hand. We have here a perfect illustration of the work of a school of English decretists, passing through several hands within the space of a very few years: many glosses reveal a knowledge of Huguccio's teaching (*c.* 1188-90);[60] and, although no pontiff later than Gregory VIII (1187) has so far been positively identified by name in the glosses,[61] there is one reference to a letter of Celestine III, of 17 June 1193;[62] research has so far disclosed no use of Bernard of Pavia's *Compilatio prima* (*c.* 1190-1), which was certainly familiar to leading English canonists at the close of the century; but, on the other hand, there is clear use of a systematic decretal collection, closely related to the Anglo-Norman *Tanner*, which in its extant version includes letters of Celestine III and Innocent III in an appendix.[63] Here is a manuscript of remarkable interest and value, perhaps unsurpassed of its type for any of the schools of canonists of its time. A vast work of research remains to be devoted to it, of which perhaps the most fruitful course would be the differen-

---

[59] Clear examples of gloss strata in different hands are found on Caius MS 676, fols 10ra, 103^v, 104^r, 104^v, 136^r, 154^v, 183^v, 188rb, 193^v, *et passim*.

[60] Cf. n. 81, below.

[61] Caius MS 676, fol. 134ra: 'GG. 8 antequam esset papa.'

[62] *Ibid.* fol. 57va: 'In extra. Prudentiam. par. Quinto': cf. *Tanner*, Appendix 1e, JL 17019, 17 June 1193.

[63] Cf. Holtzmann, *Sammlung Tanner* 143-5.

tiation and extraction of the various gloss strata, and the complementary
task of gathering together the scattered glosses of cognate origin.

Kuttner and Rathbone argued that the Caius glosses were the work of the
school of John of Tynemouth, composed substantially in the form of a *repor-
tatio* of his lectures; and in this context they linked the glosses with the *Ques-
tiones Londinenses* in the British Museum MS Royal 9 E. VII.[64] Further research tends now to confirm their suggestions, but reveals at the same time
the complexity of the glosses in their origins, and provides a warning against
too close an association of their composition with any single canonist. The
citations of John's teachings are certainly very numerous, being discovered
on a cursory survey in at least one hundred marginal columns, in which John
is identified as *Jo.d ti., Jo.de ti., Jo.ti, J.* and so forth.[65] In most instances
references to his views appear in the third person, but in a few places his
siglum is found at the end of a paragraph, suggesting a direct quotation from
his work.[66] The glosses also contain numerous comments in the first person:
'credo tamen', 'dico indifferens', 'nec ego audeo concedere', 'sed ego genera-
liter intelligo', 'hoc dico', 'rogo' and many others of a similar kind;[67] and
it is possible that some of these statements are attributable to him; but the
evidence here is inconclusive, for most of such references are quite unidentified.
Master Simon of Southwell, another English canonist and a colleague of John,
is cited in at least fourteen passages, being identified as *S'd S'*, or *S'de S'*, or
S' simply.[68] The identification of John and Simon as influential commentators is already well established, and they are known to have been the teachers
of Thomas of Marlborough. John's glosses clearly outweigh those of Simon
in the Caius MS, but in an interesting way their views are often placed together
on knotty points of law, sometimes for their varying interpretations, and at

---

[64] Kuttner and Rathbone, *Anglo-Norman Canonists* 317-27 and 340-2.

[65] Caius MS 676, fols. 1ra, 6rb, 19va, 20va, 22va, 22vb, 27va, 35va, 39rb, 40vb, 42v (bot), 48ra,
50r (bot), 50va, 56ra, 58va, 68ra, 69rb, 70ra, 75rb, 76rb, 76vb, 77vb, 78rb, 78vb, 79ra, 83ra, 83va,
88vb, 93vb, 97ra, 97v (bot), 98vb, 105ra, 112vb, 113rb, 116ra, 119vb, 126rb, 127rb, 127vb, 128ra,
139vb, 140ra, 142va, 145rb, 147ra, 147rb, 148rb, 149ra, 147v (bot), 149va, 151ra, 154rb, 165va,
165vb, 165v (bot), 166ra, 168ra, 168rb, 169vb, 170rb, 177va, 178v (bot), 180rb, 180vb, 181ra,
181r (bot), 182r (bot), 183r (bot), 183rb, 184v (bot), 185r (bot), 185vb, 188v (top), 190r (top),
190r (bot), 193r (top), 193v (bot), 194ra, 194rb, 195vb, 196rb, 196v (top), 197ra, 198ra, 215v
(bot), 216r (top), 217r (bot), 218r (top), and 223 ra. The lists of references in this and subsequent footnotes are not exhaustive.

[66] The siglum *Jo. ti.* at the end of paragraphs is found on fols. 181ra, 181va, 216r (top) and
elsewhere.

[67] Examples of first-person comments are on fols. 39vb, 42v (bot), 85va, 104va, 110v, 115vb,
132rb, 144ra, 144va, 181r (bot), 184v (bot), 215vb, 216rb, and elsewhere.

[68] Fols. 22va, 22vb, 99va, 116v, 131ra, 140va, 144vb, 145rb, 147v (bot), 149va, 167ra, 181vb,
193ra, 194ra, 195vb, 197vb and 198ra.

others for their agreement.[69] There are also at least two citations from the writings of John of Cornwall, appearing here as *Jo. Cornub.*;[70] and there is one paragraph from Nicholas of Aquila's work, ending with his siglum *N. đ aqᵗ.*[71] It is perhaps also this same Nicholas who is referred to in a further paragraph as *Nich. đ e.*[72] The concluding folios of the manuscript are particularly rich in attributions to English canonists, and various passages appear with terminal sigla, though some of these have not yet been identified: one paragraph is attributed to *Bar.*, perhaps Bartholomew, and two to *p.*[73]

References to famous continental canonists abound in these glosses: there are numerous discussions of Gratian's own *dicta*, several of which are adversely criticised;[74] many *paleae* are noted, and some so called, and Paucapalea is mentioned on at least one occasion;[75] Alexander III is identified, as canonist or pope, in many forms: including *Alex.*, *alex.*, *Alex.3*, *Roll'*, *R'ol.*, *R.* and *al.*;[76] Rufinus is cited, but surprisingly slightly;[77] no reference to Stephen of Tournai has so far been discovered; Johannes Faventinus is drawn on extremely frequently, often in association with or in contrast to Gandulfus;[78]

---

[69] Examples of glosses citing both John and Simon are on fols. 22ᵛᵇ, 99ᵛᵃ, 116ʳᵃ, 131ʳᵃ, 140ᵛᵃ, 147ᵛ (bot), 145ʳᵇ, 149ᵛᵃ, 193ʳᵃ, 194ʳᵃ and elsewhere.

[70] Fols. 99ʳᵇ, 196ʳᵇ, cf. E. Rathbone, 'John of Cornwall: A Brief Biography,' RTAM 17 (1950) 51-3.

[71] Fol. 129ᵛᵃ. [72] Fol. 198ʳᵃ.

[73] For *Bar.* see fol. 216ʳ (top); for *p.* see fol. 216ʳᵇ. It is possible that the letters *S'* and *C*, which often appear at the end of references, are also sigla in some instances. A highly interesting reference, written in a florid hand of a much later date, is found on fol. 159ᵛ (bot): 'no pro libello Po. (? Ro.) de Brecheham'; and adjacent to this is the comment: 'arguitur quod non imputatur clerico si ad defensionem iuris sui vocat milites et aliquis occidatur.' It is conceivable that these references allude to Roger of Brecham, an Oxford clerk, who stabbed a townsman in a town-and-gown riot in the High Street on 23 Feb. 1298: cf. H. E. Salter, *Medieval Archives of the University of Oxford* I (Oxford 1920) 44.

[74] Fols. 1ʳᵃ, 9ʳᵇ, 61ʳᵃ, 64ᵛᵃ, 69ʳᵇ, 78ʳᵃ, 80ʳᵃ, 83ᵛᵃ, 84ʳᵃ, 84ᵛᵃ, 93ʳᵃ, 104ʳᵃ, 108ʳᵃ, 126ᵛᵃ, 132ᵛᵃ, 137ʳᵇ, 140ʳᵃ, 142ʳᵇ, 142ᵛᵇ, 144ᵛᵇ, 145ʳᵇ, 150ʳᵃ, 155ᵛᵇ, 181ʳᵃ, 187ᵛᵃ, 189ʳᵇ, 194ʳᵇ, 197ᵛᵃ and 198ʳᵃ.

[75] Examples of *paleae* are found on fols. 9ʳᵇ, 42ᵛᵃ (three chapters added at bottom of fol. and called 'palea') and elsewhere; for 'Pacopalea', see fol. 109ᵛᵇ.

[76] Fols. 15ᵛᵇ, 114ʳᵃ, 133ᵛ (bot), 178ᵛ (bot), 179ʳᵃ, 181ᵛᵇ, 182ʳᵃ, 183ʳ(bot), and 187ᵛᵃ.

[77] Fols. 187ᵛᵃ, 187ᵛᵇ, 191ʳᵇ, 194ʳᵇ, and 215ᵛᵇ.

[78] For Johannes Faventinus; see fols. 17ᵛ(top), 19ᵛᵃ, 20ᵛᵃ, 27ᵛᵃ, 31ʳᵃ, 31ʳᵇ, 43ᵛᵇ, 48ᵛᵇ, 49ʳᵃ, 60ᵛᵃ, 61ᵛᵃ, 61ᵛᵇ, 62ʳᵃ, 63ᵛᵇ, 64ʳᵃ, 64ʳᵇ, 64ᵛᵃ, 65ʳᵇ, 66ᵛᵃ, 69ᵛᵇ, 74ᵛᵇ, 75ᵛᵃ, 76ᵛᵇ, 77ʳᵃ, 79ʳᵇ, 80ᵛᵃ, 80ᵛᵇ, 81ʳᵃ, 83ʳᵃ, 83ᵛᵃ, 94ʳᵇ, 95ᵛᵃ, 97ʳᵃ, 97ᵛ(bot), 98ʳᵃ, 99ʳᵃ, 99ʳᵇ, 104ᵛ(top), 104ᵛᵃ, 106ʳ (bot), 108ᵛᵇ, 110ᵛ, 112ᵛᵃ, 113ᵛᵇ, 121ᵛᵃ, 122ᵛᵃ, 122ᵛᵇ, 123ʳᵃ, 128ʳᵃ, 140ʳᵃ, 141ʳᵇ, 168ʳᵃ, 168ᵛᵃ, 169ᵛᵇ, 181ᵛᵇ, 183ʳᵇ, 183ʳᵃ, 185ᵛᵇ, 186ʳᵇ, 187ᵛᵃ, 194ʳᵇ, 195ᵛᵇ, 197ʳᵃ, 215ᵛ(top) and 219ʳᵇ; and for Gandulfus, see fols. 6ʳᵇ, 19ᵛᵃ, 20ʳᵃ, 27ᵛᵃ, 31ʳᵇ, 32ʳᵃ, 43ᵛᵇ, 48ᵛᵇ, 49ʳᵃ, 60ᵛᵃ, 63ᵛᵇ, 64ʳᵃ, 64ʳᵇ, 64ᵛᵃ, 65ʳᵇ, 66ᵛᵃ, 67ʳᵃ, 69ʳᵇ, 74ᵛᵇ, 76ᵛᵇ, 77ʳᵃ, 81ʳᵃ, 83ʳᵃ, 84ʳᵃ, 85ʳᵃ, 95ᵛᵃ, 104ᵛ(top), 113ᵛᵇ, 114ʳᵇ, 115ᵛᵇ, 122ᵛᵃ, 127ʳᵇ, 128ʳᵃ, 137ᵛᵃ, 138ʳᵇ, 140ʳᵃ, 150ᵛᵃ, 162ᵛᵃ, 165ᵛᵇ, 168ʳᵃ, 168ᵛᵃ, 178ᵛ (bot), 181ʳᵇ, 181ᵛᵇ, 183ʳᵇ, 196ʳᵇ, 197ʳᵃ, 206ʳᵃ, 215ᵛᵇ, 217ʳ(bot), 219ʳᵇ and 221ᵛᵇ.

Cardinalis and Bazianus are used;[79] Albertinus is mentioned once as such, and once retrospectively as Gregory VIII;[80] Huguccio is quoted many times through the volume.[81] There are frequent references to *Jo.*, without further identification: in most instances Johannes Faventinus is almost certainly intended.[82] The interesting suggestion has been made that the many references to *al.* may in some instances be applicable to Alanus, but no further evidence has been yet discovered to support this theory: in several contexts Alexander III seems a more likely candidate; in most instances the generic 'alii' is the most plausible meaning.[83] In addition to the canonists, many theologians and writers of the period are quoted, mainly from the French schools, but some with English connexions: Bernard of Clairvaux,[84] Peter Comestor,[85] Gilbert de la Porrée,[86] Hugh of St. Victor,[87] Peter the Chanter,[88] Robert Pullen[89] and Bartholomew;[90] one rare reference is made to the little-known Paganus of Corbeil, whose very existence was only recently rediscovered by the researches of the late Msgr. Landgraf.[91] The early fathers of the Church are sometimes cited: Tertullian,[92] John Chrysostom,[93] Jerome,[94] Ambrose,[95] Augustine of Hippo,[96] Gregory the Great,[97] Augustine of Canterbury[98] and Bede;[99] while the classical Latin authors are represented by Juvenal,[100] Horace,[101] Cicero,[102] Martial,[103] Terence[104] and Seneca.[105] Roman civil

---

[79] For Cardinalis, see fols. 134ra, 136va, 149ra, 168ra, 181ra, 181r(bot), 181va, 181vb, 182ra, 182r(bot), 183ra, 186rb, 187va, 187vb, 194rb, 196rb, 196v(top) and 206ra; and for Bazianus, see fols. 55vb, 115vb, 185r(bot) and 185va.

[80] Fols. 134ra and 187va.

[81] Fols. 5rb, 31ra, 52rb, 55vb, 71rb, 76vb, 78vb, 80vb, 90ra, 93vb, 97ra, 97v(bot), 101rb, 104ra, 104v(top), 122ra, 133v(bot), 134ra, 134rb, 138ra, 140ra, 140rb, 145rb, 178vb, 179rb, 180rb, 180vb, 181ra. 182rb, 183rb, 185r(bot), 185va, 188ra, 188vb, 189rb and 198ra.

[82] Fols. 20ra, 50r(bot), 60va, 63vb, 64ra, 64rb, 66va, 67ra, 108v(bot), 136va-b, 139v(bot), 183rb, 187va, 187vb, 189rb and 200vb.

[83] Kuttner and Rathbone, *Anglo-Norman Canonists* 317; cf fols 21va, 31ra, 80vb, 134ra, 136va, 142vb, 143rb, 144vb, 178va, 181ra, 183rb, 187va and 187vb; in such an instance as fol. 187vb, 'Ruf. et al. et Jo.' it seems probable that Alexander III is intended.

[84] Fol. 53v.   [85] Fols. 182ra. and 182vb.

[86] Fols. 115ra. and 154rb.   [87] Fol. 63ra

[88] Fols. 63rb, 165v(bot), 167ra, 195rb, 217rb and 218r(top).

[89] Fol. 165v(bot).   [90] Fols. 126rb, 201va and 216r(top).

[91] Fol. 218va; cf A. M Landgraf, 'Untersuchungen zur Gelehrtengeschichte des 12. Jahrhunderts,' *Miscellanea Giovanni Mercati* II (*Studi e Testi* 122; Vatican City 1946) 259-81; see also J. de Ghellinck, *Le Mouvement théologique du XIIe siècle* (2nd ed. Bruges 1948) 271 n. 4.

[92] Fol. 191vb.   [93] Fol. 189ra.   [94] Fols. 85ra and 135vb.

[95] Fol. 182ra.   [96] Fols. 63rb, 84ra, 126rb, 148va and 183v.

[97] Fol. 59rb, 126rb, 132rb and 142vb.   [98] Fol. 132rb,

[99] Fol. 162vb.   [100] Fol. 23vb.   [101] Fol. 113rb.

[102] Fols. 2ra, 46ra and 126ra.   [103] Fol. 191rb.

[104] Fol. 124ra.   [105] Fols. 128vb, 162va and 167ra.

law figures in an important way in the glosses: quite apart from many references to the standard civilian textbooks, famous *dicta* from Roman law are introduced in discussions, and Papinian is cited in one instance.[106] Among twelfth-century civilians, Placentinus,[107] Martinus,[108] Bulgarus[109] and John of Cremona (Johannes Bassianus)[110] are mentioned; and the views of Vacarius are cited on at least four occasions.[111] A point of further interest is that many of the gloss references are made in arabic numerals.[112] All these examples have been assembled on a merely provisional survey of the manuscript, but they suffice to show the width of knowledge of works of all kinds possessed by these English canonists of the late-twelfth century.

Apart from the knowledge which they disclose of their authors' sources and professional background, the English glosses have also their intrinsic canonical interest, often with a topical or regional emphasis in context or illustration. These matters will be dealt with more fully on a future occasion, but one final point remains of particular relevance in this report: the use made by the English glossators of contemporary decretal collections. It has already been shown that the glosses reveal at times a knowledge of a systematic decretal collection, closely related to the *Tanner* Collection though not in fact to the extant Tanner MS.[113] A more detailed study confirms this view but also enables the discussion to be taken further. Briefly, it can be said that the glossators cited from their decretal collection in three ways: most simply by the incipit of the decretal letter alone; alternatively by the decretal incipit, following the title of the part of the collection in which it was found; and, most precisely, by the numerical identification of book, title and chapter, or incipit, of the decretal collection in hand. The most significant evidence is clearly of the third kind: thus Kuttner and Rathbone were able to equate the Caius MS reference ' In extra. l(ibro) 6 ti.1. Meminimus' with *Tanner* 7.1.1; the correspondence is exact, since Holtzmann called the *proeemium* of the Tanner Collection 'Book I', so that the book numbers in his printed analysis are too high by one in each case; and *Meminimus* is the opening chapter in *Tanner* 7(6).1.[114] Further examples can now be listed from the Caius MS to support this identification: thus ' In extra. Li.5 t.1. Si quis rei'

---

[106] For Roman law references, see fols. 1r, 4va, 14ra, 110v, 121vb, 122vb, 123ra, 130ra, 142vb, 144vb, 167vb, 169vb, 187va, 189va, 190rb *et passim*; the reference to Papinian is on fol. 130ra.

[107] Fols. 137rb and 188va. [108] Fols. 107rb, 107va, 137rb and 137va.

[109] Fols. 78ra, 95va, 107va and 137rb. [110] Fols. 107va, 115vb and 137rb.

[111] Fols. 1r, 4va, 14ra and 142vb.

[112] Fols. 9rb, 39vb, 57vb, 61ra, 71rb, 76va, 87rb, 108v(bot), 109rb, 110v, 132rb, 133v(bot), 134ra, 135vb, 138ra, 140ra, 142v, 143rb, 143va, 144ra, 144vb, 145rb, 186ra, 187va, 198ra *et passim*.

[113] Kuttner and Rathbone, *Anglo-Norman Canonists* 340-1.

[114] *Ibid.* 340, par. 5; cf. also Appendix C, below.

agrees with *Tanner* 6(5).1.2;[115] and so forth. On the other hand, there are textual variants between the manuscripts, and the titles do not exactly correspond; in some instances the rubrics are omitted entirely from the Tanner MS but cited in the Caius gloss.[116] The most valuable example so far discovered is in an extended gloss in the Caius MS dealing with canonical problems affecting the religious orders and their tithe privileges:[117] within a single paragraph at the foot of one folio there are no less than five numerical identifications of decretals in a collection, apart from others referred to by titles and incipits or by incipits only. Of eleven identified items included in this single paragraph, all are found within the space of three columns in the Tanner MS, and within two adjacent titles in the *Tanner* analysis; they are all found between the limits *Tanner* 3.13.3 and 3.14.12 (in Holtzmann's numeration) as follows: 14.2, 14.6, 13.3, 13.4, 14.1, 14.3, 14.5, 14.3, 14.11, 14.1 and 14.12. Where these items are numerically identified in the Caius gloss, they differ consistently from the *Tanner* numeration in two respects: the book numbers vary by one, for the reason explained above; and the title numbers vary by one in every case.[118] It is clear, therefore, that the collection being used by the Caius glossator, though running in parallel agreement with *Tanner* itself at this stage, diverged slightly in the numeration of its titles. On the other hand, here is a perfect picture of an English glossator composing his comments in the Caius MS with a close relation of *Tanner* open beside him.

In conclusion, by selecting as few examples as has been done in this report, a necessarily disjointed and incomplete impression must result; yet the evidence is perhaps sufficient to provide some insight into the profoundly significant developments of canon law in England in the later-twelfth century and the contribution which English canonists made to the overall growth of canon law for the Western Church at that time. In his study on the English Church in the twelfth century Zachary Brooke concluded his survey of canonical manuscripts used in England with the arrival of Gratian's *Decretum*, thinking it unnecessary to enquire beyond that stage. So far was this from being a valid viewpoint that the most interesting period in English canonical history, what may be called the 'English period' in the history of canon law, was only then beginning.

University of London,
King's College.

---

[115] Fol. 57ᵛᵃ; a list of similar examples is given in Appendix C, below.
[116] Cf. variations listed in Appendix C, below.
[117] *Ibid.* par. 15; cf. Caius MS fol. 133ᵛ (bot), and Holtzmann, *Sammlung Tanner* 118-19.
[118] Cf. Appendix C, below: Comparative Table.

APPENDIX A

Collation of William of Canterbury's version of Becket's defense of clerical privilege with extracts from the *Decretum Gratiani* and the *Summa* of Rufinus. The first column provides a transcription of an unbroken passage from William's *Vita et Passio S. Thome* in the Winchester College MS 4, pp. 20ᵃ-23ᵃ. The second column is composed of extracts from Gratian and Rufinus in the Friedberg and Singer editions respectively: the citations from Rufinus are identified by name and page in postscript square brackets, and all other references are to the *Decretum Gratiani*.

William of Canterbury

[Winchester College MS 4, p. 20ᵃ] Porro nec in his finibus lis et ira subsedit, sed progressa est alterutrum mersum caput.

Rex enim clericos homicidas, fures, lathrones, sicarios, aut aliis flagitiis deditos, ad seculare iudicium trahebat, ut confessi vel convicti de crimine, officio suo privarentur, privati curie traderentur. Archiepiscopus vero, quid cui iudici liceat in causis considerans, nichil invenit, quod habeat in ecclesiastica causa criminali, potestas secularis, que de divinis rebus diffinire non potest, iuxta constitutionem illam: [Rubric] Quod clericus non est trahendus ad seculare iudicium:

Si crimen ecclesiasticum est, tunc secundum canones ab episcopo suo causarum examinatio et pena procedat, nullam communionem aliis iudicibus in huiusmodi causis habentibus. Crimen ecclesiasticum est, de quo concilium Cartaginense statuit dicens: Diffinimus eum rite ad accusationem [p. 20ᵇ] non admitti, qui postea quam excommunicatus fuerit, in ipsa adhuc excommunicatione constitutus, sive sit clericus sive laicus, accusare voluerit.

Omnes etiam infamie maculis aspersi, id est, histriones aut turpitudinibus subiecte persone, heretici etiam sive pagani, sive iudei ab accusatione prohibentur.

Sed nec de crimine forensi iudex secularis cognoscere potest, si clericus clericum vel laicum pulset, qui non potest accusa-

Gratian and Rufinus

Ad secularia iudicia nullus clericus est pertrahendus. [C. 11 q. 1 c. 5 *rubr.*]

Sin autem crimen ecclesiasticum est, tunc secundum canones ab episcopo suo causae examinatio et pena procedat, nullam communionem aliis iudicibus in huiusmodi causis habentibus. [C. 11 q. 1 c. 45 § 2]

In concilio Cartaginensi VII ... Diffinimus, eum rite ad accusationem non admitti, qui posteaquam excommunicatus fuerit, in ipsa adhuc excommunicatione constitutus, sive sit clericus sive laicus, accusare voluerit.

Omnes etiam infamiae maculis aspersi, id est histriones aut turpitudinibus subiectae personae, heretici etiam, sive pagani sive Judei, ab accusatione prohibentur. [C. 4 q. 1 c. 1]

Denique in criminali causa forensi multa differentia adhibenda est in his, qui conveniunt vel conveniuntur. Refert hic enim,

tionem proponere ante secularem iudicem, sicut cautum est Agatensi concilio:

Clericum nullus presumat apud secularem iudicem episcopo non permittente pulsare; sed si pulsatus fuerit non respondeat nec proponat, nec audeat criminale negotium in iudicio seculari proponere.

Secundum concilium Milevitanum causam perdet et a communione excludetur, videlicet:

Inolita presumptio usque adeo illicitis ausibus additum patefecit, ut clerici clericos suo relicto pontifice ad iudicia publica pertrahant. Proinde [p. 21ª] statuimus, ut hoc de cetero non presumatur. Si quis hoc presumpserit facere, conventum et causam perdat, et a communione efficiatur extraneus.

Est autem crimen forense, cuius examinatio et condemnatio ad secularem iudicem pertinere solet, ut crimen lese maiestatis, et incendiorum, et huiusmodi.

Si vero clericus in criminali forensi pulsetur a laico,

canones ei clementius in hac causa provident, ut non trahatur ad forensem disceptationem, ut Gaius papa scribit:

utrum clericus clericum, vel laicus laicum, vel laicus clericum, vel clericus laicum conveniat. Si enim sit clericus qui accusat de crimine forensi vel clericum vel laicum, non potest accusationem proponere apud iudicem secularem; unde dicitur in concilio Agathensi quod clericus non audeat proponere criminale negotium in iudicio seculari, ut infra e. q. cap. Clericum (17). [Rufinus, ed. Singer 307-8]

Item in Concilio Agatensi legitur. Episcopo non permittente apud secularem iudicem clericus pulsari non debet.

Clericum nullus presumat apud secularem iudicem episcopo non permittente pulsare; sed, si pulsatus fuerit, non respondeat nec proponat, nec audeat criminale negotium in iudicio seculari proponere. [C. 11 q. 1 c. 17 and 47]

Secundum concilium Milevitanum causam perdat et a communione excludatur, ut infra ead. q. c. Inolita(42). [Rufinus 308]

Item ex Concilio Milevitano: Qui pena feriatur clericus clericum ad secularia iudicia pertrahens. Inolita presumptio usque adeo illicitis ausibus additum patefecit, ut clerici clericos, relicto suo pontifice, ad iudicia publica pertrahant. Proinde statuimus ut hoc de cetero non presumatur. Si quis hoc presumpserit facere, conventus et causam perdat, et a communione efficiatur extraneus. [C. 11 q. 1 c. 42]

Est autem crimen forense illud, cuius examinatio et condempnatio ad secularem iudicem pertinet, ut crimen lese maiestatis et incendiorum et alia quorum exempla sunt infinita. [Rufinus 307]

Si autem ipse laicus in hac parte pulset clericum, tunc secundum autenticum poterit eum ad secularem iudicem trahere, ita tamen ut iudex secularis non ante puniat clericum criminis convictum, quam a suo episcopo dignitate privetur, ut infra e.q.c. Si quis cum clerico (45). Canones tamen in hac causa clericis clementius provident, ut scilicet etiam in ista causa criminali non possint trahi ad forense iudicium, ut infra cap. I et IV notatur. [Rufinus 308]

Ordinarii iudices publicam iurisdictionem habent ab imperatore, ut presides. Extraordinarii nullam iurisdictionem habent ex officio suo, sed ex delegatione, nec delegati.

Nemo unquam episcopum aut reliquos clericos apud iudicem secularem accusare presumat.

Et item Theodosius et Arcadius:

Continua lege sancimus ut nullus episcoporum, vel eorum qui necessitatibus ecclesie serviunt, ad iudicia sive ordinariorum sive extraordinariorum iudicum [p. 21b] pertrahatur. Habent illi suos iudices, nec quicquam his publicis est commune cum legibus. Item Constantinus presidens in sancta synodo que apud Nicenam congregata est, cum querelam quorumdam conspiceret, coram se deferendam, ait: Vos a nemine diiudicari potestis, quia ad solius Dei iudicium reservabimini.

Idem asserit Adrianus:

Clericus sive laicus, si crimine aut lite pulsatus fuerit, non alibi quam in foro suo provocatus audiatur.

Nisi cum permissione proprii episcopi;

qui quamvis permiserit, clericus tamen cogendus non est, si noluerit, sicut quorundam habet opinio. Item illud Agatensis concilii quod supra positum est.

Et illud Gregorii:

Fratris et coepiscopi nostri Felicis, et Quiriaci abbatis relatione cognovimus quod in insula Sardinia sacerdotes a laicis iudicibus opprimantur, et fraternitatem tuam ministri sui despiciant; dumque solum a vobis simplicitati studetur, quantum videmus disciplina negligitur.

Quod clericus apud seculares iudices accusandus non sit, Gaius Papa scribit, dicens: Nemo umquam episcopum aut reliquos clericos apud iudicem secularem accusare presumat. [C. 11 q. 1 c. 1]

Item Valentinianus, Theodosius et Archadius. Ad secularia iudicia nullus clericus est pertrahendus. Continua lege sancimus, ut nullus episcoporum vel eorum, qui ecclesiae necessitatibus serviunt, ad iudicia sive ordinariorum sive extraordinariorum iudicium pertrahantur. Habent illi suos iudices, nec quicquam his publicis est commune cum legibus. Item Constantinus presidens in sancta sinodo, que apud Nicenam congregata est, cum querelam quorumdam conspiceret coram se deferendam, ait: Vos a nemine diiudicari potestis, quia ad Dei iudicium solius reservamini [C. 11 q. 1 c. 5] et item illud Adriani : Clericus sive laicus, infra e. q. cap. antepenult. et penultimum. [Rufinus 308]

Unde Adrianus Papa ait: Non nisi in foro suo clericus audiatur. Clericus sive laicus, si crimine aut lite pulsatus fuerit, non alibi quam in foro suo provocatus audiatur. [C. 11 q. 1 c. 48]

Nisi cum permissione proprii episcopi, ut infra ead. q. c. II., item illud: Clericum nullus (17), et item illud Gregorii : Fratris (40). Sed quid, si episcopus permiserit, clericus tamen trahi noluerit? Et putem clericum in hac parte non esse cogendum [Rufinus 308-9]

A laicis iudicibus clerici non sunt obprimendi. Idem [scil. Gregorius] Ianuario Episc. Karalitano (lib. III, ep. 26, a. 594): Fratris et coepiscopi nostri Felicis, et Quiriaci abbatis relatione cognovimus eo quod in insula Sardinia sacerdotes a laicis iudicibus obprimantur, et fraternitatem tuam ministri tui despiciant, dumque solum simplicitati a vobis studetur, quantum videmus disciplina negligitur. [C. 11 q. 1 c. 40]

Denique perpendit archiepiscopus quod cum clericus apud non suum iudicem convenitur, [p. 22ᵃ] aut invitus trahitur, aut sponte vadit. Si invitus trahitur et contra eum sentencia fertur, nulla vires habet, ut Adrianus papa dicit:

In clericorum causa huiusmodi forma servetur, ut nequaquam eorum sententia a non suo iudice dicta constringat.

Si autem sponte ierit, fueritque causa criminalis, deponatur, etiamsi a iudice seculari innocens pronunciatus fuerit. Si autem civilis forensis fuerit dabitur ei optio, ut si vicerit apud secularem iudicem, causam perdat aut officium; quod habetur ex concilio Cartaginensi:

Placuit ut quisquis episcoporum, presbiterorum et diaconorum sive clericorum, cum in ecclesia ei crimen fuerit intentum, vel civilis causa fuerit commota, si derelicto ecclesiastico iudicio publicis iudiciis purgari voluerit, etiam si pro ipso lata fuerit sententia, locum suum amittat, et hoc in criminali actione. In civili vero perdat quod evicit, si iocum suum optinere maluerit.

Si autem contra eum lata fuerit sentencia, tunc ipsa firma erit, non propter [p. 22b] auctoritatem secularis iudicii, sed propter odium contumacis clerici. Nichilominus tamen condemnabitur ab officio.

Hec considerans archiepiscopus, clericos infames, non nisi apud ecclesiasticum iudicem permittebat conveniri. Ubi convicti proprie dignitatis officio spoliarentur, non mutilarentur, quia non iudicat Deus bis in idipsum, vel ne forte duplici pena multati, laicis infamibus conditione viderentur inferiores. Sed si post degradationem relaberentur in consimile flagicium, secundum

Denique notandum est quod cum clericus apud non suum iudicem convenitur, aut invitus trahitur, aut sponte vadit. Si invitus trahitur et contra eum sententia fertur, lata contra eum sententia nullas vires habebit, ut infra e.q.cap. penult. et supra Cs. III. q. VIII. c. I. [Rufinus 309] De eodem [scil. Non nisi in foro suo clericus audiatur]. Idem [scil. Adrianus papa].

In clericorum causa huiusmodi forma servetur, ut nequaquam eorum sententia non a suo iudice dicta constringat. [C. 11 q. 1 c. 49]

Si autem sponte ierit fueritque causa criminalis, deponatur, etiam si a iudice seculari innocens pronuntietur. Si autem civilis utique forensis, dabitur ei optio, ut, si vicerit apud secularem iudicem, aut perdat causam aut amittat officium, ut infra e.q. c. Placuit (43). [Rufinus 309]

Clericus apud civilem iudicem iudicari non debet. Item ex Concilio Cartaginensi III. Placuit, ut quisquis episcoporum, presbiterorum et diaconorum, seu clericorum, cum in ecclesia ei crimen fuerit intentum, vel civilis causa fuerit commota, si derelicto ecclesiastico iudicio publicis iudiciis purgari voluerit, etiam si pro ipso fuerit lata sententia, locum suum amittat. Et hoc in criminali actione. In civili vero perdat quod evicit, si locum suum obtinere maluerit. [C. 11 q. 1 c. 43]

Si autem contra eum fuerit lata sentencia, tunc ipsa firma erit, non propter auctoritatem secularis iudicii, sed pro odio contumacis clerici; nichilominus tamen condemnabitur ab officio. Et hoc potest obtineri ex similitudine illius paragraphi: Sed istud Augustini, infra Cs. XXIV. qu. I (Dict. a. c. 40). [Rufinus 309-10]

publicas leges a seculari iudice punirentur.
Non enim decebat ut dicebat, quamvis
inordinatos inordinate iudicari. Hec et
huiusmodi regis iram accendebant, cui com-
plures malivoli fomitem subministrabant,
ut in dies augeretur, profectum suum in
defectu ecclesie constituentes. Et iam ira
preceps ferebatur, per diuturnitatem temporis invalescens, et in odium vergebat.
Quapropter episcopi non reminiscentes se
super [p. 23a] gentes et regna ad evellenda
viciorum plantaria constitutos, non modo
non sumpserunt scutum fidei, ut starent
pro domo Domini in die prelii, sed et po-
suerunt corpus suum in terra ut fierent
via transeunti. Nichilominus tamen, vir
accepte potestatis memor, Deo sibique re-
lictus, immobilis permanebat. Egerat abies
in altum radices suas, et licet defluentibus
ramis suis, tamen ad turbinem ventorum
deici non potuit.

APPENDIX B

Analyses, with Comparative Tables, of selected parts of the 'Cheltenham'
Collection: *Cheltenhamensis*, British Museum Egerton MS 2819, fols. 17vb-102ra.
In the 'Cheltenham' MS, titles and decretal incipits are rubricated; initial
letters of decretals are alternately blue and red; and there is occasional marginal
glossing.

(a) *Analysis*

I. De simoniacis et indebitis exactionibus tam in ecclesiasticis quam castris
et scolis regendis. De transactionibus et patronatu in quibus quandoque
notatur simonia. [fol. 17vb

1. Vigilan'i (Vigiliensi) episcopo. [18ra
   Cum sit Romana . . . potes.
   JL 14126. — 1159-81.

2. Tolet(ano) archiepiscopo.
   De hoc autem . . . retinere.
   JL 14110. — 1159-81.

3. Eborac(ensi) archiepiscopo. [18rb
   Cum essent . . . permittatis.
   JL 13883. — 1159-81.

4. Excestrensi episcopo. [18va
   Insinuatum est . . . deierare.
   JL 13843. — 1159-81. *Lips.*: 'Cistrensi episcopo.'

5. Lucius III.
   Matheus cardinalis secreta . . . patiatur.
   JL: 14547. — 1181. *App.* 40.4: 'Turonensi archiepiscopo.'

6. Nemo presbiterorum . . . est.   [18vb
   Cap. Hincm. Rem. c. 13; *Greg.* 5.3.14. *Lips.:* 'Alexander papa III.'

7. Wigorn(iensi episcopo) et priori de Pant.
   Querelam monachorum . . . exequatur.
   JL 13165. — 1163-79: 'Rogerio Wigorniensi episcopo et priori Panteiano.'
   Lips.: 'Vig. ep. et de Pantera priori.'

8. Ea que de avaricie . . . exequatur.   [19ra
   JL 14172. — 1159-81.

9. In concilio turonensi.   [19rb
   Non satis inutiliter . . . auget.
   Tours 1163. Mansi c. 6.

10. Deusdedit papa.   [19va
    Tanta est labes . . . meretrix.
    Cap. incert.; *Greg.* 5.3.6.

11. Si dominus magister . . . exorandus.
    Cap. incert.; *Greg.* 5.3.3. *Lips.:* 'Pascalis papa II.'

12. In concilio turonensi.
    Quoniam in quibusdam . . . percellatur.
    Tours 1163: Mansi c. 7.

13. In concilio turonensi.   [19vb
    Quoniam enormis . . . habeatur.
    Tours 1163: Mansi, c. 5.

14. Wintoniensi episcopo.
    Pervenit ad audientiam . . . abstinebunt.
    JL 14192. — 1159-81.

15. Rc. (Ricardo) Cantuariensi archiepiscopo.   [20ra
    Licet iuxta . . . percellas.
    JL 14315. — 1174-81.

16. Couventrensi episcopo.   [20rb
    Mandamus vobis . . . facere.
    JL 13926. — 1159-81. *Lips.:* 'Idem ep. Conventrensi et abbati Castrensi.'

(b) *Comparative Table*

Collating the opening items of the 'Cheltenham' Collection with the Bamberg and Leipzig Collections and with *Compilatio prima.*

Chelt.	Bamb.	Lips.	Comp. I
1.1	1.1	1.1	5.2.9
2	2	2	10
3	3	3	11
4	4	4	12
5	[5]	5	21

6	5	6	13
7	6	7	14
8	7	8	15
9	8	9	7
10	9	10	16
11	10	11	3
12	2.1	2.1	3.2
13	2	2	3
14	-	4.2	27.1
15	4.1	1	32.3
16	3	4	4

Note on Comparative Table: The exact correspondence between *Chelt.* and *Lips.* ceases after *Chelt.* 1.16; the first book of *Chelt.* continues to c. 22, fol. 21^r, where the second book begins under the rubric: 'De capellanis castrorum.' The opening title of *Lips.* is 'De symonia et ne merces pro ecclesiae consecratione requiratur vel pro monachatione ecclesiae vel pro sacramentis ecclesiae, et quod apostolica sedes absque symonia possit investire de prima vacante in ecclesia'; it has 19 chapters, of which cc. 12-19 are unknown in *Chelt.* tit. 1. The second title of *Lips.* is 'Ne prelati vices suas sub annuo pretio aliis committant ad causas terminandas, vel sub annuo pretio presbiteri ad ecclesiarum regimen statuantur, licet ecclesia sub annuo censu dari possit'; it has 3 chapters, of which c. 3 is unknown in *Chelt.* tit. 1. The third title of *Lips.* is 'Ne aliquid exigatur pro licentia docendi'; it has 2 chapters, neither of which is found in *Chelt.* 1.1-16, but *Lips.* 3.2 = *Chelt.* 1.20. The fourth title of *Lips.* is 'Ne clerici illicitis exactionibus vel talleis vexentur. Ne clerici vel laici pecuniaria mulctentur'; it has 4 chapters, of which all but c. 3 are found in *Chelt.* tit. 1. Summing up: *Chelt.* 1.1-16 = *Lips.* 1.1-11, 2.1-2, 4.2, 1 and 4; *Lips.* 1.12-19, 2.3 3.1-2 and 4.3 are missing from *Chelt.* 1.1-16; and conversely *Chelt.* 1.17-22 are lacking in *Lips.* tit. 1-4, except that *Chelt.* 1.20 = *Lips.* 3.2. Despite their differences, the close relationship between the two collections is clearly demonstrated.

(c) *Analysis*

A book of marriage decretals begins in the 'Cheltenham' Collection on fol. 43ra, but the rubricated title is lacking in the MS. The close correspondence between the 'Cheltenham' and Worcester Collections will be seen in the following analysis and comparative table.

[De matrimonio.]   [fol. 43ra

1. Veniens ad nos lator . . . iniungas.
   JL 14215. — 1159-81. *Wig.*: 'Exoniensi episcopo.'

2. Winton(iensi), Herefor(densi), Baton(iensi) episcopis.
   Ad audientiam apostolatus . . . fecerunt.
   JL 14311. — 1159-81.

3. Wintoniensi et Hereforden(si) episcopis.   [43va
   Pervenit ad nos . . . compellatis.
   JL 13901. — 1159-81.

4. Abbati de Fontibus et magistro Vacario.   [43vb
   Significavit nobis . . . uxorem.
   JL 13937. — 1159-81.

5. Decano et Lincoln(iensi) capitulo.   [44ra
   Cum institisset . . . gravamen.
   JL 13983. — 1159-81.

6. Exoniensi episcopo.
   Cum sis preditus . . . transeat.   [44rb
   JL 13899. — 1159-81.

7. Wintoniensi episcopo.
   Consuluit nos fraternitas . . . iniungenda.
   JL 14136. — 1159-81.

8. Capitulo Maguntine ecclesie.   [44va
   Consuluit nos dilectio . . . licuerit.
   Not in JL. — 1159-81.

9. Herefordensi episcopo.
   Litteras tue . . . permittas.
   JL 13947. — 1159-81.

10. Wigunensi (Wigorniensi) episcopo.   [44vb
    Ad aures nostras . . . conferri.
    (a) Ad aures nostras . . . tractare.
    (b) Illas vero . . . conferri.
    JL 14104. — 1159-81.

11. Astiniensi electo vel offa.   [45ra
    Singulorum consultationibus . . . reportare.
    JL 12636. — 8 April 1173-6. *Wig.:* 'Astionensi electo.'

12. Exoniensi episcopo.
    Meminimus nos . . . potuerit.
    JL 13917. — 1159-81.

13. Eidem.   [45rb
    Super hoc quod . . . coniungant.
    (a) Super hoc quod . . . servetur.
    (b) De peregrinationis . . . dispensare.
    (c) Preterea hii . . . coniungant.
    JL 13907, 13916 and 13903. — 1159-81.

14. Episcopo et canonicis et populo Tremulano.   [45va
    Cum inter J. . . . inferri.
    JL 14194. — 1159-81.

15. Fri' Henrico et Bot' episcopo.   [45vb
    Quoniam sicut . . . exceptionem.
    (a) Quoniam sicut . . . dimittenda.
    (b) Super hoc vero . . . prohibetur.
    (c) Leprosis autem . . . exceptionem.
    JL 13773. — 1159-81. *Wig.:* 'Baiocensi episcopo.'

16. Pictavensi episcopo. [46ra
Veniens ad nos lator . . . accipere.
JL 14058. — 1159-81.

17. Toletano episcopo.
Lator presentium . . . separetur. [46rb
JL 14120. — 1159-81.

18. Biriensi (*margin:* vel Vigiliensi) episcopo.]46va
Ex publico instrumento . . . transire.
JL 13787. — 1159-79. *Wig.:* 'Brixiensi episcopo.'

19. Panormitano archidiacono. [46vb
Veniens ad presentium . . . habeat.
JL 14165. — 1159-81. *Wig.:* 'Panormitano arch(iepiscopo).'

20. Si autem vir . . . promittat.
(a) Si autem vir . . . patrocinari.
(b) De cetero laicos . . . admitti.
(c) Et si clerici . . . videtur.
(d) Si vero coram . . . removendi.
(e) De adulteriis . . . conterrere.
(f) Porro si clericus . . . subsecuta.
(g) In causis vero . . .disputari.
(h) De quarta vero . . . admittit.
(i) De presbitero . . . extitisset.
(k) Presbiterum autem . . . expirasse.
(l) Querenti etiam . . . promittat.
JL 14091 and 13946. — 1174-6. *Wig.:* 'Salernitano archiepiscopo: Licet preter.'

21. Exoniensi episcopo. [47vb
Pervenit ad audientiam . . . terminare.
JL 14214. — 1162-81. *Wig.:* 'Barth(olomeo) Exoniensi episcopo.'

22. Eidem (Bartholomeo Exoniensi) episcopo. [48ra
Ex presentium latoris . . . procedes.
JL 13900. — 1162-81.

23. Wigorniensi episcopo.
Conquestus est nobis . . . percellatis.
JL 14167. — 1159-81. *Wig.:* 'Exoniensi et Wigorniensi episcopis.'

24. Archiepiscopo Terratensi. [48rb
Significasti nobis . . . admitti.
(a) Significasti nobis . . . comisisse.
(b) Super eo quod . . . admitti.
JL 14107. — 1159-81. *Wig.:* 'Teraconensi episcopo.'

25. Eboracensi Archiepiscopo.
Licet contineatur . . . possunt.
JL 13887. — 1159-81.

26. Cantuariensi Arc(h)iepiscopo. [48va
De hoc quod . . . ministrare.

(a) De hoc quod . . . generare.
(b) Quod autem quesivisti . . . ministrare.
JL 13793. — 1159-81. Marginal rubric: 'Sub pretextu appellationis adulterium committendus.'

27. Exoniensi episcopo. [48vb
De illis qui infra . . . consensum.
(a) De illis qui infra . . . separari.
(b) Utrum autem . . . consensum.
JL 13767. — 1159-81. *Wig.:* 'Bath(oniensi) episcopo.'

28. Cassiano episcopo.
Ex litteris tuis . . . ignorent.
JL 13838. — 1159-81. *Wig.:* 'Cassiano abbati.'

29. Lucensi episcopo. [49rb
Consuluit nos tua . . . promovendus.
(a) Consuluit nos tua . . . dissolvit.
(b) De cetero quod . . . promovendus.
JL 14005. — 1159-81.

30. Trecensi episcopo.
Ex questione G. . . . decidas.
Not in JL. — 1159-81.

31. Eborardo Paduano episcopo [49va
Sollicitudini apostolice . . . constare.
(a) Sollicitudini apostolice . . . restitui.
(b) De muliere vero . . . respondere.
(c) Illos autem qui . . . constare.
JL 14235. — 1159-81.

32. Eboracensi archiepiscopo. [49vb
Accessit ad presentiam . . . licet etc ut supra e. c. licet.
JL 13887. — 1159-81. Cf. *Chelt.* c. 25, above.

33. Ex questione E. . . . exhibeat. [50ra
JL 13766. — 1159-81.

34. Paduano episcopo.
Littere quas nobis . . . copulari.
JL 14055. — 1159-81.

35. Cassiensi abbati. [50rb
Ad aures nostras . . . incestum.
JL 14164. — 1159-81.

36. Exoniensi et Wintoniensi episcopis.
Causam que vertitur . . . expirare. [50va
(a) Causam que . . . presumpsit.
(b) Ceterum si adversarius . . . expirare.
JL 13932. — 1159-81. *Wig.:* 'Exoniensi et Wintoniensi et abbati Fordensi.'

37. Lator presentium W. . . . manere. [50vb
JL 14036. — 1159-81. *Wig.:* 'Norwicensi episcopo et T. et H. archidiaconis.'

38. Magolonensi episcopo.   [51ra
    Significavit nobis . . . decidas.
    JL 13746. — 1159-81. *Wig.:* 'Meldelsi episcopo.'

39. Cantuariensi archiepiscopo.   [51rb
    Ex litteris quas . . . compellas.
    JL 13793. — 1159-81. Marginal rubrics: 'princ. pars supra fol. ii. De hoc
    quod consulere. Causam non esse remittendam ad eum a quo appellatur.'
    Cf. *Chelt.* c. 26, above.

At this point the correspondence between the 'Cheltenham' and Worcester
Collections is interrupted, and is not resumed until fol. 54vb, with *Wig.* 2. 1,
2, 7 and 8.

(d) *Comparative Table*

Collating the sequences of marriage decretals in the 'Cheltenham' and Worcester Collections.

Chelt.	*Wig.*		*Chelt.*	*Wig.*
1	1.11		21	1. 29
2	7		22	30
3	4		23	31
4	5		24a	32
5	6		b	-
6	8		25	33
7	9		26ab	34bc
8	12		27ab	35
9	13		28	36
10ab	14ab		29	41
11	15		30	7. 55
12	16		31abc	1. 38abc
13abc	17abc		32	37
14	18		33	39
15abc	19abc		34	40
16	20		35	42
17	21		36ab	43ab
18	22		37	44
19	23		38	45
20a-l	28 $\begin{cases} c\text{-}g \\ i\text{-}q \end{cases}$		39	34a

APPENDIX C

References to decretal collections cited in glosses in the Caius College, Cambridge, MS 676. [All references to *Tanner* are according to Holtzmann's numeration, for which see above p. 376].

1. Fol. 40ra: 'In extra. De prescriptione. De quarta': *Tanner* 5.6.1, JL 14091,
   1174-6; the title heading is lacking in the Tanner MS.

2. Fol. 40ᵛᵃ: 'In extra. Clericum sine auctoritate episcopi. Ex frequentibus': *Tanner* 2.6.4, JL 13817, 1159-81; the full title in Tanner is: 'Clericum sine auctoritate episcopi non [posse] constituere ecclesiam suam censuariam vel ecclesiam occupare vel in alium transferre.'

3. Fol. 44ʳᵇ: 'In extra. De potestate iudicis ordinarii. Ad hoc': *Tanner* 4.2.12b, JL 14349, 1159-81; the Tanner title is: 'De officio et potestate iudicis ordinarii.'

4. Fol. 44ʳᵇ: 'In extra. De depositione clericorum. Quia quidam clerici': *Tanner* 2.15.20, JL 14197, conc. West. 1175 c. 5, cf. conc. Tours c. 7; the Tanner title is: 'De depositione clericorum et dispensatione circa eosdem.'

5. Fol. 52ᵛᵇ: 'In extra. De iure patronatus. Illud': *Tanner* 6.3.5, JL 14154, 1159-81.

6. Fol. 57ᵛᵃ: 'In extra. De depositione clericorum. Sacerdotibus': *Tanner* 2.15.16,JL 8959, 26 Nov. 1146; cf. par. 4, above.

7. Fol. 57ᵛᵃ: 'Li. 5 t. 1. Si quis rei': *Tanner* 6.1.2, JL 14219, 1159-81; the Tanner title is: 'De confirmatione utili et inutili et rescriptis suspectis et rescripti interpretatione'; as explained above, the book numbers in the Tanner analysis must be reduced by one for comparative purposes.

8. Fol. 57ᵛᵃ: 'In extra. Prudentiam. par. Quinto': *Tanner* App. 1e, JL 17019, 17 June 1193.

9. Fol. 58ᵛᵃ: 'In extra li. 5. ca. i'; cf. par. 7, above.

10. Fol. 75ᵛᵇ: 'In extra. De testibus. De cetero': *Tanner* 5.4.7, JL 14091, 1172-4; the Tanner title is: 'De testibus et attestationibus et publicis instrumentis.'

11. Fol. 76ʳᵇ: 'In extra. De appellationibus et primo q.s.e.a. [= quis sit effectus appellationis.] Preterea': *Tanner* 5.7.5 and 11 (5 = JL 14152, 1159-81; 11, not in JL, 1159-81, *Sang.* 6.8.13); the title heading is lacking in the Tanner MS.

12. Fol. 77ʳ(bot): 'In extra. De appellationibus et primo. Significaverunt': *Tanner* 5.7.6, JL 13799, 1159-81; cf. par.11, above.
'In extra. j. De officio et potestate iudicis delegati. Consultationibus': *Tanner* 4.3.18, JL 12636, 8 April 1173-6.
'In extra. De officio iudicis ordinarii. Quesitum': *Tanner* 4.2.2, JL 13583, 1159-81; cf. par. 3 above.
'In extra. De divortio propter adulterium. Significasti': *Tanner* 7.7.2, JL 14107, 1159-81.
'In extra. t.e. [= De divortio propter adulterium]. Latrix presentium': *Tanner* 7.7.3, not in JL, 1159-81.
'In extra. De appellationibus. Proposuit': *Tanner* 5.7.8, JL 14350, 1159-81; cf. par. 11, above.

13. Fol. 78ᵛᵇ: 'Ut in extra. De simonia. Insinuatum': *Tanner* 2.1.4, JL 13843, 1159-81; the Tanner title is 'De symonia et ne pro sacramentis vel beneficiis ecclesiasticis conferendis merces recipiantur.'

14. Fol. 80ʳ(bot): 'In extra. De officio et potestate iudicis delegati. Cum tibi sit': *Tanner* 4.3.1, JL 13991, 1159-81.

15. Fol. 133ᵛ(bot): 'In extra. De decimis. Novum': *Tanner* 3.14.2, JL 6605; the Tanner title is 'De decimis a monachis prestandis vel non prestandis et de pensionibus ecclesiarum sibi debitis non augendis.'

'In extra. De decimis. Licet de benignitate': Tanner 3.14.6, JL 14068, 1159-81.
'Dec. li.II.c.xij. Cum homines. Intelleximus': Tanner 3.13.3 and 4 (3= JL 13928, 1159-81; 4 = JL 13862, 1159-81); the Tanner title is 'De decimis dandis et non commutandis.'
'In deč. li.ij.t.xiij.c.j.p(ar). accipientes ad firmam . . . Fraternitatem': Tanner 3.14.1 and 3 (1= JL 14032, 1159-81; 3 = JL 13873, 1159-81).
'In deč. l.ij.xiij. Ex parte': Tanner 3.14.5, JL 14117, 1159-81.
'In deč. l.ij.t.xiij. Fraternitatem': Tanner 3.14.3, as above.
'est illa decretal. Dilecti. l.ij.t.xiii.c.j.': Tanner 3.14.1, as above.
'In extra. De decimis . . . Ex multiplici . . . Dilecti . . . Commisse': Tanner 3.14.11, 1 and 12 (11 = JL 14144, 1159-81; 1 = JL 14023, 1159-81; 12 = JL 11660, 1162-70: for this decretal, Tanner has the incorrect incipit Commissum).

Comparative Table

Collating eleven decretal references in Caius MS 676, fol. 133^v(bot) with Tanner 3.13 and 3.14; cf. par. 15, above.

	Caius MS	Tanner
1	No number given	3.14.2
2	No number given	14.6
3	2.12–	13.3
4	12–	13.4
5	13.1	14.1
6	13–	14.3
7	13–	14.5
8	13–	14.3
9	No number given	14.11
10	No number given	14.1
11	No number given	14.12

Additional Note (to p. 384 above). — In MS Egerton 2819 at least one folio is missing between fol. 42^v (which ends abruptly in the midst of a text) and fol. 43^r. It is for this reason that the series of decretals on marriage begins without a rubric; indeed, it can be shown that five decretals preceded the present c. 1, for on fol. 52rb the first lines of the decretal JL 14311 (above, c. 2) are repeated, breaking off with the cross-reference, 'supra capitulo vii^o ad audientiam apostolatus nostri.' [From the papers and photostats of the Holtzmann Estate communicated by S. Kuttner.]

XII

RICHARD OF ILCHESTER,
ROYAL SERVANT AND BISHOP

IN his *Ymagines Historiarum*, Ralph de Diceto paused in his chronicle of Henry II's reign to reflect on the circumstances and significance of the appointment of three chief justices of the realm in 1179. Ever anxious for the efficient and impartial administration of the law, Henry had diligently sought out lovers of justice who would not be corrupted by high office; he tried, without success, many classes of men: abbots, earls, tenants-in-chief, members of his household, even his closest personal advisers. When at last all else had failed, he raised his eyes to heaven; and, passing over those who could be swayed by worldly influences, he resorted to the sanctuary of God, and appointed as archjusticiars of his realm the bishops of Winchester, Ely and Norwich. If his earlier choices had shown too little respect for him, an earthly king, these at least would act in careful fear of God, the King of kings. And if it should be argued that in assuming this task the bishops would act in despite of the strict letter of canon law, there could be urged in reply the constraint of the king and his good intentions, pleasing alike to God and men.[1]

No extract could suggest more significantly than this the complex interplay of secular and ecclesiastical interests in late twelfth-century England, or warn more sharply against too facile a judgment on their respective merits. King Henry's reputation as a monarch deeply concerned with order and legal progress is too firmly rooted to require any false vindication; and Diceto was a man of moderation, loyal to the king but zealous also in defence of the clerical order. Yet his commentary is, at least to some

[1] Ralph de Diceto, *Opera Historica*, ed. W. Stubbs, i (Rolls Series, 1876), pp. 434–35.

2

extent, misleading and exaggerated in its assessment of the royal reasoning. For the bishops in question were Richard of Ilchester, formerly archdeacon of Poitiers and ubiquitous aide of the king in his long quarrel with Becket and its aftermath; Geoffrey Ridel, formerly archdeacon of Canterbury, the 'archidiabolus noster' of the Becket correspondence; and John of Oxford, 'usurper' dean of Salisbury and hated 'jurator' of the schismatical council of Würzburg in 1165. Each had been excommunicated on at least one occasion by Becket; and all were prelates who had secured their sees in reward for long and faithful service to the king, as also to act as instruments of royal influence in the Church.[1]

The known details of Richard of Ilchester's career are co-terminous with the reign of Henry II: he emerges clearly first as clerk in the royal service, appearing as 'scriptor Curiae' in the first pipe roll of Henry II's reign;[2] by 1163 at the latest he was archdeacon of Poitiers,[3] to which the treasurership of Poitiers was added at a date unknown;[4] and by that time he was firmly established in the inner counsels of the king. Thereafter, his influence spread swiftly and ever more pervasively through every level and branch of royal service: envoy to the pope and bishops, to emperor and kings, executant of royal policies in the Angevin continental lands, baron of the Exchequer and itinerant judge in many English shires. From 1173 he was bishop of the immensely rich and influential see of Winchester, while advancing still higher in the central administration of secular government. His closing years, from c. 1185–86, were a period of little recorded activity,

[1] For the excommunication of Richard and John at Vézelay, 12 June 1166, see *Materials [for the History of Thomas Becket]*, ed. J. C. Robertson, v (Rolls Series, 1881), pp. 383, 388, 394–95, etc.; of Richard again and Geoffrey, 13 April and 29 May 1169, *ibid.*, vi (1882), pp. 594, 601, etc.; of Geoffrey again, papal confirmation, 10 September 1170, *ibid.*, vii (1885), p. 358. For John as 'jurator', *ibid.*, vi. 177; for Geoffrey as 'archidiabolus', *ibid.*, vii. 20, 59, etc. The present essay is preliminary to a full treatment of the careers of these three important servants of Henry II. My thanks are due to Mr I. P. Shaw for many helpful suggestions on Richard's career.

[2] *The Great Rolls of the Pipe for the Second, Third and Fourth Years of the Reign of King Henry II*, ed. J. Hunter (London, 1844), pp. 30, 31, 47, 121 and 122.

[3] P[ipe] R[oll] 9 Hen[ry] II (1162–63), p. 26. For all Henry II PR refs., see *Publications of the Pipe Roll Society*, 30 vols. (London, 1884–1925).

[4] Diceto, i. 319.

the result it would seem of advancing years or declining health, and he died in 1188, a few short months before his royal master.

His early background is almost entirely unknown. He was born and grew to manhood in the diocese of Bath,[1] perhaps near Ilchester. A variety of surnames has been attached to him— Toclyve, Hokelin, Tokelin, Le Poer or Poore and More; and, although there is little conclusive evidence for any of these, the case for Tokelin is perhaps the strongest.[2] The attribution of the name Le Poer is clearly very significant: his illegitimate son Herbert, later archdeacon of Canterbury and bishop of Salisbury from 1194, is known by the name;[3] as also is Richard of Salisbury, bishop from 1217. Historians have seen grounds here for suggesting a link with Roger of Salisbury, Nigel of Ely and Richard FitzNeal, key figures in English fiscal administration through the century.[4] But the only positive family identification is with Gilbert Foliot, bishop successively of Hereford and London, who expressly called Richard kinsman in two letters.[5] A story in the *Life of St Nectan* throws unsuspected light on Richard's origins, and suggests a possible source of advancement through the Gloucester household, in which Richard Tokelin, later bishop of Winchester, was a notary, apparently during Stephen's reign.[6]

[1] *Ibid.*, i. 319.

[2] *Dictionary of National Biography*, xvi (1909), p. 1080; cf. ref. to the *Life of St Nectan*, below, and also the marginal identification in B[ritish] M[useum], Cotton MS. Claudius B.ii, fo. 206ʳ: 'Iste fuit Ricardus Tokelin, postea Wintoniensis episcopus'.

[3] D. Knowles, *The Episcopal Colleagues of Archbishop Thomas Becket* (Cambridge, 1951), p. 38; C. R. Cheney, *From Becket to Langton* (Manchester, 1956), p. 27. The disputed point that Herbert was Richard's son seems greatly strengthened by the royal confirmation (Dec. 1175–Mar. 1182) of a grant made by Richard, archdeacon of Poitiers, and 'Herbert his son'; the confirmation is attested by Richard, bishop of Winchester, and Herbert, archdeacon of Canterbury: cf. L. Delisle, *Recueil des Actes de Henri II*, ii (Paris, 1920), pp. 175–76.

[4] [Richard FitzNeal,] *Dialogus de Scaccario*, [ed. Charles Johnson (London, 1950),] xiv–xv.

[5] *Materials*, vi. 453–55; Gilbert Foliot, *Epistolae*, ed. J. A. Giles, i (Oxford, 1845), pp. 247–48.

[6] *Life of St Nectan*, trans. G. H. Doble (Cornish Saints Series, no. 45, Torquay, 1941), pp. 21–22. It is conceivable that Henry II and Richard were known to one another at an early date, since Henry, when a boy, was himself for a while in the custody of Earl Robert at Bristol. I am indebted

4

Charter evidence and common family names in the households of Earls Robert and William of Gloucester and of Richard, when bishop of Winchester, lend credibility to this partly hagiographical story.[1]

I. *Secular Administration*

Many types of evidence combine to provide a pattern of Richard's career, and demonstrate his rise to a dominant place in the fiscal and judicial administration of England and, for short periods, of Normandy. The charters are chiefly useful in showing his presence and precedence in the royal household, his journeys with the king or on royal service. Eyton and Delisle together listed roughly seventy charters connected in some way with Richard, mainly through his attestations;[2] but these can be substantially supplemented from unprinted cartularies.[3] The charters range in time from early 1159, when Richard attested a charter with Becket at Rouen,[4] until 10 April 1185 when he witnessed at Dover a great charter with personal seal and autograph signature.[5] The English charters are dated mainly at the royal seats of Westminster, Winchester and Woodstock, but a substantial number were issued in Henry's continental lands in the years 1166–75, 1177–78 and 1180.[6] In a few cases Richard appears as sole witness

---

to Mr A. Tomkinson for valuable information and advice on the Gloucester household.

[1] *E.g.*, Gregory de Turri was in the service of Earls Robert and William, and Jordan de Turri was in the *familia* of Richard of Winchester: *cf.* *PR 23 Hen. II*, p. 25; Hugh de Gundeville was constable of Earl Robert, and William de Gundeville was in Richard's *familia*: *cf.* p. 6, n. 11, below and also *PR 24 Hen. II*, p. 55. A royal charter to Richard of Poitiers, concerning Hartland Abbey in late 1165, included Richard Pincerna among its witnesses; both Hartland and Richard Pincerna appear in the same context as Richard Tokelin in the *Life of St Nectan*, pp. 21–22. *Cf.* R. W. Eyton, *Court, Household and Itinerary of King Henry II* (London, 1878), pp. 87–88.

[2] Eyton, *op. cit.*, pp. 44, 60, 84–85, 96 *et passim*; Delisle, *ed. cit.*, 402, 403–4, 417, 439–40 *et passim*.

[3] A detailed report on these charters will be published later.

[4] Eyton, *op. cit.*, p. 44.   [5] *Ibid.*, p. 263; Delisle, *ed. cit.*, pp. 258–60.

[6] For charters of English provenance, see Eyton, *op. cit.*, pp. 60, 77, 84–85 *et passim*. For those of continental provenance in the periods cited, *ibid.*, pp. 96, 158, 159, 177, 219, 221, 233 and 235; Delisle, *ed. cit.*, i. 402, 403–4, 417, 442–43, 456–57, 458–59, 459–60; ii. 11–12, 15–17, 37–38, 63–64, 88–89 and 285–86.

to a royal charter,[1] and in an impressively large proportion he is first or second attestator.[2] An interesting insight into precedence is revealed by the change of order in witnessing between Richard and Geoffrey Ridel on their elections to Winchester and Ely in 1173: until that date Geoffrey, archdeacon of Canterbury, invariably attested first; thereafter Richard, elect or bishop of Winchester, preceded him.[3] At all times John of Oxford appears, if at all, after these;[4] and on John's election to Norwich in 1175 the form of precedence was established as Winchester, Ely and Norwich.[5] After Richard's elevation to Winchester in 1173, only persons of great dignity normally appear in lists before him: the king, papal legates, patriarchs and superior prelates.[6] Most of the charters are grants, settlements and confirmations, with little particular relevance to Richard himself, except that they record his participation in royal affairs; a few are personal to him, being issued by him or granted to him,[7] and three original charters preserve his personal seal.[8] Some charters show Richard with the king on occasions of much historical interest, such as the agreement between the kings of England and Connaught in 1175;[9] between England and France at Ivry in 1177;[10] or the introduction of the order of Fontevrault at Amesbury in 1177.[11] Richard is first in the list of those present when the king's will was drawn up at Bishop's Waltham, one of Richard's manors as bishop of

[1] Eyton, *op. cit.*, p. 85; Delisle, *ed. cit.*, i. 524, 527 and 528.

[2] Attesting first, Delisle, *ed. cit.*, i. 402, 403 and 417; attesting second, *ibid.*, 442–43, 456–57, 458–59, 459–60, etc.

[3] *Cf. ibid.*, i. 459–60: 'Testibus G. archidiacono Cantuariensi, R. archidiacono Pictavensi . . .' and *ibid.*, ii. 11–12: 'Testibus . . . R. Wintoniensi, G. Elyensi electis . . .'

[4] Eyton, *op. cit.*, pp. 84–85, 159 *et passim.*

[5] *E.g., ibid.*, 202. The question of ecclesiastical precedence was clearly involved in the sequence of charter witnesses, but seems not entirely to explain it in all instances.

[6] For examples of Richard not appearing first, see *ibid.*, pp. 190, 192 and 203 (following Gilbert of London); Delisle, *ed. cit.*, ii. 37–38, 60–62 (Treaty of Ivry), 113–16, 120–22, 234 and 258–60.

[7] Charters granted by Richard include two in L. Delisle, *Chronique de Robert de Torigni*, ii (Rouen, 1872), pp. 308–09; see also *idem, Recueil des Actes*, ii. 175–76 and 258–60.

[8] *Ibid.*, intro., p. 434 and ii. 258; and St Bartholomew's Hospital, Old Deed 1283 (information kindly supplied by Professor C. R. Cheney).

[9] Delisle, *ed. cit.*, ii. 45–46.   [10] *Ibid.*, 60–62.   [11] *Ibid.*, 113–16.

6

Winchester, in 1182 and was named as executor for two of its clauses.[1]

Without exception, every pipe roll of Henry II's reign throws some light on Richard's interests or activities. His income of 40/– from the mill at Ilchester is entered on the earliest roll,[2] and continued with only rare adjustments until the first roll of Richard I.[3] From 1162–63 he is referred to in the rolls as archdeacon of Poitiers,[4] and thereafter frequently identified as 'archidiaconus Pictaviensis' or 'Archidiaconus' simply.[5] From that year also he is seen increasingly accounting for expenses and disbursement in the royal service. Nothing demonstrates his rise in royal trust and favour more strikingly than the passing into his hands of rich and important charges. Together with Richard d'Aumerie, he appears in the 1166–67 roll as 'custos' of the vacant see of Lincoln, in which capacity he reappears annually until the election of the illegitimate Geoffrey in 1173.[6] In the same roll he is seen accounting for the honour of Montacute, on the death of Richard of Montacute, and continued to do so until the appearance of the heir in the roll of 1178–79.[7] The wealthy see of Winchester was placed in his hands after the death of Henry of Blois in 1171[8] and with it the vacant abbey of Glastonbury fell to his custody the same year.[9] In 1173 he secured the see of Winchester in his own right, and the rolls of 1172–73 and 1173–74 record this transition;[10] and with these changes the accounts of Lincoln and Winchester automatically lapse from the rolls. An entry of some incidental interest in the Lincoln accounts while Richard was 'custos' is the annual payment of £10 to Herbert of Ilchester, doubtless Richard's son;[11] and the roll for 1172–73 shows William

[1] Delisle, ed. cit., ii. 219–21.   [2] PR 2 Hen. II, p. 30.

[3] The Great Roll of the Pipe for the First Year of the Reign of King Richard I, ed. J. Hunter (London, 1844), p. 146.

[4] PR 9 Hen. II, p. 26.   [5] PR 10 Hen. II, p. 10; 11 Hen. II, p. 18; etc.

[6] PR 13 Hen. II, pp. 57–58; 14 Hen. II, p. 76; 15 Hen. II, p. 44; 16 Hen. II, p. 151; 17 Hen. II, p. 111; 18 Hen. II, p. 95; 19 Hen. II, p. 140.

[7] PR 13 Hen. II, pp. 148–49; 14 Hen. II, p. 140; 15 Hen. II, p. 2; 16 Hen. II, p. 113; 17 Hen. II, p. 12; 18 Hen. II, p. 72; 19 Hen. II, p. 191; 20 Hen. II, p. 16; 21 Hen. II, p. 22; 22 Hen. II, p. 154; 23 Hen. II, p. 18; 24 Hen. II, p. 39.

[8] PR 18 Hen. II, p. 85; and 19 Hen. II, p. 57.

[9] PR 18 Hen. II, p. 75; and 19 Hen. II, p. 197.

[10] PR 19 Hen. II, pp. 57 and 197; and 20 Hen. II, pp. 15–16.

[11] PR 13 Hen. II, p. 58; and 14 Hen. II, p. 77.

de Gundeville, Richard's clerk, in actual management of much of his business.[1]

An important extension of Richard's activities is recorded in the roll for 1167–68, where he appears as itinerant justice in numerous English shires in the south and west: London and Middlesex, Cambridge and Huntingdon, Hampshire, Sussex and Kent, in all areas in the company of Guy of Waltham and Reginald of Warenne, and additionally with William Bassett or Henry FitzGerald in some.[2] In all entries Richard's name appears first in the list. A preliminary view of the rolls suggests that Richard continued to visit all these areas, with some additions, until 1171–72;[3] but this is a misleading impression due to the outstanding accounts being transmitted year by year under their original headings. Nevertheless, he did act in companies of justices in Leicester and Warwick and in Nottinghamshire and Derby in 1168–69;[4] in Essex and Herts, Surrey and Sussex in 1169–70;[5] and alone in Northamptonshire in the same year.[6] In point of fact the 'placita archidiaconi Pictaviensis' continued to be enrolled in a diminishing number of counties until 1178–79, in which year all outstanding accounts were finally settled.[7]

Although Richard's appearance with his colleagues on these circuits first appears in the roll for 1167–68, it seems nevertheless that they were mainly instrumental in giving effect to the assize of 1166.[8] References in the rolls to a 'rotulus archidiaconi Pictaviensis' and later a 'rotulus episcopi Wintoniensis' have given rise to much speculation and controversy, but the evidence is meagre and the problems of interpretation of these records remain unresolved.[9] A scrutiny of the rolls of the reign reveals so far

[1] PR 19 Hen. II, pp. 57, 140 and 197.
[2] PR 14 Hen. II, pp. 4, 26, 43, 54, 105, 182, 195, 214 and 218.
[3] E.g., for PR 15 Hen. II, pp. 27, 58, 63, 75, 101, 126, 147, 154, 164, 168 and 172.   [4] Ibid., pp. 27 and 63.
[5] PR 16 Hen. II, pp. 109 and 137.   [6] Ibid., p. 22.
[7] After 1173: PR 20 Hen. II, pp. 4, 5, 42, 64, 119 and 128; 21 Hen. II, pp. 83, 114, 140, 190, 204, 205 and 216; 22 Hen. II, pp. 63, 71, 190, 208 and 213; 23 Hen. II, pp. 127, 167, 180, 193 and 204; 24 Hen. II, pp. 22 and 132; 25 Hen. II, pp. 3 and 121.
[8] J. Boussard, Le Gouvernement d'Henri II Plantegenêt (Paris, 1956), pp. 497–98; H. G. Richardson and G. O. Sayles, The Governance of Mediaeval England from the Conquest to Magna Carta (Edinburgh, 1963), pp. 200, n. 2, and 203.
[9] J. E. A. Jolliffe, 'The Camera Regis under Henry II', Eng[lish]

8

only three cases in which the 'rotulus' is mentioned—twice in
Norfolk and Suffolk, and once in Cornwall—though each case
is transmitted through a number of years until a settlement.[1]

The comparative absence from the pipe rolls of information on
Richard's judicial work after the early 1170's may be explained
on several grounds. His share in itinerant jurisdiction had apparently ceased, and there is no clear evidence of pleas resulting from
his appointment as one of the three chief justices in 1179, when
he was placed at the head of a panel of five judges with oversight
of nine of the southern English shires.[2] It may well be that
Richard's episcopal office restricted his involvement in the judicial
business of the secular courts, as canon law strictly required,
though this was not an effective bar to his appointment in 1179.[3]
On the other hand, there is ample evidence of his immersion
in the central government of the realm and on important business
overseas. His greatness in the Exchequer at the time is glowingly
attested by FitzNeal, who speaks of his earlier great skill in the
writing of rolls and writs, of his securing copies of all summonses,
checking originals and so forth; now he sits 'ex officio but by a
new ordinance' next to the presiding Justiciar.[4] The Treasurer
cannot speak too highly of him: 'He is a great man and should
not be busied except in important affairs.'[5] Moreover, it is well
known that Henry experimented in setting up central panels of
judges in and after 1178, and there is little doubt that Richard
shared in this. Certain it is that he is found on several occasions
between 1180 and 1183 sitting at Westminster or at the Exchequer
with other justices: the feet of fines record the reaching of final
concords in his presence.[6]

Hist[orical] Rev[iew], lxviii (1953), pp. 18–19; H. G. Richardson, 'The
Chamber under Henry II', *ibid.*, lxix (1954), p. 604; *idem* and Sayles, *op. cit.*,
p. 233.

[1] (i) *PR 9 Hen. II*, p. 29; *10 Hen. II*, p. 34; *11 Hen. II*, p. 4; *12 Hen. II*,
p. 18. (ii) *13 Hen. II*, p. 34; *14 Hen. II*, p. 16; *15 Hen. II*, p. 2; *16 Hen. II*,
p. 3. (iii) *22 Hen. II*, p. 151; *23 Hen. II*, p. 91.

[2] *Gesta Regis Henrici Secundi*, ed. W. Stubbs, i (Rolls Series, 1867),
pp. 238–39.

[3] But *cf.* Diceto, i. 434–35; and R. Foreville, *L'Église et la Royauté en
Angleterre sous Henri II Plantagenet* (Paris 1943), pp. 474–75.

[4] *Dialogus de Scaccario*, pp. 17, 26–27 and 74.   [5] *Ibid.*, p. 27.

[6] Eyton, *op. cit.*, pp. 237, 244, 249 and 251; *Feet of Fines, 1182–96*, PR Soc.
Publications, xvii (1894), pp. 1 and 2; see Boussard, *op. cit.*, p. 560.

No less distinguished were Richard's political services to the king in those same years and his unique position in moments of great crisis and in special commissions. In a situation of acute anxiety during the troubles in England in 1174, Henry's supporters choose Richard before all others to advise the king and counsel his return. No one, as Diceto relates it, could speak to the king more intimately, more urgently or more effectively; the Normans, seeing his arrival, wondered what further recourse could remain to the English but to send to Normandy the Tower of London.[1] Two years later, on the death of the Norman justiciar, William de Courcey, Richard returned to Normandy on a mission of the highest importance, marking, in Haskins's judgment, a turning point in the constitutional history of the Duchy.[2] The whole care of Normandy was entrusted to him: among other tasks, he carried through a thorough reorganization of the Exchequer, presided over assizes, laid tallages on Norman towns and seized castles into his hands. The disorganization resulting from the campaigns of 1173–74 was eliminated, and the fiscal roll of 1176, which is not extant, served as a basis for many years to come.[3] In Boussard's view the power and eminence of William FitzRalph, who succeeded Richard as Norman justiciar, resulted from Richard's work;[4] and Richard himself is described in a Norman charter of the period as 'post regem iudex et maior justitia'.[5] He returned to Normandy once more in 1180, and the first surviving roll of the ducal Exchequer, dating from that year, shows proof, if only scanty, of his resumption of his earlier interests.[6]

II. The Becket Conflict and its Aftermath

Richard was already highly placed in the royal *familia* when the struggle between Henry II and Becket broke out in England

[1] Diceto, i. 381–82.
[2] C. H. Haskins, *Norman Institutions* (Cambridge, 1925), pp. 174–76.
[3] *Loc. cit.*; Boussard, *op. cit.*, pp. 369–70 and 512–13; Sir Maurice Powicke, *The Loss of Normandy, 1189–1204* (Manchester, 2nd edn, 1961), pp. 51 and 54–55.
[4] Boussard, *op. cit.*, p. 513; whether or not Richard himself can be technically styled Justiciar, or Seneschal, has been the subject of some debate.
[5] Haskins, *op. cit.*, pp. 327–28.
[6] *Magni Rotuli Scaccarii Normanniae sub Regibus Angliae*, ed. T. Stapleton,

10

in 1163–64; and in that crisis he soon became a principal instrument of royal policies. Early evidence of his role in the story can perhaps be found in the letters of John, bishop of Poitiers, to Becket reporting on the gathering storm in Henry's continental lands. One of John's letters speaks of 'Luscus noster', the eye of whose mind God had blinded, arriving in Poitiers with Simon de Tournebu, to enforce new royal mandates of unheard of harshness.[1] A further letter speaks of 'Luscus' coming back to Poitiers, 'ad nos reversus', and summoning the army of Aquitaine against a possible French invasion[2]. This 'Luscus' has been variously identified as Richard de Luci or Richard of Ilchester, but there is much to be said for the latter identification: the tone and expression of the bishop of Poitiers would accord very well with his speaking contemptuously of his own archdeacon; and it is a fact that Simon de Tournebu is later found in Richard's company in the Norman reforms of 1176–78.[3]

But quite apart from matters of speculation, it is perfectly clear that Richard played a central part in the early negotiations. Diceto speaks of his sharing with Arnulf of Lisieux the task of presenting the king's case to Alexander III, then in exile in France: six times within three months they endured the perils of the sea, but without success,[4] though a moderating letter of the pope to Becket mentions Richard as one of Henry's envoys in the negotiations for the legateship of York.[5] It is not surprising, in view of Richard's nominally lowly office at the time, that his name does not figure in the list of great persons witnessing the Constitutions of Clarendon; but after Becket's flight, he was swiftly dispatched with the bishop of London and the earl of Arundel to present the king's case to the French court,[6] and then included in an imposing company of envoys on a similar mission to the pope.[7] Very early he was designated a hostile influence in the Becket correspondence, as a leading promoter of royal measures against the archbishop: Becket himself so named

---

i (London, 1840), pp. xxix, lxxxv and 74; Haskins, *op. cit.*, pp. 174–76; Boussard, *op. cit.*, p. 513 and n. 2.

[1] *Materials*, v. 38.   [2] *Ibid.*, v. 115.

[3] Eyton, *op. cit.*, pp. 206 and 209. For Simon, see also Delisle, *ed. cit.*, i.90, 91, 406, 415, 416, 426, 430, 448, 465; ii. 32, 89, 90, 108 and 126.

[4] Diceto, i. 312.

[5] *Materials*, v. 85.   [6] *Ibid.*, iv. 58.   [7] *Ibid.*, iv. 60–61.

Richard together with Roger of York and Gilbert of London in a letter of 1164.[1] And in a fascinating letter, at Christmas of the same year, Nicholas of Mont Rouen reported to the exiled Becket that the Queen Mother had been instructed by Richard in her criticisms of the shortcomings of the clergy of the time: being a woman of tyrant stock, she approved of some of Henry's constitutions, but regretted that he had seen fit to set them down.[2]

Richard's loyal service to the king involved him in more serious censures in 1165 and after. As envoy to Frederick I after the negotiations for the Saxon marriage, he travelled to Germany with John of Oxford and Rainald Dassell, elect of Cologne, and took part in the schismatical council of Würzburg on 22 May 1165, which abjured Alexander III and adhered to the newly elected anti-pope Paschal. Letters of Frederick I and Henry II lend support to the circumstantial reports of the meeting.[3] Here was a situation of great perplexity, opportunity and danger. Historians are not wanting who interpret Henry's policy as one of great astuteness in exploiting a delicate situation vis-à-vis the pope and Becket. The upshot of the matter was that Becket, at Vézelay on Whit Sunday 1166, excommunicated John of Oxford, Richard and the other English participants: a decision then confirmed by the pope.[4] Richard did not receive this sentence very happily, and seemed surprised by the archbishop's action. One of the most illuminating letters of the affair records Diceto's gently but firmly instructing his friend to accept the sentence with humility and not to set himself up against the law, providing a bad example to the destruction of many.[5] Richard indeed seems to have escaped the degree of obloquy which concentrated on John of Oxford, and was released from the ban by the papal legate in 1167.[6]

A remarkable feature throughout the controversy is the extent to which Richard remained a point of common recourse for partisans on both sides. His value to the king's supporters is clearly self-evident; but he appears not to have alienated all

[1] *Ibid.*, i. 47–48.   [2] *Ibid.*, v. 150.
[3] *Ibid.*, v. 182–84 and 428–29; *cf.* Foreville, *op. cit.*, pp. 170–75.
[4] *Materials*, i. 61; v. 388, 390 and 392.
[5] Diceto, i. 319–20. For the authorship of this letter, see *ibid.*, ii. 282.
[6] *Ibid.*, vi. 321.

members of Becket's entourage. Again, as we have noticed elsewhere, there was widespread recognition of his intimate influence with the king; and many persons, of whatever persuasion, were doubtless anxious to retain his favour and intercession. The letters of John of Salisbury are particularly revealing here; two letters to Richard in 1166 blend many divergent elements: sympathy for the excommunicated Richard, gentle allusion to his vulnerable actions, concern for John's own return to England and reconciliation with the king, hopes for peace between king and archbishop, protestations nevertheless of loyalty to the latter.[1] These letters are neatly complemented by two others to Ralph Niger, in which John promises to use whatever influence he has with Becket to bend him to Richard's favour, and regrets his own failure to secure Richard's intercession on his own behalf: Ralph should seek to influence him to the paths of justice and deal with him in charity despite his excommunication.[2] Nevertheless, John wrote to Bartholomew of Exeter that Richard and his companions of Würzburg had been justly censured;[3] and in 1168 a letter of Gilbert Foliot, in quite a different context, touched on Richard's continuing royal service, asking 'his dear kinsman' and his fellow justices not to usurp the jurisdiction of the Church over criminous clerks.[4]

Richard was deeply committed in the heightening crisis of Becket's final years, being placed under the ban of the archbishop for a second time in 1169.[5] He attended a meeting convened by Foliot in London to organize an appeal against Becket;[6] and one of the most moving letters of the time reveals Odo of Canterbury abjectly appealing to Richard to be released from pressure to join in the action against his spiritual father and archbishop.[7] Together with Richard de Luci and Geoffrey Ridel, Richard was commissioned by Henry II to bring the harsh constitutions of 1169 into England;[8] and he was fully involved in the preparations for the coronation of the young king on 14 June 1170, being found in the young king's company both before and after the ceremony.[9] He avoided Becket, on the latter's return in December,[10] and was absent from England at the time of the murder, though Eyton's

[1] *Materials*, v. 331–34 and 347–52. [2] *Ibid.*, vi. 1–5 and 5–8.
[3] *Ibid.*, v. 383. [4] *Ibid.*, vi. 453–55. [5] *Ibid.*, vi. 594 and 601.
[6] *Ibid.*, vi. 606. [7] *Ibid.*, vii. 52–56; cf. Foreville, *op. cit.*, p. 192.
[8] *Materials*, vii. 147. [9] *Ibid.*, vii. 310 and 389. [10] *Ibid.*, iii. 120.

statement that he was in the papal court at Frascati when the news arrived there seems based on a misreading of the inscriptions of letters of English envoys there at the time.[1]

Now, just as Arnulf and Richard had acted for the king in the papal negotiations at the outbreak of the dispute, so also, with Reginald of Salisbury, they played an important role in the negotiations for a settlement. They appear in a leading, and apparently conciliatory, way in the resumption of negotiations broken off at Savigny in 1172, concluding in the famous agreement at Avranches later in the year.[2] Reginald and Richard were among the king's closest advisers in ecclesiastical matters in the years following Becket's death. But if the clearly constructive part which Richard then played, coupled with certain of his later words when bishop, has induced some historians to detect in him a change of heart, induced by the martyr's death and subsequent miracles,[3] this was certainly reconciled with his continuing service to the king. He it was who announced the abortive election of Roger of Bec to Canterbury at Lambeth in 1173, in the king's absence, taking an initiative between contending factions, for the sake of peace.[4]

His own election to the see of Winchester in 1173 provides a focus of almost every theme of interest in our story. There can be no doubt that the elections to six vacant sees in that year reveal Henry's determination to create a strong basis of support and loyalty for himself within the bench of bishops at that moment: Richard himself, Geoffrey Ridel, Geoffrey Plantagenet, Reginald of Salisbury, Robert of Oxford and John of Chichester were promoted to Winchester, Ely, Lincoln, Bath, Hereford and Chichester respectively.[5] The first four at least were long experienced and tested in the royal service.[6] It is conceivable that Henry would have pursued this policy in any eventuality, but the very serious domestic and political troubles brewing at that time doubtless strengthened his resolution. The young king denounced the elections to Alexander III as in derogation of his own position; because the persecutors of the martyr were promoted to ecclesi-

[1] Cf. Eyton, op. cit., p. 153, and Materials, vii. 457–78.

[2] Ibid., iv. 414; cf. Foreville, op. cit., p. 337.

[3] E.g., Giraldus Cambrensis, Opera, ed. J. F. Dimock, vii (Rolls Series, 1877), pp. 69–70.   [4] Diceto, i. 354.

[5] Ibid., i. 367–68.   [6] Foreville, op. cit., pp. 370–71 and 379–84.

astical honours; and because the freedom of canonical election
was being abused. With particular reference to Richard he cited
the oft-quoted writ of his father to the Winchester electors:
'I order you to hold a free election, but nevertheless forbid you
to elect anyone but Richard, my clerk, the archdeacon of
Poitiers.'[1] No doubt all of the younger Henry's allegations were
true, but Alexander accepted the elections as canonically proper
and an imposing corpus of testimonials for Richard survives from
the pens of Foliot,[2] John of Salisbury[3] and Bartholomew of
Exeter.[4] For many reasons a different spirit was at work, in
Church and State alike, from that in Becket's day.

III. *Richard as Bishop*

Whether or not Richard, as bishop of Winchester, played any
significant part in the development of canon law in England has
never yet been the subject of serious examination. The question
is of exceptional interest in view of the leading role he played in
the king's service during and after the Becket dispute, because of
his own extensive legal experience and distinguished reputation,
and even more so because his years as bishop witnessed the
most fruitful contributions ever made by English canonists to the
law of the Universal Church.[5] It is true that Richard figures
prominently in the correspondence and chronicles of the period
in matters of obvious canonical interest, but often, significantly
enough, in a sense which reveals the continuation into his
episcopal career of the implementation of royal policies.

We have noted above that Richard, while archdeacon of
Poitiers and a royal justice, was admonished by Gilbert Foliot,
with Becket in exile, for an infringement of the Church's jurisdiction over criminous clerks.[6] A well-known letter of Archbishop
Richard in 1176, addressed to the bishops of Winchester, Ely and

---

[1] Foreville, *op. cit.*, p. 379; M. Bouquet, *Recueil des Historiens des Gaules et
de la France*, xiv (Paris, 1806), p. 645.

[2] Gilbert Foliot, *Epistolae*, ed. cit., i. 247–48.

[3] John of Salisbury, *Epistolae*, ed. J. A. Giles, ii (Oxford, 1848), pp. 276–
278; *epp.* 313–15.

[4] Bartholomew of Exeter, *ibid.*, ii. 279–80: *epp.* 316–17.

[5] C. Duggan, *Twelfth-Century Decretal Collections and their Importance
in English History* (London, 1963), pp. 118–51.

[6] *Materials*, vi. 453–55.

Norwich, affords an interesting complement to this. The letter complains of the avoidance of punishment by the slayers of clerks: the secular sword should be called in to supplement the Church's jurisdiction; there would be no double punishment if what was begun by one jurisdiction should be completed by the other.[1] This was a strange doctrine, said Zachary Brooke, for St Thomas's successor.[2] But it was not quite as strange as Brooke had imagined. Both Becket and Richard were contending for the Church's interests in contexts which were entirely different; the context as well as the comment must be carefully evaluated.[3] Brooke certainly understated the matter in describing the recipients of Archbishop Richard's letter as three bishops who had formerly been opponents of Becket;[4] they were still deeply committed in royal administration, and were to be the three archjusticiars of Henry's appointment two years later;[5] and it is highly significant that Archbishop Richard's letter was addressed jointly to them. The legate Pierleoni was negotiating with Henry II in England between late October 1175 and early July 1176;[6] and the king's letter to Alexander III on the conclusion of these transactions deals with the punishment of the slayers of clerks and with the problem of criminous clerks as quite separate matters.[7] It is tempting to conclude that Richard of Dover's letter to Richard of Ilchester and his companions played some part in the

[1] *Ibid.*, vii. 561–64.

[2] Z. N. Brooke, *The English Church and the Papacy from the Conquest to the reign of John* (Cambridge, 1931), pp. 219–20; see also now H. M. Mayr-Harting, 'Henry II and the Papacy', *Journal of Ecclesiastical History*, xvi (1965), p. 44.

[3] Becket took his stand in defence of clerical privilege against secular curtailment of it, not against the secular enforcement of an ecclesiastical judgment; canonical tradition allowed that recourse might be had to the secular power at the Church's discretion or to make effective judgments in the Church's interests. Becket was not contending against that tradition. Richard was likewise concerned with clerical interests: to defend clerks against attacks made on them with impunity; once more the secular power could make effective a judgment to the Church's benefit. It may be thought that Becket and Richard used ill-chosen arguments, in emphasizing the 'double punishment' thesis, but their policies were equally reconcilable with canonical tradition. *Cf.* C. Duggan, 'The Becket Dispute and the Criminous Clerks', *Bulletin of the Institute of Historical Research*, xxxv (1962), pp. 1–28.

[4] Brooke, *op. cit.*, p. 219.   [5] Diceto, i. 434–35.

[6] *Ibid.*, 402–3 and 410; *cf.* Foreville, *op. cit.*, pp. 426–28.

[7] Diceto, i. 410.

solution of these vexatious questions; and likewise that Richard of Ilchester contributed at this stage also to the settlement of outstanding problems between the two jurisdictions, as he had done at Avranches in the earlier stage of the settlement.

Two years later, in a letter dated 1 October 1178, Alexander III wrote to Richard of Winchester and Gilbert of London on the question of conflicting jurisdictions over land tenure. A mere fragment of this letter survives, in Diceto's *Ymagines Historiarum*, but it is of great importance in the working out of rival claims of Church and State in England at that period.[1] In clause IX of the Constitutions of Clarendon Henry II had attempted in 1164 to lay down the procedure for dealing with lay fees, ruling that the question of whether disputed land was held by frankalmoign or lay fee should be decided before the king's justice on the recognition of a jury. This procedure gave its form to the assize *utrum*, whose origins A. L. Poole has detected in the reign of Stephen.[2] It is not surprising that this solution in favour of secular jurisdiction was resisted by the Church. Nevertheless, the letter of 1178 shows the pope conceding the king's claims: having decided that it pertained to the king to decide matters of possession, and also to avoid injury to the king's honour, Alexander mandated the bishops to leave judgment of possession to the king. It is not easy to be sure of Richard's part in the circumstances giving rise to this letter, as it is unlikely, from everything we know of him, that he would attempt to exercise in practice jurisdiction obnoxious to the king; but the interesting suggestion has been made by Foreville that the bishops of London and Winchester received the papal mandate because of the association of their sees with the most common venues of the royal court.[3] At all events, here was one vexed issue, in which Richard was involved as bishop, which was decisively resolved in the secular interest.

In all the instances cited above Richard is seen acting in situations which have an obvious canonical importance, but in the special area of Church–State conflicts. It was natural enough that he would be involved in these affairs; and these aspects of his

---

[1] Diceto, i. 427–28.
[2] A. L. Poole, *From Domesday Book to Magna Carta* (Oxford, 2nd edn, 1955), pp. 156–57; for an excellent survey of this question, see R. C. Van Caenegem, *Royal Writs in England from the Conquest to Glanvill*, Selden Society, lxxvii (1958–59), pp. 325–30.   [3] Foreville, *op. cit.*, p. 442.

work are known through non-canonical sources. It is in the more strictly ecclesiastical setting that his place in the history of canon law has passed unnoticed. It comes as a surprise therefore to discover that several canonical rulings which he elicited from Alexander III secured a permanent place in the corpus of medieval canon law through their absorption into twelfth-century decretal collections and thence into the official Gregorian *Decretales* of 1234. At least seven chapters in the 1234 collection were received by Richard; they are scattered widely through the books and deal with a very broad range of topics: papal rescripts, the office of judge delegate, appeals, tithe payments, rights of patronage, the duty of education, and so forth.[1] Further chapters in Bernard of Pavia's *Compilatio Prima* (*post* 1191) also received by Richard but not assumed into the Gregorian collection, deal with still further points of law.[2] An understanding of the way in which papal decretals were incorporated in professional collections and transmitted from one to another easily explains why this aspect of Richard's work has passed unnoticed, for he is not identified as the recipient of these letters in the official book of canon law or in Jaffé's standard *Regesta* of papal letters.[3] The principal defects of the later derivative canonical sources are the absence of accurate historical details in inscriptions, names and dates, the excision of passages of non-juridical importance, and the dismemberment of long letters into component fragments. For reliable historical data it is best to go back to the most primitive collections, dating from the mid-1170's, and the early systematic collections, of a slightly later period. Their seminal period coincided with Richard's episcopate, and the majority of those early works were composed in England.[4]

The earliest English collections show little trace of Richard's influence: the two most ancient works, the Worcester II and Belvoir Collections, completed soon after 1175, include no

---

[1] *Corpus Iuris Canonici*, ed. E. Friedberg, ii (Leipzig, 1881): *Decretales Gregorii IX*, 1. 3. 3; 1. 28. 3; 1. 29. 6; 2. 28. 22; 3. 30. 6; 3. 38. 8; 5. 5. 2.

[2] *Quinque Compilationes Antiquae*, ed. E. Friedberg (Leipzig, 1882): *Compilatio Prima*, 3. 33. 9; 4. 1. 2; 5. 15. 6. The date of composition of *Compilatio Prima* is estimated as not earlier than March 1192.

[3] P. Jaffé, *Regesta Pontificum Romanorum*, ii (Leipzig, 2nd edn 1888), nos. (JL)14151–58 are all listed simply 'Wintoniensi episcopo', under Alexander III's pontifical years 1159–81.

[4] Duggan, *op. cit.*, pp. 66–117.

decretals addressed to Winchester.[1] The Canterbury Collection, c. 1179–81, has one long papal rescript, *Quamvis simus*, of several component chapters in which Alexander III is seen instructing Richard in a range of problems, involving general principles in canon law and canonical procedure; this manuscript dates the letter at Venice on 21 July 1177.[2] The same decretal is found in the Rochester Collection, completed in stages between c.1179–81 and in or after 1193, together with two further rescripts of possible Ricardian provenance, dealing with particular cases of papal delegation.[3] The Royal Collection, post 1181, has six chapters received by Richard, but they are in reality component parts of *Quamvis simus*, which has been dissected and its fragments distributed.[4] The growing practice of decretal dismemberment in this way reduces the value of detailed statistical analysis in the later collections. But the general conclusion is valid that, as the total corpus of Alexander III's decretals increased in the professional collections, so did the number of cases in which Richard can be seen acting in a judicial capacity. Thus the Cheltenham Collection, c. 1193 or later, has at least nine letters received by Richard, either alone or in company with other judges;[5] the Tanner Collection, of slightly later date, has about twenty scattered chapters, though several of these are not whole letters;[6] the Frankfurt Collection has approximately the same number in its basic transcription and four further items in its marginal additions.[7]

These letters for the most part show Richard acting as a papal judge delegate, of which office indeed he had had experience even

[1] Duggan, pp. 69–73 and 152–62.

[2] *Ibid.*, pp. 73–76 and 162–73; for *Quamvis simus*, *ibid.*, p. 164, no. 20 (JL 14152, 14154 and 14156): 'Dat. Venet. in Rivo Alto XII Kal. Augusti'. *Cf.* B[ritish] M[useum], Royal MS. 10 B. IV, fos. 45vb–46va.

[3] Duggan, *op. cit.*, pp. 76–78 and 173–87; *cf.* nos. 31, 37 and 72: the Winchester inscription of this last item is probably false.

[4] B.M., Royal MS. 15 B. IV, fos. 107^v, 109^r and 109^v–110^r.

[5] B.M., Egerton MS. 2819, fos. 19vb, 43ra, 43va, 50rb, 66ra, 76ra, 79vb, 85vb and 99vb; further items are of possible Winchester provenance.

[6] Oxford Bodley Tanner MS. 8, fos. 591^a–720; analysed by W. Holtzmann, 'Die Dekretalensammlungen des 12. Jahrhunderts; 1. Die Sammlung Tanner', *Festschrift zur Feier des 200jährigen Bestehens der Akad. der Wissenschaften in Göttingen, Phil.-Hist. Kl.* (1951), pp. 83–145, nos. 2. 3. 1; 2. 11. 4; 2. 14. 1; 3. 10. 1; 3. 13. 2; etc.

[7] B.M., Egerton MS. 2901, fos. 7^r, 9^r, 16^v, 17^r, 28^v, etc.

as archdeacon of Poitiers. On at least one occasion he appeared as a judicial colleague of each of the bishops of Hereford, Exeter and Bath, possibly also of London and Norwich, and with the abbot of Ford.[1] The letters, several of which are positively linked with Richard for the first time on the evidence of the decretal collections, were dispatched mostly within the limits of the period from 1174 to 1181, the year of Alexander III's death; one or two letters only were sent by Alexander's successor Lucius III;[2] and nothing to Richard is found in the canonical sources after 1185. The problems dealt with range through marriage questions, tithe payment, clerical status, judicial procedure and so forth. In view of the outstanding interest of the decretal *Quamvis simus*, it is worth examining its contents in further detail. In reply to a series of questions put to Alexander by Richard, the pope in this letter laid down a series of rulings on the admissibility of subdelegation of papal jurisdiction; on the deferment of cases commissioned 'appellatione postposita'; on the non-constraint of witnesses; on churches granted by laymen, when not yet vacant; and on the rights of perpetual vicars. These are questions which could naturally arise in the course of the delegated office; and Richard's great experience in other spheres would still further prompt his interest in the procedural problems. But the letter is even more interesting than it may appear at first sight. It may well be wondered if Richard's vast preoccupations with other duties, including the king's affairs, left him much time for the personal fulfilment of these papal commissions, and further if he had a particularly individual reason for seeking papal guidance on the subdelegation of cases. When it is remembered that the Canterbury Collection reveals that Alexander dispatched this important letter from Venice on 21 July 1177, whereas Richard was totally immersed in fiscal and judicial administration in Normandy from September 1176 until March 1178,[3] the theory is strengthened that Richard in fact conducted his ecclesiastical jurisdiction in part at least through the canonists in his household; and this in turn provides an interesting sidelight on the claim made by Peter of

---

[1] JL 13932, 14311, etc.

[2] *Tanner*, 2. 14. 1; Holtzmann, *loc. cit.*, pp. 111–12; B.M., Egerton MS. 2819, fo. 99vb.

[3] Eyton, *op. cit.*, pp. 206 and 222; *cf.* p. 9, nn. 2–5 above.

Blois that Richard of Winchester was the first to introduce the bishop's Official into England.[1]

In attempting a final estimate of Richard's place in the development of canon law in England, an important distinction must be made between the application of the law through Church courts and the machinery of justice on the one hand, and the professional work of the canonists in codification and literary commentary on the other. In the first of these respects, there is no doubt that Richard, as papal judge delegate and in his office as diocesan ordinary, played some part in the forward movement of ecclesiastical jurisdiction at that time; it is much more open to doubt if he made any significant personal contribution to the latter. While it is true that certain letters received by Richard were recognized by canonists as having particular importance and suitable therefore for inclusion in canonical collections—and that is why Richard's decretals found their way ultimately into the Gregorian collection—there is insufficient evidence at present to prove that Richard's work stimulated individual collectors in his circle to any marked degree, though one or two surviving decretal collections reveal a possible Winchester influence.[2] It is in any case almost certain that Richard received far fewer papal commissions than distinguished judges delegate of the quality of Roger of Worcester or Bartholomew of Exeter.

'Bishop Richard of good memory departed to the Lord' on 21 December 1188.[3] For several years the traces of his former power had slowly faded from the records of all kinds. It is a fitting conclusion to his record of faithful service to the king that the chronicler's final notice of his life is of Henry's visit to Richard on his estate of Merewell in the Isle of Wight.[4] For more than twenty years of Henry's reign most threads of English history had passed at some time through his hands. Exceptional skill in the detail of administration, unusual energy in the execution of

---

[1] R. W. Southern, 'Some New Letters of Peter of Blois', *Eng. Hist. Rev.*, liii (1938), p. 412 and n. 7; Cheney, *Becket to Langton*, p. 147 and n. 2.

[2] The B.M. Egerton MS. 2901 will be discussed in a separate study, together with a critical edition of the Winchester decretals of the period and a report on the canonists in the Winchester household.

[3] *Annales Monastici*, ed. H. R. Luard, ii (Rolls Series, 1864), p. 63; *Gesta Regis Henrici Secundi, ed. cit.*, ii. 58.   [4] Diceto, ii. 40–41.

his office, patience and persuasiveness in diplomacy, integrity and constancy according to his concept of his duty: these are the qualities which made him an almost indispensable servant of the king through so long a period. It is a curious paradox that, despite the richness of evidence of his influence, an insight into his own thoughts and personality persistently eludes us. No letters or writings of his own survive, except very rarely in brief and indirect citations. Yet a sense of great respect grows with increased familiarity with his work. His greatest faculty appears in effective execution rather than in a creative or originating capacity. His importance in the history of English secular institutions is broadly manifest; his role in ecclesiastical affairs is more open to interpretation. It is difficult to escape the conclusion that for several years after his elevation to the see of Winchester he was among the most decisive personalities in the English State. It was in those years that a general pattern of harmonious compromise between the rival jurisdictions of Church and State was worked out. Richard was almost uniquely fitted to facilitate this transition, and the situation in England after Becket's martyrdom provided an unusually favourable opportunity. Knowles has written with significant implication 'What Henry could have achieved after 1162 with an archbishop as pliant as his Chancellor had been and with a hierarchy recruited from men of the type of Geoffrey Ridel, John of Oxford and Richard of Ilchester must remain a matter of conjecture.'[1] But Richard came at last to the full extent of his influence in a fundamentally altered situation. Cheney has rightly said that the years after the Avranches settlement of 1172 were a period of effective adjustment and reconciliation between the two powers.[2] And it is clear that Richard of Ilchester played an important part in that achievement.

King's College London

[1] Knowles, *op. cit.*, pp. 155–56.
[2] Cheney, *op. cit.*, p. 108; *cf.* C. Duggan, 'From the Conquest to the Death of John', in C. H. Lawrence, ed., *The English Church and the Papacy in the Middle Ages* (London, 1965), pp. 87–93 and 108–13.

XIII

BISHOP JOHN AND ARCHDEACON RICHARD OF POITIERS
THEIR ROLES IN THE BECKET DISPUTE AND ITS AFTERMATH

The debt which English scholars in the twelfth century owed to the schools of France is surely self-evident, for it was in these together with the pre-eminent law schools of Bologna that almost everything intellectually creative and illuminating in the island originated at that time. And it is no less evident that the debt to France of the Western Church under papal guidance, in the pontificate of Alexander III, and of the English Church in particular in the archiepiscopate of St Thomas of Canterbury, would be hard to over-estimate. It was most appropriate therefore that the grateful Alexander dispatched the Golden Rose as a mark of signal affection to the *rex Christianissimus*, king Louis VII of France, who had afforded him refuge in exile in the early years of the perilous schism which followed the contested papal election of 1159, [1] just as later the king gave succour to St Thomas in exile after the Councils of Clarendon and Northampton in 1164. [2] In the famous circular letter of March 1173, announcing the canonization of the martyred Becket, Alexander began his eulogy of St Thomas with the words 'Redolet Anglia fragrantia et virtute miraculorum et signorum quae per merita illius sancti et reverendi viri Thomae', [3] and it is not altogether unfitting that among the numerous copies of this letter still surviving one decretal collection contains the erroneous but strangely just transcription 'Redolet Anglia et Francia virtute'. [4] For these and many similar reasons, it is above all suitable that French scholars should have conceived and organized this international colloquium in commemoration of St Thomas's canonization. It is sometimes believed that king Henry II provided an impetus to the schools in England by recalling English scholars from France during Becket's exile. [5] Certainly, it is now a welcome experience for scholars to come to France from England to

---

1. Cf. Alexander III's letter *Ex antiqua Romanorum*, under March 1163 in P. JAFFE, *Regesta Pontificum Romanorum*, 2 vols. (2nd ed. G. Wattenbach, S. Löwenfeld, F. Kaltenbrunner and P. Ewald, Leipzig, 1885 and 1888), t. II, n. 10826; items in the *Regesta* for our period are subsequently identified by the abbreviation JL. Cf. also C. DUGGAN, 'English Canonists and the *Appendix Concilii Lateranensis* : with an Analysis of the St John's, Cambridge, MS. 148', *Traditio*, vol. XVIII (1962), p. 459-468, esp. p. 463 and 467-468; *idem*, 'Golden Rose', *New Catholic Encyclopedia*, New York, 1967, vol. 6, p. 599-600.
2. Among recent accounts of the councils and exile, cf. D. KNOWLES, *Thomas Becket*, London, 1970, p. 77-134.
3. *Redolet Anglia* : JL 12203 and 12204, March 12th

and 13th, and JL 12218, April 2nd, 1173; cf. C. DUGGAN, *English Canonists*, p. 463 and 466-468. For a printed text, cf. *Materials for the History of Thomas Becket*, vol. VII, edd. J. C. ROBERTSON and J. B. SHEPPARD, London, 1885, p. 547-548, (Rolls Series).
4. Vatican MS. Ottob. Lat. 3027, fols. 109 r-v. This MS. is one of three known copies of the *Collectio Brugensis*, but the letter is not found in the two codices analysed in E. FRIEDBERG, *Die Canones-sammlungen zwischen Gratian und Bernhard von Pavia*, Leipzig, 1897 (Graz reprint 1958), p. 170, at *Brug.* 59.3.
5. Cf. H. RASHDALL, *The Universities of Europe in the Middle Ages*, 3 vols. (revised and edd. F. M. Powicke and A. B. Emden, Oxford, 1936), vol. III, p. 29-31, and Appendix I, p. 465-476, with special reference to Paris and Oxford.

72

share in this commemoration, the more so since no comparable memorial has seemingly been arranged in England, where the canonization has passed comparatively unnoticed, whereas the eighth-centenary of St Thomas's dramatic martyrdom was remembered with devotion in many churches and places in England associated with him, [6] although from the liturgical and devotional viewpoint the canonization may be judged by far the more important.

Within the context of these general reflections, the history of two leading ecclesiastics of the church of Poitiers is of outstanding interest in an examination of the Becket dispute, for its bishop John and its archdeacon Richard, both appointed to their offices at Poitiers from England, may justly be considered as classic exponents of the opposing forces. [7] Moreover, they mirrored in France the polarity of tensions created in England at Canterbury itself in the persons of the archbishop Thomas and his successor as archdeacon, Geoffrey Ridel, from 1163. Archdeacon Geoffrey of Canterbury, later bishop of Ely, was a faithful instrument of Henry II's policies, alike in their secular and ecclesiastical aspects, and as such came into repeated conflict with the archbishop: he is referred to as 'archidiabolus noster' in the Becket correspondence and was excommunicated by Becket on two occasions. [8] In remarkably similar circumstances, his friend and close colleague in the royal administration, Richard of Ilchester, later bishop of Winchester, was archdeacon of Poitiers from 1163. Richard also emerges prominently as a hostile figure in the Becket *Materials*, and was likewise excommunicated twice by the archbishop, [9] whereas the bishop of Poitiers, consecrated by Alexander III in 1163, was John of Canterbury, sometimes called of Poitiers, or John aux Bellesmains, or with some ambiguity John of Belmeis. [10] John was among the earliest of Becket's clerical colleagues and with some variations of emphasis remained among his staunchest supporters. Later he became primate of Gaul, as archbishop of Lyon, from which eminence he retired in old age to die a simple monk of Clairvaux in the pontificate of Innocent III. We have therefore this extraordinary situation that both at Canterbury and at Poitiers, which was among the most powerful sees in Henry II's continental empire, the prelate and his archdeacon were on opposite sides in the dispute.

The origins of John of Poitiers are obscure, but he is generally accepted as a native of Kent and almost certainly of Canterbury itself; [11] his brilliant ascent was through his ser-

---

6. Most notably at Canterbury: cf. *1170-1970* : « St Thomas Becket », ed. H. WADDAMS, in *The Canterbury Cathedral Chronicle*, no. 65, Canterbury, 1970. To record a merely personal experience, the present writer spoke in the course of 1970 at several places associated with St Thomas : cf. C. DUGGAN, 'The Significance of the Becket Dispute in the History of the English Church', *Ampleforth Journal*, vol. LXXV (1970), p. 365-375; idem, *Thomas of London : an Address in Commemoration of St Thomas of Canterbury*, printed for the Mercers' Company, 1971. For Professor RAYMONDE FOREVILLE's address in commemoration of St Thomas, given at Poitiers in December 1970, cf. 'Mort et survie de saint Thomas Becket', *Cahiers de Civilisation Médiévale*, vol. XIV, no. 1 (1971), p. 21-38. An excellent survey on the secondary literature concerning the Becket dispute was published in the United States in 1970 : J. W. ALEXANDER, 'The Becket Controversy in Recent Historiography', *The Journal of British Studies*, vol. IX, no. 2 (May 1970), p. 1-26.

7. There are useful but partly outdated articles on John and Richard in *The Dictionary of National Biography* : for John, cf. vol. 2 (1908), edd. L. STEPHEN and S. LEE, p. 196-198, art. by T. A. ARCHER; for Richard, cf. vol. 16 (1909), ed. S. LEE, p. 1080-1083, art. by KATE NORGATE. The most comprehensive study so far on John is by

PH. POUZET, *L'Anglais Jean dit Bellesmains*, Lyon, 1927; the most recent essay on Richard is C. DUGGAN, 'Richard of Ilchester, Royal Servant and Bishop', *Transactions of the Royal Historical Society*, 5th series, vol. 16 (1966), p. 1-21.

8. C. DUGGAN, *Richard of Ilchester*, p. 2, and n. 1.

9. *Ibid.*, p. 2, and n. 1. It is not suggested that either Geoffrey or Richard was much involved in archidiaconal functions in the dioceses of Canterbury and Poitiers; their appointments to these benefices were in compensation for their services to the king.

10. POUZET, *op. cit.*, p. 7-8; the form Belmeis is ambiguous because of its possession by the Belmeis family which was so influential in the chapter of St Paul's in London. Bishop Richard Belmeis preferred to promote Ralph de Diceto rather than John to the archdeaconry of Middlesex in 1152 : cf. RALPH DE DICETO, *Opera Historica*, vol. I, ed. W. Stubbs, London, 1876, p. xx-xxx, (Rolls Series). For John's consecration by pope, *ibid.*, p. 311.

11. POUZET, *op. cit.*, p. 9, assembles several contemporary references to John's English origins, including Walter Map's specific allusion to Canterbury as his birthplace: 'Natus a Cantuaria'. Certainly John is described in

vices to the Church. On Becket's entry into archbishop Theobald's *familia* in 1143-1144, John was already established there in a position of some importance, and a friendship grew between these two and also the young Roger of Pont-l'Évêque, later archbishop of York and in that office one of Becket's principal adversaries within the English Church. [12] All three were destined to become archbishops and metropolitans; indeed, Avrom Saltman, Theobald's biographer, has noted that this distinguished household included no less than four future archbishops and six bishops, among whom several played an important part in secular as well as ecclesiastical administration. [13] John is recorded as a witness to 13 surviving charters of Theobald, sometimes together with Thomas and Roger, with John of Salisbury and other learned and able clerks. [14] In 1152 he failed to secure the archdeaconry of Middlesex, in spite of papal support, against bishop Richard of London's nominee, Ralph de Diceto; [15] but he obtained the treasurership of York in 1153-1154, [16] shortly before Roger of Pont-l'Évêque became the northern metropolitan.

It is clear that John had already attracted the favourable notice of the Roman curia; and in this period he is recognized as a firm defender of ecclesiastical liberties, an upholder of the papal primacy, a canonist of some importance, and a defender of the prerogatives of Canterbury, of which he remained a zealous *alumnus* in spite of his northern appointment. The identity of his position with that of Becket later is obvious enough. Nor is it without interest that Gilbert Foliot, successively bishop of Hereford from 1148 and bishop of London from 1163, had slightingly referred to John of Canterbury's zeal for the apostolic see as early as c. 1146, when as abbot of Gloucester he had rejected an offer of help from John. In view of Gilbert's later hostility to Becket in a similar vein, the inscription of his letter to John of Canterbury at that early date is worth transcription: 'Sedulo maiestatis apostolice defensori domno Iohanni de Cantuaria frater Gilebertus Gloecestrie dictus abbas, sales si placet suos intra fines modestie modo laudabili cohibere.'[17]

John's election to the see of Poitiers in 1162 has been a subject of some debate. The statement of William FitzStephen that Henry II had secured this promotion to remove from Becket's side so powerful an aide is not convincing; [18] it is much more likely, in view of the political and ecclesiastical importance of Poitiers, that John's selection was part of Henry's strategy in determining ecclesiastical appointments throughout his dominions at that time. [19] If this evaluation is correct, then John's elevation should be compared with

charter attestations and in epistolary inscriptions as 'de Cantuaria', as is evidenced by extracts cited later in the present paper. I am indebted to Dr William Urry for the information that the location of John's family residence can in all probability be identified in the city of Canterbury.

12. WILLIAM OF CANTERBURY, *Materials*, vol. I (1875), p. 4; WILLIAM FITZSTEPHEN, *ibid.*, vol. III (1877), p. 16. For modern discussions of these details, cf. POUZET, p. 11-13, and most recent volumes on Becket's career.
13. A. SALTMAN, *Theobald, Archbishop of Canterbury*, University of London : Athlone Press, 1956, p. 165.
14. *Ibid.*, charters 51, 55, 61, 63, 86, 146, 147, 151, 165, 182, 252, 255 and 310; cf. also *ibid.*, Supplementary Document F. Notice in particular the interesting attestation for 1154 in charter 182: 'Testibus Rogero Eboracensi electo et Johanne Eboracensi thesaurario et Thoma Londoniensi et Johanne Saresbiriensi et Ricardo Castel apud Cantuariam anno ab incarnacione domini mcliiii°.'
15. RALPH DE DICETO, vol. I, p. XXIX-XXX. It is probable that John secured the favour of the papal curia through his missions in Theobald's company,

and possibly also through association with Becket: cf. POUZET, *op. cit.*, p. 14-15.
16. John was certainly treasurer of York by 1154, succeeding in that office Hugh du Puiset, who was consecrated bishop of Durham on December 20th 1153. Cf. SALTMAN, *op. cit.*, p. 119-122, and *ibid.*, charters 51 and 182, dated respectively 1153-54 and 1154: in each of these charters John attests as treasurer of York, whereas Roger of Pont-l'Évêque attests as archdeacon of Canterbury in 51 but as elect of York in 182.
17. *The Letters and Charters of Gilbert Foliot*, edd. A. MOREY and C.N.L. BROOKE, Cambridge, 1967, letter 57, p. 93-94.
18. WILLIAM FITZSTEPHEN, p. 46 : William asserted that the king removed from Becket's side both John of Salisbury and John of Canterbury, then treasurer of York, by sending the former into exile and promoting the latter to the see of Poitiers. Historians are not easily convinced of the validity of this interpretation: cf. POUZET, *op. cit.*, p. 20-21.
19. R. FOREVILLE, *L'Église et la Royauté en Angleterre sous Henri II Plantagenêt*, Paris, 1943, p. 97-99 and 118-119.

that of Becket himself in England the same year. [20] Nevertheless, the later actions of John and Thomas were not in total harmony at all times: John's earliest letters to Thomas are of unflinching support, of warnings of the perils facing the Church, of encouragement to the archbishop not to yield, and even of readiness to suffer exile with him, or before him, in defence of the rights of the Church. [21] But in the event John remained on good terms with the king and served him loyally. In the central and concluding stages of the dispute he played some part in seeking to remove dissensions, receiving from John of Salisbury a sympathetic expression of hope that the failure of his efforts to secure Becket's participation in a meeting with Henry might not redound upon himself to his discredit with the king, [22] and accepting from Becket in the final phases the firm but gentle rebuke of a friend. [23] There is little doubt that John remained fundamentally loyal to the archbishop on basic principles and also in practice, despite the reservations expressed by John of Salisbury to the measures adopted in 1169, concerning John's intervention in the negotiations at that time. [24] It is rather the position of John of Salisbury in these complex relationships which is ambiguous and which merits further scrutiny. [25]

Richard of Ilchester's role is more easy to define briefly. [26] As in the case of John of Canterbury, his origins also are uncertain, but an early phase of his career can be traced in the household of the earl of Gloucester, where it is possible he may first have met the later Henry II. [27] He was certainly related to Gilbert Foliot, and possibly also to the family of Roger of Salisbury and Nigel of Ely. [28] He is recorded as being 'scriptor curiae' from the second year of Henry II's reign, [29] and may well have been associated with Becket at an early stage of the latter's chancellorship: Thomas and Richard together with other witnesses attested a royal confirmation at Rouen in 1159, [30] and it is even suggested that Becket shared in the promotion of Richard to a position of greater influence in the royal administration. By 1163 at the latest he was archdeacon of Poitiers; [31] and throughout the following years he was one of the inner circle of the king's agents and administrators, collaborating with such magnates as the justiciar Richard de Lucy and with other royal

20. Cf. RALPH DE DICETO, vol. I, p. 306-308: Ralph makes explicit comparison with the archbishops of Mainz and Cologne as imperial archchancellors, and records Henry's anger at Becket's resignation of the chancellorship on election to Canterbury.

21. For John of Poitiers' letters to Becket in the early stages of the dispute, cf. Materials, vol. V (1881), letters 25, 35, 60 and 116, respectively p. 37-41, 55-57, 110-116 and 220-224. Notice especially letter 35, p. 57, sub anno 1163: 'Ego, sicut a multis mihi proponitur, non modo similem, sed duriorem calculum exspecto, utinam exsilii vestri particeps futurus aut praevius.' (Throughout the present essay, extracts from printed sources follow the spelling and form of literation of the volumes used; where manuscripts are cited, the original spelling is retained.)

22. Cf. Materials, vol. VI (1882), letter 457, p. 498-501, John of Salisbury to John of Poitiers, sub anno 1169, esp. p. 500-501: 'Timeo vero ne vobis apud eum (scil. regem) nocuerit fides et officiositas vestra, eo quod colloquium, sicut ad honorem et voluntatem ejus volebatis, non potuistis a Cantuariensi archiepiscopo impetrare.' See ibid., vol. VII (1885), letter 557, p. 65-66, also John of Salisbury to John of Poitiers, sub anno 1169.

23. Ibid., vol. VI, letter 454, p. 493-494, archbishop Thomas to John of Poitiers, sub anno 1169. The inscription ends: 'Thomas, eadem gratia Cantuariensis ecclesiae minister humilis, salutem, et se totum'; the letter begins:

'Carissime, ut quid fecistis nobis sic?' Despite the strong note of reproach through the letter, it is balanced by expressions of affection: 'Hoc modo, carissime, ab invicem discessimus... Unde et vos, dimidium animae nostrae, scire volumus...'

24. Ibid., letter 456, p. 496-498, John of Salisbury to the commissioners Simon and Engelbert, sub anno 1169, esp. p. 497: 'Sed ecce ex litteris quas nuper accepi luce clarius patet quia et legatio domini Pictavensis procurata est in fraudem ecclesiae et nostram.' Cf. ibid., letter 461, p. 506-513, John of Salisbury to Bartholomew of Exeter, sub anno 1169, esp. p. 510-511.

25. A careful study is still required of the many letters of John of Salisbury surviving from this period, because of the diversity of opinion which they seem to contain.

26. The details summarized in this paragraph are treated more fully with critical apparatus in C. DUGGAN, Richard of Ilchester.

27. Ibid., p. 3, and n. 6; and p. 4, and n. 1.

28. Ibid., p. 3.

29. The Great Rolls of the Pipe for the Second, Third and Fourth Years of the Reign of Henry II, ed. J. HUNTER, London, 1844, p. 30, 31, 47, 121 and 122.

30. R. W. EYTON, Court, Household, and Itinerary of King Henry II, London, 1878, p. 44.

31. Publications of the Pipe Roll Society, 30 vols., London, 1884-1925: Pipe Roll 9 Henry II (1162-63), p. 26. Cf. RALPH DE DICETO, vol. I, p. 319.

servants such as Geoffrey Ridel and John of Oxford. He helped to advance the king's cause in negotiations with the pope in 1164, [32] was present at the schismatical council of Würzburg in 1165, for which in part he was excommunicated by Becket in 1166; [33] he was a principal agent in Henry's plan to implement the odious and harsh constitutions of 1169, [34] and shared in the arrangements for the coronation of the young Henry in 1170, in derogation of the rights of the exiled archbishop of Canterbury. [35] On the other hand, he is seen engaged with similar effectiveness in negotiations leading to the Compromise of Avranches in 1172, [36] and possibly also in the agreement with the papal legate Pierleoni in 1175-1176. [37] Meanwhile he had been elected bishop of Winchester in 1173, and he died in the closing days of 1188. It is almost certain that two later bishops of Salisbury, Herbert and Richard Poore, were his illegitimate sons. [38] Throughout this active and distinguished career, he was above all a loyal servant to the king, and this is true both before and after his elevation to one of the most important sees in England.

An opening confrontation in the deepening crisis between ecclesiastical and secular jurisdictions in Henry II's reign took place at Poitiers in the years 1163-1164, which almost certainly involved both John and Richard, and in such a way that their contrasting roles are very clearly defined. There arrived at Poitiers in that period royal commissioners charged to impose edicts 'of unheard of harshness', restricting the operation of the church courts in certain stated areas. [39] Historians still differ in their judgments on the date of the incident, the identity of the principal commissioner, and the significance of the royal edicts within the context of the wider disharmony between ecclesiastical and secular jurisdictions. The principal evidence is found in two letters of John to Becket, in which he speaks of two separate visits by the commissioners, led by a certain 'Luscus noster', the eye of whose mind God had blinded, a royal official not more precisely identified but clearly unbeholden to John and Becket at that time. [40]

As far as the date is concerned, the second half of 1163 is almost positively established for the first visit and the first half of 1164 for the second, on internal evidence within the letters. The first letter records that 'Luscus noster' brought the edicts to Poitiers shortly after the feast of St Peter and St Paul, that is after June 29th, [41] but it shows no awareness of a serious breach in England; the second letter, which has indeed been dated at June 22nd 1164, [42] refers to 'Luscus noster... ad nos reversus', [43] and is clearly written in the knowledge of a menacing crisis in England, and almost certainly that of Clarendon in late-January 1164 and its aftermath [44]. As for the identity of 'Luscus noster', the editor of the Becket *Materials* and the biographer of John of Poitiers, respectively Robertson and Pouzet, [45] typify those

32. C. DUGGAN, *Richard of Ilchester*, p. 10-11.

33. *Ibid.*, p. 11.

34. *Ibid.*, p. 12. For the constitutions of 1169, see M.D. KNOWLES, ANNE J. DUGGAN and C.N.L. BROOKE, 'Henry II's Supplement' to the Constitutions of Clarendon', *English Historical Review*, vol. LXXXVII (1972), p. 757-771.

35. ANNE J. DUGGAN (published under maiden-name HESLIN), 'The Coronation of the Young King in 1170', *Studies in Church History*, vol. II, 1965, p. 165-178.

36. C. DUGGAN, *Richard of Ilchester*, p. 13.

37. *Ibid.*, p. 14-16.

38. *Ibid.*, p. 3, and n. 3.

39. *Materials*, vol. V, p. 38: 'propter novorum mandatorum inauditam duritiam...'; the 'mandata' are listed on p. 38-39.

40. *Ibid.*, letters 25 and 60, respectively p. 37-41 and 110-116; cf. p. 38: 'Luscus noster, cujus et mentis oculum

penitus excaecavit Deus'; and p. 115: 'quia Luscus noster, qui, licet in plenitudine potestatis, non tamen in plenitudine luminis, ad nos reversus est'.

41. *Ibid.*, p. 38: 'Illi enim paucis diebus post natalem apostolorum Pictavium venerant'.

42. *Ibid.*, p. 110.

43. *Ibid.*, p. 115.

44. *Ibid.*, p. 112.

45. ROBERTSON, *ibid.*, p. 38, n. a; and p. 115, margin. POUZET, *op. cit.*, p. 29; POUZET assumes that Luscus was Richard de Lucy: 'dont le nom et l'infirmité expliquent les jeux de mots', the reference being to a physical defect in the justiciar's vision. H.G. RICHARDSON and G. O. SAYLES also assume, with some circumstantial evidence, that Richard de Lucy was the royal commissioner: *Law and Legislation from Aethelberht to Magna Carta*, Edinburgh, 1966, p. 62-63, n. 7. The arguments in the present essay are not significantly affected by the problem of identification.

scholars who see in this demeaning expression a verbal play on the name of the justiciar Richard de Lucy, whereas Eyton and Kate Norgate and (more recently) the present writer have put the case for Richard of Ilchester, combining in himself the roles of king's commissioner and archdeacon of the diocese.[46] But the problem of identity is perhaps not among the most important aspects of this conflict, since it is easily shown that both Richard de Lucy and Richard of Ilchester were heavily committed in promoting the royal interests at that time.[47] Therefore, whether directly or indirectly, both bishop John and archdeacon Richard were implicated in this most significant incident.

Certainly it was a most significant incident, and it is hard to see on what acceptable grounds several historians have minimized the importance of the edicts, particularly within the broader canvas of Henry II's policies of resuming his jurisdictional rights, both secular and ecclesiastical, as he saw them. On this issue, Professor Foreville's assessment is more persuasive than the somewhat neutral views of Pouzet and the surprisingly simplistic arguments of the scholarly Richardson and Sayles, who concluded that the notion of a royal concerted attack on ecclesiastical privileges 'has no basis'.[48] A close scrutiny of Henry's actions both within England and in his continental possessions, in the vital matter of securing his own appointments, together with the resuming of his jurisdictional rights and promulgating edicts defining their extent, makes much more reasonable the judgment that a distinct objective was in view in those years.[49] John's letter of late 1163 to Becket only very slightly antedates the crisis in England, which came to its dramatic *dénouement* at Clarendon and Northampton in 1164. It cannot be questioned that John took grave exception to the promulgation of the royal edicts, and his letter is suffused with his deep concern and his understanding of the implications of the local action for the Church Universal.[50]

The edicts of Poitiers did not refer to the problem of criminous clerks, which was then reaching a crisis point of controversy in England, where Becket's defence of the clerical *privilegium fori* provided a focal point in the wider dispute between Henry II and the archbishop. No *ex professo* canonical scholar would now seriously challenge the judgment that Becket had a far stronger case in canon law than did his opponents, though there are distinguished political historians who have yet to be persuaded of this. A well-known case involving archdeacon Osbert of York reveals the contest over clerical immunity in full process in 1156 in Theobald's day, being retraceable in its origins back into Stephen's reign.[51] In the modern historiography of this problem, Professor Foreville as early as 1943 advanced persuasive arguments in favour of the canonical validity of Becket's stand, but English scholars were not then ready for the most part to receive such an interpretation.[52] The present writer published an essay in 1962 surveying the canonical antecedents of Becket's arguments, including evidence that John of Salisbury defended the principle of clerical immunity in his *Policraticus* in 1159, using the 'double punishment' theory

46. EYTON, *op. cit.*, p. 70-71; NORGATE, *art. cit.*, p. 1080; C. DUGGAN, *Richard of Ilchester*, p. 10.

47. For an excellent study of the judicial and administrative activities of Richard de Lucy and Richard of Ilchester, cf. RICHARDSON and SAYLES, *The Governance of Mediaeval England from the Conquest to Magna Carta*, Edinburgh, 1963, esp. p. 285-320; and by the same authors, *Law and Legislation*, p. 62-63. Cf. also F. WEST, *The Justiciarship in England, 1066-1232*, Cambridge, 1966, p. 50-57.

48. RICHARDSON and SAYLES, *Law and Legislation*, p. 62-63, n. 7. Various interpretations of the evidence are briefly discussed by ALEXANDER, *art. cit.*, p. 23.

49. FOREVILLE, *L'Église et la Royauté*, p. 99, 118-119 and 142-143.

50. Cf. *Materials*, vol. V, p. 37-41; notice esp. p. 40 : 'Adjeci etiam, quod si forte apud eos certi mihi consilii certa forma non appareret, illud Senonis in secretario domini papae non esset inutile explorare.'

51. *The Letters of John of Salisbury*, vol. I, edd. W. J. MILLOR and H. E. BUTLER, revised by C.N.L. BROOKE, London and Edinburgh, 1955, letter 16, *sub anno* 1156 p. 26-27, and Appendix III, p. 258-262, 'Nelson's Medieval Texts'.

52. FOREVILLE, *L'Église et la Royauté*, esp. chapter III: 'Le Conflit Juridique de 1164. Les Constitutions de Clarendon et le Droit Canon', p. 122-161.

associated most familiarly with Becket himself, in a work dedicated to the latter while still chancellor to king Henry II; [53] and in a further essay in 1965 revealed by a collation of texts in collateral columns that William of Canterbury's very early *Vita et Passio Sancti Thome* (c. 1172-4) records Becket's alleged defence of clerical immunity as a substantially verbatim conflation of canons selected from the *Decretum Gratiani* (c. 1141) and the *Summa Decretorum* (c. 1157-9) of Rufinus, the two foremost Bolognese works of that time. [54] There is now much wider acceptance among ecclesiastical historians of an evaluation more favourable to Becket, as evidenced by the latest writings of Professor David Knowles, [55] and a recent work of fine theological scholarship by Dr Beryl Smalley. [56] It must therefore be finally accepted that Becket's views were neither doctrinally unsound nor original to him.

This brief excursus on the criminous clerks dispute provides a further backcloth to the careers of John of Canterbury and Richard of Ilchester, since on this point also each is seen as an upholder of one of the two opposing interests. No one defended the immunity of clerks more stoutly than John of Canterbury, while still treasurer of York, as the Scarborough case in 1158 makes clear. The details of this story are inserted retrospectively in William FitzStephen's *Vita Sancti Thomae*, in juxtaposition to his account of Becket's similar stand in 1163-1164. [57] The case concerned alleged extortions by the dean of Scarborough, and was heard at York in the presence of leading prelates and secular magnates. In defence of the *privilegium fori* John secured the support of the clergy present, to the anger of the justiciar Richard de Lucy and subsequently that of Henry II, by denying any jurisdiction in these circumstances to the king. To de Lucy's question : 'Quid ergo domino regi judicabitis, in cujus iste incidit constitutionem?', John succinctly replied : 'Nihil, quia clericus est'. [58] And it was consistent with this conception that John, when bishop of Poitiers and after Becket's death, took action in defence of clerical privilege in an incident during the revolt of 1173-1174 : the younger Henry had condemned to death a clerk accused of espionage on behalf of Henry II, but the bishop of Poitiers intervened to save his life. [59]

In contrast, Richard of Ilchester, as a loyal aide of the king, clearly followed a different course of action. It is especially significant to notice a request which he received on this issue from his kinsman Foliot c. 1168-1169, while Becket was in exile in France. In a letter addressed to Richard and other royal justices, Foliot sought to secure the immunity of two clerks, a deacon and an acolyte, who had been arrested by the secular officers. The letter is tactfully phrased, but its implications for Foliot's support of clerical privilege and Richard's share in its curtailment are clear : 'supplico quatinus... ecclesiastica cohercendos iurisdictione restituatis, ne cum multa bene gesseritis, in hoc solo aduersus ordinem ecclesiasticum manum grauiter extendendo, uestre notam glorie inferatis'. [60] The time of the implied reproach and the person of the critic heighten the significance of this example.

---

53. C. DUGGAN, 'The Becket Dispute and the Criminous Clerks', *Bulletin of the Institute of Historical Research*, vol. XXXV (1962), p. 1-28; for John of Salisbury, *ibid.*, p. 17-18.

54. C. DUGGAN, 'The Reception of Canon Law in England in the Later-Twelfth Century', *Monumenta Iuris Canonici*, Series C: Subsidia I, Vatican City, 1965, p. 359-365 and Appendix A, p. 378-382.

55. KNOWLES, *Thomas Becket*, esp. p. 77-100, and 165-171; *idem*, 'Archbishop Thomas Becket — the Saint', *Canterbury Cathedral Chronicle*, no. 65, 1970, p. 5-21.

56. B. SMALLEY, *The Becket Conflict and the Schools*, Oxford, 1973; and by the same author: '*Privilegium Fori* : un Dialogue entre la Théologie et le Droit Canon au XIIe siècle', *Atti del II Congresso Internazionale della Società Italiana di Storia del Diritto*, Florence, 1971, p. 749-755.

57. WILLIAM FITZSTEPHEN, p. 43-45.

58. *Ibid.*, p. 44-45; FitzStephen's account, concluding with a reference to the death of the king's brother Geoffrey, fixes the date of the Scarborough incident in 1158.

59. Cf. POUZET, *op. cit.*, p. 19 and n. 2. Of the Scarborough case, POUZET writes: 'On voit avec quelle courageuse indépendance notre personnage avait défendu les immunités de son ordre en matière de justice, au risque de s'aliéner un monarque facilement irritable et de caractère violent'; and of the incident in the troubles of 1173-4, he speaks of John's 'défense d'un clerc accusé d'espionnage et à qui son intervention sauva la vie.'

60. *Materials*, vol. VI, letter 433, p. 453-455; and *The Letters and Charters of Gilbert Foliot*, letter 197, p. 268-269. Our citation from the text is taken from the latter and more recent edition; two versions of the letter survive, of which one was probably a draft.

Nor is it irrelevant to notice further that archbishop Richard of Canterbury addressed his letter of 1176, touching the punishment of murderers of clerks, to the bishops of Winchester, Ely and Norwich, who were at that date none other than Richard of Ilchester, Geoffrey Ridel and John of Oxford, three of king Henry's most assiduous and loyal administrators, who obtained their sees in reward for these services and continued in their secular administrative capacities after election to their bishoprics. [61] This was the letter in which archbishop Richard rejected the use of the 'double punishment' theory when it was turned against the interests of the clergy, an argument sometimes (but unconvincingly) cited to show that Becket's theory was not accepted by his successor.

It would not be disputed that Becket's martyrdom and subsequent enrolment in the catalogue of saints played an important part in the development of the process of canonization in relation to papal authority. More than thirty years ago, Professor Stephan Kuttner published a seminal article on the papal right of reservation in declaring canonization, distinguishing the stages of canonization and solemn translation of the saint's remains; [62] and in England, Dean Eric Kemp has published two related scholarly studies. [63] But as research makes progress on the Becket materials and the canonical sources, further evidence comes to light and clearer insights are secured. The lavish epistolary sources from the years immediately after the martyrdom bring out ever more clearly the strong and widespread feeling that in such a matter recourse should be had to the pope for authorization. The letters of archbishop William of Sens, of John of Salisbury, Herbert of Bosham and others, the two-way correspondence between the papal legates and Alexander III on the one hand and the promoters of the martyr's cult on the other: these are merely among the most familiar examples. [64]

We should not expect to find Richard of Ilchester among the leading supplicants on Becket's behalf; it is even possible that he should rather be sought among those who attempted in the royal interest to stifle the movement before it made much progress. [65] But one of the earliest important documents in support of Thomas's canonization was John of Salisbury's letter *Ex insperato*, addressed to John of Poitiers in 1171, recording the circumstances of the archbishop's death, deploying arguments in favour of his canonization, but concluding with a discourse on the inadmissibility of recognition of the martyr's status before a papal decision. [66] With due respect for the English scholar who has contributed most to the study of canonization, Dean Kemp surely softens misleadingly the feelings of the pope himself on this subject, in writing that of seven papal letters issued between Becket's death and the canonization, and mentioning Thomas, only one refers to him specifically as a martyr, and that generally in these letters 'the archbishop's death is treated as an ordinary piece of violence'. [67] That single letter was issued at Tusculum as early as May 14th 1171, and speaks of Thomas 'cujus anima Deo, sicut credimus, pretioso martyrio dedicata in coelis cum sanctis habitat', while the other letters are liberally sprinkled with phrases of horror and indignation: 'instinctu diabolico praefatum Cantuariensem armata manu aggressi sunt... atrociter in propria ecclesia occiderunt... Quod utique tanto majori animos audientium horribilitate perfundit, et eis, qui tantae atrocitatis

---

61. *Materials*, vol. VII, letter 794 p. 561-564; cf. C. DUGGAN, *Richard of Ilchester*, p. 14-16, esp. p. 15, n. 3.

62. S. KUTTNER, ' La Réserve papale du droit de canonisation ', *Revue historique de droit français et étranger*, 4th series, vol. XVII (1938), p. 172-228.

63. E. W. KEMP, ' Pope Alexander III and the canonization of saints ', *Transactions of the Royal Historical Society*, 4th series, vol. 27 (1945), p. 13-28; *idem*, *Canonization and Authority in the Western Church*, Oxford,

1948: for the Becket canonization, cf. p. 86-89. 64. Among numerous relevant letters, cf. *Materials*, vol. VII, letters 740, 743, 748, 757, 769, 770, etc. For the later history of the cult, cf. FOREVILLE, *Le Jubilé de Saint Thomas Becket : 1220-1470*, Paris, 1958.

65. C. DUGGAN, *Thomas of London*, p. 8. Cf. *Thómas saga erkibyskups*, vol. II, ed., E. MAGNÚSSON, London, 1883, p. 90-91, (Rolls Series).

66. *Materials*, vol. VII, p. 462-470.

67. KEMP, *Canonization and Authority*, p. 87.

occasio' *et cetera.* [68]   One wonders what resources of language Alexander had at his disposal for describing acts of violence which he considered less ordinary.   On the other hand, a letter not previously printed, but now discovered in two English decretal collections, illustrates clearly the pope's prudence in seeking reliable reports through his legates, before committing himself to a solemn decision in a cause with which he certainly sympathized. [69]

Any approach to the record of miracles, which allegedly multiplied through the martyr's intercession, cannot be simply historical.   But with that caveat, St Thomas was generous alike to friend and foe in his beneficence: miracles are recorded in connexion with both John of Poitiers and Richard of Ilchester, and even with Gilbert of London. [70] These miracles are not for the most part of spectacular character: John speaks of a miracle worked on his return from a pilgrimage to the martyr's tomb at Canterbury, when extinguished candles were mysteriously rekindled in the course of a religious ceremony, [71] and William of Canterbury mentions Richard of Ilchester, when bishop of Winchester, in narrating the story of a miracle by which king Henry's falcons were cured. [72]   More interesting, through its conscious purpose of authentication, is a letter of John of Poitiers confirming a reported miracle at Périgueux, when a condemned man was saved from death at the very moment of execution on appeal for the martyr's aid. [73]   Both John of Poitiers and John of Salisbury took pains to vouch for the truth of the miracles they recorded, in the evident realization that their credibility might be questioned. [74]   Most of these stories disclose more of the mystique and adulation which St Thomas's death inspired, and of the desire to amass an imposing corpus of *exempla*, than of historical fact.   But such aspirations and mental attitudes are themselves an historical phenomenon of the highest significance. [75]

The bitterness of the dispute was passed or was at least receding.   Not only were all kinds of men—partisans or opponents of Becket, clerks or laymen, persons of noble or lowly estate—the beneficiaries of his favour after his death; they became equally with the passing of time participators in his *cultus*.   It is not surprising that John of Poitiers promoted this movement: on several occasions he travelled with devotion to Canterbury, for the first time at least as early as 1174, and even into the period of his retirement in old age in 1194. [76]   He completed a collegiate church, dedicated jointly in honour of Our Lady and St Thomas of Canterbury, in his archiepiscopal see at Lyon, where he succeeded the saintly Guichard, who as abbot of Pontigny had provided a refuge for Becket in the

68. *Alexandri III Opera Omnia*, ed. J.-P. MIGNE, in *Patrologiae Cursus Completus : Series Latina* (subsequently identified as *Pat. Lat.*), vol. CC, Paris, 1855. Alexander's letter including the phrase 'pretioso martyrio dedicata' is no. 790, addressed to the archbishop of Tours, his suffragans and other ecclesiastics of his province; the other six letters are nᵒˢ 788, 789, 794, 798, 995 and 1014.

69. The letter is found in two closely-related manuscripts of the Worcester Family of decretal collections : *Cottoniana* 4. 32 and *Petrihusensis* 3.32. An edition of this letter has been prepared for publication shortly; meanwhile, cf. JL 12199 and 12200, March 10th 1173.

70. It is recorded that Foliot was cured from serious illness by St Thomas : cf. WILLIAM OF CANTERBURY, p. 251-252; notice William's comment : 'Quis nostris aut aliis temporibus suo sanguine suum potavit et sanavit adversarium? Martyrum hic solus sibi vendicat hoc privilegium.'

71. *Ibid.*, p. 438 : a letter of John to the prior and monks of Christchurch, Canterbury; for this and other recorded miracles linked with John, cf. POUZET, *op. cit.*, p. 41-42.

72. WILLIAM OF CANTERBURY, p. 528-529.

73. *Ibid.*, p. 369-373, esp. p. 372-373 for John's letter of confirmation to prior Odo of Canterbury : ' Quorum omnium firmum testimonium praesentium latores vobis perhibere poterunt'.

74. This is best illustrated in John of Salisbury's letter *Ex insperato* to John of Poitiers in 1171; cf. *Materials*, VII, p. 462-470, esp. p. 468-469, the discussion of miracles concluding : 'Quae profecto nulla ratione scribere praesumpsissem, nisi me super his fides oculata certissimum reddidisset. '

75. Cf. C. DUGGAN, *The Significance of the Becket Dispute*, p. 365-366.

76. For John's visit to Canterbury in 1174, cf. POUZET, *op. cit.*, p. 41; STEPHEN OF TOURNAI, *Pat. Lat.*, vol. CCXI, letter 25, col. 328; and WILLIAM OF CANTERBURY, p. 438. For his pilgrimage in 1194, cf. RALPH DE DICETO, vol. II, p. 120; John had resigned as archbishop of Lyon in 1193.

early phase of his exile. [77] It is even surmised that Guichard's cultivation of devotion to St Thomas at Lyon influenced its chapter to choose John, Thomas's 'most dear friend', as Guichard's successor. But Richard of Ilchester, at an early date as bishop of Winchester, also gave his assent and advice for the construction of a chapel in honour of St Thomas at Portsea, [78] and Gilbert of London endowed the hospital of St Thomas, which through the centuries was to have so illustrious a history; [79] but these acts have little significance in disclosing the true feelings of the latter prelates while Becket was still embattled.

In evaluating the contribution made by John of Poitiers and Richard of Ilchester to the further development of relations between *regnum* and *sacerdotium* and of ecclesiastical jurisdiction after Becket's death, two principal considerations are necessary for a fully satisfactory assessment. Each, in isolation, provides merely a partial picture. There is the pragmatic question of their involvement in the political affairs of their time, in particular disputes and litigation, in their personal relations with secular rulers, and so forth; and for many political historians this is understandably the primary interest. But there is also the crucial question from a spiritual and ecclesiastical viewpoint of their influence as religious leaders, theologians, liturgists and canonists; and it is easily demonstrable that in the long view the latter is more important for the Church. There is little reason to doubt that in the former category each of our bishops played a helpful and positive part in achieving the closer harmony which was gradually attained in the greatly altered situation following Becket's murder, though with different emphases and from different motives. As far as Richard is concerned, it is sufficient to mention briefly again his share in the negotiations leading to the Compromise of Avranches in 1172, in the difficult electoral dispute over the Canterbury vacancy in 1173, his own elevation to the see of Winchester in the same year, and his probable intervention in the diplomacy preceding the settlement with the papal legate in 1175-1176. [80]

At the same time, it is clear that Richard was a political prelate, who certainly continued to devote a large part of his considerable abilities to the service of the state; there is little concrete evidence of the spiritual or religious leader in his episcopal career. It is true that several distinguished clerics wrote from time to time in praise of his qualities of character and his virtues, most notably in support of his election to Winchester in 1173. Among those who wrote on his behalf at that time were Gilbert of London, not surprisingly, but also Bartholomew of Exeter and John of Salisbury.[81] John of Salisbury had already adopted a somewhat ambivalent attitude to Richard, recognizing and sometimes seeking his powerful intercession with the king during the period of Becket's exile, while writing simultaneously to other friends that Becket's actions against Richard were fully justified.[82] But John surely went too far in commending Richard to the papal notary Gratian in these terms: 'praefato martyri devotos esse constat dilectionis vestrae secure audeam commendare. Horum unus est et numerandus in primis, venerabilis vir Ricardus Wintoniensis electus, quondam Pictavensis archidiaconus, pupillorum pater, et moerentium consolator, fautor ecclesiasticae libertatis, justitiae cultor, et iniquitatis adversarius'.[83] In the sequel Richard acquired a reputation for liberality to the poor and for good works,

77. POUZET, *op. cit.*, p. 78.

78. Southwick Cartulary I, Hampshire Record Office lM54/1, fol. 17vᵒ; I am indebted for this reference to Mr Patrick Hase.

79. *The Letters and Charters of Gilbert Foliot*, charter 452, p. 482, *sub annis* 1173-c. 1180 : '... ad construendum xenodochium quod in honore Dei et beati Thome martiris Lundonie apud Sudwerc' ad pauperum et infirmorum susceptionem... '

80. C. DUGGAN, *Richard of Ilchester*, p. 13-16.

81. *The Letters and Charters of Gilbert Foliot*, letter 223, p. 297; JOHN OF SALISBURY, *Epistolae*, ed. J.A. Giles, Oxford, 1848, letters 313-317, p. 276-280.

82. Cf. *Materials*, vol. VI, letters 227 and 228, p. 1-8, *sub anno* 1166 : John of Salisbury to Ralph Niger; *ibid.*, vol. V, letter 194, p. 376-386, esp. p. 383, *sub anno* 1166 : John of Salisbury to Bartholomew of Exeter : ' ... allegatis variis causis et justis, excommunicavit Ricardum Pictavensem archidiaconum, et Ricardum de Luci, ... '

83. JOHN OF SALISBURY, *Pat. Lat.*, vol. CXCIX, col. 371.

but the panegyrics he received in 1173 as a defender of the *libertas ecclesiae* are much less convincing than the young king's complaint to the pope that the persecutors of the martyr were being elevated to the English bishoprics.[84] And it is hard to accept simply at face value the statement of Giraldus Cambrensis that Richard, as bishop of Winchester, acknowledged that he had misjudged Becket's character in his lifetime, and complained that all that the martyr strove for could have been secured, had not his success been wasted through the weakness of his successor, Richard of Dover.[85]

With John of Poitiers there is no such ambiguity. Without diminishing his sacerdotal office or forsaking his principles, he loyally served king Henry in the strategically and politically important diocese committed to his charge: on the one hand he was an effective servant of the king, even in military matters, in Poitou;[86] on the other, he was engaged in defence of the doctrinal integrity of the Church in confounding the heretics of Toulouse.[87] It is possible that he secured his dignity as legate of the apostolic see in 1174 in recognition of the vital part he played in the work of reconciliation between *regnum* and *sacerdotium* which had by then been achieved in the English king's dominions.[88] To the congratulations of Stephen of Tournai, he narrowly avoided becoming archbishop of Narbonne, to be elevated to the exalted office of primate of Gaul, as archbishop of Lyon.[89] He was in fact elected to Narbonne, but on his journey to the papal curia, pope Lucius III preferred to appoint him to the more senior see. The fragmentary reconstructions of the papal registers of the period, which rarely survive in original before the pontificate of Innocent III disclose John's concern, first as bishop of Poitiers and then as archbishop of Lyon, with the normal pastoral duties of his office: in settling marriage disputes, in resolving dissensions between religious houses, and so forth.[90] At last he freely laid down his high office to retire into scholarly and spiritual reflection at Clairvaux; and from this closing phase of his life two letters of Innocent III to John, in 1202 and 1203, show that matchless guardian of the Western faith expounding sacramental and doctrinal questions of fundamental importance: the doctrine of the Eucharist, with specific reference to the dogma of transubstantiation, and the complex mystery of the Holy Trinity.[91] In the culmination of their careers, therefore, we see in Richard and John two very contrasting facets of the Church in the aftermath of the Becket dispute, a contrast of perennial significance for the Church: the great administrator, useful for the continued order of Christian society; and the saintly ascetic, by no means unversed in public affairs, without whom that society would lose its meaning.

84. *Recueil des Historiens des Gaules et de la France*, ed. M. BOUQUET, Paris, vol. XIV, 1806, p. 645.
85. *Giraldi Cambrensis Opera*, vol. VII, ed. J. F. DIMOCK, London, 1877, p. 69-70, (Rolls Series); bishop Richard of Winchester is quoted thus : 'Multum decepti fuimus de homine illo... Quia si successor ejus decimam partem bonitatis et probitatis habuisset, nullum ecclesia de articulis illis amisisset. '
86. RALPH DE DICETO, vol. I, p. 407, *sub anno* 1176 : ' Johannes Pictavensis episcopus, auxiliariis undique convocatis, stipendiariorum numerositate collecta, juncto sibi Theobaldo Chabot qui princeps erat militiae Ricardi ducis Aquitanorum... Sicque salus in manu clericorum data satis evidenter ostendit plerisque non animos deesse sed arma. '
87. PETRUS SANCTI CHRYSOGONI, *Pat. Lat.*, vol. CXCIX, letter 3, cols. 1119-1124, *sub anno* 1178.
88. POUZET, *op. cit.*, p. 41-42; cf. the letter of Stephen of Tournai, cited above : *Pat. Lat.*, vol. CCXI, letter 25, col. 328.

89. STEPHEN OF TOURNAI, *Pat. Lat.*, vol. CCXI, letter 75, cols. 373-374: '... religioso saltu praeambula Narbonensem electum prima sedes Galliarum sibi vindicat Lugdunensis. Admirabilis et amabilis est ecclesiarum ludus iste...'
90. Cf. Alexander III to John, bishop of Poitiers: JL 14058 and 14059; Clement III to John, archbishop of Lyon : JL 16579 and 16580; Celestine III to John, archbishop of Lyon: JL 16820.
91. INNOCENT III, *Pat. Lat.*, vol. CCXIV, *Regestorum Lib. V*, letter 121, cols. 1118-1123; *ibid.*, vol. CCXV, *Regestorum Lib. VI*, letter 193, cols. 213-220; these long letters from Innocent III to John, *quondam* archbishop of Lyon, deal respectively in 1202 and 1203 discussions on the Eucharistic and Trinitarian doctrines, among other subjects. Cf. also *ibid.*, vol. CCXIV, *Regestorum Lib. V*, letter 62, cols. 1032-1033, *sub anno* 1202, in which Innocent responds to John's request from Clairvaux for a form of collect and other prayers in honour of St Bernard.

Their respective roles in the technical development of canon law, through which the papacy achieved in practice the most extensive expression of its ideological supremacy, above all in the pontificate of Innocent III, are more difficult to judge. In a preliminary survey of canonical manuscripts the present writer suggested in 1965 that the professional decretal collections of the later-twelfth century contained about twenty decretals, or parts of decretals, received by Richard as bishop of Winchester.[92] The work now continuing on all known decretal collections of the pre-*Compilatio prima* period substantiates that earlier estimate. There survive in fact exactly twenty decretals, some composed of several sections, received at Winchester, in the whole corpus of decretal manuscripts; but not all were addressed to Richard. Some were sent to the bishop of Winchester alone, others to the bishop in association with episcopal colleagues; one antedates Richard's episcopate, one is addressed to his successor, and two identify the archdeacon of Winchester as their recipient; a further decretal was received by Richard as archdeacon of Poitiers.[93] Their contents cover a wide range of episcopal and judicial activities, and one includes a strong rebuke from pope Lucius III to Richard of Winchester for failing to allow canonical purgation to the deacon of Bookham, following the death of the bishop's own nephew.[94] In contrast, the collections preserve only six decretals to John: four while he was bishop of Poitiers and two while archbishop of Lyon.[95] These comparative statistics may suggest to the unpractised observer that Richard was more active than John in the promotion of canon law, which would be very remarkable in the light of our knowledge of their careers as recorded in other sources. But that deduction would be quite misleading, since it is virtually certain that the provenance of the archetypal collections and the circumstances of their compilation explain the relative numbers of letters to any recipient now surviving in the professional decretal sources.[96]

The present brief essay provides merely a starting point for a more thorough examination of the careers of these two great men, but the evidence discussed above, of the greatly differing attitudes which they assumed on selected problems, justifies the claim made at the outset that in John and Richard two of the most powerful forces in the governance of Western Christian society in their time, the ecclesiastical and the secular concepts of authority, are significantly symbolized. During the prelude to the Becket dispute and in its course, each revealed through his actions and primary loyalties the essential character of one side of the controversy. John was in the vanguard of the hierocratic and canonical reformers of the post-Gregorian Church, and this judgment is not substantially weakened by the mediatory attitude which he adopted when the crisis between king and archbishop seemed unduly prolonged and intractable. Richard exemplified at least as clearly as any of his contemporaries the rising class of skilled and devoted administrators in the service of secular rulers. In the aftermath of the controversy, each played a constructive role in the process by which an acceptable balance of interests was attained. Nevertheless, it could

92. C. Duggan, *Richard of Ilchester*, p. 17-18.

93. A *regesta* of all decretals to England in the twelfth-century collections is in course of preparation by myself, while a similar *regesta* of all decretals to France is being prepared by Professor Stanley Chodorow; simultaneously, we are jointly working on an edition of all decretals still unprinted. These projects are made possible by the generous hospitality of Professor Stephan Kuttner, President of the Institute of Medieval Canon Law, in the University of California at Berkeley. The invaluable papers of the late Professor Walther Holtzmann are now in the Institute at Berkeley.

94. JL 15206: Lucius III to bishop Richard of Winchester, 1181-5.

95. These figures for Poitiers and Lyon are provisional, pending the completion of Professor Chodorow's *regesta* for France. Only two of the four letters to Poitiers are listed in Jaffe: JL 14058 and 14059; but both letters to Lyon are listed: JL 16580 and 17661.

96. Cf. C. Duggan, *Twelfth-Century Decretal Collections and their Importance in English History*, University of London: Athlone Press, 1963, p. 140-151; *idem*, 'English Decretals in Continental Primitive Collections: with Special Reference to the Primitive Collection of Alcobaça', *Studia Gratiana*, vol. XIV, 1967 : *Collectanea Stephan Kuttner*, vol. IV, p. 51-72.

hardly be questioned that John adhered throughout his career more closely to the principles for which St Thomas died, or that his was the less worldly and more spiritual character. Even in that moment of desolation for Becket in 1169, when many of his supporters including John, counselled compromise, the archbishop's reproach to the bishop of Poitiers was couched in terms of affection: 'Carissime, ut quid fecistis nobis sic? Ut quid nos et vos strangulastis?'[97] It is obvious that both Richard and John were men of remarkable talents, but Richard seems in retrospect the less colourful and less humane personality; in comparison with John, he appears somewhat cold and detached, despite his great influence and unremitting activities. There are indeed legends with moral and pastoral implications touching Richard's later career, but it would be hard to conceive in his case the growth of so moving a story as that which Hoveden narrates in connexion with John: when bishop William of Ely fell ill and died at Poitiers in 1197, the figure of Christ on the crucifix of St Martial in the cathedral church seemed to weep; the people said that this had happened twice before: once when a former bishop of the city had died, and a second time when John departed from his diocese of Poitiers for the last time.[98]

---

97. *Materials*, vol. VI, letter 454, p. 493-494.

98. ROGER OF HOVEDEN, *Chronica*, ed. W. STUBBS, vol. IV, 1871, p. 17, (Rolls Series).

XIV

RALPH DE DICETO, HENRY II AND BECKET WITH AN APPENDIX ON DECRETAL LETTERS

THROUGH MANY YEARS' REFLECTION on the reign of Henry II and the Becket dispute, the unique value of Ralph de Diceto's historical writings has become ever more apparent. It is not surprising that Dr Beryl Smalley has made the well-judged comment in her volume on the intellectual background of the controversy: 'The dean of St Paul's is jogging my elbow. Master Ralph of Diss has a right to the last word, since he crops up at each stage of the conflict, and then he narrated it in his *Histories*.'[1] The indispensable starting point for a fresh evaluation of Diceto's work is still the erudite two-volume edition published by Stubbs almost exactly one hundred years ago.[2] But, despite his characteristic learning in introductions and textual presentation, there are evident limitations in the deductions he drew from Diceto's personal associations, and more importantly in his knowledge of the sources available to the author, and the complex intellectual and psychological insights which the *opera omnia* disclose. It would indeed be strange if some restatement were not now necessary, in view of the many relevant monographs published meanwhile by political historians, experts in textual transmission, biblical and canonical scholars, and paleographers studying anew the superb surviving manuscripts, two of which were almost certainly products of the St Paul's scriptorium in the closing years of Diceto's own administration (as Stubbs himself showed), the Lambeth MS 8 being in all probability a transcription of the author's final revision, and perhaps his personal possession.[3] Happily, the necessary reappraisal is making rapid progress. In two studies Dr Smalley has discussed Diceto's stance in the Becket affair, with special emphasis on his historical method and technique, and on his place in

---

[1] B. Smalley, *The Becket Conflict and the Schools* (Oxford, 1973), pp. 230–4.
[2] *Radulfi de Diceto decani Lundoniensis Opera Historica* (hereafter Diceto), ed. W. Stubbs, R.S. (2 vols., London, 1876).
[3] *Ibid.*, I, pp. lxxxviii–c, esp. lxxxviii–xc.

the writing of history.[4] And Dr Grover Zinn has followed further one of her suggestions to demonstrate Diceto's indebtedness to Hugh of St Victor's *Chronicon* in his own *Abbreviationes Chronicorum*.[5] The purpose of the present essay is to give notice of a broad revision of Diceto's treatment of the Becket dispute, which will seek to determine his principal literary, epistolary and legal sources, and so to evaluate more surely his record of the causes, course and consequences of the affair.[6]

The conventional view of Diceto's standpoint as historian of Becket's career and martyrdom is that of an essentially moderate and conciliatory observer. As Dr Chibnall has well expressed it, despite his Angevin leanings, he gave a very fair and balanced account of the controversy.[7] But any such simple statement must conceal the subtle and elusive character of his writings, and particularly of his principal historical composition, the *Ymagines Historiarum*.[8] His scholarly formation was completed in the schools of Paris, and his skill in administration was secured in the chapter of St Paul's, where he was archdeacon of Middlesex from 1152 and dean from 1180 until his death in 1202.[9] He was a man of intelligence, keen perception, sensitivity and all-round ability, with an innate concern for order and a respect for authority. He seems above all a man who withdrew by natural inclination from confrontation and radical positions. Circumstances placed him at a delicate intersecting point of many lines of contrasting influences and ideologies, and found in him an unusual confluence of

[4] Smalley, *Becket Conflict*, pp. 230–4, and *Historians in the Middle Ages* (London, 1974), pp. 114–19.

[5] Grover A. Zinn, Jr, 'The Influence of Hugh of St Victor's *Chronicon* on the *Abbreviationes Chronicorum* by Ralph of Diceto', *Speculum*, LII (1977), pp. 38–61. There is an excellent recent survey of Diceto's life and works in A. Gransden, *Historical Writing in England c.550 to c.1317* (London, 1974), esp. pp. 230–6 and Plate VII, in which several points are touched upon which concern the special emphasis of this essay. See also C. N. L. Brooke and G. Keir, *London 800–1216: the Shaping of a City* (London, 1975), pp. 350–6 and Plate 51.

[6] For a brief survey of the controversy, cf. C. Duggan, 'The Significance of the Becket Dispute in the History of the English Church', *Ampleforth Journal*, LXXV (1970), pp. 365–75. The best recent biography of the archbishop is by D. Knowles, *Thomas Becket* (London, 1970). The largest and most learned survey of the whole subject is still that by R. Foreville, *L'Église et la royauté en Angleterre sous Henri II Plantagenet* (Paris, 1943).

[7] M. M. Chibnall, 'Ralph of Diceto', *New Catholic Encyclopedia* (15 vols., New York, 1967), XII, pp. 70–1.

[8] Diceto, I, pp. 289–440, and II, pp. 1–174.

[9] *Ibid.*, I, pp. x–lxxxiii, *passim*; Smalley, *Becket Conflict*, p. 230 and n. 53; A. Morey and C. N. L. Brooke, *Gilbert Foliot and his Letters* (Cambridge, 1965), and *The Letters and Charters of Gilbert Foliot* (Cambridge, 1967), *passim*; D. E. Greenway, 'The Succession to Ralph de Diceto, Dean of St Paul's', *Bulletin of the Institute of Historical Research*, XXXIX (1966), pp. 86–95, and *John Le Neve, Fasti Ecclesiae Anglicanae, 1066–1300: I. St Paul's, London* (London, 1968), *passim*.

Diceto, Henry II and Becket

personal relationships. His wide circle of patrons and friends included partisans both of Henry II and of Becket, as well as others who avoided with prudence a positive or exclusive attachment to either.[10] His close links with Foliot, bishop of London and most hostile of Becket's episcopal colleagues, did not unduly colour his record of their quarrel.[11] He shared the doctrinal orthodoxy of the English Church of the period, and accepted axiomatically the ascendant jurisdictional authority of the papacy. He wrote 'de fide nostra' as a matter of course in connection with the refutation of heresy,[12] and in his short treatise De Dupplici Potestate he distinguished in a familiar contemporary fashion the two swords of spiritual and temporal power, while duly stressing the inherited Petrine character of the papal office, with its superior faculty of binding and loosing, 'quoniam anima dignior est quam corpus'.[13] At the same time, his loyalty and fidelity to his lawful secular lord were deeply rooted, and he was on intimate terms with the king's most powerful and familiar supporters.[14]

Despite his discretion and his ability to treat of divisive matters with circumspection, he was a man of very positive attitudes. His multiplex loyalties and antipathies are seldom concealed. As a leading ecclesiastic, he reveals an implicit acceptance of the unity of Western Christendom under the pope, a concern for clerical privilege in general and for the rights of the Church in England, commitment to the pre-eminence of the Canterbury province within the English Church, and anxious care for the precedence of his own London diocese.[15] In secular matters, his loyalty was manifestly secured to the English Crown, and very

[10] Cf. C. Duggan, 'Richard of Ilchester, Royal Servant and Bishop', Transactions of the Royal Historical Society, 5th series, XVI (1966), pp. 1–21, esp. pp. 1–2 and 8–14.

[11] Note his inclusion in the Ymagines Historiarum of items 8, 9, 14 and 15, Appendix I, below; all four letters contain material critical of Foliot's actions.

[12] Diceto, I, p. 295. It should be emphasised that Diceto's work is highly derivative: the passage cited is taken verbatim from Robert of Torigni; cf. Chronicles of the Reigns of Stephen, Henry II, and Richard I: Chronica Roberti de Torigneio, abbatis Monasterii Sancti Michaelis in Periculo Maris, ed. R. Howlett, R.S. (4 vols., London, 1884–9), IV (1889), p. 168.

[13] Diceto, II, p. 180.

[14] Ibid., introductions to vols. I and II, passim; note especially II, pp. xxxi–xxxii; cf. C. Duggan, 'Richard of Ilchester', as in n. 10, above.

[15] Examples of all these basic attitudes are found too frequently to list here. The exercise of papal authority within the Western Church is taken for granted, rather than expounded enthusiastically, in the summoning of councils, the granting of the pallium, the confirming of appointments, the canonisation of Becket, the reception of appeals, the commissioning of legates and judges, and in numerous other ways (the brief treatise De Dupplici Potestate is already cited in n. 13 above, and an indented reference at the 1175 'concilium regionale' of Westminster notes: 'Solius papae est concilium generale, Romanae ecclesiae et Constantinopolitanae est concilium universale', Diceto, I, p. 399). A striking example of Diceto's recognition of the Petrine

strikingly to Henry II in person, to established political authority, and to a regime of social law and order. In a more personal way, his stability and reliability are witnessed in his relations with colleagues and friends, who appear to have valued his counsel – his letter of restraint to Richard of Ilchester at an emotional moment of crisis in 1166 is a notable instance of these qualities.[16] But his prejudices are no less evident. His comments unfold the Canterbury subject's condescension to the province of York, the London dean's circumscription of the aspirations of the bishops of Winchester and Rochester, and an English contempt for the French monarchy and the French people, from whom he seemingly excludes the continental subjects of the Angevin king of England.[17] The Becket dispute brought into sharp focus the problems arising from such diverse and sometimes conflicting sentiments, at a time of exceptional crisis in relations between ecclesiastical and secular interests in a unitary Christian society, and his version of that crisis is found in the *Ymagines Historiarum* and more compactly in the *Series Causae inter Henricum Regem et Thomam Archiepiscopum*, the latter providing an unusually clear and brief survey of the controversy on the basis of a sequence of texts distributed through the relevant years in the larger work.[18]

From the plateau of relative tranquillity when the *Ymagines* was completed, Diceto portrays the conflict in a deceptively detached manner, in contrast with the emotive atmosphere captured in the hagiographical and epistolary sources, an atmosphere often charged

doctrine of papal power, together with his willingness to criticise a particular papal decision, occurs *ibid.*, II, p. 165. The records of the dispute at Clarendon in 1164 and the reconciliations of 1172 and 1175-6 reveal a concern for clerical rights, *ibid.*, pp. 312–13, 351–2, 402–3 and 410. Assertions of the pre-eminence of Canterbury within the English Church are evident in the record of the Council of Tours in 1163 and the triple dignity acquired by Archbishop Richard in 1174, *ibid.*, pp. 310 and 390; indeed one of Diceto's special *signa in margine posita* identifies important sections 'De privilegiis Cantuariensis ecclesiae', *ibid.*, p. 4. His assumption of the distinction of London is nowhere better illustrated than in a passage on episcopal precedence at Becket's consecration, or in another on Foliot's translation from Hereford to London, the 'civitas regalis sedes' as Alexander III's letter describes it, *ibid.*, pp. 306–7 and 309.

[16] *Ibid.*, pp. 319–20.

[17] For ecclesiastical matters, cf. n. 15, above. Stubbs discussed the possibility that Diceto was himself of French origins (cf. *ibid.*, xvii–xx), but concluded nevertheless that 'Ralph was an Englishman of the period of amalgamation'. There is no doubt that Ralph speaks disparagingly of the French king and his subjects on many occasions, notably during the war of 1173-4: cf. *ibid.*, pp. 372, 375, 386–7, 394 *et passim*; but a more favourable comment appears at times, as when Louis VII visited the martyr's tomb at Canterbury in 1179: *ibid.*, pp. 432–4. For a note on loyalty to Henry II in Maine and Anjou, cf. *ibid.*, pp. 379–80.

[18] For the distributed passages in the *Ymagines*, cf. *ibid.*, pp. 307-14, 329 and 337; for the *Series Causae*, cf. *ibid.*, II, pp. 279-85.

Diceto, Henry II and Becket

with tensions, drama, tragedy and terror.[19] It is certain that he reconstructed the earlier part of the *Ymagines* from sources already existing.
He used the *Chronica* of Robert of Torigni for material down to 1162.[20]
For the Becket conflict he drew on archival material available to him,
selecting from hagiographical works and letter collections, perhaps to
some extent from his own records preserved from that time, and from
the experience and files of his many influential friends. It is essentially
a work of editing and selection, composed retrospectively by one who
was personally involved in the situation he is recreating, and who was
present on some of the occasions to which he refers.[21] It is only later,
from c.1180 when he became dean of St Paul's, that his history acquires
a quality of immediacy and takes on a more personal and more complete character. And herein lies the fascination of his handling of the
Becket question. It is difficult to penetrate with any sense of certainty
into his own thoughts on the matter, whether at the time of the
original crisis or at the moment of his choosing and dissecting the
documents many years later. To take a single example: his account of
Becket's distress at Northampton in October 1164 is admittedly
expressed in terms of sympathetic sorrow for the archbishop, but we
would not suspect that this was the occasion of which William
FitzStephen wrote: 'Similiter et Radulphus de Dicito . . . plurimum ea
die ibi lacrymatus est.'[22] This element of self-effacement increases the
character of ambivalent detachment in Diceto's treatment of delicate
areas of conflict.

Yet there is no concealment of his loyalty to Henry II, or of his
admiration of the king's qualities, energy and statesmanlike policies.
And this devotion is a necessary backcloth to his view of the conflict
between Henry and Becket. The king is the very pattern of the just
and clement ruler – 'a tyrannide semper oculos deflexit et animum'.[23]
He is shrewd in evaluation of his adversaries' motives, but ready to act

[19] A striking example of the sense of terror created at points of crisis is recorded in the letter
Mandatum vestrum, which envoys of Thomas sent him from England before his return in late
1170 (note especially its postscript): *Materials for the History of Thomas Becket* (hereafter *Materials*),
eds. J. C. Robertson and J. B. Sheppard, R.S. (7 vols., London, 1875–85), VII (1885), pp. 389–93,
ep. 717.

[20] Diceto, II, pp. x–xii and 291–306; Chibnall, above, n.7, pp. 70–1.

[21] He was involved in negotiations leading to Foliot's translation in 1163 (Diceto, I, pp. xxxviii–
xxxix and 309), was present at Northampton in 1164 (*ibid.*, pp. xlii–xliii), and was consulted
by Richard of Ilchester on the latter's excommunication in 1166 (*ibid.*, pp. xliii–xliv and 319–
20); and numerous similar examples can be cited throughout Diceto's career. The point is well
discussed in Stubbs's introduction: I, introd., *passim*.

[22] Cf. Diceto, I, pp. 313–14, and FitzStephen, *Materials*, III (1877), p. 59.

[23] Diceto, I, p. 394.

to his own disadvantage for the general good or through family piety –
'Francos igitur vel dona ferentes evitasse debuerat' (a double thrust
here in adapting the Virgilian phrase to scorn the French).[24] So great
is his power and skill in government that the young King Philip of
France is reportedly advised to model himself upon him – 'ut igitur in
amministratione regni tanti principis informaretur exemplo'.[25] Lengthy
panegyrics extol the king's thirst and quest for justice, as also his
devoted care for the welfare and education of his children.[26] In a passage
of exceptional interest, Diceto attributes to the king both strength of
character and psychological insights, reflected in a conscious assumption of outward confidence in the face of heightening perils.[27] This is
the ruler whom he sees in hostility to his own spiritual father. Even in
this context, he registered important points in Henry's favour. Thus,
as Diceto has it, Henry won the approbation of many by his offer to
submit the quarrel to arbitration (though on his own terms) in 1169 –
'ita rex Angliae, qui prius odium in se plurimorum conflaverat, in hoc
verbo plurium favorem adeptus est'.[28] Likewise, he accepts from his
epistolary sources that, on hearing of Becket's murder, Henry offered
forthwith to submit to the Church's judgment and accept its verdict.[29]

There is no need to doubt the sincerity of Diceto's high praise of the
king. It would be over-simple to attribute it either to regard for a
powerful patron or to fear of retribution. Diceto's final draft was
completed after Henry's death, though the work of composition
was begun earlier. Other contemporary writers, notably Giraldus
Cambrensis and Ralph Niger, spoke without inhibition on the king's
public and private conduct. For Giraldus, the king was a notorious
adulterer, lacking in respect for God, a hammer of the Church and
born to its destruction – 'ecclesiae malleus et filius in perniciem natus'.[30]
The fair-minded William of Newburgh attributed a measure of blame
to archbishop and king alike, judging that no advantage came from
Becket's actions, but that rather they inflamed the wrath of the king
and brought many misfortunes in their train.[31] He concluded that the
acts of 'that venerable man' were not to be praised, though they
resulted from commendable zeal; but Henry's attitude to Becket

---

[24] *Ibid.*, p. 394.
[25] *Ibid.*, II, pp. 7–8.
[26] *Ibid.*, I, pp. 434–7, and II, pp. 17–18.
[27] *Ibid.*, I, pp. 373–4.
[28] *Ibid.*, pp. 336–7.
[29] *Ibid.*, p. 345.
[30] *Giraldi Cambrensis Opera*, edd. J. S. Brewer, J. F. Dimock and G. F. Warner, R.S. (8 vols.,
London, 1861–91), VIII (1891), *De principis instructione liber*, p. 160.
[31] *Chronicles of the Reigns of Stephen, Henry II, and Richard I*, ed. Howlett, I (1884), *Willelmi Parvi,
canonici de Novoburgo, Historia Rerum Anglicarum*, pp. 142–3 and 281.

Diceto, Henry II and Becket

also exceeded the bounds of moderation in its unreasoned rage – 'in absentem irrationabiliter saeviens, et plusquam deceret principem, effrenato furori indulgens'. In his general survey of the reign, William reflected that Henry's later misfortunes were in part the result of his failure to the end to abate the fierceness of his unhappy hostility to Becket (an unusually truthful record of the king's implacable enmity), and hoped that a happier fortune would be Henry's in another life.[32] Diceto's appraisal of the dispute stands quite apart from such positive statements, and in seeking to bridge the gulf between the two protagonists he presents an enigma. In a subtle passage, Professor Warren speaks of Diceto's doing his best for his friend, the king, and concludes that 'he seems to be writing on the defensive, as if he knew men would find it hard to believe him'.[33]

Indeed it is in his narrative treatment of Becket, both as a person and as the unflinching upholder of principle, that Diceto is most elusive and perplexing. If his position vis-à-vis the king was one of loyalty and admiration, his account of Becket's long ordeal and death is expressed with respect and reverence, though without evident warmth. Again, it would be over-simple to explain this approach as simply sharing in a general ex post facto devotion to the martyr and canonised saint. He had an expert knowledge of ecclesiastical law and the rights of the Church, which he himself defended on occasions; he clearly knew when customary policies or exceptional incidents were infringements of canon law, even if he sometimes considered a deviation from the strict law to be a matter of common sense or wisdom. There is no reason to doubt that he agreed with Becket on the controverted juristic principles, as did the English bishops in general. On single issues emerging in the course of the quarrel, he may well have seen in Becket a champion of claims close to his own heart, as in the rivalry between Canterbury and York. He did not believe in the subjection of the Church to secular domination, and such phrases as the libertas ecclesiae were not without important meaning to him. But he did not seek or support emotional and violent solutions to difficult problems, above all when he felt sympathy for both sides in the great dispute. If it is a truism that all men are to some extent the products of their age and environment, Diceto is nevertheless a striking example. He was a well-favoured member of the privileged strata in the English society

[32] Ibid., p. 281.
[33] W. L. Warren, Henry II (London, 1973), pp. 214–15.

of his day, and a product of that network of family and social connections which provided many of the influential English ecclesiastics in his period – the ramifications of patronage by the Belmeis and Foliot families in his own London chapter clearly illustrate this factor.[34] To such a man, the growing tension between the ever more confident claims of canonists and theologians on the one hand, and the consolidation of traditional secular kingship, with its politico-theological infrastructure, on the other, was unwelcome and feared, and imperfectly understood.[35] This is a familiar and recurring predicament in Christian society, which must be recognised as the essential framework of the Becket dispute in its deepest sense, but as the explanation also of the minor part played within it by a clerk like the dean of St Paul's.

It was entirely natural to Diceto that secular and ecclesiastical leaders should work in harmony. It was familiar and customary, and mutually beneficial. He knew that canon law placed limitations on the secular activities of clerks, but Becket's refusal to continue in the office of chancellor on becoming archbishop in 1162 not only alienated the king – 'quod altius in cor regis ascendit' – but contrasted with the dual roles of the archbishops of Mainz and Cologne, who functioned also as arch-chancellors in the Empire.[36] In the same way, Henry's choice of the bishops of Winchester, Ely and Norwich as arch-justiciars of the realm in 1179 was admittedly 'contra canonum instituta', but seemed justified by the king's pursuit of incorruptible judges and followed a precedent in the career of Roger of Salisbury in the reign of Henry I.[37] Diceto's comments on the appointments of 1179 may well appear ingenuous to some, and he was certainly treading a razor's edge in describing Richard of Ilchester, Geoffrey Ridel and John of Oxford

---

[34] Diceto, I, pp. xx–xxx and xxxv–xl; C. N. L. Brooke, 'The Composition of the Chapter of St Paul's, 1086–1163', *Cambridge Historical Journal*, x (1951), pp. 111–32; *idem*, 'The Deans of St Paul's, *c.*1090–1499', *Bulletin of the Institute of Historical Research*, xxix (1956), pp. 231–44; *idem* and Morey, *Gilbert Foliot and his Letters*, and *Letters and Charters of Gilbert Foliot*, *passim*. Cf. A. T. Bannister, *The Cathedral Church of Hereford* (London, 1924), pp. 37–46, on 'The Rule of the Foliots' at Hereford.

[35] For the complex theological and ideological background, cf. Smalley, *Becket Conflict*. See now the important volume of essays: R. Foreville, ed., *Thomas Becket*, Actes du Colloque International de Sédières, August 1973 (Paris, 1975), e.g., J. Châtillon, 'Thomas Becket et les Victorins', pp. 89–101; and A. Graboïs, 'L'Idéal de la royauté biblique dans la pensée de Thomas Becket', pp. 103–10, together with discussions of both papers, *ibid.*, pp. 127–32. In a wider context, the studies by P. Classen are of outstanding importance: cf. his *Gerhoch von Reichersberg* (Wiesbaden, 1960); see also S. Chodorow, *Christian Political Theory and Church Politics in the Mid-Twelfth Century* (Berkeley, 1972).

[36] Diceto, I, pp. 307–8.

[37] *Ibid.*, pp. 434–5; this passage is discussed in C. Duggan, *Richard of Ilchester*, pp. 1–2.

Diceto, Henry II and Becket

(the bishops in question) as standing for the 'sanctuariam Dei'; but his general argument is readily understandable and was widespread among his contemporaries. In view of the central importance of canonical questions in the Becket dispute, Diceto's interest in canon law is clearly crucial. He was at once alert when some unusual point of law arose, or where infractions of basic principles cut across his own experience or that of his associates. In some such cases he cited in the *Ymagines* relevant precedents culled from the *Decretum* of Ivo of Chartres, and made cross-references to these same topics in a transcription of Ivo's preface, incorporated in his own *Abbreviationes Chronicorum*.[38] A few problems drew his special attention: the consecration of priests' sons and their succeeding in their fathers' churches, ecclesiastical restoration after deposition, and the translation of bishops from one see to another.[39] This last question was of immediate interest to him, by reason of Foliot's translation from Hereford to London, in which Diceto was himself involved, and other problems were familiar to him in the exercise of his office.[40] Yet he reveals in the *Ymagines* less direct concern with canon law and ecclesiastical legislation than we might expect. His treatment of the important conciliar business at Tours (1163), Westminster (1175) and the Lateran (1179) is surprisingly slight.[41]

The principal stages of the quarrel between Henry II and Becket are well known and need not be restated here, but Diceto's selection of texts and details requires evaluation, and provides at the same time an unusually succinct account. His record is set out most clearly in the *Series Causae inter Henricum Regem et Thomam Archiepiscopum*, devoted exclusively to the dispute and sent by him to the religious of Saint Colombe at Sens, which had provided a refuge for Becket in exile, after his departure from Pontigny. The work opens with Thomas's elevation to Canterbury and his resignation of the chancellorship in 1162, proceeds through the crisis and its aftermath to the canonisation in 1173, and concludes with a postilla on the devotion shown to the saint by magnates and prelates of France.[42] As noted already, the *Series*

---

[38] Diceto, I, pp. 32–3, esp. *ad finem*.   [39] *Ibid.*, pp. 305, 298, 309 and 413.
[40] *Ibid.*, pp. xxxviii–xl and 309, for the Foliot translation.
[41] *Ibid.*, pp. 310, 399 and 429–30. He provides no information on the canons of the 1163 council; of the Westminster Council, he says with brief significance 'Statuta concilii si bene revolveris perpauca reperies quae tibi corpus canonum incorporare non possit'; and of the important 1179 Lateran Council, he comments 'plurima memoriae plurimum commendanda statuta sunt ibi, de quibus saltem inseramus paucissima', adding merely two brief extracts dealing respectively with plurality and the privilege of Templars and Hospitallers in interdicted churches.
[42] *Ibid.*, II, pp. 279–85, for the *Series Causae*; cf. *Ymagines, ibid.*, I, pp. 307–14, 329 and 337.

Causae is in effect an integration of numerous relevant passages distributed through the annalistic strata of the *Ymagines*. In each work, high points of crisis are numbered in order of chronology and marked with the special symbol of two letters C, linked back to back, and defined in a prefatory table to the *Abbreviationes Chronicorum* by the phrase 'De controversiis inter regnum et sacerdotium'.[43] Thirteen passages are picked out in this way in the edition of the *Series Causae*, with one further and later item similarly designated in the *Ymagines*.[44] The phrase is apt in one obvious sense, but the use of the sign (one of Diceto's 'signa in margine posita') is limited, denoting a choice of incidents confined to the Becket dispute, almost entirely to its early phases, and wholly within the limits 1162-9. This is a narrower vision than the phrase suggests. The topics signalised are these: the voluntary resignation of the chancellorship by Becket, his enforced resignation of the Canterbury archdeaconry, resistance to his authority by Clarembald of St Augustine's, tenurial disputes between the archbishop and Earl Roger de Clare and William de Ros (concerning holdings in Kent), the king's reaction to the excommunication of William of Eynsford in an advowson dispute, his efforts to win to his side the pope in exile in France, the Council of Clarendon, the debate over criminous clerks, Thomas's abortive attempt to leave England after Clarendon, his dispute with John the Marshal over a property matter, and the ensuing crisis at the Council of Northampton. These first twelve stages mark the evolving crisis to October 1164, and thereafter the marginal sign is used only twice: once for a garbled reference to papal legates in 1166 (an apparent confusion of names and dates), and finally for the failure of attempts at reconciliation between the king and archbishop in 1169.[45] It could hardly be said that Diceto's use of his own marking device is comprehensive, yet it is strikingly effective in disclosing the nature of the quarrel and its diverse facets in the opening phases, as

---

[43] For Diceto's explanation and list of his *signa in margine posita*, cf. the preface to his *Abbreviationes Chronicorum*, *ibid.*, pp. 3-4. For Dr Smalley's discussion of this device, cf. references in n. 4, above.

[44] Diceto, I, p. 337; the symbol is not given at the corresponding position in II, p. 283.

[45] Diceto's account of the failure of negotiations for a reconciliation in 1166 is inaccurate, *ibid.*, I, p. 329. He refers to an abortive meeting of the papal legates William of Pavia and John of Naples with Henry and Becket at Montmirail in that year. William and John are not otherwise recorded as acting jointly, though William and Otto were involved in two meetings in late 1167 (firstly between Gisors and Trie, and secondly at Argentan); and there was a conference at Montmirail in January 1169, but the papal representatives there were Bernard de Corilo and Prior Simon of Mont Dieu. For a general discussion of Diceto's dating (excluding the present example), cf. *ibid.*, II, pp. xxxii-xlv.

Diceto, Henry II and Becket

these appeared to a closely-involved observer. Though couched in the language of a neutral record, his account reveals the devious methods adopted by the king in his response to Becket's stand. Diceto's narrative clearly shows how both ecclesiastical and secular persons, especially in Kent, seized the opportunity afforded by Becket's fall from royal favour to resist his authority or lordship, to advance their own interests and contribute to his distress and humiliation; and it is evident that they could count on the king's support in this. Diceto's narrative in general is of exceptional value in combining evidence both of the jurisdictional problems involved in the dispute (advowsons, clerical privilege, excommunication of tenants-in-chief and so forth) and the numerous personal and material factors which helped to shape the actual course of events. And the sequence of paragraphs marked for special emphasis presents such evidence even more directly.

But, in assessing Diceto's role as historian of the Becket dispute, it is at once apparent that many essential features are omitted or insufficiently explained. From his record, we should have a wholly inadequate knowledge of the complex legal arguments advanced at Clarendon in 1164 and no evidence at all of the *in terrorem* constitutions of 1169, to mention just two examples.[46] On the other hand, we find a fair and accurate summary of the points of agreement reached at Avranches in 1172 and the unique survival of Henry II's letter to Alexander III in 1176, following Pierleoni's mission as papal legate and marking the second decisive stage of reconciliation after Becket's death.[47] Diceto was much dependent on epistolary records for his reconstruction of the story, and his selection from the very large number of letters available was limited and fragmentary, but without partisan emphasis. Some letters are set out formally as such, with addresses and *incipits*, and transcribed verbatim, though not always in full. Others are adapted in a paraphrased version and incorporated without identification of source into his own composition. Many passages of seeming narrative or comment can be shown to be derived from letters in this way. At critical phases, he appears to seek a balance in the choice of texts, to

[46] *Ibid.*, I, pp. 312–13, for the Council of Clarendon; the record is extremely brief, but important for the criminous clerks dispute. The latest discussion (with texts) of the 1169 constitutions is by M. D. Knowles, A. J. Duggan and C. N. L. Brooke, 'Henry II's Supplement to the Constitutions of Clarendon', *EHR*, LXXXVII (1972), pp. 757–71.

[47] Diceto, I, pp. 351–2, 402–3 and 410. For the Avranches settlement, Diceto was probably using the text of a communication from the papal legates, Albert and Theodwin, to Henry II (cf. item 30, Appendix I, below), but his letter from Henry II to the pope in 1176 is among the most valuable of his records not otherwise known.

disclose the arguments of each side, as in his account of representations made to the pope in 1164, or in the selection of important letters from the year 1166.[48] The latter include Becket's famous and didactic *Desiderio desideravi* to the king, a letter of profound ideological interest, and his condemnatory *Mirandum et vehementer* to Gilbert Foliot.[49] These are hardly matched in power by the Canterbury suffragans' *Quae vestro pater*, reproachfully addressed to Becket, and Diceto omits Foliot's *Multiplicem*, the most important of all epistolary attacks on the archbishop.[50] The author's own letter to Richard of Ilchester in the same year, *Si tactus inconsulto*, perfectly exemplifies his personal moderation and respect for the due process of law, in advising Richard to accept with humility the sentence of excommunication imposed by Becket on Richard and others at Vézelay, though he dates the sentence inaccurately.[51] The letter is of further interest, since its contextual commentary makes no mention of the presence of the excommunicates at the schismatical council at Würzburg in 1165, which was specifically stressed in their condemnation. This *suppressio veri*, like the omission of *Multiplicem*, may well reflect the exercise of editorial tact.[52]

As far as the strictly jurisdictional issues are concerned, there can be little doubt that Diceto judged Becket's canonical arguments to be well grounded. His passage on the criminous clerks debate is of the utmost value in its brevity and precision. He makes crystal clear the king's procedural proposals for dealing with felonous clerks, and states the general episcopal dissent from this policy – 'Rex Anglorum volens in singulis ... In contrarium sentiebant episcopi *etc.*' There is no hint here of peculiarity in Becket's opposition to the king's plan.[53] And he

---

[48] Diceto, I, pp. 314–17 (cf. items 3 and 4, Appendix I, below), and 319–28 (cf. items 5–9, Appendix I, below).

[49] Diceto, I, pp. 320–1 and 323–5.

[50] *Ibid.*, pp. 321–3. For *Multiplicem*, cf. Knowles, *The Episcopal Colleagues of Archbishop Thomas Becket* (Cambridge, 1951), pp 171–80; Morey and Brooke, *Gilbert Foliot and his Letters*, pp. 166–87; and for the text, *eidem*, *Letters and Charters of Gilbert Foliot*, pp. 229–43, ep. 170.

[51] Diceto, I, pp. 318–20. Diceto records that the excommunications were promulgated on Ascension Day, whereas the correct dating is Whit Sunday. The *Ymagines* preserves the letter *Si tactus inconsulto* as addressed to Richard of Ilchester 'ab amico' (*ibid.*, p. 319, with editorial note 'Possibly by our author himself'), but the *Series Causae* places the matter beyond dispute with the addition 'Radulfo scilicet de Diceto' (*ibid.*, II, p. 282).

[52] *Ibid.*, I, p. 318. Diceto records that the excommunicates were condemned as observers, defenders and instigators of the *avitae consuetudines*; it is a serious omission that the presence of some at the schismatical council is not recorded by Diceto, since the verdict linked the interests of both Alexander III and Becket, of the Roman and the English Churches.

[53] *Ibid.*, p. 313. For discussion of the criminous clerks dispute in its canonical setting, cf. C. Duggan, 'The Becket Dispute and the Criminous Clerks', *Bulletin of the Institute of Historical Research*, XXXV (1962), pp. 1–28; *idem*, 'The Becket Dispute: William of Canterbury and

Diceto, Henry II and Becket

alone completes the story of this issue with a transcription of Henry's formal statement of the terms of the compromise in 1176.[54] Despite his friendship for the king and Foliot, he inserts letters of papal and archiepiscopal reproach to both, and his documented narrative of the circumstances of the Young King's coronation in 1170 and of the gathering storms preceding Becket's murder tilt the balance of sympathy rather in Thomas's favour.[55] But his ambivalence and caution are seen once more, when speaking of Henry's reactions to Becket's death. He records a measure of blame attributed by some personally to the king for the outrage, quoting the aged Henry of Winchester's stern rebuke to the king – 'qui eum pro morte gloriosi martyris increpavit durissime' – as well as the impassioned denunciation of the murder by Archbishop William of Sens.[56] At the same time, there is an unconvincing note in his statement of Henry's remorse at the moment of hearing of Becket's fate: even among conventional claims of the king's regrets, credulity is taken beyond reasonable limits by such excusatory comments as that Henry was blameless – 'nisi forte in hoc delictum sit, quod adhuc minus diligere credebatur archiepiscopum'.[57] This is an almost stunning understatement, but in this passage he is closely following a well-known letter by Arnulf of Lisieux, his old friend and Becket's adversary: the language is Arnulf's, not his own.[58] A seldom-noticed letter from the king proves that his immediate chief anxiety was that harmful repercussions should not adversely affect himself. The letter is entirely devoid of compassion for the victim, who indeed continues to be censured even in death.[59] Nevertheless, it is clear that Diceto strove to tread a path between contentious and prejudiced positions. It was earlier remarked that he achieved a notably objective summation, the more so in view of the complications of loyalties and

Clerical Privilege', in *The Reception of Canon Law in England in the Later-Twelfth Century*, Monumenta Iuris Canonici, Series C: Subsidia I (Vatican City, 1965), pp. 359–65 and 378–82; *idem*, 'Bishop John and Archdeacon Richard of Poitiers: Their Roles in the Becket Dispute and its Aftermath', in Foreville, ed., *Thomas Becket*, pp. 71–83, esp. pp. 76–8. For varied recent judgments, cf. Knowles, *Thomas Becket*, pp. 77–87; Smalley, *Becket Conflict*, pp. 124–37; Warren, *Henry II*, pp. 459–70, 480–1 and 537–42.   [54] Diceto, I, p. 410.

[55] *Ibid.*, pp. 332–5 and 338–41 (cf. items 13–16, 20, 22 and 23, Appendix I, below). On the coronation, cf. A. J. Duggan (A. J. Heslin), 'The Coronation of the Young King in 1170', *SCH*, II (1965), pp. 165–78.

[56] Diceto, I, pp. 347–8.   [57] *Ibid.*, p. 345.

[58] *Materials*, VII, pp. 438–9, ep. 738 (cf. item 25, Appendix I, below).

[59] *Materials*, VII, p. 440, ep. 739. This letter was not known in the collections of Becket correspondence, but is found inserted at the foot of a folio in the Avranches decretal collection (from Mont St Michel), Avranches, Bibl. de la Ville, MS 149; its significance and authenticity are discussed by C. Duggan, in Foreville, ed., *Thomas Becket*, pp. 192–3.

duties briefly discussed in this essay. It must be recognised that his silences and omissions are as significant as his assertions, and that he composed his account largely on a basis of documents selected from epistolary archives, documents which he dismembered and dissected at will.[60] Yet, if we had Diceto's version of the Becket dispute in isolation, none other surviving, the more favourable verdict between the opposing parties would be awarded to Becket, and with some reluctance against our author's friends. But it would be a finely balanced judgment.

APPENDIX I

LIST OF LETTERS, SPEECHES AND RELATED DOCUMENTS, USED IN THE 'YMAGINES HISTORIARUM' FOR THE PERIOD 1163-73

It is plain that Diceto relied extensively on epistolary sources for the years from Becket's elevation as archbishop to his canonisation. Substantial sections are composed almost entirely of transcriptions, abbreviations or paraphrases of letters, sometimes very freely rendered. The list below cites such letters, whether they have been clearly set out as documents or have been identified as sources of seemingly narrative passages, together with a small number of allocutions or reports. Others may yet be discovered by further research. The list is drawn up as follows: where a letter is formally transcribed as such, its *incipit* in Diceto's version is stated first, followed by the true *incipit* in parentheses if the opening has been truncated. Where a letter has been adapted or woven into the narrative, the opening and closing phrases of Diceto's adaptation are given first, and the item is marked with an asterisk; the original letter is then identified. The sender and recipient are named wherever possible, the page location in the first volume of the printed edition (RD) is noted, with the year in which Diceto places the item. Where appropriate, the number of the original in Robertson's edition of the Becket Materials (BM) is given, and its number in Jaffé's *Regesta Pontificum Romanorum* (JL) in the case of a papal letter. Finally, the correct date is noted, or the closest approximation to the true date is suggested on the basis of internal and circumstantial evidence. More exact dating may be achieved later in some cases. The list is set out in order of appearance in the *Ymagines*, but Diceto's dating is not always correct; a few items are seriously misplaced.

1. *Ex litteris karissimi:* Alexander III to the London chapter, RD 309 (1163), JL 10838, 19 March 1163.
2. *Ex antiqua Romanorum:* Alexander III to Louis VII, RD 310–11 (1163), JL 10826, 1 March 1163.

[60] Diceto's access to the archives of Gilbert Foliot has been frequently assumed, and will be further discussed by A. Duggan; see also *eadem, Thomas Becket: a textual history of his letters* (Oxford, 1980). For collections of papal letters, cf. C. Duggan, *Twelfth-Century Decretal Collections and their Importance in English History*, University of London Historical Studies XII (London, 1963).

Diceto, Henry II and Becket

3. 'Inter Thomam ... parentaret' (*Medicinae potius*): royal envoys to the pope in consistory at Sens, RD 314–15 (1164); extract from *Medicinae potius*: 'enemies of Thomas' to Alexander III and cardinals, BM ep.73; allocution in the papal consistory, early November 1164 (perhaps drafted in England, late October).

4. 'Ad audientiam tuam ... repertor': allocution by Thomas in the presence of Alexander III, RD 316–17 (1164), BM ep.74, mid-November 1164.

5. *Si tactus inconsulto*: Diceto to Richard of Ilchester, RD 319–20 (1166), BM ep.211, in or shortly after late June 1166.

6. *Desiderio desideravi*: Thomas to Henry II, RD 320–1 (1166), BM ep.154, April–May 1166.

7. *Quae vestro pater*: Canterbury suffragans *et al.* to Thomas, RD 321–3 (1166), BM ep.205, *c.*24 June 1166.

8. *Mirandum et vehementer*: Thomas to Gilbert Foliot, RD 323–5 (1166), BM ep.224, in or after July 1166.

9. *Fraternitatis vestrae*: Thomas to his suffragans, RD 326–8 (1166), BM ep.223, in or after July 1166.

10. *Praedecessorum nostrorum* (*In apostolicae sedis*): Alexander III to Thomas, RD 330 (1167), BM ep.170, JL 11268, 8 April 1166.

11. *Cum clerum plurimum*: anonymous report on council of Würzburg, RD 331 (1168): to Alexander III; BM ep.99: 'De schismatis innovatione'. RD address and text appropriate for letter to the pope, but BM text suggests this improbable; cf. BM ep.98, *Imperator cum principes*, letter of similar content from a friend to Alexander III. End of May 1165 or (more probably) soon after.

12. *Mandatum vestrum*: Gilbert Foliot to Alexander III, RD 331–2 (1168), BM ep.108, late July or early August 1165.

13. *Quam paterne*: Alexander III to Henry II, RD 332–3 (1169), BM ep.423, JL 11404, 22 May 1168.

14. *Excessus vestros*: Thomas to Gilbert Foliot, RD 333 (1169), BM ep.479, *c.*April 1169.

15. *Vestram non debet*: Thomas to the dean, archdeacon and clergy of London, RD 334 (1169), BM ep.488, 13 April 1169.

16. *Serenitatem tuam* (*Ex naturali ratione*): Alexander III to Henry II, RD 334–5 (1169), BM ep.492, JL 11621, 10 May 1169.

*17. 'Siquidem dignitas ... consequatur' (*Nuntios et litteras*): Norman bishops and clergy to Alexander III, RD 336 (18 November 1169), BM ep.567, after 8 September 1169.

18. 'Hoc petimus ... permittat': petition of Thomas to Henry II, presented at Montmartre, RD 336 (18 November 1169), BM ep.604, 18 November 1169; incorporated also in *Omnem operam*, report on the Montmartre conference by Vivian to Alexander III, BM ep.607.

19. *Rotomagensi archiepiscopo* (*Quod tibi ad praesens*): Alexander III to Gilbert Foliot, RD 337–8 (1170), BM ep.627, JL 11716, 12 February 1170.

20. *Illius dignitatis*: Alexander III to the archbishop of York and all the bishops of England, RD 338 (before June 1170), BM ep.169, JL 11267, 5 April 1166.

21. *Sciatis quod Thomas:* Henry II to the Young King, RD 339 (1170), BM ep.690, c.15 October 1170.

22. *Cum filium suum (Licet commendabiles):* Alexander III to Roger of York and Hugh of Durham, RD 339–40 (1170), BM ep.701, JL 11836, 16 September 1170.

23. *Cum karissimus filius (Oportuerat vos):* Alexander III to the bishops of London, Salisbury, Exeter, Chester, Rochester, St Asaph and Llandaff, RD 340–1 (1170), BM ep.700, JL 11835, 16 September 1170.

24. *Adductus est (Quam iustis):* Thomas to Alexander III, RD 341–2 (1170), BM ep.723, early December 1170; extracted also from *Quam iustis:* 'Evocavit rex . . . episcoporum', RD 342.

*25. 'Rex Anglorum . . . repromisit' (*Cum apud regem*):* Arnulf of Lisieux to Alexander III, RD 345 (1171), BM ep.738, early January 1171.

*26. 'Missi sunt nuncii . . . foverent', RD 345–6 (1171), constructed largely from passages in *Noverit vestra,* BM ep.750, 28 March 1171 and *Qui fuerint primi,* BM ep.751, April 1171: respectively, royal envoys' report to Henry II and royal envoy's letter to Richard of Ilchester.

27. *Vestro apostolatui:* William of Sens to Alexander III, RD 347–8 (1171), BM ep.740, January 1171.

*28. 'Rotro Rotomagensis . . . restitutus', RD 348 (1171), probably paraphrased from *Et ipsa loci:* Alexander III to Rotrou of Rouen and the bishop of Amiens, BM ep.763, JL 11908, 23 October 1171.

*29. 'Rotro Rotomagensis . . . ecclesiam', RD 351 (1172), probably paraphrased from *Fraternitati vestrae:* Alexander III to Rotrou of Rouen and the bishop of Amiens, BM ep.767, JL 12143, 28 February 1172.

*30. 'Post longos . . . promisit', RD 351–2 (1172), probably paraphrased from *Ne in dubium:* Albert and Theodwin to Henry II, BM ep.772, on or after 21 May 1172.

31. *Inspirante Illo:* Albert and Theodwin to clerks and monks of vacant churches in England, RD 366–7 (1173), BM ep.789, late 1172 or early 1173.

32. *Redolet Anglia:* Alexander III to the prelates, clergy and people of England, RD 369–70 (13 March 1173), BM ep.785 (12 March 1173); cf. JL 12203 and 12204, 12 and 13 March 1173; cf. also JL 12218, 2 April 1173: Alexander III to William of Sens.

APPENDIX II

DICETO AND THE SOURCES OF CANON LAW, WITH PARTICULAR REFERENCE TO DECRETAL LETTERS[61]

The present essay has indicated only very briefly the interest of Ralph de Diceto in questions of canon law and his use of canonical sources. This is a major topic which will be explored in a separate study. Meanwhile, the importance of the *Ymagines Historiarum* for the criminous clerks controversy and for the two principal phases of

---

[61] This section is appended in recognition of the special debt owed by CD to Walter Ullmann, under whose guidance his interest in the decretal collections first began.

Diceto, Henry II and Becket

reconciliation following Becket's death, in 1172 and 1175–6, should be emphasised. Likewise, his comments on the jurisdictional conflicts and on problems arising from a strict application of canonical principles in the political climate of his day are most illuminating. It is necessary to investigate further his use of the more formative books of canon law, of Gratian and the new decretal collections, with which it must be assumed he was familiar, and his approach to conciliar edicts. But it will be revealing also to examine the extent of his personal involvement in the administration of canon law. His duties as archdeacon of Middlesex and later as dean of St Paul's drew him into the routine business of the Church courts, but he was also the recipient of papal mandates and commissions, and acted occasionally as a papal judge delegate. A few examples must suffice here to illustrate both his own use of papal decretals as a chronicler and also the importance of letters which he himself received.

(a) *Nos attendentes* (JL 13106) and *Causam que inter* (JL 14002)

The mandate *Nos attendentes*, from Alexander III to the bishops of London and Winchester, is found in the *Ymagines Historiarum* under the date 1 October 1178. This date establishes the recipients as Gilbert Foliot and Richard of Ilchester, both of whom were on terms of close familiarity with Diceto. It is a brief passage which asserts that questions of property are subject to the king's jurisdiction, not to that of the Church. Noting that King Henry has been much disturbed in this matter, the pope orders the bishops to leave the judgment of possessions to the king. Stubbs remarked that this was an original document, not otherwise known, and it was listed in the *Regesta* from this single source (JL 13106). The papal ruling is of such evident importance for the history of jurisdictional conflicts that scholars have frequently been drawn to its evaluation. Its context has remained unknown. One striking theory is that Alexander III here laid down a general principle of law, advisedly to two English prelates of special influence.[62] But it can now be shown that *Nos attendentes* is an excerpt from the marriage decretal *Causam que inter*, which Alexander III sent to Gilbert and Richard. The decretal records one phase in a great marriage dispute involving the Arderne (or de Ardenna) family. It is found in sixteen decretal collections, including the *Appendix Concilii Lateranensis* (33.4) and the Gregorian *Decretales* (4.17.7). It is separately registered in the *Regesta* (JL 14002), and must be read with a further decretal, *Causam que vertitur*, to the Bishops Bartholomew of Exeter and Richard of Winchester and Abbot Baldwin of Ford (JL 13932: in thirteen decretal collections; cf. *Decretales* 1.29.17, 4.17.4, and 2.14.3). *Causam que vertitur* records a later stage in the same dispute, and includes a new papal ruling notwithstanding previous references to the question of possession and the king's court.[63] It is therefore clear that Diceto's *Nos attendentes* is misleadingly abbreviated, since it records a judgment in a particular case and was not devised as a considered statement of general principle. Neither marriage decretal was dated more narrowly than 1159–81 in the *Regesta*, though Holtzmann in

---

[62] Cf. C. Duggan, *Richard of Ilchester*, p. 16.
[63] The Arderne case is discussed in A. Morey, *Bartholomew of Exeter: bishop and canonist* (Cambridge, 1937), pp. 68–70.

his unpublished index reduced the limits to 1174–81, the *terminus a quo* being decided by Richard's consecration as bishop of Winchester in 1174.[64] The combined evidence of the decretal collections and Diceto's entry shows that *Nos attendentes* is part of *Causam que inter*, that JL 13106 and 14002 are therefore one and the same letter, whose date is 1 October 1178, and that *Causam que vertitur* (JL 13932) was issued between that date and Alexander III's death in 1181. The identity of the core of *Causam que inter* and *Nos attendentes* is made clear in Document A, below.

(b) *Audito laudabili* (JL 13897) and *Dignum est* (JL 14183)

The papal dispensation *Audito laudabili* is placed by Diceto at the close of December 1189, though it was issued by Alexander III, and cannot therefore be later than 1181. It is addressed to the Archdeacon Richard of Ely, and grants that he could by papal indulgence proceed to an ecclesiastical benefice or dignity, despite his illegitimacy. It was doubtless inserted at that point as an appropriate preface to the record of Richard's consecration as bishop of London on 31 December 1189.[65] Stubbs noted that the letter could not have been issued after 1181, and concluded that it came into Diceto's hands at the time of Richard's consecration, which is indeed one possible explanation. Richard was the famous FitzNeal, treasurer to King Henry II and author of the *Dialogus de Scaccario*. He was archdeacon of Ely from c.1158, a canon of London by 1181, and dean of Lincoln from c.December 1183. He was nominated for the bishopric of Lincoln in 1186, but unsuccessfully, and became bishop of London in 1189, as noted here.[66] At which stage in his career Richard obtained the papal dispensation has not been determined. Charles Johnson argued that Richard became archdeacon about 1160 and 'must have received his dispensation from Alexander III' at that time.[67] If the more recent view is correct that Richard was archdeacon from c.1158, he could not have been granted the indulgence to proceed to that office by Alexander III (1159–81). Moreover, the form of address in Diceto's record raises a query, since it names Richard as archdeacon in a letter granting him permission to accept an ecclesiastical benefice and rank in the future. This problem lies open for further study, but it may be conjectured that Richard secured the papal letter in expectation of higher preferment. The address and dating could point to the London canonry, which might also explain Diceto's possession of a copy. In the absence of firmer evidence, the grant can be dated only by the limits of Alexander III's pontificate, as it is listed from this source in the *Regesta* (JL 13897).

---

[64] For this reference and other decretal discussions, thanks are due to Professor Stephan Kuttner for generous access to the Holtzmann papers in the Institute of Medieval Canon Law in the University of California at Berkeley. Full details of all known decretal collections of the twelfth century, their manuscript locations, editions, analyses and secondary literature are now provided in C. R. Cheney and Mary G. Cheney, eds., *Studies in the Collections of Twelfth-Century Decretals: from the papers of the late Walther Holtzmann* (Vatican City, 1979). All collections cited in the present paper are fully documented in this volume.   [65] Diceto, II, pp. 74–5.

[66] For the most recent details of Richard's career, cf. D. E. Greenway, *John Le Neve, Fasti Ecclesiae Anglicanae, 1066–1300: Lincoln* (London, 1977), p. 9. His various offices were noted by Diceto, II, p. 69.

[67] *Dialogus de Scaccario*, ed. Charles Johnson (Nelson's Medieval Texts: London, 1950), p. xv.

Diceto, Henry II and Becket

Now *Audito laudabili* should be compared with the decretal *Dignum est*, which deals with an identical dispensation and is found only in the three systematic collections *Tanner* (3.12.5), *Francofortana* (12.7), and *Compilatio Prima* (1.9.9), which latter affords an edited text.[68] This letter is also listed in the *Regesta* for Alexander III's pontifical years, its recipient being uncertain (JL 14183: 'Cuidam' and 'Eboracensi archiepiscopo perperam inscribitur'). It was not part of the main transcription in *Tanner*, where it was inserted later with a shortened text, and was added to one codex of *Compilatio Prima*. Both these sources record an address from Alexander III to the archbishop of York, which cannot be reconciled with the dispensation. The evidence of the *Francofortana* codices is unhelpful – one has an uncertain reading, except that Alexander is named as the sender, and the others associate the text with the 1179 Lateran Council, which is seemingly a scribal error. In these circumstances the context of *Dignum est* has lacked a solution. Holtzmann pondered the election of Geoffrey, illegitimate son of Henry II, to York in 1191 as a possible solution, but rightly decided against it. The presence of the letter in the *Francofortana* collections would rule out a date as late as Geoffrey's election to York, and the York address cannot be accurate. Nor is an address to Lincoln acceptable. Geoffrey was elected to Lincoln in 1173, when he was already an archdeacon, but he was also then under age, and Diceto records that Alexander III granted a delayed dispensation 'tam aetatis quam nativitatis' in 1175 (RD I, 392–3 and 401). A collation of the decretal *Dignum est* with Diceto's text *Audito laudabili* provides a very convincing explanation. The FitzNeal dispensation is almost certainly part of the decretal *Dignum est*. By the same reasoning, JL 13897 and 14183 are one and the same letter, recording variants of the papal dispensation sent to Richard of Ely sometime within the limits of Alexander III's pontificate. The false address to York could conceivably spring from a scribe's misreading of Archdeacon Richard of Ely as Archbishop Roger of York (cf. 'R. elien. archi.' and 'R. eboracen. archi.'). Similarities in the careers of Richard and Geoffrey could likewise give rise to a mistake. The possibility must be allowed that Alexander III issued identically phrased letters to meet comparable situations, and therefore that two distinct letters are in consideration. But the collation of *Dignum est* and *Audito laudabili* in Document B, below, reveals their striking similarity, and justifies the proposal that they are derivatives from a single text.

(c) *Retulit nobis* and *Indignum est* (JL 15172 and 15177)

The foregoing examples have shown how Diceto's excerpts from papal letters may be freshly examined in the light of more recent studies on the decretals. The latter also disclose his involvement in delegated jurisdiction. He was quite possibly the Archdeacon R. of London commissioned with Gilbert Foliot by Alexander III in the letter *Significatum est nobis* (JL 14222: 1163–81), but the identification is uncertain, since there were other Archdeacons R. in the London diocese at that time. The decretal mandated action against clerical and lay incontinence in the area subject to

---

[68] E. Friedberg, *Quinque Compilationes Antiquae necnon Compilatio Lipsiensis* (Leipzig, 1882), p. 5.

them.[69] He was certainly the recipient of a number of commissions by Lucius III (1181–5), when he was dean of St Paul's. Jointly with his Archdeacon Nicholas, he settled a dispute between St Bartholomew's Hospital and Peter of Wakering over the church of Little Wakering in Essex, in the years c.1182–6.[70] Among the letters which he received from Lucius, the decretal *Retulit nobis* is of exceptional interest. As noted already, Dr Smalley remarked that Diceto 'has a right to the last word' on the Becket dispute.[71] By a strange chance, he was quite literally a recipient of the last word in the Gregorian *Decretales*, the most important official collection of canon law in the middle ages, though his identity there would pass unnoticed. The closing entry in the *Decretales* appears under the title 'De regulis iuris', with a chapter rubric 'Pro spiritualibus homagium non praestatur' (5.41.11). The total entry under these headings is 'Lucius III. Indignum est et a Romanae ecclesiae consuetudine alienum, ut pro spiritualibus facere quis homagium compellatur.' It is found in this form both in the sixteenth-century edition by the *Correctores Romani* and in the standard nineteenth-century edition by Friedberg. But Friedberg drew on the evidence of additional manuscripts and other collections, which provided a fuller text and a further *incipit*, *Retulit nobis*. His critical apparatus recorded the discovery of various corrupted versions of the address: 'decano Bidea et abbati de Fi', 'Eborac. archiep. et Lendon. decano et abb. de Filien.' and 'Eborac. archiep. et decano Lundon. et abb. de Fi.'. From these sources the letter was listed in the *Regesta* (JL 15172), with both *incipits*, *Retulit nobis* and *Indignum est*. But a further entry in the *Regesta* (JL 15177) refers to a letter *Retulit nobis*, transcribed in the Paris B.N. MS 16992, fo.220. This letter deals with the same matter as the decretal, with an address 'Episcopo Herefordensi et abbati de Faversham'. From this evidence it seemed likely that the archbishop of York, the bishop of Hereford, the dean of London and the abbot of Faversham provided a list of possible recipients, that JL 15172 and 15177 were derived from a single letter, and that *Indignum est* is a fragment of *Retulit nobis*, stating an important juristic principle excerpted from a longer letter dealing with an individual case. These conjectures prove mostly correct, except that the inclusion of the archbishop of York is an error and his name must be deleted. The letter is found in ten decretal collections. The complete text is preserved only in *Cheltenhamensis* (14.7), but mostly also in *Sangermanensis* (3.9.2 and 10.78), *Abrincensis* (3.6.1), *Alanus* (5.14.1) and *Fuldensis* (5.17.2). The correct address is 'Lucius III Herefordensi episcopo et decano Londoniensi et abbati de Faversham', and the decretal is 'Retulit nobis . . . appellavit', concerning an important dispute between the bishop of Chichester and his archdeacon. The complete letter is printed for the first time in Document C, below.[72] Since the dating limits are determined by Lucius III's pontificate, the recipients were

---

[69] The latter is found only in the *Belverensis* decretal collection, contained in an important volume of Foliot materials: cf. C. Duggan, *Twelfth-Century Decretal Collections*, pp. 71–3 and 155–62: cf. no.2.6, p. 158.

[70] Morey and Brooke, *Letters and Charters of Gilbert Foliot*, pp. 452–3.

[71] Smalley, *Becket Conflict*, p. 230.

[72] The case is discussed in its historical setting in *The Acta of the Bishops of Chichester*, ed. H. Mayr-Harting, Canterbury and York Society CXXX (Torquay, 1962), pp. 50–1.

Diceto, Henry II and Becket

Bishop Robert Foliot of Hereford, Dean Ralph de Diceto of St Paul's, and Abbot Guerric of Faversham. The disputants in the case were Bishop Seffrid II of Chichester and Archdeacon Jocelin of Lewes.[73]

APPENDIX III

DOCUMENTS

A Collation of *Causam que inter* and *Nos attendentes*; cf. Appendix IIa above. The version of *Causam que inter* supplied here is a composite text, based principally on *Wigorniensis* (7.9), with improved personal names derived from *Roffensis* (60). The greater part of the letter was transmitted to the *Decretales* (4.17.7). The text of *Nos attendentes* is reproduced from the edition of the *Ymagines Historiarum* (RD 1.427–8).

Causam que inter	*Nos attendentes*
Causam, que inter *a*Francum et R. de Ardena super eo quod Agatha*a* mater iamdicti R. dicitur non fuisse de legitimo matrimonio nata agitari dinoscitur, experientie vestre commisimus terminandam. Verum quoniam litteris nostris inseri fecimus ut predicto R. possessionem omnium eorum quorum possessor extitit quando avus suus iter Ierosolimam proficiendi*b* arripuit ante principalis cause ingressum feceritis*c* appellatione cessante restitui, si eadem possessione fuisset per violentiam spoliatus, nos*d* attendentes quod ad regem pertineat, non ad ecclesiam, de talibus possessionibus iudicare, ne videamur iuri *e*et dignitati carissimi in Christo filii nostri Henrici*e* regis Anglorum detrahere, qui sicut accepimus commotus est et turbatus, quod de possessionibus scripsimus, *f*cum ipsarum iudicium ad se asserat pertinere,*f* volumus et fraternitati vestre mandamus ut regi possessionum iudicium relinquentes de causa principali, videlicet utrum predicta mulier de legitimo	Nos attendentes quod ad regem pertineat, non ad ecclesiam, de possessionibus iudicare, ne videamur iuri et dignitati karissimi in Christo filii nostri H. illustris Anglorum regis detrahere, qui sicut accepimus commotus est et turbatur, quod de possessionibus scripsimus, cum earum iudicium ad se asserat pertinere, volumus et fraternitati vestre mandamus, ut regi possessionum iudicium relinquatis.

a–a R. et F. super eo quod *Wig.* and *Decretales* (X); Francum et R. de Ardena super nativitate ipsius R. . . . utrum Agath(a) mater R. *etc Roff.*   *b* proficiscendi X   *c* faceretis X   *d* om. *Wig.* *e–e* om. *Wig.*   *f–f* om. Wig.

matrimonio fuerat nata, plenius
cognoscatis et appellatione remota
secundum formam aliarum litterarum
nostrarum terminetis, licet videatur
incongruum quod matrimonium matris
prefati R. impetatur,[g] quod ea vivente
non fuit ut dicitur impetitum.

Data Tusculani kalendis Octobris.

g impetratur *Wig.*

B Collation of *Dignum est* and *Audito laudabili*; cf. Appendix IIb above. The text of
Dignum est is taken from the *Francofortana codices* (12.7). *Audito laudabili* is repro-
duced from the edition of the *Ymagines Historiarum* (RD 2.74–5: 'Alexander papa
III[tius] Ricardo Elyensi archidiacono').

[a]*Dignum est*	*Audito laudabili*
Dignum est et rationi consentaneum ut qui litterarum scientia sunt prediti et honestatis moribus ornati preroga- tivam favoris et gratie nostre obtineant et speciali privilegio decorentur honoris.	
Inde est quod de te laudabili multorum testimonio audito, quod videlicet scientia litterarum et honestatis moribus sis ornatus, tibi de consueta clementia et benignitate apostolice sedis indul- gemus ut, si aliqua ecclesia annuente domino te ad beneficium vel dignitatem quamlibet vocaverit, non obstante quia non es de legitimo matrimonio natus, libere valeas ad beneficium vel digni- tatem assumi. Ita tamen ut, que tibi de speciali beneficio indulgemus, non debeant aliis in posterum legem prefigere, nec in exemplum deduci, statuentes ut nulli omnino homini liceat hanc paginam nostre concess- ionis infringere et ei aliquatenus contraire. Si quis etc.	Audito laudabili multorum testimonio, quod scientia litterarum et honestatis moribus sis adornatus, tibi de consueta clementia et benignitate sedis apostolice indul- gemus ut, si aliqua ecclesia annuente Deo te ad beneficium vel dignitatem quamlibet vocaverit, non obstante quia non es de legitimo matrimonio natus, libere valeas ad beneficium vel digni- tatem assumi.

a inscription in *Tanner* (3.12.5): Al. III Ebor. arch.; in *Compilatio Prima* (1.9.9): Idem (*scil.*
Alexander III) Eboracensi archiepiscopo; in the Frankfurt, Troyes, and St Maximin codices of
Francofortana (12.7): ex concilio Lateranensi; the Rouen codex has the ambiguous reading: li aleẍ.
III. An adjacent letter in *Tanner* (3.12.6) and *Francofortana* (12.6) is addressed to the bishop-elect
(Geoffrey) of Lincoln: JL 13982. As noted already, the text is a later addition in *Tanner*, trans-
cribed at the foot of the folio; it stops short at 'legem prefigere'. Friedberg's edition of *Compilatio*

Diceto, Henry II and Becket

C The text of *Retulit nobis*; cf. Appendix IIc above. This text is based on *Cheltenhamensis* (14.7), *Sangermanensis* (3.9.2 and 10.78), *Abrincensis* (3.6.1), *Frag. Riccardianum* (55), and *Compilatio Secunda* (5.13.2). Among decretal sources, the complete text is found only in *Chelt.*; only paragraph [b] was transmitted to the *Decretales*; and paragraph [c] has not been found elsewhere in print.*

Retulit nobis

Lucius III Herefordensi episcopo et decano Lundoniensi et abbati de Faversham.

1181–5

[a] Retulit nobis dilectus filius noster Jocelinus archidiaconus Cicestrensis quod, cum canonice archidiaconatum Cicestrensem possideat, eius episcopus pro eo quod decanatum tanquam quem sibi credit de iure competere vendicare laborat, ipsi prorsus infestus iura ipsius minuere et que ad archidiaconatum de consuetudine et iure spectare noscuntur turbare et subtrahere post appellationem ad sedem apostolicam factam non desistit. Preterea homagium ab eo et fidelitatem novam pro sua voluntate requirit. Volentes igitur paci et iustitie ipsius archidiaconi paterna dilectione providere, discretioni vestre per apostolica scripta precipiendo mandamus quatinus inquisita diligentius veritate, si eum predecessori episcopo et successoribus eius fidelitatem iurasse constiterit, iam dictum episcopum ex parte nostra moneatis et ecclesiastica censura nullius appellatione obstante auctoritate nostra cogatis ut iura archidiaconatus integra archidiaconum sine contradictione possidere permittat, et ab exactione homagii et fidelitatis omnino desistat.

[b] Indignum siquidem est et a Romane ecclesie consuetudine alienum ut pro spiritualibus facere homagium quisquam compellatur.

[c] Si que vero post appellationem factam vel postquam archidiaconus iter arripuit ad sedem apostolicam veniendi circa eum vel possessiones suas videritis innovata vel mutata, omnia in eum statum appellatione remota reducatis in quo fuisse constiterit quando archidiaconus appellavit.

Prima notes that the text is in the Augustiniana edition but otherwise missing, except that it appears as a marginal addition in cod. Friburgensis 361a. The transmission of the text in the decretal collections merits further study.

* In addition to the collections listed above, the following also contain parts of the decretal: *Dunelmensis Secunda* (151b), *Alanus* (5.14.1), *Fuldensis* (5.17.2), *Compilatio Prima* (5.37.13), and *Decretales* (5.41.11).

XV

FROM THE CONQUEST TO THE DEATH OF JOHN

THE period from the Norman Conquest to the death of John marks a decisive turning point in the history of Anglo-papal relations. In no previous age were the affairs of the English Church so closely interwoven with those of the Western Church as a whole; and in no other phase did English ecclesiastics exert a more pervasive influence on the ideological and canonical developments which buttressed the rise of papal supremacy over the entire Church. For England, the period opened with the arrival of the Norman conquerors bearing a papal banner, yet resolute in their determination to resist the implications which that impressive symbol contained. It ended with the Angevin John conceding defeat after a protracted and bitter struggle with Innocent III, taking the Crusader's vow and yielding his kingdom to the pope in feudal subjection. Within these limits, three archbishops of Canterbury—Anselm, Becket and Langton—suffered long periods of exile in circumstances reflecting the clash of royal and papal interests, while Becket further endured the ultimate penalty of martyrdom in his own cathedral. The only English pope in the history of the Church, Adrian IV, reigned in the central years of the period. Beginning with Robert Pullen, English ecclesiastics were found for the first time in the college of cardinals in the mid-twelfth century; Englishmen, from King Edward the Confessor to St. Thomas of Canterbury, were inscribed in the catalogue of the saints with formal papal approval. Papal legates *a latere* appeared in England on many occasions with temporary jurisdiction to deal with particular situations; and English prelates were also appointed as papal legates with less specific commissions. With the advance of the twelfth century, papal judges delegate were named in ever-increasing numbers to deal with problems of law and to settle disputes by virtue of the pope's universal jurisdiction: a development which also reflected the swelling stream of appeals from England to the Roman Curia. Englishmen, many of them no longer known to us, shared in the intensive and creative growth of canon law, sometimes with lasting results for the Western Church as a whole. These channels of interrelation were of mutual concern and advantage: the English Church contributed to the increase of papal influence, just as it bore itself the imprint of the rising papal power.

It follows that no history of the English Church in the period is intelligible except in both its insular and its continental frameworks. This rather obvious judgement might appear at first superfluous, were it not that many existing commentaries are weakened by too great a preoccupation with local conditions and a failure to recognize the common pattern in the growth of the Church both in England and elsewhere in Europe simultaneously. Thus, the reforms of the English Church in the later-eleventh century and the introduction of the Investiture Dispute into England are matters which are naturally and validly linked with the policies of the first three Norman kings; but crucial and epoch-making changes for the whole of the Western Church coincided in time with the Norman Conquest of England; and, in one form or another, the issues they posed would certainly have been raised in England, independently of the change of the English dynasty. Had this conceivably not been so, the English Church would have proved a striking exception to the general pattern of the Western Church at the time. Nevertheless, the precise evolution of events was conditioned by the policies assumed by secular and ecclesiastical leaders in England in the light of the existing circumstances. Again, it is a commonplace judgement to consider the reign of Stephen as an intermission of weakness in English secular government, coming between the strong rules of Henry I and his grandson Henry II; according to this theory, in a period of unprecedented opportunity, the English Church advanced to a position of great strength and many-sided privilege: a position which Henry II felt naturally constrained to challenge. But Stephen's reign ran parallel in time with a phase of remarkable development in papal centralization and jurisdiction, especially through the agency of canon law, throughout the Church. This was the age which witnessed a vital point of departure in the history of ecclesiastical law: the 'Great Divide' between *ius antiquum* and *ius novum*, marked by the completion of Gratian's *Decretum* at Bologna, *c.* 1140–1. Clearly, both the local and the general factors played their part.

The Becket dispute is among the most familiar stories in English history; and conventionally the clash of personalities which it involved has formed the principal focus of interest in numerous evaluations of the contest. Alternatively, a diligent scrutiny of the life and practices of the English Church, its traditions and customs, and of the policies of the English kings affecting these, has provided an important yet entirely insular foundation for other assessments. Yet Becket expressed and championed the ascendant ideology of the popes and canon lawyers of the mid-twelfth century; and the conflict of secular and ecclesiastical interests and jurisdictions, which revolved in England round his personality, was also reflected in many other parts of the contemporary Church: in Sicily and Hungary, to mention but two examples, and in the reawakening of the papal-imperial struggle between Alexander III and Frederick Barbarossa. The English dispute was complex and has given rise to many contrasting interpretations, but it can never be understood divorced from its European context. Lastly, to cite one final instance, the affairs of the English Church in the reign of John involved repeated papal intervention so directly that their briefest outlines will serve to illustrate this general theme: Langton was appointed archbishop of Canterbury and consecrated by Innocent III against the wish of the king; the English kingdom was subjected to interdict for resistance to the papal action; the king himself was excommunicated at first and threatened later with deposition; papal authority and local secular problems, expressed in the baronial opposition to John, were intermingled in the struggle for the Charter and its subsequent condemnation by the pope; and the period ended, as mentioned above, with John's surrender and

68

his submitting the kingdom to papal feudal overlordship. Nevertheless, throughout this well-known story, the basic tenets and principles on which the papacy acted were independent of the particular problems of the English kingdom, and can be accurately judged only against the wider background of Innocent's conception of the papal office and the place of the English Church within the *totum corpus* of Western Christianity.

The fortunes of the papacy itself form, therefore, the necessary backcloth to our story: within the limits of this long period of one and a half centuries, the plenitude of papal power advanced from confident, though frequently resisted, definition to a very high point of practical realization. At the outset, Gregory VII crystallized the essential principles of many centuries of doctrinal and ideological growth touching the themes of sacerdotal superiority in Christian Society and of papal supremacy over the Universal Church. But, despite his immense achievements and the lasting influence of his transcendent personality, his policies were often contradicted and frustrated in his own lifetime; and, despite the decisive and formative phase which his pontificate is retrospectively seen to mark in the evolution of the Church's history, Gregory died in fact in exile, with much of his work in temporary ruins. The principles for which he fought were not fully realized in practice for many decades. Mainly through the influence of theological and canonical exposition on the theoretical plane, and on the practical level through the ever-increasing efficiency of the administrative and judicial machinery of the Curia, the popes of the twelfth century rose to a peak of prestige and authority, until with Innocent III a Christian ethos was attained in which the *plenitudo potestatis* was, in Haller's striking phrase, not merely an exorbitant pretension of the pope, but the belief of the century. Through the long path by which this summit of power was reached, the fluctuations of papal successes and failures conditioned relations between the popes individually and the Churches and rulers in the separate countries. Axiomatically, a strong ruler, as was William I or Henry II in England, resisted ecclesiastical pretensions with greater success than would otherwise have been the case; and, conversely, the problems confronting a given pope, such as Alexander

III in his dangerous contest with Frederick I, induced a temporary or diplomatic abatement of the widest papal claims and an opportunity which secular rulers elsewhere could be expected to exploit. Nevertheless, despite all such vicissitudes of papal fortune, the total story is one of gradual and inexorable papal advance throughout the period, within which the power of the papacy over the Church as a whole, as over the Church in England in particular, increased beyond all previous recognition, whatever qualification of this judgement may seem appropriate in any narrower context.

Some aspects of papal history from the mid-eleventh century affected the life of the English Church so intimately that their nature and evolution must be briefly mentioned. In the first place, the twin and interlocking movements of Church reform and the Investiture Contest permeated by degrees into every province of the Western Church. In its narrowest and technical meaning, the Investiture Contest was the product of a papal reaction against long centuries of secular control of the Church at all its levels, exercised chiefly through a decisive voice in the selection of ecclesiastical officials. The Germanic traditions of a proprietary church system, or *Eigenkirchenwesen*, and of regional churches subject to the control of their local rulers, or *Landeskirchentum*, resulted in such officials becoming increasingly subject to secular rulers and magnates and at the same time involved in secular business; and, as a corollary of this, bishops became important property holders and influential ministers in royal and feudal administration: a development reflected most directly in their dual possession of spiritual office and material benefice. Both Church and State drew benefit in some respects from this co-operation; and secular rulers came naturally to expect some measure of control over the activities of the Church in their dominions and over the appointment of the more important ecclesiastical officials. But a new situation resulted from the spiritual and juridical reform movements of the eleventh century, which upset the existing and traditional delicate balance. The papacy had fallen on evil days by that time, and the nomination of the popes themselves had passed into the control of the Italian and Roman factions. This regrettable situation was amended by an intervention of the German ruler Henry III, who at the synod of Sutri in 1046 secured the deposition of rival claimants for the papal title, and in the person of Clement II inaugurated a line of popes of far superior character and suitability for their office. This secular action was viewed in retrospect by reforming ecclesiastics as an unlawful usurpation.

Nevertheless, the papacy, being itself reformed from without, went forward now to take the initiative in a broad and deeply-penetrating reform of almost every aspect of its life and that of the whole Church; the work of Leo IX, Nicholas II and Gregory VII in particular, taken up and further developed by Urban II, was of outstanding importance. With the reforming movement now pushed forward on a very wide front, the investiture question revolved within it round a single but highly significant problem: to the clerical reformers it seemed an intolerable abuse that bishops and other ecclesiastics should be invested with the symbols of their rank, dependent essentially on its spiritual functions, by secular persons, while, for the historical reasons already mentioned above, secular rulers felt unable to distinguish so sharply the spiritual and material competence of the holders of these important positions. For itself, the papacy cast off the constraints of external secular pressure in the matter of papal elections, and by a decree of Nicholas II in the Lenten Synod of 1059 placed for the future their effective control in the hands of the cardinal bishops. Then Gregory VII, from 1075, and Urban II laid down rules prohibiting the practice of lay investiture at all levels in the Church; and these injunctions were repeated from time to time by their successors. The most dramatic dispute resulting from these measures took place between two series of popes and emperors, spanning the period from 1076 until 1122, and ending in the Concordat of Worms in the latter year. During that long period, the issue was contested in England also, within the space of a very few years, in the reigns of Rufus and Henry I, while Anselm was archbishop of Canterbury; and an agreement was reached between Anselm and Henry I in 1107, comparable in terms with the more famous agreement at Worms referred to above.

But however important the Investiture Contest appears in

political history, it was in fact merely symptomatic of far deeper problems in the interplay of secular and ecclesiastical forces in the period. It was, in Tellenbach's familiar judgement, not simply a dispute over investitures, but 'a struggle for right order in the world': a struggle for all that was summed up in the Gregorian concept of *iustitia*, or righteousness and true order in Christian Society.[1] The intervention of the emperor Henry III could not have produced such far-reaching results, paradoxically so injurious in their consequences to the imperial power itself, had not already-existing currents of reform in the Church provided a promising foundation. These currents were mainly of a spiritual and juristic nature. The revivified spirituality of the Church, which was basic to any authentic religious reformation, is recognized most clearly in the history of the religious orders in the period: above all, though not exclusively, in the earliest phases in the expansion and influence of the Cluniac movement from the early-tenth century, and later attaining an all-pervasive penetration of the life of the Church through the rise of the Cistercian movement in the twelfth. This new religious zeal, with its characteristic emphasis on the monastic virtues and disciplines, conditioned the general state of the Church as well as, in a more particular way, the minds of such leading reformers as Peter Damian and Gregory VII himself. It played a vital role in effecting a wider movement of reform, and was in the event itself still further stimulated by it.

But in producing an efficient instrument of reform and a means of expressing its manifold aspects in concrete terms, the growth of canon law was even more important. Jedin has recently argued that the historical transition marked out by the ending of the old canon law, and the emergence of the new, is more significant in fact than the conventional classification of historical epochs; and, from a different viewpoint, Knowles has suggested that canon law was soon to eclipse, if only for a time, theology itself as an influential discipline in the Church. The canonical tradition had never in fact died out since the early centuries; but, in a more proximate con-

---

[1] For a stimulating, if controversial, account of the Investiture Contest, see G. Tellenbach, *Church, State and Christian Society at the Time of the Investiture Contest*, trans. R. P. Bennett, Oxford (1948).

72

text, the canonical background of Gregorian Reform and its impact on twelfth-century developments can be retraced in its origins to the publication of the pseudo-Isidorian collection in the mid-ninth century, a fountain-head of canonical transmission from that time, through the proliferation of collections in the hands of the eleventh-century reformers, and culminating in the *Decretum* of Gratian in the mid-twelfth century.[2] From that time, at least until the pontificate of John XXII at Avignon, every significant pope was also an experienced canon lawyer, and papal policies were firmly based on canonical principles. For good or ill, the power of the medieval papacy at the peak of its prestige and influence was realized and made effective by canon law. These are essential reflections in considering the relations between the Roman Curia and the separate countries comprising the Western Church.

The reciprocal interchange of influence between the English Church and the papacy is revealed, against this background, in the crucial matter of ecclesiastical appointments. It was a typical feature of the policies of the reforming popes to foster canonical elections and to seek an increasing measure of influence over the selection, or at least to confirm the selection, of ecclesiastical officials. At its highest level, this policy was demonstrated in the papal promotion of the authority and jurisdiction of primates and metropolitans, not as representatives of separate *Landeskirchen*, but as powerful instruments by which the highly centralized government of the Church could be applied in its component parts; and so the symbolical importance of the pallium was increasingly stressed, with the requirement that archbishops should receive from the pope himself this token of their metropolitical office. Papal concern with the application of these principles to the English

---

[2] The *Pseudo-Isidore*, more generally known as the False or Forged Decretals, was one of the most decisive works in the history of canon law. Compiled in Frankish lands, probably at Reims or Le Mans *c.* 847–52, it incorporated both supposititious papal decretals from the early Christian centuries and genuine later canons. Among its author's motives were the consolidation of clerical privilege in Christian society and that of papal authority over the whole Church; and for these themes the collection exercised great influence on subsequent canonical collections. For further details, see A. van Hove, *Prolegomena ad Codicem Iuris Canonici*, Malines-Rome (1945), pp. 305–11; W. Ullmann, *The Growth of Papal Government in the Middle Ages*, Methuen (1955), pp. 180–9; etc.

Church was already evident in the twenty years preceding the Norman Conquest, simultaneously with the exertion of papal pressure, by popes Leo IX and Nicholas II, in the matter of episcopal elections. The anti-pope Benedict X had granted the pallium to the schismatical Stigand of Canterbury; and Nicholas II later granted the same to Ealdred of York, dispatching papal legates at the same time to settle related problems. But, after the Conquest, the process and habit of seeking such papal approbation became an issue of still more importance: in 1071 both Lanfranc of Canterbury and Thomas of York travelled to Rome for their pallia, while Lanfranc had accepted his appointment at the explicit command of the pope. A crisis arose, following Anselm's election, when Rufus obstructed at Rockingham Anselm's request for permission to journey to Rome for papal confirmation with the pallium. Nevertheless, Anselm received the essential symbol from the hands of a papal legate in his own cathedral in 1095, and Rufus's plans were circumvented. For the following century, a few examples only may be chosen from the many to illustrate the continuing interest of this papal prerogative: in Stephen's reign Theobald was elected to Canterbury by royal agreement with the papal legate, Alberic of Ostia; a disputed election to York resulted in the intervention of four successive popes, until William Fitzherbert was deposed in 1147 by Eugenius III, in favour of Henry Murdac, though the papal decision was frustrated in practice by the English king. In the reign of Henry II, Becket consented in 1162 to accept the province of Canterbury at the insistence of the king in agreement with the legate, Henry of Pisa, and English representatives including John of Salisbury and John of Poitiers, later distinguished adherents of Becket in his quarrel with the king, journeyed to the papal court to secure his pallium[3]; his successor, Richard of Dover, was elected in 1174 and travelled to Italy, where he was consecrated at Anagni by Alexander III, receiving the pallium from the pope in person; papal approval, together with the pallium, was freely granted by Lucius III to Baldwin of Ford and Worcester, who succeeded Richard in 1184.

[3] Cf. W. Stubbs, ed., *Radulfi de Diceto Opera Historica*, Rolls Series, 2 vols. (1876), I, 307; John of Poitiers was treasurer of York at that time.

74

And, most striking instance of all, in the reign of John, Stephen Langton was chosen and consecrated archbishop of Canterbury at Viterbo by Innocent III in 1207, following a disputed election which was quashed by the pope; though it was not until 1212 that John was induced to submit to the papal decision.

It is obvious that royal interests were also deeply involved in these matters. The person selected was normally the choice of the king, and in practice a large measure of co-operation was achieved between both parties. Yet it is significant that in a small number of critically disputed cases the papal action proved eventually the more successful even against the king. On the other hand, in the matter of episcopal elections the principle and practical value of papal approval were increasingly recognized, although the process of such elections provided a focus of recurring conflicts, above all during the investiture quarrel in Anselm's day, and in the Becket dispute over the Constitutions of Clarendon in 1164; and in the mainstream of development the royal will was in general the decisive factor. Nevertheless, papal influence percolated ever more deeply and pervasively through all levels of the English Church with the advance of the century, extending at last to all kinds of ecclesiastical appointments: of deans and archdeacons, of rectors and even monastic officials. The beginnings of the papal practice of granting expectative favours for benefices not yet vacant, the early traces of papal provisions, the granting of benefices to Italian or curial clerics: all these significant trends can be traced in England before the close of the century.[4]

But the problem of canonical elections provoked the use of a sword of two edges, since the legality of papal elections was often itself in dispute in the period. Gradually, through many crises, there evolved the basic canonical rules which were designed to place beyond question the validity of papal elections in the future. In 1059, in the context of ecclesiastical reforms already described, the decree *In Nomine Domini* of Nicholas II confirmed the electoral powers of the cardinal bishops, in consultation with the rest of the cardinal clergy. Yet the following century witnessed re-

---

[4] These matters are fully discussed in C. R. Cheney, *From Becket to Langton*, Manchester University Press (1956), esp. pp. 75–82.

peated conflicts within the electoral body, reflecting frequently the pressures of secular rulers, with the result that schism became endemic in the Church. After a long and dangerous instance of such confusion, the canon *Licet de vitanda* of Alexander III, in the Lateran Council of 1179, established the principle of a two-thirds majority of the total body of cardinals. Henceforth there could be no uncertainty concerning the legality of a given election; but a further problem arose through the scandal of extended vacancies, when the lawful electors were unable to reach a decision. And so the matter was finally settled in the decree *Ubi periculum* of Gregory X, at the Council of Lyons in 1274, which accepted in canon law the constraints of the conclave.

It follows that the period of this chapter, down to 1179, was one of exceptional danger for the papacy: between 1045 and 1179, no less than thirteen antipopes fractured the unity of the Church, in contrast with ten claimants of doubtful validity in the preceding four and a half centuries, and only one in the following two hundred years down to the outbreak of the Great Schism in 1378. This crisis of authority in the Church sprang in large measure from the conflicts of ecclesiastical and secular interests, as in the Investiture Contest or in the papal-Sicilian issues in the reign of Roger II. But for all secular rulers of the period a problem of choice, and at the same time an opportunity for the advancement of their separate ambitions, resulted. Thus, for England, the German creation of the antipope Clement III against Gregory VII in 1080 provided William I and Lanfranc with an occasion to arrest the promotion of Gregorian claims over the English Church, which fitted in very well with their general concept of ecclesiastical independence; and in the event they adopted a policy at first of hesitation and finally of neutrality. The problem was continued into the reign of William II, when Anselm succeeded Lanfranc, and the question arose of the recognition of Urban II by the English Church; this finally William agreed to approve, while obstructing Anselm's wish to visit the pope in person, as described above. Thereafter, the English Church, with royal agreement, supported the legitimate popes in similar conflicts. Nevertheless, the attitude assumed by English rulers proved of vital concern to the papacy, and frequently of political advantage to the English kings themselves. A difficult period for the Church opened with the double election of Innocent II and Anacletus II in 1130; but Henry I, in common with the French and German rulers, supported the ultimately successful Innocent, whose rival was sustained by forces in Italy and, in an important way, by Roger II of Sicily; and the schism lasted until 1138.

A still more difficult phase began with the death of Adrian IV in 1159, when against the newly and legitimately elected Alexander III, a line of antipopes was inaugurated by Frederick I; and a relentless conflict continued for almost twenty years until 1177: an experience clearly instrumental in provoking Alexander's electoral decree in 1179. In this schism also the English king supported the lawful claimant, refusing to accept Frederick's choice of Victor IV, at the Council of Pavia in 1160. But for many years Alexander was confronted with enormous difficulties: at times in exile from Rome, and even from Italy; often in danger of violent defeat at the hands of his German adversaries; and burdened with great expenses to sustain his fight and compensate for the loss of important revenues. Henry II was able to gain much profit by a diplomatic use of this crisis; and it is a matter of the highest significance that the papal schism covered the period of the Becket dispute in England. At the height of the English conflict, Henry's emissaries John of Oxford and Richard of Ilchester attended the schismatical Diet of Würzburg in 1165, and in somewhat obscure circumstances pledged support for the antipope Pascal III; in addition to which it is known that Henry wrote to the Imperial chancellor in 1166 of the possible transference of his allegiance from Alexander. In this context, Alexander is often accused of having adopted a weak and vacillating policy, of being lukewarm or even reluctant in his support of the English archbishop; but, in assessing his role in the insular conflict, it is vital to recall the problems which pressed more immediately and more persistently on him. The papal-imperial agreement at Venice in 1177 ended the series of crises which had revolved so long round the problem of papal elections. Meanwhile the wheel had turned full circle in England when Henry sought Alexander's support in his own dangerous crisis in the rising of 1173-4, conceding at that moment of peril, according to one admittedly questionable record, even the feudal subjection of his kingdom to the pope.[5]

With some of the major themes of contemporary papal and English ecclesiastical history established, it is feasible now to attempt a chronological sketch of Anglo-papal relations from the Conquest to the death of John. The overall trend is one of gradual extension and ramification of papal influence in England, with many setbacks and against frequent opposition: a gradually rising plane, broken by three peaks of crisis: the first in the time of Lanfranc and more particularly of Anselm, the second in that of Becket, and the third in the days of Langton. At each of these moments a major break-through of papal policy was achieved in dramatic circumstances. The intervening periods were not intrinsically less significant; indeed, in a less spectacular way, it was in those very phases of comparative quiet that the practical working out of ecclesiastical and secular issues was achieved; and, in the event, for the long-term fortunes of the Church and its relationship with secular law and government, these periods were to prove by far the more productive. But it is not possible to believe that the extent of the Church's success within the wider framework could have been achieved without the exceptional effort made in the periods of open conflict.

An earlier view that a radical change in Anglo-papal relations was accomplished by the Norman Conquest is no longer acceptable without substantial qualification. It is evident from the foregoing arguments that a coincidence in time explains, to some extent at least, the participation of the English Church in a wider movement. But more than this, it has also been clearly shown that the late Anglo-Saxon Church was by no means as moribund as

[5] The record of an alleged letter of Henry II written during the crisis is preserved by Peter of Blois, but its authenticity is doubtful. On the other hand, Duchesne's edition of the Life of Alexander III by Cardinal Bozo discusses variant MS readings of the Avranches Settlement of 1172 as found in Bozo MSS. The later MSS attribute to Henry II an undertaking very suggestive of feudal submission to the pope, but Duchesne's judgement is against this version, as being a possible interpolation; cf. L. Duchesne, *Liber Pontificalis*, Paris (2nd ed., 1955), Tome II, p. 426, n.1.

78

was previously imagined, that it was not at all isolated from contact with the papal Curia, and that the early seeds of reform had already been planted in it. The corollary of this thesis is that certain familiar measures of the immediately post-Conquest period have conventionally received a disproportionate emphasis. A more balanced view, revealing both innovation and continuity, has now been achieved, notably by Darlington and Barlow among more recent scholars.[6] A single example will serve to clarify this point: the *Northumbrian Priests' Law* of *c.* 1020 affords evidence for the existence and operation of canon law in ecclesiastical courts, reducing to some extent the significance of the Conqueror's oft-quoted writ dealing with the separation of ecclesiastical and secular jurisdictions. In the same way, the concern of the reforming papacy with the English Church from the time of Leo IX has already been noticed. Nevertheless, it is true that the Normans conquered the island with papal approval, at a moment when the archbishop of Canterbury, Stigand, was in a canonically vulnerable position. They came, moreover, with a tradition of support for ecclesiastical reform on the continent; and there is no doubt that, in spite of the limits which the Conqueror wished to impose on the ideological aspects of papal policy, an important drive forward in the general reform of the Church was the inevitable result of the change of political direction. It is more fitting to speak therefore of a swifter application of reform and advance of the Church as a result of the Conquest, an acceleration of a movement which was already set in motion.

The policies and personalities of the first post-Conquest kings and archbishops require a similar evaluation. The Conqueror is rightly seen as a conscientious supporter of ecclesiastical and moral reform, in contrast with his son, William Rufus, who was disinterested in spiritual and moral questions, a despoiler of Church property and an oppressor of ecclesiastical persons. The deterioration of relations between *regnum* and *sacerdotium* which took place in England with the transition from one reign to the other

[6] Cf. R. R. Darlington, *The Norman Conquest*, Creighton Lecture in History 1962, Athlone Press (1963), esp. pp. 13–18; for the latest detailed study of the immediately pre-Conquest Church, see F. Barlow, *The English Church, 1000–1066*, Longmans (1963).

is partly explained by this altered royal attitude. At the same time, Lanfranc, the Conqueror's coadjutor at Canterbury, was in sympathy with the king's ecclesiastical policies, including his determination to govern effectively his *Landeskirche* in England, to set up the ring-fence round his dominions, to erect a barrier between the island and the continent, and thus to control the interchange both of ideas and of persons between the English Church and the Roman Curia. Whereas Anselm, Lanfranc's successor, was imbued with the very spirit of Gregorian Reform in all its aspects; therefore, for him, the reform of the regional Church in detail, though important, was no longer sufficient, and the denial of the fullest papal claims was an intolerable burden. In these circumstances, the happy co-operation which had existed between William I and Lanfranc was no longer feasible. The change was accomplished by a twofold and contrary transmutation: the royal policy had deteriorated through abuse to corruption, while the archiepiscopal purpose had risen from a moral and merely ecclesiastical level to a full theocratic and ideological programme. There is much that is true and illuminating in this theory, though in several aspects it is an insufficient, and even over-simple, explanation. To mention one obvious example: the papal programme had itself gained further momentum in the meanwhile.

The Conqueror's attitude was unambiguous enough. The judgement of Zachary Brooke seems somewhat generous in the circumstances. For Brooke, William 'was naturally devout and, like his fellow countrymen of Southern Italy, filled with a deep regard for the papal office'; yet his own analysis of William's dealings with the papacy suggests the actions of a ruler of realistic and understandably practical self-interest: the pope's support was useful at the time of the Conquest, and papal legates were necessary in the early transitional stages; but there was no hesitation on William's part in rejecting whatever aspects of papal policy were subsequently unwelcome to him. Gregory urged against him the fullest papal theories, claims which in their origins were retraceable to Gelasius I: 'As I have to answer for you at the awful judgement, in the interests of your own salvation, ought you, can you, avoid immediate obedience to me?' No king, not even a pagan king, Gregory claimed with some exaggeration, had opposed him in William's fashion. The latter agreed to contribute the traditional Peter's Pence to the support of the papacy, but utterly rejected the implications of tribute and feudal subjection which might be inferred from it: his predecessors, he firmly asserted, had not done fealty to the popes, nor had he promised to so do at the time of the Conquest. Therefore, despite his support for the ecclesiastical reforms in detail, the political aspects of reform were obscured in his reign in England: the investiture decrees remained a dead letter in William's dominions, and he ended his reign in easy neutrality between rival claimants for the papal title. Rufus continued the policies of his father, in this respect, in confronting the inroads of papal influence attempted in his kingdom, but without the Conqueror's compensating qualities: he was a persecutor of the Church and no supporter of spiritual and ecclesiastical reformation; and therefore he alienated many who otherwise might have supported him in the more political aspects of the question. But it is clear that Anselm regarded his curtailment of papal authority and his resistance to the developing canon law as the critical issue: Rufus had acted, in Anselm's judgement, contrary to the law of God in arrogating to himself the adjudication of papal elections and in resisting the application of the investiture decrees.

In contrast, the conventional distinction drawn between the policies of Lanfranc and Anselm is both valid and over-simple. It is important to stress the qualities they had in common as well as their differences: both were Italians who came to England as monks from the Norman abbey of Bec; both were great scholars of international reputation whose fame was established independently of their archiepiscopal office; both were imbued with the spirit of the reforms of the time, and acquainted at formative phases in their careers with popes or future popes, members of the papal Curia and leading reformers; both fully accepted the prevailing theories of papal supremacy, even if Lanfranc supported the limitation of the theories at times in practice. Lanfranc was a distinguished theologian and perhaps a product of the law schools of Italy, though an earlier view that he was numbered among the *causidici* in the schools of Roman law at Pavia has now been seriously challenged.[7] His later career as primate of the Church in England reveals his continuing interest in canon law and its general application; no work was more congenial to the promotion of all that the Gregorian reformers stood for than the *Pseudo-Isidore*, whose derivative collection Lanfranc certainly used in England. At the same time, he undoubtedly modified the rigour of some of the reforming policies in detail, such as the absolute insistence on clerical celibacy, without questioning their validity. He likewise accepted in full the right of appeal by ecclesiastics to the papal Curia, but simultaneously distinguished the secular interests which might make an appeal inappropriate. He fully supported the Conqueror's limitation of papal encroachments, and emphasized in particular situations his rights as metropolitan rather than the superior authority of the pope. His attitude was therefore to some extent ambivalent; and the interesting suggestion has been made that his coldness to Gregory VII resulted in part from the latter's earlier obstruction, as Archdeacon Hildebrand, of Lanfranc's project to build up a kind of patriarchate for the British Isles under his own control.[8] No doubt his attitude was compounded of many varied factors, and the common assumption is too facile that his difference of outlook from that of Anselm was largely explicable because Anselm was born a generation later.

But Anselm was more obviously a zealous adherent of the most advanced Gregorian party: a distinguished theologian and, paradoxically, less experienced in legal studies than his predecessor. He displayed in his attitude to the papacy, and on all the main planks of the papal reform programme, a complete acceptance of the Gregorian theories: his conflict was joined with Rufus on such key issues as the papal confirmation of his own election, the receipt of the pallium, and the recognition at the same time of the validity of Urban II's election. In the event, Anselm's resulting period of exile, from 1097, broke down the barriers which the Conqueror

---

[7] On this see R. W. Southern, 'Lanfranc of Bec and Berengar of Tours', in R. W. Hunt *et al.*, edd., *Studies in Medieval History presented to F. M. Powicke*, Oxford (1948), pp. 27–48, esp. pp. 28–30.

[8] This is suggested by E. Amann and A. Gaudel in 'Lanfranc', *Dictionnaire de Théologie Catholique*, Paris, VIII, ii (1925), col. 2562.

had erected, brought Anselm himself even more directly in touch with the central stream of reform at Church councils in Italy, at Bari and Rome in 1098 and 1099 respectively, from which he returned on Henry I's accession in 1100 determined more than ever to uphold the principles for which he had accepted exile. Meanwhile, with hardly less significance, signs of a wider movement were evident among the English bishops towards the recognition of an effective papal authority over elections, appeals and similar related questions. Herbert of Losinga, bishop of Thetford, travelled to Rome in 1093, resigned his bishopric on the grounds that his election in 1091 was tainted with simony, and accepted it back from the hands of Urban II; the bishops of Hereford and Salisbury, who had previously dissociated themselves from Anselm's actions, now moved over to his side, just as the bishops-elect of Winchester and Hereford later refused to accept investiture from Henry I, and likewise aligned themselves with Anselm.

The Investiture Contest was thus brought into England in the reign of William II; and the beginnings of a grouping of ecclesiastical leaders round Anselm and in support of the most advanced papal programme are clearly seen. It was an advantage to Henry I to receive back Anselm initially into favour, but the investiture issue was quickly resurrected, leading to Anselm's second exile and thus to the compromise worked out finally in 1107. The agreement was in the form of a compact in which each side gained some measure of success: Henry accepted that the symbols of investiture, the episcopal ring and staff, should not be conferred by a layman, but the bishops would nevertheless be elected in his court or chapel; and he ensured in practice that the homage of a bishop-elect would take place before his consecration. In its turn, the Church had secured the formal royal concession of the canonical principle that investiture was in essence a spiritual matter, though it may well be thought that in substance the greater gain was made by the king. The English compromise was accepted by Pascal II, the reigning pontiff, after a long series of difficult negotiations, and foreshadowed the very similar agreement at the papal-imperial level at the Concordat of Worms in 1122. But it would be idle to think that these agreements on the specific question of investitures resolved the basic conflicts of which it was merely symptomatic. The Becket dispute in mid-twelfth-century England, as well as the re-emergence of the papal-imperial struggle in the days of Barbarossa, revealed in a very true sense the posing of the same elemental questions in an altered situation.

Meanwhile, Henry I adopted a position *vis á vis* the Church in England logically transitional between the policies of his father, William I, and his grandson, Henry II. All three were strong kings who moved forward in many areas of mutual co-operation with the Church, yet with varying degrees of success for their plans to limit the extent of papal intervention in their kingdom. The barriers which the Conqueror erected were breached at certain vantage points in the reign of Henry I, but they were by no means destroyed altogether. Recourse was had to Rome for the pallium for Archbishop Ralph in 1114, but in circumstances which provoked the complaints of the pope over lack of consultation and the obstructions which were placed in the way of inter-communication: Pascal II wrote a letter of protest in 1115 with specific reference to papal letters, legates, appeals to the Curia, and the translation of bishops without papal consent. Nevertheless, the practice of appeals later made significant headway, of which the *Liber Landavensis* provides convincing evidence. The appointment of legates assumed a heightened importance. A total of nine legates were appointed during the reign: among these, the legate Anselm was commissioned in 1116, but detained in Normandy for three years; with uncertain results, Henry I sought papal agreement in 1119 to limit the scope of legatine action in England; the commission of John of Crema in 1125 was of outstanding importance, and he held a legatine council at Westminster in that year. A measure of compromise was reached when Honorius II granted the status of legate to Archbishop William of Canterbury in 1126; and William convened a legatine council, with royal approval, in the following year. Throughout the same period, various disputes occasioned the departure of English ecclesiastics for the Roman Curia, with a resulting continuous contact with papal policies at their centre of formulation; the re-emergence of the Canterbury and York dispute over the primacy is a particularly revealing instance. These few examples suggest a tangible advance of papal influence in England in the reign of Henry I, yet they must still be viewed against a general background of royal control over a very wide area of the Church's activities, as in the vital matter of episcopal elections, mentioned above: in Henry's reign, quite apart from his effective voice in the selection of candidates, bishoprics were sometimes kept vacant for long periods, and the practice of simony remained a scandal.

A less qualified judgement is appropriate to the progress made by the English Church in Stephen's reign, for there is no doubt that the desired freedom of the Church, the *libertas ecclesiae*, was approached in decisive strides at that time. Stephen owed much to the Church for its support of his own accession; and in his coronation charter of 1136, which echoed the tenor of that of Henry I, he promised redress of the principal abuses touching ecclesiastical appointments, possessions and jurisdiction. Foremost among these undertakings was the promise that episcopal elections would be canonical and free from taint of simony. It is generally accepted that Stephen at first respected these commitments, but later deviated from them as opportunity arose. Nevertheless, the reception of papal influence was ever more evident. Stephen indeed had acknowledged the papal confirmation of his own election, though it was not until 1138 that Innocent II, harassed by an eight-years' conflict with the antipope Anacletus II, was free to take a more positive line with the Church in England. Then Alberic of Ostia arrived to resume the work of John of Crema in the previous reign, and to hold a legatine council dealing with Church reforms by a clear assertion of papal authority. In the following year the dispute between Stephen and Matilda was argued by their supporters in the presence of the pope at the Lateran Council; in 1139 also, Stephen's brother, Henry of Winchester, was created legate for the English Church, of which he was the dominant figure until his commission lapsed with the death of Innocent II in 1143, to be resumed in the person of Archbishop Theobald until his death in 1161.

These two contrasting figures, Henry and Theobald, were second to none in the application of papal jurisdiction and centralized administration in England. It is no longer possible to accept Henry of Huntingdon's statement that appeals to the Roman Curia were first made under Henry of Winchester, for there is ample evidence of them earlier; but it is possible that papal judges delegate with explicit commissions and mandates can first be clearly traced from this time. The *Liber Eliensis* affords valuable evidence of the operation of ecclesiastical jurisdiction, as in the Stetchworth dispute, involving Gilbert Foliot of Hereford and Archbishop Theobald as ecclesiastical judges. Foliot, who was later to be translated to London with papal approval and to play a leading role in the Becket dispute, was elected to Hereford in 1148, and consecrated by Theobald outside England, without reference to Stephen but at the command of the pope. Nevertheless, the English bishops present at the consecration dissociated themselves from the proceedings, and Foliot himself swore fealty to the king on returning to England. Meanwhile, English prelates had attended the Lateran Council in 1139, and others attended the Council of Reims in 1148. Stephen's intention to prevent the primate from attending the latter was abortive; and, despite their nominal reconciliation, this incident was symptomatic of deteriorating relations between the papacy and influential English bishops on the one hand, and Stephen and his dynasty on the other. The coronation of Eustace, Stephen's heir, was forbidden in 1152 and the Angevin succession in 1154, in the person of Henry II, was greatly facilitated by this alignment of interests.

The problems confronting Stephen in the political sphere, and his resulting weakness compared with the Conqueror and Henry I, as well as with Henry II who succeeded him, have influenced too decisively the conventional views of his reign, since no less significant were the wider developments in the Church as a whole under papal guidance in the period. This factor has been mentioned above in the introductory section, and need only be briefly repeated here. The increasing efficiency of papal jurisdiction through the reception of appeals and the appointment of judges delegate spread evenly through the Western Church at the time, and was in no way peculiar to Stephen's kingdom. The vital developments in papal conciliar legislation, and in the codification and interpretation of canon law, associated above all with the great school at Bologna and with the *Decretum* of Gratian, were destined to infiltrate gradually into all the provinces of the Western Church. Scholars and ecclesiastics from England were increasingly involved in such advances, frequently participating in a creative way. Many English theologians and canonists studied and taught in the schools on the continent: Robert Pullen became cardinal and Chancellor of the Roman Church in 1144; Hilary of Chichester served in the papal chancery in 1146; Bozo, later cardinal, served there from 1149; in which year also Nicholas Breakspear was created cardinal, to be raised to the papal throne as Adrian IV in 1154; many of the later protagonists in the spectacular controversy of Henry II's reign were in the early phases of their careers during that of Stephen.

The rapid expansion of the monastic and canonical orders throughout Europe, and within England in full proportion, contributed beyond measure to the increase of papal influence. In this context, the growth of the Cistercian Order, as explained already, was of outstanding importance: the advance of papal power in the mid-twelfth century in the extent of its permeation of the Church was at least in part linked with the higher pitch of religious fervour achieved by the Cistercians. The great moral force of St. Bernard, especially in French society, had its counterparts in England too; and English society was confronted for the first time on a very large scale by an order decisively conceived on a supra-national basis, and markedly detached from the structure of the feudal kingdom. At the same time, the religious orders in general proved the natural and constant allies of the papacy, with which many contracted a special and immediate relationship, and almost all found it useful to seek regular confirmation of their privileges and possessions by the highest ecclesiastical authority. It is now generally recognized that the archiepiscopate of Theobald provided the prelude to the more dramatic events of Becket's career: the advance of canonical learning, mentioned above, was fostered in an important way in Theobald's household; and many of the individual points of conflict which were later to make up the controversy between Henry II and Becket were already exposed in the closing years of Theobald's life. Moreover, Theobald was seen presiding as master of the English Church, as in his legatine council of 1151; and the period witnessed numerous and increasing instances of a two-way traffic between England and the Curia: judicial problems and disputed elections, such as that of Richard Belmeis to London in 1152, were referred to the papal court for a decision. This was itself a measure of the inroads which papal policies had made in England during Stephen's reign and of the extent to which the stronger policies of the Anglo-Norman kings had been dissipated. It was Henry II's objective to attempt to restore the previously-existing conditions, to put back the clock, to reconstitute the conditions which prevailed in the time of his grandfather. But neither in England nor on the continent could the changes of many years be forgotten, and there was something unrealistic in the appeal, however accurate and understandable, to the customs of a superseded period.

It was in this situation that there was fought out one of the most famous conflicts of secular and ecclesiastical forces in Christian history. The strands of English and papal history are so interwoven in Henry II's reign that only a ruthless selection of the most important elements is possible in this chapter. There is no doubt that Henry selected Becket as primate in the expectation that the former association of William I and Lanfranc, to their mutual advantage, would be re-created; and this was natural in recollection of the important political role which had been filled by English prelates down to that time, while contemporaries noted how in a wider canvas the German rulers enjoyed a similar relationship with the archbishops of Mainz and Cologne as imperial chancellors. But this expectation was not to be realized. The conflict which ensued will not be understood if the vision is narrowed to the particular points at issue at any given stage of the controversy. If this were done, it would be possible to argue that personal differences between Becket and Henry were of primary importance; or that material interests, such as the Canterbury properties, dominated Becket's policies; or that primatial notions of prestige and power in the English Church lay at the root of Becket's relations with the English episcopate. All these elements are present in the story and have their importance; but they could not explain why, for instance, Alexander III, despite the difficulties of his own position and his reluctance at times to be committed to the full rigour of Becket's logic, nevertheless associated Becket with Lucas of Gran as the twin buttresses of the Church's liberties.

This is not to make a moral judgement for or against the archbishop or the king: both their policies are explicable in the framework of their thought processes. It is possible in retrospect to sympathize either with the one or the other, while fully accepting and understanding the views of both. On the one hand, there is the background of relentlessly advancing canon law and papal ideology already described, together with the spiritual and religious climate reflected in the dynamic monastic movements of the period; on the other, there are the concepts of medieval kingship and the increasingly self-conscious theories of royal justice and its practical realization. Both these major streams of development were swelling and flowing more swiftly through the century. The intellectual ferment of the age must also be considered, especially the legal and theoretical strands of the so-called twelfth-century renaissance, which was reaching in these respects a peak of achievement in the second half of the century: an intensively creative period in the history of law, whether of canon law and Roman law, or of the regional laws of the various kingdoms. It was virtually inescapable that difficulties, in various forms, would arise as the separate concepts of jurisdiction and legal systems clashed at their many points of overlapping interests.

Henry, in his coronation charter of 1154, had promised to preserve the freedom of the Church. And, while Theobald lived, an open conflict was averted; but there is ample evidence that the aged archbishop was increasingly disquieted by indications of a firmer royal policy. Meanwhile, Henry had thrown his support on the side of Alexander III in the papal schism which opened in 1159; and, in the early phase of Becket's rule, the English Church was seen in harmonious relationship with the exiled pope: both archbishops, of Canterbury and York, attended the Council of Tours in 1163, with a number of English bishops. A widening area of disagreement between Becket and the king rose, however, to a crisis over the question of criminous clerks in 1163, and culminated in Henry's sixteen points programme in the Constitutions of Clarendon in 1164. By these clauses Henry sought formal recognition of the customs regulating relations between royal and ecclesiastical interests as established by the Norman kings. These were the *avitae consuetudines*, the customs of his grandfather; and there is general agreement that his claim was valid on almost all points as to the matter of historical fact. Some of the clauses necessarily involved relations with the papacy, others dealt more specifically with politico-ecclesiastical questions within the kingdom. One vital clause aimed to make the departure of ecclesiastics from England to the continent subject to the king's consent; a further clause cut short the appellate system of ecclesiastical courts at the provincial level, so that recourse should not be had to the papal Curia except at the will of the king; the famous third clause embodied the royal plan to ensure the secular constraint of criminous clerks; yet another clause dealt with ecclesiastical vacancies and electoral procedure. There is no doubt that Henry made a tactical mistake in seeking to extort a sealed acceptance of these requirements, which could not be reconciled with the existing state of the Church's law. He would almost certainly have been able to enforce his will, at least on several points, in practice. Becket, for his part, was adamant in his refusal to agree to such conditions, apart from a temporary vacillation under heavy pressure. For Becket the appeal to custom was quite irrelevant. Echoing directly the words of Gregory VII in the previous century, he argued that Christ had said 'I am the truth'; He had never said 'I am the custom'.

In canon law there is little doubt that Becket was fully justified in the attitude he assumed in opposing the constitutions.[9] But the English bishops, though basically in agreement with him, were not prepared, for various reasons, to support him *in extremis*. The pope, too, was in a perilous phase of his struggle with Barbarossa, and would doubtless have preferred to avoid the English issue alto-

[9] Cf. C. Duggan, 'The Becket Dispute and the Criminous Clerks', *Bulletin of the Institute of Historical Research*, XXXV (1962), pp. 1–28.

gether at that moment. Nevertheless, when confronted directly with Henry's constitutions, he condemned ten outright, while being prepared to tolerate six. The archbishop's exile, his absence in France for six years filled with difficult negotiations and abortive attempts to work out a solution of the quarrel, the final reconciliation and return to England, his martyrdom at Canterbury in 1170, and his canonization by Alexander III in 1173: all these are very familiar details. Relations between England and the papal Curia continued at a high and sometimes anxious level of activity throughout. Alexander's rulings varied in their precision and firmness in some proportion to his own fluctuating fortunes in his struggle with Frederick I; and Henry was not averse to exploiting Alexander's difficulties by the threat of defecting to Pascal III. Constantly, letters were exchanged between both parties in the English dispute on the one hand and the Roman Curia on the other; paradoxically the quarrel increased this intercommunication, which Henry made no attempt to curtail. Meanwhile, Alexander had also to deal diplomatically with the re-emergence of the Canterbury and York dispute, which was brought to a pitch of crisis by Roger of York's coronation of the young king, Henry's son, in 1170 while Becket was still in exile, in derogation of Becket's rights and in opposition to the papal prohibitions. And all the while the routine contacts were maintained, to some extent, between English religious houses and ecclesiastical judges and the papal Curia.

Henry averted the threat of serious papal reprisals for Becket's murder, and his reconciliation with the Church was achieved in two main stages. The Compromise of Avranches in 1172 included royal promises of acts of penance in atonement for the outrage, which Henry swore he had neither wished nor contrived, and policy undertakings in connection with specified points in dispute during the quarrel. He promised to repeal the customs introduced in his time against the Church in his kingdom, though he protested to Bartholomew of Exeter that he considered these very few or even none at all; and he promised also to allow freedom of appeals to the Curia unless injury to his own position was thereby threatened. There was no explicit reference to the Clarendon Constitutions, nor was there mention of the subject of criminous clerks. A letter of Alexander III to Henry, recording the terms of agreement, survives in transcription, from which it is clear that the pope was much concerned to have them officially registered for future reference. Three years later, the legate Pierleoni arrived in England in 1175, and further disputed points were settled by the following year. On this occasion a letter of Henry II to Alexander is extant, agreeing to the elimination of various outstanding abuses touching vacancies and the persons and rights of clerks, and most significantly accepting the principle of clerical immunity from secular justice, with the exceptions of charges relating to lay fees or transgressions of the forest law. Meanwhile, other facets of Anglo-papal relations were revealed by Henry's appeal for papal support in his period of great danger during the rising of 1173–4, and by the young king's dealings with the pope in an attempt to assert his royal position, *vis à vis* his father. In many ways Henry continued to keep a firm grip on the English Church, in spite of several important concessions. Three of his most loyal aides in the contest with Becket were elected to the sees of Winchester, Norwich and Ely in the years of the post-Becket settlement: they were respectively Richard of Ilchester, John of Oxford and Geoffrey Ridel. In such ways as these, Henry was seen to achieve some of the vital objects which he had pursued at Clarendon in 1164. Nor did he faithfully fulfil the promises he had made to the papal legates in 1172 and 1175–6, as the prolongation of episcopal vacancies affords striking testimony.

Historians have variously assessed the results of the compacts between Henry II and the papacy after Becket's martyrdom. For Zachary Brooke, the main theme was a posthumous victory for the archbishop, with the defeat of Henry's attempt to reconstruct the barrier policy of his ancestors, and the opening up of England for the first time to the full impact of canon law after a period of isolation. For Cheney, the Compromise of Avranches settled nothing, in the sense that royal policy seemed not significantly changed by the precise terms of the agreement; and he has adduced impressive evidence in support of the thesis that the period after Avranches was one of 'effective adjustment, with give and take between the two jurisdictions'. For Morey, the importance of the settlement was rather that it permitted the English Church to go forward participating fully in the overall advance of the Western Church, whereas this result might otherwise have been imperilled. In two respects, Brooke's thesis is no longer acceptable, since the English Church had clearly not been isolated before the compromise; and his use of decretal evidence as the main element of proof in his argument is now known to have been misconceived. Apart from this important proviso, the various views are not as irreconcilable as they may seem at first consideration, and are in fact complementary facets of a single whole.

The twelfth century was not an age of unconditional surrender: victory of Church or monarchy on one point did not necessarily entail the same result on others. In this respect, Cheney's view is clearly valid: each side gained some points and surrendered others. It is difficult not to believe that the Church, under papal guidance, gained a great victory in the matter of routine appeals to the Roman Curia: the striking evidence of the decretals which poured into England from the early 1170's (as they did into other countries also) and the ever-expanding jurisdiction of the papal judges delegate prove that the two-way traffic between the English courts Christian and the Curia had now become a constant factor and altogether a matter of course, whatever evidence there may be of royal curtailment of it in specific instances. On the vexed question of criminous clerks, the Church gained recognition of a highly-prized principle, but conceded certain exceptions in return. On other debated matters, the Church failed utterly to establish its position against secular opposition. The question of advowsons, the *ius praesentandi*, affords a significant example of the secular law in practice winning a victory over the law of the Church;[10] and in many other ways, as already indicated, the English king was able to canalize or curtail its full operation. But the canon law in England made dramatic strides forward in the decades following Becket's death: the activities of the English judges delegate and of the canonists in the circles of distinguished English bishops were

[10] J. W. Gray, 'The ius praesentandi in England from the Constitutions of Clarendon to Bracton', *English Historical Review*, LXVII (1952), pp. 481–509.

unsurpassed in some respects elsewhere in Europe at that period, of which developments the work of the English decretal collectors provides a major and permanently important illustration. Papal legislation then flowed into England: Archbishop Richard cited Alexander's decretals in his provincial council of 1175; the canons of the 1179 Lateran Council, which English bishops attended, were brought back immediately into England, and transcribed in numerous manuscripts within a year or two of their promulgation; papal decretal letters enforced some of the Lateran rulings in England before Alexander's death in 1181; swift and frequent interchange between the schools of English and continental canonists is abundantly recorded in the manuscripts surviving from the period. Archbishops Richard and Baldwin are frequently judged inadequate successors to Becket, from an ecclesiastical or papal viewpoint, but in the application of canon law throughout the kingdom there is irrefutable evidence of its steady and effective growth throughout their time.

Between Alexander's death in 1181 and the accession of Innocent III in 1198, the Church was ruled by a succession of five pontiffs whose reigns were individually too short to leave any decisive mark on the central government of the Church or on the course of papal relations with the separate countries, yet they can by no means be dismissed as a series of ineffective old men. The papacy then moved forward into a more placid period, the schisms were left behind; new problems arose in connection with heresies, the promotion of a Crusade and many other such matters. But there was no serious interruption or reversal of the trends of papal policies already established: Urban III had been in Becket's circle in the days of his great quarrel with Henry II; and Celestine III had acquired vast experience as a papal legate in his earlier career as Cardinal Hyacinth. Legates continued to arrive in England to deal with special problems; judges delegate were appointed in large numbers to deal with English disputes; several important *causes célèbres*, often involving great religious houses, took English ecclesiastics to plead their cases in the papal Curia. The practice became regular of English archbishops receiving commissions as papal legates by virtue of their office: Richard, Baldwin, Hubert

94

Walter, as well as Longchamp of Ely, were created legates in the closing quarter of the century. Relations between the monarch and the papacy also developed further in circumstances of mutual advantage. Transitionally, from the reign of Richard to that of John, the archiepiscopate of Hubert Walter is judged by many historians as a model of the way in which harmonious relations could be maintained between *regnum* and *sacerdotium*. Hubert was at times chief justiciar, chancellor and vice-regent in secular government, as well as primate and papal legate in ecclesiastical affairs; but this was a deviation from the ideal of a Christian bishop in canon law, and it may also be thought that the earlier struggles had helped to make possible the *modus vivendi* as it existed in practice under Hubert, which otherwise might not have been achieved with a comparable balance of interests.

The death of Innocent III in July 1216, and that of John in October of the same year, marked the end of an epoch in the history of Anglo-papal relations, whose final phase was centred on the opening years of Langton's archiepiscopate: in particular on the circumstances of his appointment and its aftermath, and on the triangular relationship between archbishop, pope and king at the time of *Magna Carta*. On the death of Hubert Walter in 1205, the monks of Christ Church elected Reginald, their subprior, to the vacant see, to be opposed by John de Gray, bishop of Norwich, the king's nominee. The double nomination passed in due course within the purview of the papal Curia, whereupon Innocent rejected both the rival claimants and consecrated Langton, a distinguished English theologian from the schools of Paris and a curial cardinal at the time of his nomination. In the long quarrel which ensued, a further familiar crisis in English history, issues of critical importance for royal-papal relations were raised, involving not only the principle of canonical elections, but also the specific question whether or not the king could exercise a final veto in the choice of a bishop. The ultimate success of the pope in these circumstances was therefore a development of the utmost significance; and an important by-product of the struggle was the charter of freedom of elections secured in the period between Langton's acceptance in England and his later divergence with the king in the conflict for *Magna Carta*. But these successes were not quickly attained: the king long resisted the papal action and prevented the archbishop's entry into England. Innocent was no less adamant, and it was John's misfortune to be confronted by one of the most resolute and decisive popes in the Church's history. England was placed under interdict in 1208; the king was excommunicated in 1209, and threatened finally with deposition in 1212. And since these developments coincided with a deterioration in Anglo-French relations, which Philip Augustus was ever ready to exploit, John was at length constrained to yield to the pope.

Meanwhile the English Church had been seriously deprived of spiritual guidance at the highest level. In addition to Langton himself, the archbishop of York was also absent from England; the bishops of London, Ely and Worcester left after imposing the interdict; some bishoprics were vacant; further ecclesiastics quitted the country following the more serious penalty of John's excommunication in 1209. Nevertheless, negotiations between Innocent and John were never entirely interrupted, until, finally in 1213, John submitted to the complex of pressures described above, and surrendered his kingdoms of England and Ireland to the pope, receiving them back in return for an annual tribute. The most striking element in the king's submission was the oath of fealty which he took, together with his promise to do homage should he later meet the pope in person. The agreement was formally ratified in St. Paul's Cathedral in the presence of the legate, Cardinal Nicholas, and sealed with a golden bull; and thus the interdict ended in 1214. A paradoxical result was that, when Langton eventually arrived to assume his duties, his former relentless opponent was now in the fullest papal favour, as the feudal dependant of the pope. In the struggle which shortly took place between the king and his magnates, culminating in the sealing of the Charter in 1215, Langton played a leading and moderating role, only to incur in the end the disfavour of Innocent for failing to support the king in this new situation and likewise to condemn his opponents. In the course of this crisis, the issue had been referred to the pope 'since he is lord of England'; and Innocent had declared against the magnates as being conspirators and rebels. But Langton was unwilling to pronounce the sentences of excommunication against them, and was suspended in consequence by the bishop of Winchester and the papal legate. Thus Langton passed into exile for a second period. And, when he returned, both Innocent and John were dead, and papal legates were taking now a dominant part in the government of England in the minority of Henry III.

'That the English Church may be free and enjoy its rights in full and its liberties unimpaired': whatever policy Innocent felt it prudent to pursue in relation to John, his feudal vassal and a committed Crusader, he could not be expected to dissent from this opening clause of the Charter of 1215. But his actions in the English quarrel can be assessed only in the full comprehension of his role as the conscious and supremely confident leader of Western Christendom: Vicar of Christ, mediator between God and men, judge of all men but judged by none, arbiter of all human affairs as well in temporal as in spiritual matters. The universality of his conception, as well as the summit of papal legislative power, was most clearly demonstrated in his great Lateran Council of 1215. It is natural that politico-ecclesiastical aspects of his relations with John should chiefly attract the attention of English historians; but for Innocent these were comparatively small components in an immensely complicated mosaic. On the secular plane, his dealings with a succession of contenders for the imperial title, with the leaders of the various Christian kingdoms, and most particularly his feudal connections with the rulers of Aragon and Portugal, of Sicily and Hungary: all these factors place the English affair in a fitting proportion. But no papal policy was conceived by Innocent on merely secular considerations. If papal intervention was required in the affairs of a secular kingdom, it was because the pope had a duty to act on moral and Christian principles, because a matter of sin or injustice was involved or because peace was endangered. The letters which Innocent wrote to England in condemning the Charter show him proceeding firmly on established canonical doctrines. But quite apart from, and transcending, the major political issues, he was also the supreme judge of all Christian people, the Universal Ordinary to whom every Christian might have direct recourse. The records for England richly reveal Innocent acting throughout his pontificate in this capacity in exactly comparable fashion as he did for all Christian countries: for Ireland and Poland, for Portugal and Hungary, for Italy and Spain. In terms of purely political history, he was a great statesman, the dominant figure of his age, through whose hands passed all the main threads of development in his day. But he was also a great pope and spiritual leader 'devoted to his pastoral task . . . zealous for the faith, strong in legal science and subtle diplomacy, and tremendously active.'

In the interests of simplicity, important strands of Anglo-papal history have been touched on only incidentally in the pages above. Such a question is the primacy of the English Church, contested in the Canterbury and York disputes, for this involved at times the intervention of the pope very decisively. In its origins the problem is retraceable to the letter of Gregory I to Augustine, in which he laid down a scheme for the future organization of the English Church, divided in two provinces under archbishops at London and York, ruling that he should have precedence between these who was consecrated earlier. But, for well-known historical reasons, Canterbury secured the headship of the southern province. The question of primacy, together with various attendant problems such as professions of obedience and jurisdiction over debated dioceses, was swiftly raised by Lanfranc after his elevation, and submitted to Alexander II for adjudication. The pope entrusted the enquiry to the legate Hubert, from whom Lanfranc and Canterbury secured a favourable verdict.[11] But the victory of Canterbury was not destined to remain long unchallenged. Indeed the question of the primacy was raised again as early as Anselm's

[11] The brief account given here of the complex history of the Canterbury-York rivalry is necessarily incomplete. The seminal period from the Conquest to the third decade of the twelfth century is now reviewed in an important study by R. W. Southern on 'The Canterbury Forgeries', *EHR*, LXXIII (1958), pp. 193–226. Southern argues that Lanfranc's success was achieved by his own force of character and persuasiveness, and through the support of the king; he rejects the view that the Canterbury case was argued in Lanfranc's lifetime on a basis of the well-known Canterbury forgeries, which he believes to have been fabricated in or about 1120 and brought forward after January 1121. The intervening period was one of repeated efforts by York to reverse the favourable decision secured by Lanfranc.

consecration in 1093, which occasion Southern notes as the first defeat suffered by Canterbury in the long struggle destined ultimately to cancel the success achieved by Lanfranc in the exceptionally favourable circumstances of his time. And although the papacy supported Anselm's primacy for obvious reasons of mutual interdependence, the altered relations between archbishops and king, after Anselm's death, together with an increasing papal understanding of the English rivalry and its background, led to a more favourable consideration being given by the popes to the claims of York. One curious resulting situation was that Thurstan of York, a former royal servant, vigorously fought for the independence of the northern province, supported now by a series of popes, while the claims of Canterbury were defended by the king. On this occasion, victory was adjudged to York by Honorius II in 1126, by which time the falsity of the Canterbury case had been sufficiently revealed. Inevitably, contacts between England and the Curia were developed in an important way as a result of these extended negotiations, which are recorded in a lively and fascinating version, sympathetic to York, by Hugh the Chanter.

The issue was raised once more in the reign of Henry II, and contested then in bitter fashion between Becket and Roger of York, to be continued by Becket's successors. The problem was complicated still further in Becket's lifetime by the ambitions of Gilbert Foliot, as bishop of London, the foremost of Becket's opponents among the English episcopate.[12] It seems certain that Foliot, a bishop of outstanding ability and reputation, was resentful of Becket's accession to a position for which he might consider himself the better qualified; and there is evidence that the Gregorian plan that London, rather than Canterbury, should be head of the southern province was remembered in Foliot's interests. But there could be no real hope of success in so radical a project. The strife between Canterbury and York reached a heightened crisis with the coronation of the younger Henry by Roger of York in 1170, as explained above, in Becket's absence and in

---

[12] A critical edition of the letters of Gilbert Foliot is in an advanced stage of preparation by Professor C. N. L. Brooke and Dom Adrian Morey.

defiance of papal mandates of prohibition.[13] This act of derogation of Becket's functions proved in the event the occasion for the final drama leading at last to his murder in Canterbury Cathedral. Alexander III strove to tread his way most cautiously through this tangle of conflicting interests. His support for Becket did not exclude a dispassionate consideration of the rights of York: the diocese, though not the province, of York was explicitly omitted from the legatine jurisdiction which he granted to Canterbury in 1166. Nevertheless, the rivalry was not diminished after Becket's death, and unseemly conflicts continued to mar relations between the two archbishops: the most regrettable incident ending in confusion and physical violence in the legate's presence in 1176; in which year also Alexander once more confirmed the independence of York. A final solution to these difficulties lay only in the very remote future. But the problem left in the meantime a significant trace in canonical history, for certain decretal collections dating from the early 1180's included several papal letters touching the subject, under the title *De preeminentia Lundonensis et Eboracensis*, which some sensitive collectors later diplomatically emended in the interests of Canterbury to *De preeminentia Cantuariensis et Eboracensis*.

A further strand of interest can be traced in the very complex inter-relations between the English monarchy, the papacy and the Celtic peoples of the British Isles. Spiritual and material motives were intermingled in the policies of the Anglo-Norman and Angevin rulers affecting Ireland, Wales and Scotland; and the papal desire for the advancement of legal and administrative reforms, together with the spiritual regeneration of all Christian communities, produced an alliance of royal and papal interests. The work of Irish scholars has established the existence of a two-way traffic between the Roman Curia and Ireland in the eleventh century to a more significant degree than was previously believed. Gwynn in particular has illuminated the subject of papal influence in Ireland in the days of Gregory VII.[14] The reform of the Irish

[13] The background and implications of the coronation are discussed by Miss Anne Heslin, 'The Coronation of the Young King in 1170', *Studies in Church History*, II, Nelson (1965: in press).

[14] A. Gwynn, 'Gregory VII and the Irish Church', *Studi Gregoriani*, Rome, III (1947), pp. 105–28.

Church was initiated through a series of important councils, most notably of Cashel in 1101 and Rath Breasil in 1111, convened by papal legatine authority. But it is also clear that Anglo-Norman and papal interests progressed together in Ireland in the days when Lanfranc and Anselm consecrated Irish bishops and dealt with them on terms of implicit superiority. The arrival of the Cistercians, and their influence, diffused under Malachy's guidance, played an important part. A further great council was held at Kells in 1152 under the presidency of the legate John of Paparo, and established the territorial divisions of the Irish Church in four provinces with their suffragan sees.

Both Rome and Canterbury had played their parts in producing the results attained so far. But much remained to be done; and it was in these circumstances that Adrian IV granted to Henry II permission to invade and subdue Ireland, and promote the cause of ecclesiastical reform. The authenticity of the bull *Laudabiliter* of 1155 has been much debated, but its substantial accuracy is now generally accepted: its essential points are recorded by John of Salisbury, who took part in the negotiations, and were later confirmed in the indubitably genuine letters of Alexander III. Both papal authority and jurisdiction and Angevin political rights in the island were reconciled in this policy. The invasion itself was delayed until after Becket's death. And the ecclesiastical results of the conquest were first significantly seen in the legatine Council of Cashel in 1172, under Christian of Lismore, and by the letters exchanged in the same year between Henry II and Alexander III. These letters dealt with the state of the Irish Church and the powers of the English king to govern the island and reform its Church in accordance with the usages of the Church in England. The authority of the English king in Ireland was fully supported by the pope throughout the period which followed; nevertheless, a way was carefully left open by which the rights of the papacy over Ireland, as being within the Patrimony of St Peter, might later be more decisively asserted, and the Irish Church was not subjected to the jurisdiction of English prelates. Thus its integrity and independence were preserved. The Irish Church continued to produce its own characteristic and distinguished members, of whom

St. Laurence O'Toole (†1180) was the outstanding exemplar; but with the appointment of John Cumin to Dublin in 1182 a new type of Anglo-Norman feudal prelate was created with important results for later Irish history.

Meanwhile, Henry's measures for the reorganization and better administration of Ireland went forward with papal support: the legate Vivian reconfirmed the royal rights in a council at Dublin in 1177, in which year also Henry created his son John 'Lord of Ireland' at the Council of Oxford. Later, when John himself was reigning as king, the Angevin policy was more clearly revealed that the native Irish should be excluded, whenever possible, from the Irish sees. The attitude of which this policy was merely symptomatic created a rift between the old Gaelic and the new Anglo-Norman bishops, tending to the weakening and disruption of the Church; and the letters of Innocent III to Ireland show a concern with problems of this kind. In 1202, during a vacancy in the primatial see of Armagh, the papal legate, John of Monte Celio, convened a council at Dublin at which John sought the legate's support against Irish bishops opposed to his methods of controlling the Irish Church, though apparently without success. For Ireland, the period ended, as for England, with formal submission of the kingdom to Innocent and an agreement for the payment of an annual tribute.[15]

For Wales, the interest in this chapter centres on the claims of Canterbury to jurisdiction and primacy over the four Welsh bishoprics, and on their reciprocal claims for independence, together with the increasing efforts of St. David's to establish itself in the primacy of a separate province. It is clear that Anselm exercised an effective control over the Church in Wales from the later-eleventh century, comparable with his policy in Ireland and Scotland at the same time, as when he consecrated Urban to Llandaff in Canterbury Cathedral in 1107. This relationship was effectively maintained by his successors until the days of Theobald, when a notable bid was made by St. David's to assert its

[15] Relations between Ireland and the papacy during the pontificate of Innocent III have been greatly clarified by the studies of Rev. Fr. Patrick Dunning: cf. *idem*, 'The Letters of Innocent III to Ireland', *Traditio*, Fordham University Press, XVIII (1962), pp. 229-53, including bibliographical references.

position: in 1140 Bernard of St. David's contested Theobald's right to consecrate Maurice of Bangor and to receive an oath of obedience from him. The significance of this assertion was heightened by the eventual victory of St. David's over Llandaff in a long dispute involving letters and journeys between Wales and the papal Curia; and Urban of Llandaff had actually died in Rome on a visit *ad limina* in 1133. It is in connection with this protracted quarrel that the *Liber Landavensis* affords such striking evidence of papal-Welsh relations from 1119. But St. David's was unsuccessful in the attempt to secure a pallium; and the issue of the primacy between Canterbury and St. David's was decided *in personis* in favour of the former by Eugenius III in 1148, though leaving open the question of right.

Thus, when Becket succeeded Theobald in 1162, the Church in Wales was in legal subjection to Canterbury, with papal approval, at a moment when Henry II was maturing plans for the political subjection of the Welsh princes. The problems arising from these complex relationships were still further accentuated as a result of the Becket dispute, when the exiled archbishop was confronted by the twofold hostility of Henry II in England and Owain Gwynedd in Wales. The Bangor dispute provides a revealing insight into this situation: a troublesome vacancy followed the death of Maurice of Bangor in 1161, and the matter was not finally settled until 1177. Meanwhile, despite the efforts of Alexander III and Becket, Henry and Owain in turn obstructed an acceptable solution, the former preventing a free election in the period *c.* 1167-8, and the latter presuming even to intercept papal letters. Nevertheless, in spite of such vexing problems, Canterbury successfully maintained its metropolitical authority over the Welsh Church throughout the period. But the primacy issue was reintroduced on three further noteworthy occasions: in 1176, at the instigation of Giraldus Cambrensis, at the legatine Council of Westminster; in 1179, in the presence of Alexander III in the course of the Lateran Council; and in 1198-1203, in a most interesting and well-documented fashion, again under Giraldus's guidance, before Innocent III and commissions of papal judges delegate. The case for St. David's was stated clearly in the course of this litigation: it was urged that a metropolitan see in Wales would be to the Roman Church's advantage, and that Peter's Pence would be paid in recognition of this special relationship. Independence for the Welsh Church from the jurisdiction of Canterbury was sought, but neither the primacy nor the pallium was specifically requested. Giraldus hoped, in the event unsuccessfully, that Innocent would confer on the Welsh Church the status of a *filia specialis* which he had granted some years previously to the Church in Scotland.[16]

Affecting Scotland, too, political and ecclesiastical interests were intermingled in English policies. Questions of Church reform and conflicts of jurisdictional authority went hand in hand with the advance of Anglo-Norman and Angevin influence, and naturally attracted the concern of popes. The claims of York in particular for primacy over the Scottish dioceses provided a source of continuing controversy. Lanfranc and Thomas of York had agreed at the Council of Windsor in 1072 that all sees north of the Humber should be subject to York's metropolitical jurisdiction, but without the concurrence of the Church or the king in Scotland. Nevertheless, Calixtus II mandated the Scottish bishops in 1119 to proffer canonical obedience to York. It was therefore all the more significant that Alexander I of Scotland attempted in the following year to fill the vacant see of St. Andrews with Eadmer of Canterbury: a project which inevitably provoked the resentment of York, and was in the event frustrated. This was a phase in which the Scottish kings were clearly anxious to promote the independence of the Church in their realm from external intervention; and a necessary feature of this policy was the attempt to curtail the jurisdictional claims of York, despite the commands of the pope. Nor was the St. Andrews dispute an isolated example: John, bishop of Glasgow, persisted throughout his life in refusing to acknowledge the supremacy of York; and on his death in 1147 his successor was consecrated by Eugenius III in person, and thus the awkward issue was circumvented. The papal favour shown to York was, nevertheless, continued by Adrian IV; and the inter-

[16] I. P. Shaw, 'Giraldus Cambrensis and the Primacy of Canterbury', *Church Quarterly Review*, CXLVI (1946), pp. 82–101.

esting point has been argued that, with these claims of York accepted, the ancient Gregorian plan of a northern province of twelve suffragan sees subject to York was now for the first time, if only temporarily, realized.

But a point of departure in papal policies may be traced from Alexander III's appointment of William of Moray as papal legate in 1160; and other measures of Alexander III were consistent with a revision in the papal attitude to Anglo-Scottish ecclesiastical relations, though this did not exclude his appointment of Roger of York as legate for Scotland from 1164 until 1181. Meanwhile, a critical period had opened for Scotland with military defeat in the troubles of 1173-4, when William of Scotland participated in the loosely concerted war waged against Henry II by many of his adversaries on both sides of the Channel. The Scottish intervention ended in political disaster with the capture of the king at Alnwick in 1174. The Scottish Church also shared temporarily in this misfortune, since at the treaty of Falaise in 1174 its subjection to the English Church was included in the terms of reconciliation. But the Scottish Church lost no opportunity in reacting against this unwelcome situation, and by 1176 secured the support of Alexander III in disclaiming York's metropolitical authority, which had meanwhile been challenged also by Richard of Canterbury. A phase was now opened when papal legates and judges delegate were more active in Scotland, though not without some hindrance, as revealed very strikingly in the disputed election to St. Andrews from 1178. This vexatious conflict provoked repeated appeals to the Curia and resulting papal mandates, which were successfully resisted by the Scottish king and his nominee, until the former was himself at last excommunicated. More favourable relations were restored by Pope Lucius III and his successors: the St. Andrews dispute was concluded in 1188; and Scotland was freed by the pope from English domination, in secular and ecclesiastical spheres alike, in 1189. Meanwhile, the see of York was itself vacant for a decade, in the years 1181-91, a factor which may well have played some part in favouring Scottish interests. Pope Celestine III declared the Scottish Church a *filia specialis* of the Roman See in 1192, subject henceforth to no one but the pope or his legate *a latere*; and Scottish bishops, free from subjection either to York or Canterbury, attended the Lateran Council under Innocent III in 1215, as did their Irish colleagues.

But Knowles has rightly argued that it is not to the great political issues nor to the papal claims for temporal power that we should look for the most significant contacts between England and the continent in this period, but to the regular and systematic traffic between England and the Curia, accepted as a matter of routine and calling for no particular comment in the contemporary records. And in this respect the archives of the English monastic houses and cathedral chapters provide a source of information second to none in importance in revealing the extent and propagation of papal jurisdictional power. Unfortunately, the papal registers no longer survive for the greater part of our period: between the registers of Gregory VII and Innocent III, at its two extremities, only a brief transcript of an excerpt from the records of Alexander III is now extant. But the cartularies of the individual religious houses and those preserved by some of the cathedral chapters provide a wealth of evidence on which the course of papal policy can be accurately plotted. For England, the records of the religious houses are especially rich and revealing.[17] The spiritual revival associated with the Church Reforms of the eleventh century and the foundation of new religious orders, above all of the great Cistercian Order, as already discussed, and the rapid expansion of the orders of regular canons, blended ideally with the development of papal policies of centralization and universal guidance in spiritual as well as jurisdictional spheres.

It was not a novel idea in the Western Church that religious houses should commend themselves to the papacy in a special relationship, enjoying immediate recourse to the pope, securing papal protection of their rights and possessions, and paying in return an annual tribute; but it was a practice which was enor-

[17] A vast source of information on Anglo-papal relations is supplied by the records of the religious orders: cf. esp. D. Knowles, *The Monastic Order in England*, Cambridge (2nd ed., 1963); J. C. Dickinson, *The Origins of the Austin Canons and their Introduction into England*, London (1950); H. M. Colvin, *The White Canons in England*, Oxford (1951); etc.

mously extended in this period. In the same way, the new religious orders gradually built up a complex of rights and privileges, and found it advantageous to secure papal recognition and guarantees for these. Moreover, both great orders and individual houses plunged increasingly into litigation in defence of their claims, touching spiritual and material interests, in conflict with both ecclesiastical and secular rivals. It became the invariable custom for religious houses and cathedral chapters to seek regular papal reconfirmation of their privileges, particularly on the accession of each new pope or following a definitive ruling resulting from a specific dispute. Transcripts of papal rescripts and formal *privilegia*, papal commissions and mandates to judges delegate appointed to adjudicate between rival claimants: all these were carefully enrolled in the monastic and cathedral archives, and provide the wealth of evidence referred to above. No one has illuminated this aspect of Anglo-papal relations in the twelfth century more significantly than the late Walter Holtzmann, whose three volumes of English *Papsturkunden* include many hundreds of previously unknown papal letters to England. Such records reveal a steadily swelling stream of papal *privilegia* entering England throughout the century, throwing light both on the history of England and of the individual recipients, as well as on the overall pattern in the development of papal justice. Only a minute fraction of characteristic instances can be cited here: no less than ninety-six papal letters relating to the single house of St. Albans were dispatched from the Curia between 1122 and 1198; thirty-seven were sent in connection with the affairs of Bury St. Edmunds between 1123 and 1196; a *regesta* of the Augustinian priory of Kirkham in Yorkshire records the receipt of thirteen letters of Alexander III, privileges and mandates, touching the rights of that single, comparatively insignificant, house between 1159 and 1181. A microcosm of the whole history of the growth of Cistercian privileges and exemptions throughout the Universal Church is clearly provided by the *Papsturkunden* to English Cistercian houses, including the history of the important tithe exemption and of the various immunities from diocesan jurisdiction; the letters to Rievaulx, Byland and a host of other abbeys afford abundant evidence for these developments. No less interesting are the records of papal confirmation of special rights enjoyed by particular houses: letters to St. Albans, Westminster and St. Augustine's at Canterbury, conferring on their abbots the privilege of wearing episcopal symbols of rank; to St. Albans, again, conferring a primacy of honour among all the abbots of England out of respect for the proto-martyr; and so forth. A touching letter of Alexander III to the hermit Godric of Finchale bears witness to the pope's solicitude for his individual subjects in the English Church: he has heard of Godric's holiness, which he commends, requesting in return Godric's prayers for the well-being of the whole Church. It must be said at once, as a point of additional significance, that the *Papsturkunden* for other provinces of the Church provide an exactly comparable record of the scope and pattern of papal influence.

Maitland and Zachary Brooke established two conclusions regarding the medieval English Church which have never subsequently been seriously challenged. Maitland refuted Stubbs's thesis that the medieval canon law was not considered binding on the English Church, and drew the vital distinction between the ideals and teachings of the Church when operating freely in Christian society and the limits imposed on them by secular rulers and local interests: a distinction at no period more necessary to be remembered than when considering the creative phase of canonical developments in the twelfth and thirteenth centuries. Later, Brooke rejected the notion that the medieval terminology used in reference to the English Church reflected a separatist or even national viewpoint, at least in the sources for the eleventh and twelfth centuries which he extensively studied. The concept of an English Church, or *ecclesia Anglicana*, is especially relevant to these considerations, since its existence in this formulation is first discovered in the period considered in this chapter, when it superseded in general usage earlier phrases such as *ecclesia Angliae* or *ecclesia Anglorum*. Brooke rightly argued that the concept of an *ecclesia Anglicana* was in no sense anti-papal, that it was a natural idiom in contemporary papal theory, and that comparable formulations existed for other sections of the Western Church. At the same

time, Brooke believed that the phrase was in fact first used by
John of Salisbury and was later adopted by the popes; but further
evidence now discloses its use in papal documents at an earlier date.
No English *Landeskirche* was implied in either the curial or the
insular usage.

Such phrases as *ecclesia Anglicana*, *ecclesia Gallicana* and *ecclesia
Hibernica* certainly described with aptness the corporate sense and
interests of the Churches of the various regions, but they were not
designed or understood to imply a separateness from the *ecclesia
Romana*. On the contrary, such concepts were commonly used by
ecclesiastics to safeguard the rights of the Church against the
encroachments of secular rulers: a theory which is nowhere better .
supported than in Becket's letter *Quae in colloquio* of 1169, in which
he argued that no concession should be wrung from him *praeter
morem ecclesiae Gallicanae et Anglicanae*, urging elsewhere in the
same letter the adoption of policies 'advantageous alike to the
Roman and the English Churches', or in the opening clause of
Magna Carta in 1215, as mentioned above. Moreover, the popes ·
themselves in their decretal letters granted dispensations from the
general law in favour of the customs existing in the *ecclesia
Anglicana*; and such letters were later incorporated in canonical
collections, and canonists referred to the customs of the English
Church in their decretist glosses.

It is above all in the reception of canon law by the English
Church in the twelfth century that the flow of papal influence
into England can be most accurately estimated. A curiously
myopic view still survives, even among medievalists, that canonical studies are merely of peripheral or highly specialist interest. So
far is this from being a true opinion that the conclusion is inescapable that the canon law deeply affected the lives of all
Christians throughout the length and breadth of the Western
Church, from birth through life until death, in many of their essential functions in human society. As far as England is concerned,
a steady and continuing acquisition of canonical texts is disclosed
throughout our period, reaching a climax of extraordinary interest and initiative from the central decades of the twelfth century,
and rapidly accelerating after Becket's death. In Lanfranc's day,

if not before, the doctrine of *Pseudo-Isidore* was firmly established in England, a tradition so vital for the development of papal ideology and centralized government. Lanfranc's own collection, a derivative from *Pseudo-Isidore*, survives in the library of Trinity College in Cambridge; and many related manuscripts were housed in the libraries of English cathedral chapters in the beginning of the following century. Burchard's *Decretum*, the many collections of the Gregorian reformers, and the major works of Ivo of Chartres: all these were likewise received in England before the mid-twelfth century. The *Decretum* of Gratian, composed at Bologna c. 1140–1, came quickly into England: it was certainly known by the canonists in Theobald's household; there is textual evidence of its use by John of Salisbury in 1159 at the latest; and it formed a basis of reference in the Becket dispute from 1163. The foremost Bolognese decretists, with Rufinus at their head, were known to English authors by the early 1170's, possibly even during the Becket dispute itself; and English or Anglo-Norman canonists now began to take an initiative in the various literary exercises which typified the schools of canon law at the time.

A major historical development emerged in the mid-1170's with the beginnings of contemporary papal decretal codification, and English collectors played a dominant role in this work: of roughly fifty decretal collections surviving in the whole of Europe for the rest of the century, a large proportion are of indubitable English authorship; while of twenty-seven collections of the most primitive and formative phase of composition, no less than fifteen are the works of English collectors.[18] Not only is an original and creative achievement disclosed on the part of English canonists, but a mutual interchange of material between English and continental schools of canon law is also clearly established. English collections were widely disseminated on the continent at least as early as 1179–81; and continental collections, most notably French and Italian, were used in the same period to afforce the English collections built for the greater part from local archives. It must be

[18] C. Duggan, *Twelfth-Century Decretal Collections and Their Importance in English History*, University of London Historical Studies XII, Athlone Press (1963).

emphasized that the English works were composed by Englishmen, predominantly from letters addressed by the popes, from the pontificate of Alexander III onwards, to English recipients; and, by the reception of these insular sources into the mainstream of canonical transmission on the continent, a permanently important English imprint was left on the corpus of canon law gradually assembled for the Universal Church at that time, being officially promulgated in the *Decretales* of Gregory IX in 1234. The proportionate English contribution to the total body of canons amassed in the later-twelfth century is truly astounding: of approximately one thousand papal letters preserved in all decretal manuscripts of the period known at present, no less than four hundred were received by English or Anglo-Norman ecclesiastics within twenty years. At no other period in its history did the English Church exert so direct, extensive and lasting an influence on the law of the Church as a whole.

Meanwhile, English canonists continued to play an ever more varied role in the general developments. English clerics studied in large numbers at Bologna, and sometimes taught there, and at the schools of canon lawyers in France and in the Rhineland. Canonical works of all kinds, collections and commentaries, continued to be composed by English authors; and, conversely, the major continental works flowed into England before the close of the century: the leading decretists of the Italian schools down to Huguccio (*c.* 1188–90) were cited with natural familiarity by the 'Oxford School' of canonists in the mid-1190's. The epoch-making *Breviarium extravagantium*, or *Compilatio Prima* (*c.* 1189–91), of Bernard of Pavia was well known to English commentators at the turn of the century; and *Compilatio Secunda* (post 1215) was actually composed in Italy by John the Welshman, on a basis of two earlier collections, also made in Italy, by the Englishmen Gilbert and Alan. By which time it is obvious that English canonists were playing a leading role at the very centre of canonical jurisprudence for the Unive:sal Church.

The quickening of canonical evolution was by no means merely an academic exercise. At the highest level of ecclesiastical legislation, popes in general councils throughout the period laid down canons applicable to the whole Church. This was an epoch which may be described as that of 'the popes above the councils', to underline the decisive papal authority achieved at this stage of conciliar history. Particularly in the four great Lateran Councils of 1123, 1139, 1179 and 1215, popes were seen presiding with unchallenged authority over mighty representative assemblies, dealing with a vast range of doctrinal, moral, jurisdictional and disciplinary problems. The Fourth Lateran Council is rightly judged the highest peak of papal legislative achievement in the history of the medieval Church. But many other papal councils were also held in the period: the Italian councils of the popes of the Investiture struggle, two Councils of Reims in 1119 and 1148 respectively, the Council of Tours of 1163, and so forth. This papal legislation was paralleled by conciliar action in England,[19] in councils held by papal legatine commission or reflecting the work of the continental assemblies, many of which latter were attended by English bishops despite the desire of English kings in the period to control such attendance. The councils of Lanfranc and Anselm in 1075 and 1076, and in 1102 and 1118, respectively; five legatine councils in 1125, 1127, 1138, 1143 and 1176, the first and the third under the presidency of *legati a latere*; the council of Archbishop Theobald in 1151; the legatine councils of Hubert Walter in 1195 and 1200: all these meetings record the pattern by which a constant effort was made to implement in England the policies and reforms of the central legislation. Nor was such papal influence confined to conciliar action. The work of papal legates has been touched on in numerous contexts above. It is sufficient to add here that Tillmann has listed sixty occasions between the Conquest and the death of Innocent III on which papal legates or commissions were appointed to deal with English questions, or those in which the interests of the English king were involved; and she has selected thirty of these for particular mention. The Becket dispute provided a high-point of such activity: four major commissions of legates were appointed by Alexander III to negotiate between the parties in 1167, 1168, 1169 and early 1170, while further legates were

[19] C. N. L. Brooke, 'Canons of English Church Councils in the Early Decretal Collections', *Traditio*, XIII (1957), pp. 471–80.

commissioned to deal with the various stages of the subsequent reconciliation, especially in 1172 and 1175–6.

But no papal agents were more effective than the judges delegate, whose jurisdiction resulted from the rapid upsurge of appeals to the Roman Curia in the twelfth century, which in its turn resulted from the centralization of Church government following the eleventh-century reforms. A vast stream of appeals dealing with problems of all kinds flowed into the Curia, and an equal flood of rescripts, mandates, commissions and decretal letters, issued from the chancery in return. The popes could not hope to deal personally with the immensely increased weight of business; and there were in addition obvious advantages in settling many disputes in their place of origin. The office of the judge delegate was created to deal with this situation: the beginnings of the system can be traced in many parts of the Western Church in the opening decades of the twelfth century; and it was fully matured, with recognized procedures and common form phraseology, within the following fifty years. The delegate's jurisdiction was carefully defined and limited in scope, lapsed on the completion of the issue giving rise to the commission, and was essentially exercised by virtue of papal authority, which was transferred to the delegate for the terms of each single case. England fully shared in the various phases in the development of this system, the records being particularly rich in the decades following Becket's death. Many hundreds of papal commissions and mandates to English judges delegate were certainly issued, and large numbers of these have been preserved in transcription: some in the cartularies of religious houses or cathedral chapters, and many in a very significant way in English decretal collections; but it may be assumed that substantial numbers have also been lost.

It is now clear that the rapid spread of canon law in England from the early 1170's ran parallel with the extension of papal delegated jurisdiction, which stimulated at the same time that unique and creative English initiative in decretal codification which has been mentioned above. The judgement that these remarkable developments were primarily the work of a group of 'papalist' English canonists, supporters for the most part of Becket in the

dispute which had just been concluded, has been recently challenged, yet stands firmly rooted in the massive evidence of the
English collections, which owed their existence above all to the
decretal records of Baldwin of Ford, Bartholomew of Exeter,
Roger of Worcester and Richard of Canterbury. Bartholomew
and Roger are believed to have been commissioned by the pope
more frequently than any other English bishops of their time, and
their distinction in this respect is immortalized in Alexander III's
description of them as 'the twin lights illuminating the English
Church'; Baldwin's personal influence in decretal codification is
faithfully recorded in at least one important surviving manuscript;[20] and Richard's archives certainly provided the coherent
sequences of Canterbury decretals in many extant collections.
Whatever limitations the secular power was able to impose on
this species of papal jurisdiction in practice, the reality of its
existence and the vast scope of its application present one of the
most striking features of the life of the English Church at the close
of our period.

An adequate survey of Anglo-papal relations would treat of
many matters neglected in this essay, or dealt with only perfunc-
torily. Events in the Holy Land, the resulting appeals to the West
and the negotiations for the promotion of further Crusading
efforts; the history of canonization in the context of the papal
prerogative of authentication;[21] the history of political ideas, as
well as of theology and doctrine, and the contributions of English
scholars in these fields; the evolution of papal and episcopal diplomatic, including the increasing skill displayed in the critical
examination of official documents; the work of the papal camera
and the development of papal fiscal policies: all these are but a
selection of the many distinct additional areas of interest in which
English and papal history were to some extent intermingled. The
pattern of Anglo-papal relations throughout the long period is
complex, and no useful purpose is served by its oversimplification.

[20] British Museum MS Royal 10 A.II; cf. Duggan, 'The Trinity Collection of
Decretals and the Early Worcester Family', *Traditio*, XVII (1961), pp. 506–26.
[21] Cf. esp. E. W. Kemp, *Canonization and Authority in the Western Church*, Oxford
(1948), pp. 53–106.

On the one hand, there are the numberless proofs of the growth of papal authority and influence in the island between the Conquest and the death of John; on the other hand, it would be quite misleading to suggest that movements of thought and policy were pointed in one direction only. It is patent that royal and secular interests were often opposed to the papal progress; and it is no less obvious that the secular power was frequently able to limit or frustrate its application. It was natural that this was so, since the Church of the Gregorian Reform was in a real sense a conscious 'aggressor' against a long-established framework of Christian society, which it considered unjust. The measure of the Church's achievement must be seen against that background: not in the many individual and temporary contests which were waged now with success for the *regnum*, now for the *sacerdotium*, now ending in compromise and the division of the spoils of victory, but in the extent of the ultimate breaches which the Gregorian attack made in a powerfully entrenched existing fortress.

Nor yet were the views of ecclesiastics themselves undivided. Many bishops, while fully recognizing papal authority in theory, accepted willingly the customs which had long governed relations between ecclesiastical and secular activities in practice, considering it reasonable that Christian kings should require and exert a measure of control over the Church in their realms. Some bishops indeed were unlikely to hold a contrary viewpoint, since they were in effect the creatures of secular rulers. On the one side, there were the full papal doctrines, as advanced by Anselm and Robert Pullen, by John of Poitiers, Becket, John of Salisbury and Herbert of Bosham, by the English canonists of the later-twelfth century and by Stephen Langton at the close of the period; on the other side, there were the customs and concepts of an increasingly self-conscious secular monarchy, supported by tradition and by many ecclesiastics who for varied reasons held to a pre-Gregorian notion of the relations between *regnum* and *sacerdotium*: a dualistic ideology, identified sometimes as the Gelasian theory, through misunderstanding of Pope Gelasius's doctrine. The attitude of such bishops in England was perfectly mirrored in the writings and career of Gilbert Foliot, and summed up explicitly during the

Becket dispute in his *Multiplicem*,[22] while a distinctly anti-papal note had been recorded decades previously in the Anglo-Norman tractates, the so-called Anonymous of York, a work of probable Norman origins. But, for this one period of English history, the dominant trend in Anglo-papal relations was in favour of the papal claims in a fullness which had not previously existed, and which would progressively diminish in the following centuries. Knowles has crystallized the matter most succinctly in saying that what had in previous centuries been a union of faith, love and loyalty became now a union of law, discipline and authority while, in the ages which followed, 'though the connection with the continent and with Rome was as close as ever, the time had passed when the external influence of the papacy upon the administration of the Church in England was genial and creative.'

[22] The letter *Multiplicem* is discussed in Knowles, *The Episcopal Colleagues of Archbishop Thomas Becket*, Cambridge (1951), pp. 171–80. Professor D.C. Douglas's *William the Conqueror*, Eyre and Spottiswoode (1964), appeared too late for reference in this chapter. Where not specifically acknowledged in footnotes, my debt to many scholars is indicated in the appendix bibliography.

XVI

THOMAS OF LONDON
AN ADDRESS IN
COMMEMORATION OF
ST. THOMAS OF CANTERBURY

The ancient and familiar record of St Bede speaks of a meeting of pope Gregory I and the heathen English boy slaves in a Roman market. They were called *Angli*, he was told, which seemed appropriate to him, 'for they have the face of angels and such men should be co-heirs of the *angeli* in heaven'.[1] The work of conversion of the English people and the consolidation of the Christian faith among them attained many peaks of high achievement in the centuries which followed, but none more exalted than at that moment when pope Alexander III announced the canonization of the martyred Becket in 1173: 'Redolet Anglia fragrantia et virtute—England is filled with the fragrance and virtue of the miracles which the almighty Lord has wrought through the merits of the holy and venerable man Thomas, former archbishop of Canterbury, and the whole Christian body everywhere rejoices'.[2] Almost fifty years later, in 1220, pope Honorius III sanctioned the translation of St Thomas in words evocative of pope Gregory's comment: 'sic unus ex Anglicis, inter angelos super opera manuum Domini constitutus—thus one man from among the English has been placed among the angels'.[3] Not all of Becket's contemporaries would have agreed with this verdict in his lifetime, but the martyrdom, miracles and subsequent canonization silenced the bitter hostility which he had then encountered, and raised his reputation to an unparalleled height. The depth and universality of the devotion to St Thomas of Canterbury for the rest of the middle ages exceeded in reality all possible needs of partisan exaggeration.[4] The strife of the sixteenth century drove the cult of the martyr into temporary eclipse, until now, after the passing of so many centuries, a remarkable reawakening has been demonstrated, alike in historical and literary interest and in spiritual and devotional concern.[5]

The outlines of Becket's career are well known and can be briefly summarized.[6] He was born into a family of substantial London citizens of Norman stock about the year 1118. His early education was in the care of the Augustinian canons at Merton in Surrey, and then in London, and there is evidence of his continued studies in the distinguished schools of Paris. His most significant ecclesiastical promotion came with his appointment to the household of archbishop Theobald, following which he is reputed to have begun his canonical studies at Bologna and Auxerre. Numerous appointments and offices were conferred upon him: the church of St Mary-le-Strand was his earliest benefice, and he later acquired a living at Otford in Kent, a prebend at St Paul's, the important archdeaconry of Canterbury in 1154, the provostship of Beverley and various other benefices. Soon after the accession of king Henry II in 1154, Thomas became the royal chancellor and was thereby launched on a career of affluence and brilliance and of influence second to none in the kingdom: the splendour of his embassy to the French king Louis VII in 1158, 'in apparatu magno',[7] and his valour in the Toulouse campaign of 1159 were merely highlights in a period of political power, administrative energy and exceptional royal favour, which culminated in his elevation to the see of Canterbury in 1162, following Theobald's death in the previous year.

There is no doubt that Henry envisaged a continuation in this new phase of Becket's career of that mutual affection and effective co-operation which had marked their relationship hitherto: Becket would play for him the role which Lanfranc had played for William the Conqueror, or would reflect in England that happy co-operation between Church and State achieved in his own day by the prelates of Mainz and Cologne as arch-chancellors in Frederick Barbarossa's Empire.[8] But Henry's plan was doomed to failure, since Becket resigned forthwith the chancellorship, and the story of their relationship thereafter is one of progressive alienation, in which Becket stood out increasingly as the champion of ecclesiastical rights and jurisdiction against the threats of secular encroachment. Two meetings in 1164 sum up the essence of the crisis, both in its underlying currents of conflicting spheres of interest and in the final dissolution of their former personal harmony.[9] The Constitutions of Clarendon early in 1164 defined in 16 clauses Henry's rulings on the jurisdictional conflicts;[10] in a meeting at Northampton later in the year Henry mounted a personal and vindictive attack on Becket within a framework of feudal justice and on financial charges retrospectively brought against him in respect of incomes which he had received while he was chancellor, though he had certainly been exonerated in these matters on his elevation.[11] In this moment of undoubted peril Becket passed into exile, finding refuge for six distracted years in the French king's territories, until the brief reconciliation in 1170, which resulted in his return to Canterbury and his martyrdom there soon after.

But no such simple survey could make intelligible the dramatic impact of Becket's career or explain the universal and permanent recognition of its significance. In commemorating the martyr's death today, it would be inappropriate to appear to diminish in any way his personal stature, nor does historical objectivity make this necessary. The essential element in Becket's *cultus* is personal to him, and cannot be diminished, but the Becket dispute acquires a heightened significance through his symbolic greatness, and because of the coherence in him of personal qualities and eternal principles. A point of departure in the history of Western Christendom was marked by the emergence of the reformed papacy to the effective leadership of the Western Church in the mid-eleventh century, reflected clearly in every facet of Christian life and society.[12] The most significant consequence in a politico-ecclesiastical context was a dichotomy in Christian society, distinguishing the functions of kings and priests and their respective rights and powers, producing the contrasting polarities or tensions of *regnum* and *sacerdotium*, a problem admittedly ancient in origin but re-posed now in a particularly disquieting way. In the wider Western Church this tension resulted in such crises as the so-called Investiture Contest, in the recurring struggles between popes and emperors and in many other ways, while the Becket dispute marked merely the most violent and dramatic manifestation of the problem within the English realm.

The precise points at issue between Henry II and Becket fall into two principal categories, relating respectively to the wider freedom of the Western Church under papal guidance and to the immunities of the English Church within the kingdom. Freedom of appeals to the Roman curia and the two-way traffic of inter-communication between England and the continent, whether by papal legates entering England or by English bishops quitting the island, were the must crucial instances of the former; clerical immunity from secular jurisdiction, freedom of canonical elections, the rights of presentation to ecclesiastical benefices, and clerical incomes and properties were notable aspects of the latter.[13] For the most part these issues were not invented by Henry II; he claimed himself that they were simply the customs prevailing in the time of his grandfather, Henry I, and in all probability his claim could be substantiated on most points. His concern with these matters was entirely understandable, since, like most secular rulers, he was accustomed within the traditions of several centuries to a large measure of control over the Church in his kingdom; and in point of fact ecclesiastical and secular interests had become so closely intermingled that their absolute separation could no longer be accomplished without grave disturbance to the existing social and political structure.

In a paper delivered in Canterbury in January of this year, I spoke of the significance of the Becket controversy in the history of the Church in these words: 'The meaning of the Becket dispute for the Church lies in its witness to the strivings of the Church, in one phase of its evolution, for its freedom from secular constraint and for its own spiritual integrity, in its forthright assertion of the hallowed and therefore privileged place of the priestly element in Christian society and of the primacy of the papacy in the universal Church'.[14] If the origin and progress of the dispute are examined in all their extraordinary complexity, such a conclusion as this might seem at times obscured by personal, material, transient or regional considerations, and it would be true to say that many modern observers have focused attention too exclusively on these admittedly valid aspects of the whole. But in its essence the Becket dispute transcended these more mundane features. When at the moment of final tragedy the four knights entered the cathedral at Canterbury, Becket addressed them in these words: 'If you seek the archbishop, here I am before you . . . I am prepared to die, preferring to life the assertion of justice and the freedom of the Church'.[15] There can be little doubt that Becket was in fact prepared for martyrdom, as was testified during his lifetime and at the approach of death by the words of friend and foe alike. 'It is the cause and not the stroke which makes the martyr' had been the bitter rebuke of Gilbert, bishop of London, in 1166.[16] 'We are all sinners and not yet prepared for death. I can see no one who is freely prepared to die but you' was the fearful lament of the faithful John of Salisbury, Becket's loyal but moderate co-exile, as the very moment of Thomas's martyrdom drew nigh.[17] But the cathartic experience of imminent death imparts a clarity and authenticity to Becket's final statement.

In the presence of this distinguished assembly from Church and State alike, from the capital city, from the province of Canterbury and from the diocese of London, it seems especially fitting to draw attention, perhaps more than is usual, to those aspects of Becket's career which have a particular interest in this setting. He was Thomas of London before he became St Thomas of Canterbury, and the influence of London is evident in all stages of his life.[18] He was born in this place where the Hall of the Mercers' Company now stands; his parents were London citizens of honour and standing; when later charged with ingratitude to the king who had raised him from lowly status to such eminence he spoke with pride of his London parentage, of his 'progenitores . . . cives quidem fuerunt Lundonienses', who lived without strife in the midst of their fellow citizens and who were by no means base— 'nec omnino infimi'.[19] He spent his childhood, received part of his education and acquired his first benefice in London; as royal chancellor he was inevitably involved in affairs in and around the city, and these connexions continued to some extent after his consecration. The hagiographical and chronicle sources for his life have in notable instances a London provenance: FitzStephen's *Life* of Becket is a leading source for the social life of London in his day;[20] the *Ymagines Historiarum* of Ralph of Diceto, archdeacon of Middlesex during the controversy and later dean of St Paul's, is invaluable for its survey of the genesis of the dispute and for its aftermath;[21] the letter collections of Gilbert Foliot, bishop of London and Becket's principal clerical adversary, are plainly of central importance.[22]

Indeed, Foliot's career provides a point of convergence for many strands of interest in this story. Learned and ascetic monk of Cluny, successively abbot of Gloucester and bishop of Hereford, considered by some the most suitable and worthy successor to Theobald in 1161, Foliot stood out subsequently as Becket's leading opponent among the English bishops. His translation from Hereford to London in 1163, an unusual canonical procedure in which Becket himself played a part, reflected at once his own distinction and the importance of the place.[23] The papal letter of authorization on that occasion refers to London as a royal seat— 'Lundoniensis civitas regalis sedes sit', and records that since this city is more noble and celebrated than all the others, so in proportion the English king wished to have as its bishop a man of Foliot's qualities.[24] The most famous, perhaps notorious, denunciation of Becket's opposition to the king was destined to come from Foliot's pen in the letter *Multiplicem* in 1166.[25]

And after Becket's death his devotional *cultus* continued these links with London in an interesting way, since many notable pilgrims from overseas journeyed to Canterbury and proceeded from there to London following their devotions at the martyr's tomb. Thus, when William, archbishop of Reims, visited Canterbury in 1178, king Henry went out to meet him, accompanied him back to London and lodged him in the royal palace with honour and great expense.[26] When Philip, archbishop of Cologne, and count Philip of Flanders visited Thomas's tomb in 1184, once more the English king went forth to greet them and received them in London, in a city adorned—'civitas coronata'—on this occasion, a thing not previously seen, according to Diceto's testimony; and once more the guests were royally entertained.[27] In contrast, the pilgrim king Louis VII of France, who had afforded asylum and succour to Thomas in exile, landed at short notice at Dover in August 1178, to king Henry's evident consternation; the English king hurried to meet the first monarch of France ever to set foot in England, but on this occasion the pilgrim advanced no further than Canterbury.[28]

The splendour and glory of Canterbury shine through every facet of this story. At every turn of events Becket was deeply concerned with the privileges and rights of his see. It is all the more significant, in view of their long alienation, that the highest eulogy came from the lips of the king in a striking phrase to Becket at Fréteval, a few months only before the archbishop's death: 'nor do I doubt', said Henry, 'that the see of Canterbury is the most noble among all the churches of the West—nobilissima sit inter omnes ecclesias occidentis'.[29] But perhaps the most touching comments on this theme are found in the hagiographical literature, as very movingly phrased in the *Thómas Saga,* an Icelandic source of exceptional interest, in recording the remorse and distress which Becket suffered at Clarendon, following his temporary submission to the royal will, a story disclosing many aspects of the problem so often forgotten: the faith of those who looked to Becket as their champion, and the anguish which his resolution and seeming obstinacy sometimes concealed.[30] The *Thómas Saga* records it in this way: 'The clerk who beareth the cross before the archbishop now taketh part in the talk, and . . . muttereth lowly out of his mouth: "The king's might and will now confoundeth all things . . . No one is found who loveth rightwiseness. Only those know aught today, and are held in honour, who make themselves the servants of mighty men . . . Where shall now be found a place of abiding for innocence or resistance, or who may conquer in the fight, since the captain is felled?" ' To which Becket after sombre reflection replied: ' "Nor is it to be wondered at, that matters should go in this way, for by reason of my sins must England's holy church suffer such dishonour; for I was not chosen to this office and dignity by the church or by the clerics, nor from a cloister or a house of morals, as my predecessors and forefathers, the archbishops of Canterbury; nay rather was I taken out of the palace of the king and from among his household . . . It were therefore a judgment rightfully passed on me, to be cast with shame far away from such a holy seat".' But Thomas was not destined to be cast with shame from his seat at Canterbury, to which his passion and death brought increasing lustre, so that the later dean of St Paul's could reflect on the occasion of his successor's consecration: 'Positus est Cantuariensis archiepiscopus super candelabrum ut luceat coram hominibus—the archbishop of Canterbury is placed on high like a light to shine forth among men'.[31]

It is sometimes forgotten that Thomas's murder was not in the event occasioned by the vexatious issues discussed at Clarendon in 1164, but by a particular aspect of Canterbury's jurisdiction, namely the right of the archbishop of the southern province to crown the king. The coronation of the younger Henry, king

Henry II's son, in June 1170 was performed by Roger of York, in Becket's absence and in derogation of Canterbury's rights, in spite of its prohibition by the Pope and by Thomas in exile, which Roger claimed he had never received.[32] The resulting condemnations of the archbishop of York and the bishops of London and Salisbury, promulgated by Becket on his return to England, provoked the impassioned outburst by the king which led to Becket's death. This was the most tragic aspect of that rivalry between York and Canterbury, of ancient origin and recurring crises, which broke out anew with exceptional bitterness coincidentally with the Becket dispute, and which was still further complicated by Foliot's possibly tentative and certainly provocative proposal that the see of London should be raised to metropolitical status and thereby freed from Canterbury's jurisdiction.[33] The genesis of both these problems can be retraced to the instructions of pope Gregory I to Augustine in 601 that the English Church should in due course comprise two provinces, with archbishops at London and York, each with twelve suffragans, and that he should have precedence between the archbishops who was senior in order of consecration.[34]

It was natural that Gregory should choose London at that time as the future see of the southern province, but for well-known historical reasons that part of his plan was never fulfilled, and Canterbury increasingly through the centuries established its pre-eminence. Nevertheless, the Gregorian intentions gave ancient justification to York's claims for independence and equality, and even in some instances for precedence in honour, though under archbishops like Theodore (when there was no archbishop of York) and Lanfranc (who with the Conqueror's aid achieved an undoubted primacy) the whole English Church had been subject to Canterbury.[35] The Canterbury-York dispute was clearly not solved in Becket's lifetime, but on the contrary added a further bitterness to a situation already critically divisive. It was more surprising that the claims of London should be put forward, though it is not easy to judge how seriously they were intended by Foliot. It is obvious that the Gregorian letter was known and used in the controversy, and it is a significant detail that the ancient letter was shortly after incorporated in collections of canon law, at first under the title 'Concerning the pre-eminence of London and York', and then with the more prudent alteration 'Concerning the pre-eminence of Canterbury and York'.[36] The affair is of evident importance and added a further dimension to the complex Becket crisis, but it is hard to believe that Foliot's proposal ever had much hope of success, and after Becket's martyrdom it was never mentioned again.

The reaction to Becket's death was swift and dramatic. Among the more powerful and emotional outbursts was that of William, archbishop of Sens and Thomas's faithful friend and supporter, who appealed to the Pope to vindicate the martyr's blood, 'which cries out from England', which Alexander achieved in the best possible way with Becket's canonization in 1173.37 The cult of the martyr spread with astonishing speed and pervasiveness, largely through its intrinsic potentiality, but partly also through papal patronage and encouragement, as instanced in Alexander's letter to the bishop of Aversa in 1173, relating to him the process of canonization and speaking also of Becket's renown, 'which you have heard and the greater part of the world has recognized', recording too how through his cardinal legates, and through the archbishops and bishops not only of England and France but also of other regions, he had ordered the martyr's feastday to be celebrated.38 Centuries later, when the martyr's shrine was desecrated and his reputation temporarily tarnished, king Henry VIII formally enacted that 'from hence forth the sayde Thomas Becket shall not be esteemed, named, reputed nor called a sayncte'. In saying this, king Henry was not in fact very orginal: the *Thómas Saga* had recorded centuries earlier how, shortly after Becket's death, 'the mighty men in the country now see that the king's shame is all the more keenly felt . . . Hence it cometh, that the highest lords of the land forbid, under peril of life and limbs, any one to call archbishop Thomas a holy man or even a martyr. But the outcome of this seemeth unto learned men even to surpass most miracles, for threaten the people with all its might as the king's power would, the pilgrimages to the archbishop's grave multiply all the more, so much so, that the whole road from London to Canterbury, fifty miles, was crowded by people coming to and going fro'.39 Nor was the later Henry in the long term more successful, as the commemorations of this year amply prove. Indeed the tragic figure in this history is that of the great king Henry II, a monarch of so many noble qualities and accomplishments, who died in defeat and despair, deserted by even his closest and dearest kin. Of Henry it might be said, as also of those who surrounded him, as has been aptly said of king Edward I and his circle a century later: 'none of them was, at all seriously, called a saint. No fevers were cured at their tombs'.40

1. Cf. *Bede's Ecclesiastical History of the English People*, edd., B. Colgrave and R. A. B. Mynors, Oxford (1969), pp. 132-35.

2. *Materials for the History of Archbishop Thomas Becket*, edd., J. C. Robertson and J. B. Sheppard, 7 vols, Rolls Series 67, London (1875-85): VII, pp. 547-48.

3. *Becket Materials*, VII, pp. 582-84.

4. Cf. T. Borenius, *St Thomas Becket in Art*, London (1932); R. Foreville, *Le Jubilé de Saint Thomas Becket: 1220-1470*, Paris (1958); and D. J. Hall, *English Mediaeval Pilgrimage*, London (1965). See also now *The Canterbury Cathedral Chronicle*, No. 65, published in July 1970.

5. As evidenced by the numerous commemorative services, lectures and festivals arranged especially in Canterbury and London, but also in many parts of England and even overseas.

6. For full details, cf. R. Winston, *Thomas Becket*, London (1967), and Dom David Knowles, *Thomas Becket*, London (1970).

7. Cf. Ralph de Diceto, *Opera Historica*, ed., W. Stubbs, 2 vols, Rolls Series, London (1876): I, p. 302.

8. *Ibid.*, I, pp. 307-08.

9. The two councils are finely discussed in Knowles, *The Episcopal Colleagues of Archbishop Thomas Becket*, Cambridge (1951), pp. 53-90, and *idem*, *Thomas Becket*, pp. 77-100; see also Winston, *op. cit.*, pp. 156-96.

10. For a scholarly treatment of the legal issues, cf. R. Foreville, *L'Église et la Royauté en Angleterre sous Henri II Plantagenet, 1154-89*, Paris (1943), pp. 122-61. Cf. C. Duggan, 'The Becket Dispute and the Criminous Clerks', *Bulletin of the Institute of Historical Research*, XXXV (1962), pp. 1-28, and *idem*, 'From the Conquest to the Death of John', in *The English Church and the Papacy in the Middle Ages*, ed., C. H. Lawrence, London (1965), pp. 87-93.

11. Diceto, I, pp. 313-14.

12. Among many excellent works on this subject, cf. G. Tellenbach, *Church, State and Christian Society*, trans., R. F. Bennett, Oxford (1948), and W. Ullmann, *The Growth of Papal Government in the Middle Ages*, London (1955).

13. Cf. references in n. 10, above.

14. Now published as 'The Significance of the Becket Dispute in the History of the English Church', *Ampleforth Journal*, LXXV (1970), pp. 365-75.

15. Diceto, I, p. 343.

16. In the letter *Multiplicem*: cf. *Becket Materials*, V, p. 537.

17. Auctor Anonymus I: *Becket Materials*, IV, p. 74.

18. His early career is most fully discussed in L. B. Radford, *Thomas of London before his Consecration*, Cambridge (1894).

19. Diceto, I, p. 324: *Becket Materials*, V, p. 515.

20. William FitzStephen, *Vita Sancti Thomae*, in *Becket Materials*, III, pp. 1-154; for London, cf. esp. pp. 2-13.

21. Cf. footnotes *passim* in this paper.

22. See now A. Morey and C. N. L. Brooke, *Gilbert Foliot and his Letters*, Cambridge (1965), and *The Letters and Charters of Gilbert Foliot*, Cambridge (1967).

23. Diceto, I, p. 309; *Becket Materials*, V, pp. 24-30.

24. Diceto, I, p. 309.

25. *Becket Materials*, V, pp. 521-44; Morey and Brooke, *Gilbert Foliot and his Letters*, pp. 166-87, and *Letters and Charters*, pp. 229-43.

26. Diceto, I, p. 426.

27. *Ibid.*, II, p. 31.

28. *Ibid.*, I, pp. 432-34.

29. *Becket Materials*, VII, p. 332.

30. *Thómas saga erkibyskups*, ed., E. Magnússon, 2 vols, Rolls Series 65, London (1875-83): I, pp. 170-73. For very similar records, cf. Alan of Tewkesbury, *Becket Materials*, II, pp. 323-25, and Herbert of Bosham, *ibid.*, III, pp. 289-90.

31. Diceto, I, p. 390; cf. Matthew, 5.13-19, esp. 'Neque accendunt lucernam, et ponunt eam sub modio, sed super candelabrum, ut luceat omnibus qui in domo sunt. Sic luceat lux vestra coram hominibus, ut videant opera vestra bona, et glorificent Patrem vestrum, qui in caelis est'.

32. Cf. A. Heslin (Mrs. C. Duggan), 'The Coronation of the Young King in 1170', *Studies in Church History*, II (1965), pp. 165-78.

33. Morey and Brooke, *Gilbert Foliot and his Letters*, pp. 149-62.

34. *Bede's Ecclesiastical History*, pp. 104-07.

35. For Theodore, cf. *ibid.*, p. 332: 'isque primus erat in archiepiscopis, cui omnis Anglorum ecclesia manus dare consentiret'; for Lanfranc, cf. R. W. Southern, 'The Canterbury Forgeries', *English Historical Review*, LXXIII (1958), pp. 193-226.

36. C. Duggan, *Twelfth-Century Decretal Collections and their Importance in English History*, Athlone Press (1963), pp. 137-38.

37. For William's appeal, cf. Diceto, I, pp. 347-48; for Becket's canonization, cf. *ibid.*, I, pp. 369-70.

38. *Becket Materials*, VII, pp. 549-50.

39. *Thómas Saga*, II, p. 91.

40. R. Brentano, *York Metropolitan Jurisdiction and Papal Judges Delegate (1279-1296)* University of California Press (1959), p. 178.

ADDENDA ET CORRIGENDA

STUDY I

Additional bibliography: D.Knowles, Thomas Becket (Oxford 1970);
idem, A.J.Duggan and C.N.L. Brooke, 'Henry II's supplement to the
Constitutions of Clarendon', EHR (1972) 757-71; B.Smalley, The
Becket Conflict and the schools (Oxford 1973); R.Foreville, ed.
Thomas Becket (Paris 1975); M.G.Cheney, Roger, bishop of Worcester
Oxford 1980); A.J.Duggan, Thomas Becket: a textual history of his
letters (Oxford 1980).

STUDY II

Decretal collections: The most recent printed list of collections is in
Studies in the collections of twelfth-century decretals, from the papers
of W.Holtzmann: ed., revised and trans. C.R.Cheney and M.G.Cheney
(Monumenta Iuris Canonici, Series B: Corpus Collectionum 3, Vatican
City 1979) xx-xxxii. Two further works are now known: a fragment of
an early Worcester family collection, in the Cathedral library at
Hereford (see VII below), and a work not yet identified, at Tortosa.
For the texts of decretal letters hitherto unprinted, see Decretales
ineditae saeculi xii, from the papers of W.Holtzmann: ed. and revised
S.Chodorow and C.Duggan (MIC, B: Corpus Collectionum 4, Vatican
City, in press). On the continuing need to revise the decretal statistics
cited in this chapter, see comment to III below.

STUDY III

The final count of twelfth-century decretals must await the completion of
the Regesta decretalium saeculi xii (from Holtzmann's papers) by
Chodorow and Duggan. The regesta lists the decretals in alphabetical
order of incipits to a total of 1090, but this figure is inexact since each
item is now fixed at a given point, to achieve stability in a complex
system of references. My latest count of Alexander III's decretals to
England is 387; only two decretals in the collections were sent to Ireland,
both by Clement III. The statistical arguments in II and III are not
affected by more recent figures, but some adjustments were required to
the report on p.144.

Appendix Concilii Lateranensis (ex 1184-85): The concluding titles in
the four known versions of Appendix are discussed in P.Landau, 'Studien
zur Appendix und den Glossen in frühen systematischen Dekretalensammlungen', Bulletin of Medieval Canon Law (1979) 1-21, esp. 1-8;
for title 50, see Holtzmann-Cheney, Studies in the collections 119-20,
132-34; for Holtzmann's assessment of English decretals in French
primitive collections, ibid. 26-34. Cf. General conclusions (a) and
VIII below.

The significance attached here to the Bruges Collection (Brugensis, from 1187; see pp.145-46) seems ever more persuasive, but some details required correction. The collection was not without influence on later compilations, notably on Sangermanensis and Abrincensis (both c.1198); and the 35 decretals described as found in Brugensis alone were otherwise unknown when Friedberg first analysed the collection in Die Canones-Sammlungen (Leipzig 1897) 136-70, but most were received into later collections. On the discovery of a third codex of Brugensis (to add to the two already known at Bruges), see Holtzmann, 'Uber die Vatikanische Handschrift der Collectio Brugensis' in Collectanea Vaticana in honorem Anselmi M.Card. Albareda, Studi e Testi 219-20 (1962) 391-414; the Vatican cod.Ottobonianus lat. 3027 reveals the closest text to the original, in a manuscript from the Benedictine abbey of St Remi at Reims. It now appears that 7 decretals to Reims are found in Brugensis, but in no other collection; at least 29 further decretals to recipients in the Reims province occur in Brugensis for the first time; 13 of the latter were transmitted to Sangermanensis and Abrincensis alone. The collection includes 18 decretals addressed to the dean of Reims, some to Fulk (identified 6 times), others to his successor Ralph.

General conclusions:
(a) English decretal collections: the important contribution of English collectors in the primitive phase is everywhere recognised; the influence of English sources on some continental primitive collections is likewise established (see IX below). The English origin of the Appendix is now widely accepted, though Holtzmann seemingly retained to the end his conviction that it was Italian (see Holtzmann-Cheney, Studies in the collections 116-34; Landau, 'Die Entstehung der systematischen Dekretalensammlungen und die europäische Kanonistik des 12. Jahrhunderts', Zeitschrift der Savigny-Stiftung, Kan. Abt. 66 (1979) 120-48, esp. 128-131, with the proposal of Lincoln or Oxford as the place of composition, ex 1184-85). Tanner is now confidently described as English (1187-91), and the St Maximin codex of Francofortana was completed in England, after 1189 (Landau, ibid. 137-43 and 144-46). The importance of the Rouen school of canonists is discussed in Holtzmann-Cheney, Studies in the collections 135-207, esp. 146-51, and Landau, Die Entstehung 137-43 (on the 'Zwischenstation Rouen', and the significance of the career of Walter of Coutances).
(b) English bishops: it was not my intention to minimize the role of important prelates like Roger of York and Gilbert Foliot of London as judges delegate or recipients of decretal letters. Large numbers of papal commissions were in fact received by them, and many are found in the decretal collections. But the English collections do not suggest the use of their archives or judicial records as the immediate sources used by the collectors. That is the distinction intended between their role and that of the bishops of Exeter and Worcester, and the archbishop of Canterbury (see now M.G.Cheney, 'The Council of Westminster 1175', Studies in Church History 11 (1975) 61-68; eadem, Roger, bishop of Worcester 197-206).

(c) General history: the political implications of my challenge to the
Maitland-Brooke theory were questioned by Henry Mayr-Harting, with
special reference to the 'failure' of Henry II's policies (see 'Henry II
and the papacy, 1170-89', Journal of Ecclesiastical History 16 (1965)
39-53; my argument on this point is clarified in I 372-74 above, and
XV 90-93 below. Frank Barlow suggested that the exile of Alexander III
in France (1162-65), and his resulting close association with French and
English prelates could explain the large number of their decretals,
compared with prelates in other regions (rev. History 48 (1963) 361,
and The English Church, 1066-1154 (London 1979) 147); it could well
explain the very large numbers of letters sent to them, but could not fully
explain the unusual English collecting activity some 10-15 years later.
In a humane and gracious study, Mary Cheney has now proposed a
reconciliation between divergent earlier theories. In her view, the
contrasting arguments of Z.N.Brooke and myself respond to complementary evidence of a single complex problem. In essence, I did not argue
that the Maitland-Brooke conclusions were necessarily invalid, but that
they could not be validly reached on the evidence adduced. Both theses
recognize an unusual and important development of canon law in England
in the 1170s, but they differ in their understanding of the nature and
meaning of the evidence used (cf. M.Cheney, Roger, bishop of Worcester
208-12).

STUDY IV
Decretal collections: cf. sub nominibus Landau, Die Entstehung;
Holtzmann-Cheney, Studies in the collections; M.G.Cheney, Roger,
bishop of Worcester 197-206; G.Fransen, Les décrétales et les collec-
tions de décrétales (Typologie des sources du moyen âge occidental, 2,
Turnhout 1972).

Review of dates of decretal collections: the date of the first redaction of
Compilatio prima is now placed in 1190, the work being compiled between
ex 1188 and 1190 (see Fransen, Les décrétales 22-23; Landau, Die
Entstehung 136. The final item in Cheltenhamensis was issued in 1193
(JL 17055 and 17675, 25 July), but that is an addition in a different hand;
the main collection is dated from late 1188. Petrihusensis must be ex
1195 or later, since it includes a decretal of 7 Sept. 1195 (JL 17679 and
17614). The Appendix is now dated ex 1184-85, Tanner 1187-91, and
Sangermanensis and Abrincensis 1187-91.

That the material of Wigorniensis II (altera) was first assembled in
England was not accepted by Holtzmann, but receives recent support in
Holtzmann-Cheney, Studies in the collections 47n, and in M.G.Cheney,
Roger, bishop of Worcester 200-02. For the discovery that the supplement to the archetype in Claudiana was partly derived from a late
Appendix source, see Holtzmann-Cheney 132-34. On the English
decretals in the 'Tortosa' family, see IX below; for the early Worcester
family, VII below; for the Cheltenham collection, XI.2 below.
P.142: The folios of the Claudian Collection in the British Library have
been re-numbered; the references in 2 1.2 are now 189ra-216ra and in
1.11 191v.

STUDY V

P.194 and Pl.IV: The folio number is now 203v.

STUDY VI

Dunelmensis prima: for Holtzmann's essay on Durham MS C.III.1, fols.
5v-18r (his Dunelmensis prima, books 1-3), with analysis, see
Holtzmann-Cheney 75-99; he identified fols. 1v-5v as extracts from the
9 books of the Decretum of Burchard of Worms. He correctly noted a
'striking parallel' between sequences of decretals in book 2 and in the
Collectio Cantuariensis (Holtzmann-Cheney 79); and concluded that the
Durham Collection was assembled in England as an addition to a manuscript or exemplar, with an appendix to Gratian's Decretum, which had
been brought from Italy. Evidence of the completion of the work in the
northern province is found in two privilegia included in book 3: no.46,
a forged privilege to the monks of Lenton; no.61, a privilege to Master R.
of the church of York (see Chodorow-Duggan, Decretales ineditae nos.
78,77).

STUDY VII

Early Worcester family: two bi-folia in the Hereford Cathedral library
reveal a previously unknown fragment of an early Worcester family
member (information from Dr N.R.Ker). It is very close in appearance
and detail to Wigorniensis, and preserves material from book 7: 19-27
and 33-44 (these items were already arranged in this sequence in the
archetype). It is written in double columns, the items are numbered
and supplied with rubricated inscriptions, and sub-sections are supplied
with rubrics. Its discovery does not affect the arguments advanced in
the present chapter.

For the dating of Petrihusensis and Cheltenhamensis see Addenda to IV.
It is now known that Claustroneoburgensis is later than the death of
Alexander III in completion, since it includes at least two decretals of
Lucius III in the material which it appended to the 'Worcester' archetype
(Claustr. 302 and 319; Holtzmann also considered that 330 was issued
by Lucius III). Letters later than the death of Alexander have already
been listed as additions to the archetype in Wigorniensis (fols. 1r,2r,
2v,3r; 62v,63v; and part of a letter of Lucius III to the archbishop of
Gran, appended to book 3: JL 15196). These are all additions in
different hands from the main collection. The latest fixed date in the
archetype and in Wigorniensis itself is 23 Jan.1181 (Wigorn. 7.59).
It is generally assumed that the decretals to the bishop of Worcester in
the archetype and in Wigorniensis were received by Roger, who died
9 Aug.1179; this is probably true, but it should be noted that Wigorn.
7.59 has an internal reference to Baldwin as bishop (from Aug.1180).
The suggestion of Dr Mayr-Harting that the Wigorniensis codex, with
supplements, was compiled by or for Master Silvester is of interest,
but it is not established and does not relate to the provenance of the
archetype ('Master Silvester and the composition of the early decretal
collections', Studies in Church History 2 (1965) 186-96; cf. M.G.Cheney,

Roger, bishop of Worcester 198-200).

Adjustment to analysis: 2.21 to be dated May 1,1178-79; 2.22 to be dated 1178, was sent to Gerard; 2.23 to be dated 1154-59, was sent to Theobald of Canterbury by Adrian IV; 2.25 was sent to the abbot and to the brothers of Loroy; 2.26 was sent to the abbot and brothers of Rigny; 2.28 was sent to the bishop of Durham; 3.1 to be dated 1174-79; 3.3 to be dated 1174-81; 3.5 to be dated 1177-78; 3.6 was sent to the bishop of Zamora; 3.7 to be dated June 19,1161-79; 3.8 was sent to the archbishop of Cosenza; 3.12 & 13 was sent to the bishop of London; 3.14 to be dated 1178, was sent to the elect of Bamberg; 3.15 to be dated 1159-81; 3.19 to be dated 1172, was sent to the bishop of Exeter; 3.24 to be dated 1162-81; 4.2 to be dated January 23,1160-76; 4.3 to be dated June 3,1177; 4.4 to be dated 1162-79; 4.7 (=JL 14102) to be dated 1164-79.

STUDY VIII
The St John's Collection is now renamed Fragmentum Cantabrigiense, and in lists as Fragm. L. Holtzmann's important studies on the Appendix are now printed in Holtzmann-Cheney 116-34; for further references, see comments on III and IV above, and M.G.Cheney, Roger, bishop of Worcester 196. The Appendix, which was almost certainly an English work, drew on early continental sources, but apparently not on Parisiensis II (Landau, Die Entstehung 131 and n).

Additional notes: the sequence of canons of the Third Lateran Council in the St John's Collection (pp.464-66) agrees with that in the Cheltenham Collection, fols. 11ra-16r; the marginal comments by canons 11 and 12 (p.465) agree with those by the same canons in the Lincoln Appendix, fol. 96r. Analysis: 1.2 to be dated September 27,1177; 2.1 to be dated c. 1153; 2.2 to be dated 1125; 3.3 to be dated June 26,1174-76; 3.5 was sent to archdeacons in whose areas Ramsey abbey possessed churches; elsewhere, 3.6 is variously addressed to Lincoln, Winchester, Chester, or York; and 3.7 to Hereford, Chester, or Lincoln recipients.

STUDY IX
On the dating of the primitive collections see Addenda to IV.
Alcobacensis prima: Holtzmann's essay on this collection, with an analysis, is now printed in Holtzmann-Cheney 8-25; cf. M.G.Cheney, Roger, bishop of Worcester for a convincing argument that Alcob. 50-72 were derived from Roger of Worcester's office. The present essay demonstrated a comparable derivation from Exeter and Canterbury archives. There is no doubt that a Roman-Tortosa source was expanded with material from an English primitive collection in the completion of the Alcobaça collection. My earlier thesis that the Roman-Tortosa stock was already indebted to a different English supply has not been further examined. Correction: P.62 11.12-13 should read: the Alcobaça collection is transcribed in a single column throughout, which ends on the 21st line of the final folio verso, stopping short ...

The number of known decretal collections (p.58) is subject to continuing

revision. In Holtzmann-Cheney (xxxii) the number of primitive collections is given as 28, of which 16 are English; but the Oslo fragment
(Fragm. A) is not primitive. The numbers remain the same, through
the addition of the newly-discovered Hereford fragment of a Worcester
family collection (see VII above); the Fragm. Parisiense has not yet
been fixed within these categories (cf. Chodorow, BMCL 3 (1973) 51-55).
On the Italian collections, see Holtzmann-Cheney 35-74. The promise
of a report on the decretals relating to the church of Bungay in Suffolk
is now fulfilled (Chodorow-Duggan, Decretales ineditae, at no.46).

STUDY X
Additional bibliography: see I above; W.L.Warren, Henry II (1973);
R.M.Fraher, 'The Becket dispute and two decretist traditions', Journal
of Medieval History 4 (1978) 347-68. See also X.2 below.

My principal aim in this paper was to challenge the then-existing con-
sensus among English historians that Henry II had a better case in canon
law than Becket, and that he was not the first to use the 'double punishment' argument in defence of clerical immunity. My views largely
agreed with those of Miss Foreville. In his final assessment of the
Becket dispute, Knowles accepted this revision, though he did not consider Becket's actions prudent; Miss Smalley brought important new
insights into the affair, from her study of the theologians, as distinct
from the canonists. The canonical and theological arguments are
complementary, not contradictory; there were experts in both disciplines
in Becket's household, and some key texts are found in canonical and
theological sources. The most direct response to my conclusions in a
context of canon law has come from Richard Fraher. Using new evidence,
as well as re-examining that already known, Fraher returns to the
verdict that decretist commentaries in the relevant period accord with
Henry II's proposals. He draws a distinction between the views of the
Bolognese and Anglo-Norman commentators, before and after the controversy. His work makes necessary some corrections, notably with
reference to the Roman law text which appears as a palea at Gratian's
XI.1.45. But it does not touch the central concerns of my thesis. There
is no doubt that Becket received the historically more valid interpretation of the canons themselves, which in some cases were first found in
pseudo-Isidore; and it has been demonstrated that the 'double punishment' theory was used in defense of clerical immunity before his own
involvement in the debate, whether by canonists or theologians. Within
his chosen field of decretist commentaries, Fraher attaches insufficient
importance to the Church's discretionary rights in applying or denying
permissible procedures. This is a crucial distinction. Several substantial points of emphasis in Fraher's essay were in fact conceded in
my own work.

For two previously unknown decretals, concerning clerical privilege,
see now Chodorow-Duggan, Decretales ineditae nos. 35 and 83: no. 35
was sent by Alexander III to Henry II, arising from an individual case;

no. 83 was sent by Alexander or Lucius III to bishop John of St Andrews,
and allows a double punishment of merely tonsured clerks, if their
crimes are sufficiently grave. Corrections: 'vel confessus' was omitted after 'Et si clericus convictus' on p.3. Here and elsewhere, Licet
preter is now dated ? 1176 (pp.18,23). P.18 l.18 ff read: and imposed
a detailed course of penance; he must in future serve as acolyte,
demoted from his sub-diaconal status, but, 'because God does not
judge twice in the same matter', the pope had by dispensation granted
that he be allowed to keep his benefice in full; and he should suffer no
further vexation.

STUDY XI

For part 1, see X above.

Part 2: For the dating of collections see Addenda to IV.

The systematic source used in the Cheltenham Collection was most
probably a 'Bamberg' collection of French provenance; my use of the
term 'Bamberg-Leipzig tradition' (here and elsewhere) is therefore
more accurately expressed as Bamberg simply (Landau, Die Entstehung
145 n108). Analysis: Holtzmann called the Lateran canons (Chelt.fols.
11ra-16r) book 1; therefore my book 1 (pp.382-83) is his book 2. The
'book of marriage decretals' (pp.384-88, Chelt. 43ra-51rb) is part
of Holtzmann's book 9; as a result of the loss of folios, 9.1-5 are
missing; for a similar reason, 4 decretals are lost between fols. 46
and 47 (probably Wigorn. 1.24-27), between my nos.19 and 20; my
1-39 = Holtzmann 9.6-44. Corrections: the latter part of no.19 and
the opening of no.20 are missing (through the loss of folios, as explained
above); 19. should end "mulier-" not habeat; 20. should start "-(ca)
non posterus...habeat. Si..."; Querenti etiam (no.20 (1) is attached
to Licet preter in error, and correctly is part of Super eo quod, JL
13946. These technical adjustments do not affect the original claim that
the Cheltenham Collection drew together material from an early
Worcester family collection and from a continental systematic collection
in the Bamberg tradition. Adjustments to pp.382-83: 2. to be dated
1174-81; 3. to be dated 1175; 4. to be dated 26 June 1175; 7. to be
dated 1164-79; 8. to read "Ea que de avaricie...a vobis." and to be
dated 1 June 1160-75; 15. to be dated 26 June 1174-76; 16. to read
JL 13857. -26 June 1174-76. To pp.384-88: 1. to be dated 1162-81; 2.
to be dated 5 Feb.1175-81; 4. to be dated 30 June 1170; 6. to be dated
28 Jan.1177; 9. to be dated 6 March 1177; 10. read JL 13163 and 14132.
- 1163-79; 11. to be dated 1167-81; 12. to be dated 1162-81; 13. to be
dated 1164-65 ?; 14. to be dated 26 Sept.1167-69; 15. to be dated
1 Dec. ? 1165-66; 20. to be dated ? 1176; 21. to be dated 1162-67; 23
to be dated 5 July 1177; 25. to be dated 1175+; 26. to be dated 5 Feb.
1175-81; 27. to be dated 1174-81; 30. to be dated 1163-81; 31. to be
dated 1166-81; 32. to be dated 1175+; 34. to be dated 1166-81; 36. to
be dated 1 Oct.1178; 39. to be dated 5 Feb.1175-81. To pp. 388-89:
1. & 10. to be dated ? 1176.

Part 3: Correction: a false attribution of the citation 'Bandin.' to

Alexander III (Rolandus Bandinelli) has been deleted on p.374; on the
references to Rolandus and Alexander III, see J.T.Noonan, 'Who was
Rolandus?' in Law, Church, and Society, edd. K.Pennington and
R.Somerville (Univ. of Pennsylvania 1977) 21-48. The widespread
assumption that Alexander III was the canonist Master Rolandus is now
challenged by Professor Noonan.

STUDY XII
Parts of this study were reconsidered in XIII below; where there is a
change or development of emphasis, XIII records a revised opinion (as
for 'Luscus noster', p.10; and on decretals received by Richard, p.18).
The decretal discussed on p.16, to Richard and Gilbert Foliot of London,
is Causam que inter, JL 14002; its historical context was previously
misunderstood, since the fragment in Diceto's Ymagines historiarum
was excerpted from a marriage decretal: see XIV pp.75-76 and 79-80
below. For the dating of Compilatio Prima and Cheltenham see Addenda
to IV.

STUDY XV
Additional bibliography: more recent studies on the ecclesiastical
history of the English Church in the period of this essay are too
numerous to list; of special relevance are: M.Gibson, Lanfranc of Bec
(1978); F.Barlow, The English Church, 1066-54 (London 1979); M.Brett,
The English Church under Henry I (London: OUP 1975); J.E.Sayers,
Papal judges delegate in the province of Canterbury (London: OUP 1971);
C.R.Cheney, Pope Innocent III and England (Stuttgart 1976); Councils
and Synods, with other documents relating to the English Church II, edd.
D.Whitelock, M.Brett and C.N.L.Brooke (forthcoming). Recent studies
on the period of the Becket dispute are listed for I above. In any revision of the broad theme of this chapter, I should include a consideration
of the theologians in the English Church in the period (Anselm, Robert
Pullen, Robert of Melun, John of Cornwall, Stephen Langton).
Corrections: it is accepted that the pseudo-Isidorian collections were
made at Reims (p.72 n2: delete 'or Le Mans'); the antipope Clement
appeared out of context on p.78 (a slip; he appears correctly in 1080,
p.75); the elevation of Boso to the rank of cardinal was wrongly placed
in 1149 (p.86); the bishop of Worcester was printed as Winchester on
p.95; an awkward phrase has been replaced on p.104 line 4).

INDEX

- 5 -

INDEX OF DECRETAL COLLECTIONS

Coll. Eberbacensis (Eberbach):
IV 135,138-39,140,143; IX
53,62-65,66,68,70; XI 368

Coll. Florianensis (St Florian):
IX 61 and n.25,70; XI 369

Coll. Fontanensis (Fountains):
IV 142; VI 182; IX 69,71

Fragm.A - Fragm. Asloense
(Oslo): VII 508 n.8

Fragm.H - Fragm. Riccardianum
(Riccardi): XIV 81

Fragm.L - Fragm. Cantabrigiense
(Cambridge; also St John's
Collection): VII 506 n*; VIII
462-68

Coll. Francofortana (Frankfurt):
IV 144; V 195 and plate VIII;
VIII 463 n.29; XI 370-71; XII
18,20 n.2; XIV 77,80 and n.a

Coll. Fuldensis (Fulda): XIV
78,81 n*

Coll. Lipsiensis (Leipzig):
III 143; IV 138 and n.1; V
195; VII 507,511 and n.24;
XI 371,383-84

Coll. Orielensis (Oriel; and
Orielensis II): IX 57

Coll. Orielensis I (Oriel 1)
Bambergensis O: VIII 459

Coll. Parisiensis prima
(Paris 1): VIII 463,468b
and d; IX 60-61,70,71; XI
368,369,370

Coll. Parisiensis secunda
(Paris 2): VI 180 and n.3;
VIII 460,464,468d

Coll. Petrihusensis
(Peterhouse): IV 138,143;
VII 508 and nn.8,9, 511 and
n.20; VIII 461 and nn.18,19;
XI 370; XIII 79 n.69

Coll. Regalis (Royal): IV 136,
141-42; V 193 and plate II;
VI 182; IX 69,71; XII 18

Coll. Roffensis (Rochester):
IV 136,141; VI 182; VII
506 n*; IX 69,71; XI 368,
369; XII 18; XIV 79

Coll. Sangermanensis (St
Germain-des-Prés): IV 138;
VIII 463,468c; XI 367,370;
XIV 78,81

Coll. Seguntina (Sigüenza): IX
57

Coll. Tanneri (Tanner): IV
138; VIII 461 and n.19,463,
466 no.1n,467 1.3n,468c; XI
367,370,372,376-77; XII 18;
XIV 77,80 n.a

Coll. Trinitatis (Trinity):
IV 143; VII 506 and n.3,
507,510-13 and nn.516-26

Coll. Wigorniensis
(Worcester): IV 137,142; V
194 and plates V,VI; VII 506
n.3,507 and nn.5,6,508-16 and
nn.517-22,523-26; VIII 460-
61 and nn.12-14,467 3.5n; IX
69,71; XI 368,369,388; XIV
79-80

Coll. Wigorniensis altera
(Worcester 2): IV 135,141;
V 193 and plate I,195; VI
182; VII 506 n*; XI 367;
XII 17-18